AWAKE IN THE DARK

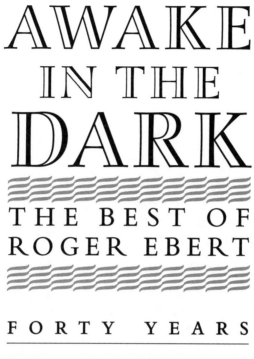

AWAKE IN THE DARK

THE BEST OF ROGER EBERT

FORTY YEARS OF REVIEWS, ESSAYS, AND INTERVIEWS

FOREWORD BY DAVID BORDWELL

THE UNIVERSITY OF CHICAGO PRESS

CHICAGO AND LONDON

Library of Congress Cataloging-in-
Publication Data

Ebert, Roger.
Awake in the dark : the best of
Roger Ebert / Roger Ebert.
p. cm.
Includes index.
ISBN 0-226-18200-2 (cloth : alk.
paper)
1. Motion pictures—Reviews.
2. Motion pictures. I. Title.
PN1995.E313 2006
791.43'75—dc22
2006008929

The University of Chicago Press, Chicago 60637
The University of Chicago Press, Ltd., London
© 2006 by The Ebert Company, Ltd.
All rights reserved. Published 2006
Paperback edition 2008
Printed in the United States of America

17 16 15 14 13 12 11 10 09 08   2 3 4 5 6

ISBN-13: 978-0-226-18200-1 (cloth)
ISBN-10: 0-226-18200-2 (cloth)
ISBN-13: 978-0-226-18201-8 (paper)
ISBN-10: 0-226-18201-0 (paper)

For Sonia and Josibiah

CONTENTS

PART 1
INTERVIEWS AND PROFILES

PART 2
THE BEST

PART 3
FOREIGN FILMS

PART 4
DOCUMENTARIES

PART 5

OVERLOOKED AND UNDERRATED

PART 6

ESSAYS AND THINK PIECES

PART 7

ON FILM CRITICISM

Symposium from *Film Comment*

All Thumbs, or, Is There a Future for Film Criticism?
BY RICHARD CORLISS

FOREWORD

Roger Ebert has blended prodigious energy, keen judgment, wide knowledge, probing insights, and a sharp sense of humor into some of the most perceptive commentary on cinema published in our time. In the tradition of George Bernard Shaw and Robert Hughes, he practices a graceful and deeply informed art journalism. Some pieces he writes are ephemeral, but nothing he writes is trivial. As he puts it in one essay, "It is not dishonorable to write for a daily deadline." His best pieces will last a long time, and we are lucky that the University of Chicago Press has chosen to preserve them.

Most obviously, this book records some high points of an extraordinary career. Ebert has become an institution. As a Pulitzer Prize–winning journalist (the first film critic so honored), he has become a mainstay of magazines and newspapers. His television show, which virtually founded television-based film reviewing, has been broadcast continually for thirty years. His books—not only of collected reviews but also of essays on larger film topics—have poured forth in a steady stream. He has taught courses on film at several universities, and he has held audiences enthralled for days with shot-by-shot analyses of classic films.

Ebert loves movies, but he also loves film. His writing incarnates cinephilia, the sheer savoring of the range and power of the medium itself, and his enthusiasm is infectious. His style isn't as pungent as, say, Dwight Macdonald's or Pauline Kael's; perhaps its closest kin is the warm, conversational tone of Donald Richie. Ebert and Richie never strain to seem smart at the expense of the films or filmmakers; even their wisecracks radiate a certain gentleness.

The essays collected here reveal Ebert to be the most thoughtful and historically informed critic writing for a general audience today. No other writer can shift, in the space of a paragraph, from an appreciation of John

Wayne to a subtle discussion of how Ozu presents movement in *Equinox Flower*. The essays are layered as very few film pieces are. A blast at colorization turns into a lyrical tribute to black-and-white cinematography, tethered to a precise explication of lighting changes in *Notorious* and *Casablanca*. No critic writing for the nonspecialist audience can move so gracefully from broad judgment to the fine grain of a movie's shots, lines, and performances. Ebert's unobtrusive craft respects the way movies engage us by their textures no less than by their stories.

Every critic has a writing persona, and most strain to create one of memorable eccentricity. Too many critics bully us to accept their tastes because of their greater expertise; one of today's most famous often launches a piece by assuring us that he championed the film or the director long before anyone else did. Ebert never intimidates. He's never clever at the expense of the movie, but neither is he utterly self-effacing. The quality he projects in his writing is that of a sensitive, curious appetite for new cinematic experience, whether coming from a blockbuster, an indie, or an import. In watching what transpires on the screen he tries to grasp, by means of his sympathetic imagination, the highest ambitions to which the film might aspire, whatever its genre or level of production. He serves the film, not his ego; his modesty doesn't dissolve his standards but reminds us of how flexible those standards are.

Some critics define themselves by what they don't like (often, it turns out, nearly everything). Ebert assesses each movie in terms of what it's trying to do, what traditions it belongs to, and what distinctive pleasures it can offer us. He is our most generous critic, capable of praising both *Howards End* and *The Bad Lieutenant*, *The Fugitive* and *Schindler's List*, *Pulp Fiction* and *Forrest Gump*. It's surprising that Ebert cites Macdonald as one of his influences, for Macdonald probably liked less than 10 percent of what he saw (and he didn't see all that much). Perhaps the lesson he passed to the young writer was the need to find an independent voice. Ebert has been resolutely unfashionable, championing Michael Apted's *Up* series as well as offbeat films like *Trouble in Mind* and *The Rapture*. He is alive to a wide range of cinematic appeals, and this breadth enables his writing to endure.

Endurance of another sort is evident from the sheer longevity of his career. Twenty-five years seems about the limit for a daily film reviewer before he or she longs to read books, any books, rather than watch a Rob Schneider movie. Each of the long-distance runners at the *Times*—Bosley Crowther, Vincent Canby, and Janet Maslin—managed to sustain their pace for nearly a quarter of a century. Meanwhile the unflagging Ebert is about to enter his fortieth year as the *Chicago Sun-Times* critic. Perhaps his marathon run has something to do with the breadth of his tastes. He can still love cinema because early on he accepted art films, mass movies, and (the hardest for most intellectual critics to stomach) middlebrow movies on their own terms, while still retaining a sense of what counts as true cinematic excellence. No one who reads the essays in the *Great Movies* volumes can doubt Ebert's commitment to the classics, but returning to his daily reviews reveals that savoring the masterpieces hasn't lessened his eagerness to spot glimmers of achievement in each weekend's releases. If a current movie will be remembered, Ebert is likely to show us why.

So this collection would be noteworthy solely on the strength of Ebert's critical accomplishments. But there's an additional value here, for *Awake in the Dark* records changes at many levels of American film history and film culture. Perhaps more than Ebert himself realizes, he chronicled major developments in how movies were made, received, and talked about.

Film criticism became a respectable branch of American journalism in the 1940s, when James Agee and Manny Farber turned their talents to it. These two very different writers set a high standard. Agee's reviews had some of the serpentine self-consciousness of *Let Us Now Praise Famous Men,* while Farber championed B pictures and avant-garde cinema in a jazzy demotic that mixed Broadway slang with art-world jargon. Significantly, both men reviewed films on a weekly or monthly basis. This set the template for serious film criticism: it would be essayistic and not merely a matter of "covering" the new releases. A weekly or monthly (or better yet, quarterly) schedule gave the reviewer enough time to ponder the film and to sculpt a nuanced response.

In the 1960s, movies became a point of intellectual interest as never before, and suddenly critics for *Esquire* and the *New Republic* and the *New Leader* and *New York Magazine* found themselves celebrities. Macdonald, John Simon, Stanley Kauffmann, and a host of less-remembered writers appeared on television, toured campuses, and published anthologies of their pieces. Indeed, it was a zesty collection of essays and reviews, *I Lost It at the Movies* (1965), that propelled Kael to the center of U.S. film culture and to a long stint at the *New Yorker*. At the time, these writers offered a tonic alternative to the power of the *Times* chief critic Bosley Crowther. Crowther's power was as immense as his tastes were deplorable. *Bonnie and Clyde* he considered "a cheap piece of bald-faced slapstick comedy," while *The Big Sleep* displayed "a not very lofty moral tone." Compared to Crowther, the new generation looked sleek and smart.

These were critics of the Greatest Generation, born between 1916 (Kauffmann) and 1925 (Simon). Versed in modern art and literature, they were sensitive to the importance of the emerging European cinema of the 1950s, but not as sympathetic to new developments in American film. A notable exception was Kael, whose passion for popular cinema kept her alert to the emergence of the New Hollywood. A younger critic, Andrew Sarris, brought more controversy to the mix. Writing first for *Film Culture*, a magazine devoted to avant-garde cinema, and then for the *Village Voice*, Sarris imported certain French notions to America. He distinguished between mise-en-scène and montage, floated the idea that an adaptation might fruitfully betray its original, and calmly expected his readers to be acquainted with directors in the *Cahiers du Cinéma* pantheon, from Jean Renoir and Roberto Rossellini to George Cukor and Nicholas Ray. His most significant gesture was the unclassifiable compendium of director essays, *The American Cinema* (published in *Film Culture* in 1963 and in book form in 1968). With this book, he redefined the way critics thought about popular cinema. While many younger writers took their style from Farber or Agee, they got their tastes from Sarris. His influence is felt today not only in his continuing critical output (now for the *New York Observer*) but also in the work of the Film Brat Generation—above all, Martin Scorsese, whose proselytizing for the Hollywood tradition has become his personal revision of the Sarris canon.

If Kael and Sarris were godmother and godfather to the Movie Generation, Ebert became its voice from within. He channeled the erudition of the weighty weekly reviewers into daily bursts of insight and enthusiasm. In the process, he articulated the baby boomers' pleasure in genre-breaking films like *Bonnie and Clyde* and *2001* and *The Last Detail* and *Nashville* while

never disdaining the best films that brought in the mainstream audiences. So he could enjoy *The Godfather, Rocky,* and *Close Encounters of the Third Kind* as much as *Taxi Driver* and *Aguirre: The Wrath of God.* Perhaps as well, his outpost in the Midwest protected him from the cycles of discipleship and apostasy ruling Manhattan film culture. With many guides but no gurus, he was free to follow his own compass.

In his pluralism, Ebert proved a more authentic cinephile than many of his contemporaries. They tied their fortunes to the Film Brats and then suffered the inevitable disappointments of the 1980s' return to studio-driven pictures. Ebert understood, I think, that the reinvention of mass-market cinema in the last two decades wasn't simply a matter of stifling the "little picture" so prized by those who long for a return to the 1970s. He realized that Steven Spielberg, Francis Ford Coppola, George Lucas, Tim Burton, Robert Zemeckis, Peter Weir, and others were, in their own ways, reinventing the studio tradition for new audiences, and doing so with admirable skill and visionary ambitions.

Ebert's oeuvre, then, is a fascinating historical record of how an exceptional intelligence reacted to massive changes in modern cinema. The reviews and essays collected here capture this flux, but so do the interviews and profiles. The latter show how rising stars like Warren Beatty and Meryl Streep were replacing the older generation, how critical hopes were pinned on nonconformists like Robert Altman and Woody Allen, and how Spielberg and Tom Hanks personified the megapicture as Scorsese and Errol Morris became emblems of the personal film.

The 1960s film boom never fizzled out; movies are still cool, to people of all ages. But a decade of information speedup has made us accustomed to instant, strident opinions. The intellectually challenging reviewing tradition maintained by other baby boomers (J. Hoberman at the *Voice,* Jonathan Rosenbaum at the *Chicago Reader*) seems ever farther from the lightspeed punditry of the Web, which favors first-response witticisms. Even the good, gray *Times* has joined the scramble, setting its reviewers blogging from Cannes and trying to increase edginess in pursuit of a younger readership. (In 2004 a *Times* reviewer memorably compared Santa's giant bag in *The Polar Express* to "an airborne scrotum." *Not* a lofty moral tone.) Above this crackle and cleverness stand Ebert's thoughtful, humane musings—

also delivered at whipcrack speed, but richer and more thoughtful and almost always more charitable.

Awake in the Dark constitutes a record of a major critic's sensibility and a precious history of our film culture over the last forty years. It is destined to sit on your shelf alongside Agee, Farber, and their very few peers.

David Bordwell

INTRODUCTION

I began my work as a film critic in 1967, although one of the pieces in this book goes back to my days on the *Daily Illini* at the University of Illinois. I had not thought to be a film critic, and indeed had few firm career plans apart from vague notions that I might someday be a political columnist or a professor of English. I came up to Chicago in September 1966 as a PhD candidate at the University of Chicago, which was kind enough to accept me although I did not have my MA from the University of Illinois; I had fulfilled all of the requirements except the foreign language, which they assured me I could take care of during the first year. It was not that I could not learn French, but that I would not: I resisted memorizing and repeating, and there was something stubborn and unyielding in my refusal that had its origins, I suspect, in the tear-stained multiplication tables over which I was drilled in grade school. To read, to listen, to watch, and to learn came easily to me, but to memorize was a loathsome enterprise. I never did get a decent grade in French.

I had done some freelance book reviewing for the *Chicago Daily News,* and applied for a job there. Herman Kogan, the arts editor, forwarded my letter to James Hoge, city editor of the *Chicago Sun-Times,* who took me out to lunch with Ken Towers, his assistant. After a chicken sandwich at Riccardo's I was hired as a feature writer on the paper's Sunday supplement.

Today students are on a "career path" beginning almost in grade school, but I must truthfully say my only object in attending college was to take literature classes because they were fun. I read books and talked and wrote about them, and got grades that let me continue to do that; I would have happily remained an undergraduate forever. To be hired by the *Sun-Times* after applying to the *Daily News* was the first of several accidents, or

strokes of good luck, that would form my future; when young people ask for career advice, I tell them there is no such thing, only the autobiography of the person they are asking, whose career was likely fashioned as much by chance as design.

Chicago in 1966 was caught up in the era of the war in Vietnam, the Beatles, hippies, flower power, psychedelic art, and always the movies. Philip Larkin assures us,

> Sexual intercourse began
> In nineteen sixty-three
> (which was rather late for me)—
> Between the end of the *Chatterley* ban
> And the Beatles' first l.p.

And the movies began for my generation at about the same time or a little earlier. The two were not unrelated. The great turning point was the French New Wave. In Champaign-Urbana I haunted the Art Theater, watching the films of François Truffaut, Jean-Luc Godard, Ingmar Bergman, Federico Fellini, the Angry Young Men and the spontaneities of John Cassavetes. Some of my curiosity was driven by sexual desire; I saw in foreign films what Hollywood never dealt with. What I also saw was a world far outside my own. In the movies as well as in the books I was reading (the Beats as much as the Russians and the Victorians) was a range of life that filled me with uneasy hungers. I wanted to go to California. I wanted to go to England, to France. I wanted to go somewhere.

In 1962 I bought a $325 charter flight to Europe and saw *La Dolce Vita* again in a theater on Piccadilly Circus and *The Third Man* on a rainy day in a smoky revival house on the Left Bank of Paris. In high school I had seen a re-release of *Citizen Kane* at the Art Theater, and by the act of watching it I learned that films were made by directors and had a style. Before then I thought they were about stars and told a story. On campus at the film societies, I saw Akira Kurosawa and Sergei Eisenstein, and was no less awed by Fred Astaire and Ginger Rogers, the Marx Brothers, Humphrey Bogart, Robert Mitchum, and Billy Wilder.

The *Daily Illini* had a film critic, a graduate student named Ron Szoke. I became editor of the paper in my senior year and had endless conversations with him, during which I felt that I had a very great deal to learn

about film. After the Sunday night screenings of international films at the Auditorium, we would all stream down the quadrangle to the basement of the Illini Union, where a professor named Gunther Marx would fascinate us with his readings of Luchino Visconti, Vittorio De Sica, Michelangelo Antonioni, and Alain Resnais. *Last Year at Marienbad,* he explained, was a working out of the theories of Claude Levi-Strauss. I did not know a thing about Claude Levi-Strauss, but was fascinated by this information, and repeated it wisely for years, all about the Lover, the Loved One, and the Authority Figure. Gunther Marx's son would grow up to be Frederick Marx, one of the makers of *Hoop Dreams.*

What I knew about film criticism, I knew from Ron Szoke and from the monthly columns of Dwight Macdonald in *Esquire.* He wrote about the movies in a way I had not experienced before, informally, angrily, with digressions and asides and the notion that sometimes they were saying something other than what they seemed to be saying.

There were no film classes at Illinois in those years. The Campus Film Society was run by Daniel Curley, a novelist, short story writer, and professor of English, whom I adopted as my mentor, signing up for every class he taught, even the writing workshop at which Larry Woiwode read his work and the rest of us simply sat there and stared at him in envy. Curley loved the movies in a personal way, and a word from him sent me to any film he mentioned. In 1965 I was returning through London after a year at the University of Cape Town, and he was there with his family on a sabbatical. We went to the Academy Cinema to see *Shakespeare Wallah,* and took the walk that later became our book *The Perfect London Walk.*

In my new job at the *Sun-Times* I wrote about bottled water, hero priests, snake charmers, fortune tellers, and the filming of *Camelot.* That was my first visit to a movie location. Josh Logan spent most of a day trying to make a lake on the back lot at Warner Brothers look green. On Monday nights, when Second City was dark, they showed underground films in the theater, and I reviewed them for the paper. I wrote obituaries of Walt Disney and Jayne Mansfield, and a memory of the children's matinees of my youth, when the coming of spring was announced by the arrival at the Princess Theater of Dan-Dan the Yo-Yo Man, an official representative of the Duncan Yo-Yo Company. He held a yo-yo contest on the theater stage. Winner got the Schwinn.

Robert Zonka, who was named the paper's feature editor the same day I was hired, became one of the best friends of a lifetime. One day in March 1967 he called me into a conference room, told me that Eleanor Keen, the paper's movie critic, was retiring, and that I was the new critic. I walked away in elation and disbelief, yet hardly suspected that this day would set the course for the rest of my life. How long could you be a movie critic, anyway? I had copies of Pauline Kael's *I Lost It at the Movies,* Arthur Knight's *The Liveliest Art,* and Andrew Sarris's *Interviews with Film Directors,* and I read them cover to cover and plunged into the business of reviewing movies.

In my very first review I was already jaded, observing of *Galia,* an obscure French film, that it "opens and closes with arty shots of the ocean, mother of us all, but in between it's pretty clear that what is washing ashore is the French New Wave." My pose in those days was one of superiority to the movies, although just when I had the exact angle of condescension calculated, a movie would open that disarmed my defenses and left me ecstatic and joyful. Two movies in those first years were crucial to me: *Bonnie and Clyde,* and *2001: A Space Odyssey.* I called both of them masterpieces when the critical tides were running against them, and about *2001* I was not only right but early, writing my review after a Los Angeles preview during which Rock Hudson walked out of the Pantages Theatre complaining audibly, "Will somebody tell me what the hell this movie is about?" My review appeared the same day as the official world premiere in Washington.

The University of Chicago had a famous film society, Doc Films, whose members seemed to have been born having already seen every movie. I met Doc members like Dave Kehr, Terry Curtis Fox, Charles Flynn. I was asked to lunch one day by Flynn and a high school student from Evanston, Todd McCarthy, later to become *Variety*'s chief critic. They were to edit the famous anthology *Kings of the Bs* together. Doc Films invited great men like John Ford to the campus, where he saw a print of *The Long Voyage Home* so chopped and scratched that he could barely bring himself to discuss it. On the North Side, Michael Kutza was in the fourth year of his Chicago Film Festival, and in November 1967 his festival showed *I Call First,* later retitled *Who's That Knocking at My Door,* the first film by a young New Yorker named Martin Scorsese. I thought it was a masterpiece.

The Clark Theater in the Loop showed daily double features, twenty-

three hours a day, seven days a week, and was run by Bruce Trinz and his assistant Jim Agnew. They told me I *had* to see certain films—not those by Orson Welles, Howard Hawks, and Alfred Hitchcock, whom I knew about, but those by Phil Karlson, Val Lewton, Rouben Mamoulian, Jean Vigo, and all the others. Through Agnew I met Jay Robert Nash, who was put on this earth as the living embodiment of the *Readers' Digest*'s Most Unforgettable Character. Through them I met Herschell Gordon Lewis, the director of *Blood Feast, The Gore Gore Girls, Two Thousand Maniacs,* and thirty-four other titles.

In later years when Lewis became a cult figure, I was asked for my memories of him, but I never saw one of his movies or discussed it with him. Instead, in the living room of the boardinghouse in Uptown where Agnew lived with his family, I sat with Agnew, Nash, Lewis, and a film booker and publicist named John West and Lewis's cinematographer, an Iranian named Alex Ameripoor, and we looked at 16 mm movies on a bed-sheet hung upon a wall. They felt an urgency to educate me. We saw *My Darling Clementine, Bride of Frankenstein,* and *Yankee Doodle Dandy,* with Nash dancing with James Cagney in front of the screen and telling me Cagney's secret was always to stand on tiptoe, so there would seem to be an eagerness about his characters as opposed to the others. When John Ford died, Agnew and Ameripoor and some others from this group drove to Los Angeles and stood at his grave and sang "Shall We Gather at the River" and drove back to Illinois again. Although Herschell Gordon Lewis was notorious as the director of violent and blood-drenched exploitation films, I remember only a thoughtful lover of the movies.

Nash went on to edit *The Motion Picture Guide,* ten thick volumes of tiny type on big two-columned pages, purporting to contain an entry on every American and most foreign films of any note. This he produced by hiring from the bar stools of O'Rourke's Pub out-of-work journalists and alcoholics with time on their hands, chaining them to primitive early IBM PCs in a townhouse he rented on Sheridan Road, and setting them to grinding out entries at slave wages. So draconian were the working conditions that when the project was completed and he commenced *The Encyclopedia of Crime,* Jeanette Hori Sullivan, the coowner of O'Rourke's, told him, "Jay, the *Encyclopedia of Crime* won't be complete unless it contains an entry on *The Motion Picture Guide.*"

These years had amounted to the education of a film critic. When I started teaching a film class at University of Chicago Extension in 1970, it was John West who advised me to use a stop-motion 16 mm projector to conduct shot-by-shot analysis of films. With the class I would spent six to eight hours stopping and starting and discussing dozens of films, and when the approach became more practical with the invention of laser discs and DVDs, I did it at film festivals all over the world. It was a direct and practical way to discuss film style, beginning not with theory but with someone calling out "Stop!" in the dark, and then a freeze-frame and a discussion of a shot, composition, camera movement, editing sequence, dialogue, performance, costume, lighting technique, or something peculiar in the shadows of the screen. I do not know that we evolved any overarching ideas about cinema, but there were times when we felt we had joined the director inside his film; I remember a Hitchcock film when there was the flash of a gunshot, and we looked at the film itself and found that one single frame had been left clear, so that the projector light would bounce from the screen.

In these sessions we learned from *Understanding Movies,* by professor Louis D. Giannetti, who offered practical insights involving compositional strategies, and, a few years later, from the several books by professors David Bordwell and Kristin Thompson, who discussed film style with the greatest insight and penetration, and showed their confidence in their knowledge by writing in clear, elegant English instead of disguising insecurity with academese. Their books were an illustration of a truth that Robert Zonka cited when editing an impenetrable piece of copy: "If you cannot write about it so that anyone who buys the paper has a reasonable chance of understanding it, you don't understand it yourself."

I went to film festivals. At New York in 1967 I met Pauline Kael and Werner Herzog and many others, but to meet those two was of lifelong importance. Kael became a close friend whose telephone calls often began with "Roger, honey, no, no, no," before she would explain why I was not only wrong but likely to do harm. Herzog by his example gave me a model for the film artist: fearless, driven by his subjects, indifferent to commercial considerations, trusting his audience to follow him anywhere. In the thirty-eight years since I saw my first Herzog film, after an outpouring of some fifty features and documentaries, he has never created a single film

that is compromised, shameful, made for pragmatic reasons, or uninterest-
ing. Even his failures are spectacular.

A year or so later, I finally met Martin Scorsese; the two of us and
Pauline Kael got half hammered in a hotel room and he talked about *Season of the Witch,* the screenplay that would become *Mean Streets.* Another
time he took me to the loft where *Woodstock* was being edited; he was
working under Thelma Schoonmaker, who would become the editor of
most of his films. Another time we went to Little Italy on the Feast of San
Genaro, and in an Italian restaurant where he had eaten since childhood he
told me of the kinds of people who would populate his films; the opening
narration of *GoodFellas* is a version of the way he remembered his childhood during that dinner.

I went to Cannes. There were only five or six American journalists
covering it at that time. The most famous was Rex Reed, then at the height
of his fame, and I remember that he was friendly and helpful and not snob-
bish toward an obscure Chicagoan. Andrew Sarris and Molly Haskell were
there, Richard and Mary Corliss from *Time,* Charles Chaplin from the *Los
Angeles Times,* Kathleen Carroll from the *New York Daily News,* George
Anthony from Toronto, and the legendary Alexander Walker from London. I remember a night in 1979 when the Machiavellian French publicist
and cineaste Pierre Rissient took us all by motorboat to Francis Ford Coppola's yacht, where Coppola made his fateful statement that he didn't
know whether or not the ending of *Apocalypse Now* worked. By not defining what he meant by "ending," he skewed half of the original reviews
of his masterpiece; critics felt compelled to provide an opinion about the
"ending" even though, in fact, he was talking only about the end titles. He
said he would show "both versions" at Cannes, because he considered the
festival "an out-of-town tryout." Andrew Sarris asked: "Where's town?"

I visited many movie sets. In those days there were no ethical qualms
about the studio paying the way, and I flew off to Sweden to watch Bergman and Bo Widerberg at work, to Rome for Fellini and Franco Zeffirelli,
to England for John Boorman and Sir Carol Reed, to Hollywood for Billy
Wilder, Henry Hathaway, Otto Preminger, Norman Jewison, John Huston, countless others, most memorably Robert Altman, who struck me as
a man whose work and life amounted to the same thing. Those were the
days before publicists kept their clients on a short leash and reduced "in-

lessly and blissfully before the screen. It means to believe, first of all, that they are worth the time. That to see three movies during a routine workday or thirty movies a week at a film festival is a good job to have. That your mood when you enter the theater is not very important, because the task of every movie is to try to change how you feel and think during its running time. That it is not important to have a "good time," but very important not to have your time wasted. That on occasion you have sat before the screen and been enraptured by the truth or beauty projected thereon. That although you may be more open to a movie whose message (if it has one) you agree with, you must be open to artistry and craftsmanship even in a movie you disagree with. A movie is not good because it arrives at conclusions you share, or bad because it does not. A movie is not about what it is about. It is about how it is about it: about the way it considers its subject matter, and about how its real subject may be quite different from the one it seems to provide. Therefore it is meaningless to prefer one genre over another. Yes, I "like" film noir more than Westerns, but that has nothing to do with any given noir or Western. If you do not "like" musicals or documentaries or silent films or foreign films or films in black and white, that is not an exercise of taste, but simply an indication that you have not yet evolved into the more compleat filmgoer that we all have waiting inside.

These observations accepted, we can now consider movies that affect us with the same power as experiences in our real lives. Such movies can be comedies as well as tragedies; to laugh deeply and sincerely is as important as to weep. What must happen is that, for a scene or for a whole film, we are swept up in thoughts and emotions not of our own making. They can reinforce our own beliefs or oppose them; which they do is not the point. During those moments we are in intimate communication with the makers of the film. We share their thoughts and feelings as if working beside them. We are being guided through an empathetic experience by those who have felt it already and now seek how best to share it with us. Consider in this context not films that are universally valued, such as the beloved silent comedies, but a film that represents values we despise, such as Leni Riefenstahl's *Triumph of the Will*. To watch her glorification of Hitler and the Nazi party is to feel what Riefenstahl felt, and therefore to understand more immediately how Hitler's appeal worked and his influence grew. You can see any number of films against Hitler and understand he is a villain, but you must see him through the eyes of his admirers to fully understand the quality of his evil and the emotions that he engendered. Without that understanding you will see him as a spectacle but not as a fact.

It is not necessary to choose such extreme examples. Consider a movie like *Singin' in the Rain,* which was made on the musical assembly line at MGM, or *Casablanca,* a product of the Hal Wallis production team at Warner Brothers. These films did not set out to be great. Those making them were not impressed by their prospects. No one on the set could have guessed that they would someday be considered among the best of all films. They begin with standard ingredients: a backstage musical, a wartime melodrama. They do not arrive at great truths. Yet they both achieve perfection of their kind because they were made by artists who found themselves at the top of their personal abilities in material perfectly suited to them, and because for reasons both deliberate and accidental, nothing happened to obscure that process. There is joy in them. There can also be joy in a perfect film that is uncompromisingly sad, like Robert Bresson's *Au Hasard Balthazar,* a film that achieves extraordinary emotional power even though its protagonist is a donkey who has little understanding of the world and no power in it, and is never in the slightest degree made "human." Balthazar functions simply as the acceptance of what happens to Balthazar.

It is a common quality of the films we "love" that we can see them an indefinite number of times. Most good films need be seen only once (films that are not good need not be seen at all). *Raiders of the Lost Ark* achieves what it intends with admirable skill and artistry, but when you have seen it, it remains seen. I have seen *Citizen Kane* perhaps a hundred times, perhaps sixty of those times with the shot-by-shot approach, and I could happily start watching it again right now. That is also true of *Vertigo, The General, Nosferatu, Aguirre: The Wrath of God, Ikiru, Pulp Fiction, Touchez Pas au Grisbi, Raging Bull, The Third Man, Rules of the Game, La Dolce Vita,* and for that matter Errol Morris's *Gates of Heaven,* a documentary about the owners and customers of pet cemeteries which I have seen dozens of times and which I think is truly bottomless; the deeper into it I look, the more humanity and sadness and truth I see, but I never get to the end of its mystery.

I do not believe Errol Morris ever has, either. Something happened during the making of that film that is beyond planning or comprehension. Something like that happens in one way or another with all of the films we love; Auden wrote about Yeats that "he became his admirers," and in some way we become these films and they become us.

PROLOGUE
DEATH OF A DREAM PALACE

DECEMBER 4, 1994

One day it was winter. The next day there was a wet restlessness in the wind, and it was March. We knew it was March because Dan-Dan the Yo-Yo Man always came to town right around St. Patrick's Day. He visited all the grade school playgrounds, driving up in his fat maroon Hudson and jumping out with the yo-yo already in the air. He passed out fliers for the annual yo-yo contest at the Princess Theater.

The yo-yo was the first of many things I failed to master in life. Oh, I could walk the dog and loop the loop. But I was never able to rock the baby, so I was always disqualified on the first Saturday, the day when every kid in Urbana was up onstage at the Princess with his yo-yo. Two weeks later, when Dan-Dan presided over the finals, a kid would win a new Schwinn bike. The kid was never me.

The Princess closed forever last month. Friends and relatives sent me clippings in the mail from the *Champaign-Urbana News-Gazette*. "The Last Picture Show in Urbana," the headline said. It was also the only picture show in Urbana. Old clippings show it was in business as early as 1915. It was the place where I learned to love the movies.

In 1950, television was still a rumor in Champaign-Urbana. Some jerk down the street might put up a big antenna and be able to drag in a test pattern from Peoria, but for everybody else, mass media meant the radio and the movies. Over in Champaign they had the Rialto, the Orpheum, the Virginia, the Park, and the Illini, which was down by the railroad station and specialized in movies about nudist camps and the mademoiselles of Gay Paree. On campus, there was the Co-Ed. In Urbana, there was the Princess, where the program changed twice a week, and there was a Kiddie Matinee on Saturdays. The Kiddie Matinee was the biggest bargain in town. For exactly nine cents, you got a double feature, five color cartoons, a newsreel, the coming attractions, and a chapter of a serial starring Batman or Sheena, Queen of the Jungle. In March, you got Dan-Dan the Yo-Yo Man.

Your parents dropped you off at noon. You waited in the alley that ran down the side of the theater. Some of the older kids had just finished their Saturday morning dance classes at Thelma Lee Rose's dance studio, which was upstairs from the theater. When the Princess doors opened, there was a mad rush for tickets and seats: front row was the best. Usually your parents gave you twenty cents, which was enough for Jujubes and popcorn, with a penny left over for the jawbreaker machine.

First came the color cartoons, five of them, each exactly six minutes long. After *Th-th-th-at's all, folks!* came the first half of the double feature, which was always a Western: Hopalong Cassidy, Rex Allen, Roy Rogers, Gene Autry, or those two slightly kinky, sinister figures, Lash LaRue and Whip Wilson, who are due to be rediscovered any day now in camp circles. Then came the serial, the newsreel ("In sunny Cypress Gardens, mermaids learn that what goes up, comes down!") and the ads for the Urbana Pure Milk Co. and Reliable Furniture. Then came the second feature, which in my memory is always a comedy starring the Bowery Boys with Huntz Hall.

For a kid in grade school, going to the movies was one of the few acts in life that you could undertake entirely on your own. You chose your own seat. You ate your own popcorn. You lived out the adventures on the screen with an intensity that no later masterpiece by Steven Spielberg or George Lucas would ever equal. You laughed, you shrieked, and when the hero even looked like he was going to kiss the girl, you groaned.

The Princess in those days was not without its ominous side. Every show started with a slide offering a five-dollar reward "for the apprehension and conviction of vandals." Then came a dire warning: "Ladies! Hang onto Your Bags! Do Not Leave Them on the Seat Next to You!" In the boys' room, which was downstairs off the lobby, junior high school kids clustered in corners and smoked cigarettes. There was running warfare between the ushers and kids who tried to sneak in through the exit door. And if you bumped against the back of the seat in front of you, some junior thug was likely to turn around and threaten you with a knuckle sandwich.

Eventually I grew too old for the Kiddie Matinees. I became one of the students at Thelma Lee Rose's, learning the fox-trot and the box step. One Friday night Miss Rose held a dance for her students, and I asked a girl from my grade at school. When we got to the doorway that led up a steep flight of stairs to her studios, I discovered to my humiliation that I had made a mistake, and the dance was not until the following week.

My date and I pooled our funds and bought tickets to *The Bridge over the River Kwai,* which was the current feature at the Princess, and it was the best movie I had ever seen in my life. And my date let me put my arm around her, and that was even better.

In the Princess Theater I saw *Lawrence of Arabia* and *The Long, Long Trailer* and Pat Boone in *April Love* and Doris Day in *Young at Heart* and hundreds of other movies. Eventually I made my way across town for *Citizen Kane* and Bergman and Fellini at the Park (which had become the Art) and *The Immoral Mr. Teas* at the Illini.

One day, after I left Champaign-Urbana for the big city to the north, I learned that the Princess had been renamed the Cinema. And it seemed to me that in the very change of name, an era had passed and a crucial mistake had been made, because who would ever rather go to the Cinema than to the Princess?

Eventually they divided the old theater into two smaller auditoriums. They experimented with cheaper ticket prices. Business fell off. The students at the nearby University of Illinois were presumably looking at videos or logged on to the Internet. A giant multiscreen megaplex opened south of town, on U.S. 45. You could walk to the Princess, but the new extravaganza wasn't even in Champaign or Urbana.

In the movie *The Last Picture Show,* the last movie shown in the local theater was *Red River,* with John Wayne. At the Cinema, the final double bill was *Ed Wood,* a comedy about a 1950s exploitation film director, and *Red Rock West,* a triple-cross film noir. The night before they closed, they took in fifty dollars. Admission was three dollars until 6 p.m. and five dollars afterward. Still the biggest bargain in town.

My first movie reviews were written for the *Daily Illini* at the University of Illinois. I asked Kit Donahue, the current publisher, to plunder the files for what could be found, and the results were reviews of *King of Kings, Two Women, Saturday Night and Sunday Morning,* and *La Dolce Vita* (below). This is not a good review and is substantially mistaken, but it is where and how I started.

The *Daily Illini* experience was one of the great times of my life. As a freshman at Illinois I had edited and published a weekly newspaper on politics and the arts, named the *Spectator*. If we'd had the wit to give it away, we would have invented the alternative weekly, but no; it struggled for a year, I sold it for two hundred dollars, and joined the *Daily Illini* as a weekly columnist.

The paper then and now was one of the great college dailies, published independently of the university and with its own clankety rotary press roaring away at 3 a.m. every morning. We had a union print shop, and dealing with the realities of professional printers and pressmen was more educational than all possible injections of journalism theory.

The writing staff was awesome; it included William Nack, later to become the great *Sports Illustrated* racing and boxing writer, who even then was addicted to horses. We had one photo engraving of a horse, which as I recall we ran to illustrate whatever horse had just won the Kentucky Derby. At least a dozen other graduates of that period of the *DI* rose to become editors, publishers, columnists, and writers.

La Dolce Vita

OCTOBER 4, 1961

There is in *La Dolce Vita* a great deal to be puzzled about, and a great deal to be impressed by, and perhaps a great deal which we as Americans will never completely understand. Yet it is a fine motion picture. And we have the feeling that even those students who sat through its three hours with a measure of boredom came away convinced that something was there. It is this something, this undefined feeling being hammered at beneath the surface of the film, which gives it power and illumination. And it is this hidden message which contains the deep and moral indictment of the depravity which *La Dolce Vita* documents.

In technical excellence, the film surpasses every production this reviewer has seen, except a few of the Ingmar Bergman classics. Photography and the musical score are together almost as important as the dialogue in conveying the unmistakable attack on "the sweet life."

This attack is also made clear in frequent symbolism, although sometimes the symbolism becomes too obvious to fit into the effortless flow of the total production. For example, in the final scene where merrymakers gather around the grotesque sea monster which represents their way of living, and then the protagonist is called by the "good" girl but cannot understand her, the symbolism is very near the surface. Yet this tangible use of symbols might account in part for *La Dolce Vita*'s fantastic success. Too often the "new wave" fails through symbolism that is simply too subtle for most moviegoers.

The acting itself is startlingly realistic, and for a very good reason: too many of the players are portraying themselves. The greatest surprise—and one of the greatest successes—in the film is the Swedish sex goddess Anita Ekberg, cast as a "typical" American motion picture star. She plays the part with a wild, unthinking abandon which far surpasses her previous roles in "B" pictures designed primarily to exploit her impressive physical attributes.

But there can be no real award for best actor or actress in the film, just as in a sense it does not seem to be a film so much as a simple record of "the sweet life." The characters, in their midnight parody of happiness, are all strangely anonymous. Only their life, their society, comes through—with a sad, burnt-out vividness that sputters briefly through a long night and then dies in the morning on the beach, dies with the sea monster who has blank, uncomprehending eyes.

In the film, the wild but bored house party comes just before the dawn. It is this party, in all its depravity, which has become one of the most widely known segments of the film. Yet it is probably the one area of "the sweet life" which misses the mark for many American audiences. The scene is meant to show a last, desperate attempt to find something beneath the whirlpool of animalism which finally engulfs them all. Yet as the girl lies still beneath the mink stole, bored and restless eyes look away—still looking.

We are afraid that too many Americans might consider this scene as a sharp, immediate event. Its message, of complete and final meaninglessness, might not come through to an audience which may not find such things particularly everyday. And so, despite the almost extreme good taste with which the scene was filmed, we are afraid that many of the thousands who queued up before the theatre had rather elementary motives.

This is excusable. We wonder how many years it has been since a film as intellectual and meaningful—and as basically moral—as *La Dolce Vita* has attracted such crowds here. We suspect it has been a very long time. The greeting it is getting is a tribute to one of the finest motion pictures of our time.

PART 1

Interviews and Profiles

INTRODUCTION

In a perfect world, movie critics would perhaps never do interviews. There is a potential conflict involved in talking with someone, even dining with them, even visiting the set of their film, and then writing a review that is intended to be objective. Many papers make a clear distinction between critics and interviewers, and at Cannes when you apply for credentials they ask if you are a "critic" or a "chronicler." I have always been both.

It was a lucky break for me, after all, that the *Sun-Times* had one person on the movie beat, me. I wrote the reviews and did the interviews. That allowed me to build up a more complete database of reviews than any other critic of the same period, and it also allowed me access to hundreds of directors and other film artists.

From time to time I would grumble about the workload, and indeed the *Sun-Times* has had many other writers involved in writing interviews, but I never wanted to give it up entirely because I was interested in talking with these people about their work. As the publicity mechanism grew more calculating, the carefree access of earlier years shrank into the Dreaded Hotel Room Interview—three minutes taped for TV in front of a poster of the movie—and these I tended to avoid. What I would not have missed were visits to the sets or locations of Sam Peckinpah, Altman, Jewison, Bergman, Fellini, Carol Reed, Henry Hathaway, dozens of others. I talked with Hitchcock, Astaire, Streep, Groucho, John Wayne, Herzog, Mitchum, both Fondas, two Hustons, Jeanne Moreau, Elizabeth Taylor, Antonioni, Mae West.

My strategy as a writer evolved during some of my early pieces for *Esquire*. In reaction I suppose to Rex Reed and Tom Wolfe, who did some fancy footwork for the magazine, I developed a deadpan style in which I simply observed my subjects as they spoke and behaved, and commented on them with understatement. The Lee Marvin piece is an example of this approach.

Warren Beatty

Gene Siskel and I hosted a tribute to Warren Beatty in the 1980s at the Toronto Film Festival. Many of those he worked with agreed to appear: Arthur Penn, Robert Towne, Jerzy Kosinski, Jack Nicholson. Beatty himself did not agree to appear. He agreed to sit in the audience next to Diane Keaton and see how the tribute went, and then, when it concluded, he would see how he felt about getting up on the stage. In the event, he did mount to the stage, but to make remarks, not to answer questions.

He is protective of himself. Once I went to interview him and as I waited in a hotel room I was asked by a publicist what I thought about Beatty's new movie. I later discovered that he was sitting on the other side of a door, listening.

In Los Angeles one day I got a message from James Toback, inviting me to visit the set of his new movie *Bugsy.* I am customarily uninformed about films in production; I don't much read the trades and the press releases, or I would have known that *Bugsy* was not precisely Toback's film. He wrote it. Barry Levinson was directing it. Warren Beatty was coproducing and starring in it. I arrived at the house, was pointed up the driveway by a production assistant, walked in behind the cameras, and was seen by Beatty:

"Roger. Uh, yeah. Hi. Yeah. How are you?" This was all clearly an evasion of the question he wanted to ask, which was, what in the hell was I doing there? It was a closed set. Toback materialized and my presence was accounted for. How Toback eventually explained his invitation to Beatty is something I have never asked him.

Do I sound critical of Beatty? The fact is that I have enormous admiration for him. He has made some great films. He was personally responsible for the existence of *Bonnie and Clyde,* and it was his decision to trust Arthur Penn after they had gone down in flames together with their pre-

3

vious film, the underrated *Mickey One* (1965). It was Beatty who persuaded Jack Warner to give the film a proper release, although several versions exist of the story about how he did that. I am proud that as a new critic I was absolutely right about the greatness of *Bonnie and Clyde* at a time when much critical opinion was against it.

I don't think Beatty owes me a thing. His job is to make the movies. He can refuse to get up on the stage if he wants to, he can listen to my opinion of his movie before he talks to me, he can suggest a luncheon interview and then take me to a hot dog stand. "I want you to personally experience the best hot dogs in Burbank," he told me. I did.

SEPTEMBER 24, 1967

LONDON—No film in the last 10 years has gotten better reviews in London than Warren Beatty's *Bonnie and Clyde,* which opened here last week and in Chicago Friday. Beatty had all the reviews clipped out and stuck in a cardboard folder, which was resting on the coffee table in his room at the Gloucester Hotel. He kept pointing to the folder as if it was an exhibit and this was a trial.

"Hard to believe," he said. "Great reviews. Tremendous reviews. One critic called it the best American movie since 'On the Waterfront.' And you know what really hurts?"

He paused, and then continued to pace up and down the yellow carpet.

"What really hurts," he said, "is that one lousy review in the *New York Times.* Bosley Crowther says your movie is a glorification of violence, a cheap display of sentimental claptrap and that's that. The *New York Times* has spoken, hallelujah."

So Beatty, who produced and starred in *Bonnie and Clyde,* was getting it off his chest at last. It was the first time he had replied to Crowther's charges, although Arthur Penn, the film's director, had a succinct word or two to pronounce about Crowther last week.

The whole *Bonnie and Clyde* controversy is something of a rarity in American movie circles. You'd probably have to go back to *Psycho* to find another Hollywood film that has generated such intense debate. There's a little war going on right now in the little world of movie critics and it's beginning to look as if Crowther is getting the worst of it.

"The man at the *New York Times* has once again blown his tiny supply of cool," Wilfrid Sheed, *Esquire*'s movie critic, wrote this week. Andrew Sarris of the *Village Voice* accused Crowther of setting back the American film industry by refusing to recognize a great film when it finally made one. *Variety* covered Crowther's attack on violence cheek by jowl with a paragraph reporting that the Legion of Decency had praised the movie for its treatment and approach.

And after Crowther, in a second article, served notice to Hollywood that he will "no longer favorably review a movie with too much violence in it," Orson Bean wrote the *Times:* "More and more it seems that a liberal is someone who will fight to the death for your right to agree with him."

The funny thing is that the storm over *Bonnie and Clyde* has blown up so quickly. This wasn't exactly a movie that everyone stood around for months with their tongues hanging out waiting to see. For a long time, *Bonnie and Clyde* was just some movie that Warren Beatty was shooting down in Texas. It was about Bonnie Parker and Clyde Barrow, two folk heroes of the 1930s, who robbed banks, killed people, and snapped each other's pictures to send in to the newspapers. The Barrow Gang, as the ads have it, "was the strangest damn gang you ever heard of."

The story sounded interesting enough, sure, but who expected much? Penn was a director with moments of brilliance but an uneven track record, and Beatty—well, everybody knew Beatty was a crazy kid, kind of eccentric, who might throw an ashtray at you.

That was the attitude until *Bonnie and Clyde* was premiered at the Montreal Film Festival, when suddenly people realized they had something to deal with here. This was probably the best American film of the year. Beatty and Penn (who would have guessed it?) had gone out into the desert and labored and brought forth a masterpiece.

Most of the people who saw the film believed so, anyway. But not Crowther. And not—for a week, anyway—Joseph Morgenstern, the critic at *Newsweek*. In an unprecedented about-face, Morgenstern panned *Bonnie and Clyde* one week, and then reversed his stand in the next issue. "I was wrong," he wrote, analyzing where he'd gone astray and praising the movie extravagantly.

The *Newsweek* episode brought a smile to Beatty's lips. "Can you picture it?" he said. "Morgenstern is honest enough to admit he changed his mind. So he goes in to the editors, and they say, Good Lord, you can't change your mind. You're a critic—you're infallible. But Morgenstern stands his ground, so they let him have his way. I'll bet some doors slammed at *Newsweek*."

So *Newsweek* came around. The other reviews were good. All except for Crowther. And it was his review that Beatty simply could not forget. He walked up and down in his hotel room, he shook his head, he picked up the clippings of the London reviews for reassurance, he talked.

"Because Crowther writes for the *New York Times*," he said, "he has influence all out of proportion to his importance. Out in the bush leagues, the theater owners, they read the *Times*. For them, Crowther is God. Everybody in the world can like a movie, and if Crowther doesn't, he kills it."

Beatty said part of the trouble might have been the audience at Montreal.

"Maybe Crowther thought when the audience cheered, it was cheering for violence. See, there are several scenes in which we carefully develop one emotion in the audience, and then—zing!—we cut very fast to the opposite emotion. So you're sitting there laughing and suddenly you look at the screen and what you're laughing at isn't very funny at all.

"That was kind of the way with Bonnie Parker and Clyde Barrow. They didn't seem to be able to see their crimes in context. They killed all these people, and it was still a game for them, a lark. What we tried to do in the movie was put the humor and the violence in the same framework, to make a point about the social climate that produced the Barrow Gang."

Beatty said he would give an example.

"Bonnie and Clyde are strictly amateurs at the hold-up game, of course. They take incredible risks for nothing at all. So remember the scene where Clyde is waving around this enormous pistol, and he's in a grocery store and all he's stealing is a sack of groceries. So the grocer fills the Kraft paper bag, and Clyde says. 'You sure you ain't got any peach pies?' And the grocer is very nervous with that thing waving in his face, and he says, 'No, sir, mister. I'm sure we ain't got any.'

"And so the audience laughs because this is so ridiculous. But just then a big fat butcher lunges at Clyde with a meat cleaver. A meat cleaver! And the audience says this isn't so funny. But then Clyde and this fat butcher roll around on the floor, and that's funny, because this butcher looks so comical and so they forget the meat cleaver, they start to laugh again. But then Clyde bashes the butcher on the side of the head—splat!—with his pistol, and then he swings back and hits him on the other side of the head—SPLAT!"

Beatty swung his hand back and forth, fast, as if the pistol were still in it. Then he leaned forward enthusiastically. "What we did," he said, "was, we quadrupled the sound level on the second splat. So it was incredibly loud and sickening. And the audience found the laugh dying on their lips. They hated us for that, hated us for playing with their emotions that way.

"But then—we change the mood again." Beatty sounded like a kid explaining a trick play around left end. "Bonnie and Clyde drive away in their touring car, and on the sound track we have Flatt and Scruggs playing 'Foggy Mountain Breakdown,' giving the whole thing kind of a carnival air. Only this time the music isn't appropriate, see? It's music that says laugh, but you can't laugh. The whole movie kind of weaves back and forth between making you laugh and making you sick."

Beatty was interrupted by a knock on the door. He admitted a bellhop, who carried a gift-wrapped present.

"Humm, probably cyanide," Beatty said, unwrapping the parcel. It was a bottle of champagne. He read the card aloud. It said, "To America's Greatest Producer."

Beatty smiled. "Well, how about that." he said. He put the champagne on the mantelpiece. Then he sat down, for the first time during the interview, and crossed his legs.

"There is one consolation," Beatty said. "At least Crowther was furious at the movie. I couldn't have taken it if he'd been indifferent. But how can you take anyone seriously in this day and age who calls a character in a movie a 'young tough?' I ask you."

Beatty was on his feet again by this time, looking out the window. He said he was only going to be in London for another day or two, and then back to Hollywood.

"A lot of people out there just kind of dismiss me as an irresponsible kid," he said. "All of Hollywood is old, old, old, for that matter. There are as many good young actors and directors in America as there are in Europe, but Hollywood shuts them out. Hollywood is afraid of young blood. It's a ghost town."

He pointed a finger and posed a question. "I'm twenty-eight years old," he said. "I'll give you five seconds to name me another Hollywood leading man under the age of thirty-five."

It was hard to do. Promising newcomers, yes, but no stars. And even later with plenty of time to think, only three names came to mind: Elvis Presley, Frankie Avalon, and George Hamilton. That's food for thought right there.

James Stewart

Frank Casey was the Warner Brothers publicist in Chicago when I became the *Sun-Times* film critic. He'd gotten his job when mayor Martin Kennelly suggested him to Jack Warner at a time when Kennelly was owed a favor. The mayor called in Frank and informed him that he was now working for Warner Brothers. Frank was not sure this was good news. He had a job at Coca-Cola.

"What can they give you that Warner Brothers can't?" asked the mayor.

"A uniform."

Shortly after I joined the paper as a feature writer, Casey announced a junket to the set of *Camelot* and the paper sent me. In those days we accepted studio junkets without a moment's thought. Casey liked my story about *Camelot* and told the editor of the paper I should be their new film critic. That had something to do with me getting the job, when it opened up. On the other hand, I was once on Casey's enemies list and did not get invited to a screening or an interview for two years. He never told me why. Then we were buddies again. It was said he had never sat through an entire movie. He once called me up and said, "Whoosis wants to know if you want to talk to Whatsis."

Casey engineered the interview with James Stewart, when I had been on the job less than a year. *Firecreek* was a Universal picture, but Stewart said he wouldn't do the junket unless Casey handled it. They had a history together. Warners loaned him out. Casey had a history with Ronald Reagan, too; as a favor to his friend Dr. Davis, he introduced the doctor's daughter Nancy to Ronnie.

At the wake at Gene and Georgetti's steak house after Casey's death, his bosses got up and told stories about his expense accounts. A waiter showed me an American Express machine. "This is the machine we used," he said, "when you had dinner here with Frank every night."

"I had dinner with Frank every night?" I said.

"Including Mondays, when we are closed."

Re-reading this James Stewart interview, I am struck by the fact that I apparently asked him why he'd never played a bad guy, and he answered me, "I just really don't know if I could play a heavy." Perhaps he was being nice to me. Certainly he knew, as I obviously did not in 1968, that he had played bad guys. By the time I wrote the piece "Mitch and Jimmy: Some Thoughts," I knew that. You learn on the job.

1968

EL PASO, TX—The morning after the world premiere of *Firecreek,* his seventieth motion picture, James Stewart pulled a maroon dressing gown on over his shirt and slacks to ward off the chill in his hotel suite.

This took a minute or so and then he returned to his chair and sat down, crossing his arms, rocking back and forth slowly, trying to frame the right words to answer the question his visitor had just posed.

"Oh, I guess I've been asked often enough when I'm going to get around to playing a bad guy," he said at last. "I never have. Seems like everyone else has taken the plunge. John Wayne. Henry Fonda."

He took another pause, and you could see the grin beginning around his eyes. It was a slow grin that took its time working around to the rest of his face. The Stewart grin.

"I don't know," he said at last. "I just really don't know if I could play a heavy. I've played heroes all my life, and now—well, it would be like playing Hamlet. It's not that you don't want to, but you just don't know if you could. I've never seriously considered it."

He sipped from a mug of black coffee. "It wouldn't be in character, would it?" he said.

James Stewart playing a bad guy? No, that wouldn't be in character. Not after Lindy, who flew the ocean, and Mr. Smith, who went to Washington, and Destry, who rode again.

"The Stewart character usually isn't aggressive enough to be a bad guy," Stewart mused. "It's all he can manage to be the good guy. He'd rather just plod along, getting through life without too much commotion, but somehow he stumbles into a dangerous situation and has to get out.

"That's the kind of character I play in *Firecreek*—a part-time sheriff who gets paid two bucks a month and doesn't want to shoot out nothing with nobody."

That was also the kind of character in *Rear Window,* wasn't it?

"Right," Stewart said. "The guy who has a broken leg, and discovers a crime by accident. He gets involved against his better judgment. For his troubles, he gets another broken leg. Some hero."

As Stewart spoke, his voice fell into the famous drawl. It is not an act. It is the way Stewart talks, and it is catching.

After five minutes with him you're likely to discover, to your embarrassment, that you're doing a Jimmy Stewart imitation.

"Don't let it bother you," Stewart said, smiling. "Sometimes I wonder if I'm doing a Jimmy Stewart imitation myself. All of this"—he waved vaguely at the suite—"wasn't planned. I'm a lazy person. By nature I would have planned a quieter life. I don't act. I react."

John Wayne said something like that about Westerns once: that they were divided into action and reaction. In the action Western, the hero says, let's chase the varmints down. In the reaction western, the hero says, let's make a plan . . .

"I make plans," Stewart said. "I think my strength on the screen is that I can react. When you think about *Rear Window,* you'll remember my role largely consisted of reacting. First Hitchcock would show what I was seeing through my binoculars. Then he'd show my face, and I'd reflect what I saw. I spent an astonishing amount of time looking into the camera and being amused, afraid, worried, curious, embarrassed, bored, the works."

Stewart recalled some of the other directors he had worked with: Frank Capra, John Ford, George Cukor, Ernest Lubitsch, Henry Hathaway, Anthony Mann. "A good director will keep the reins pulled tight," he said. "I've secretly wanted to direct a film myself, but it's a big chore and, like I say, I'm lazy. Directing is really the most creative and rewarding job in pictures. But I'm stuck in acting, I guess. I enjoy myself too much."

He divided a sweet roll into four parts, selected one, and washed it down with more coffee.

"You know what the real mystery is?" he said. "Over the years, I've learned the technique of movie acting, the craft, pretty well. I can go through the motions to my own satisfaction. But then, when it comes right down to it, none of the technique means a thing against those moments when you're in front of the camera and something takes place entirely in addition to the lines and the movements.

"John Ford always said—he's so disrespectful of everything and everybody—that most of the really good things in movies happen by accident. I think maybe he's right. You bring together competent people, and you solve the technical problems, and you try to find a solid piece of material to film. And if you have all that—THEN, maybe, something will happen. Or maybe not.

"Hitchcock and Ford both worked that way. They'd plan everything in advance, meticulously. Every detail. They'd foresee everything that could possibly be foreseen. And then, when they got us in front of the cameras, they'd sort of throw it all up for grabs, to see if anything exciting would happen. Within the technical framework, you sort of cross your fingers and wish for magic."

Stewart shook his head and allowed himself a wry smile. "I remember Ford used to have a speech. His theory of movie making. He'd say, don't talk about it. Don't analyze it. Don't rehearse it. Don't think about it. Come prepared and then get in front of the camera and do it and see how it comes out.

"Ford never rehearsed. I never like to rehearse anyway, for that matter. I learn my lines and think about them some, but if I'm doing a scene, I want to know the camera is operating. Unless the camera is moving, the scene isn't alive, and the rehearsal is technical stuff. By the time you get to the cameras, the scene is dead. Rehearsal should be limited to making sure nobody falls over any chairs.

"Directors who shoot a scene again and again aren't necessarily perfectionists. They're just waiting for that moment—that little moment, I can't put it into words—when everybody knows it was done right.

"Ford, on the other hand, always tried to shoot a scene only once, counting on spontaneity to carry the day. Sometimes it would work, sometimes it wouldn't. But it had nothing to do with improvisation in any case. The French directors like Godard who like to improvise everything are cheating themselves and their actors. They give nobody a chance to listen or react; everyone's thinking about what they're going to do next.

"But sometimes, all the same, a little moment will come when everything is right. You get involved. The sweat glands start to work. You tremble a little. And people will remember those scenes for years. They'll forget the whole movie, but remember the scene."

Stewart put his hands behind his head and leaned back in his chair, staring up at the ceiling. "I'll never forget once, we were on location in Canada, up in the ice fields," he said. "It was raining, and we had a fire; the company was trying to keep warm. An old man—he must have been seventy—came walking out of the rain and the wilderness. Out of nowhere.

"He said, Which one of you fellows is Stewart? I said I was. He said he'd seen me in a lot of picture shows. He said he remembered one scene real well. I was in a room, he said. There was a girl in the next room. There were fireflies around. I said a piece of poetry to her. The old man said he'd never forget that scene.

"Well, at the moment I couldn't remember it myself. But finally I did. That was from 'Come Live with Me,' and the girl was Hedy Lamarr, and we made it in 1941." Stewart shook his head, remembering. "A moment like that will stay with you and the whole movie will fade away," he said.

"I've been in movies for thirty years or more, and I still don't understand what goes on in this art form, but I'm beginning to accept it. People will visit a Hollywood set and see dozens of people standing around doing nothing, and they'll say, what are all these people for?

"Well, they're there because it's the most inefficient business in the world. You'll spend a whole day, maybe, getting a few seconds or a minute or two of film. At the end of several weeks or months you have all these bits of film, and the idea is to paste them together into a movie. Ford calls it crocheting. It's a slow, sticky, frustrating business, but it's worth the time we spend."

Stewart swung his arms around as if he held a camera. "All this hand-held camera business misses the point," he said. "I'm never happier than when the cameras are grinding and I'm trying something out in front of them. If it doesn't work, throw it away and try again. Maybe sometimes you'll get some film worth saving. And what the hell." The wry grin appeared again. "The film is the cheapest stuff in the whole business."

Robert Mitchum

Robert Mitchum was said to be an impossible interview, but I loved to spend time with him, because he didn't give a damn. He would say whatever he felt like saying, interview or not, didn't care if he was quoted, and would talk to you again. That's one reason he became such a larger-than-life character: He wasn't protected by hovering press agents and thirty-second sound bites.

I met him for the first time in 1967, on the Dingle Peninsula of Ireland, the location of David Lean's *Ryan's Daughter*. He was living in a rented cottage on a wind-swept coast. I'd traveled to Ireland with my Irish friend John McHugh and his younger brother Eugene, and the three of us joined Mitch in mid-drunk. That interview survives, and this one, from the set of *Going Home,* took place soon after. It ran in the *New York Times,* and caused some comment because of the implication that Mitchum was smoking pot, which he certainly was. He told me a story one day I couldn't use in the paper. It involved Trevor Howard, his costar in *Ryan's Daughter*.

"After the movie was finished and ready to be released," he said, "we were dispatched to the four winds on promotional tours. Trevor was sent to Germany. Bailey Sellig, our publicist, went along with him. Bailey got Trevor to Heathrow, where he topped up at the airport pub, bought a watch at the duty free, and then stopped at the men's room on the way to his airplane. While he was standing at the urinal, he admired his new watch, one of those digital jobs from Japan. It told you the time, day, date, month, year, atmospheric pressure, I don't know what all.

"Trevor remained topped up all during the German trip. Two weeks later, Trevor and Bailey returned to Heathrow. Trevor again felt the need to urinate, and went into either the same men's room, or one which was architecturally similar. Bailey waited in the corridor. He heard a cry of alarm. He raced inside. Trevor was standing at the urinal, looking at his watch and moaning. Bailey asked him what the matter was. *I've been pissing for two weeks,* Trevor said."

SEPTEMBER 19, 1971

MCKEESPORT, PA.—The sky hung low and dripping over the Sheraton Motor Inn, and Robert Mitchum hunched his shoulders against it and scooted around to the other side of the Mercury.

"I bought some of that lime spray," he told Tim Lawless, his friend. "Maybe she'll go for some of that lime spray."

"Lime spray," Tim said.

"You coming or staying?" Tim shouted out the window to another member of the company. "Staying?" He started the car and guided it down a ramp and onto a highway, turning left, which was, as it turned out, a fateful decision.

"This is, I would say, relaxing work," Mitchum said. "They don't push you too hard. While you're resting they say, would you mind carrying these anvils upstairs?"

"Jesus, what a lousy, crummy day," Tim said.

"And here it is only two in the afternoon," Mitchum said. "Reflect on the hours still before us. What time is the call for?"

"They're looking for you around 2:30, quarter to 3," Tim said. "You got it made."

"You know the way?" Mitchum said.

"Hell yes, I know the way," Tim said. "I was out here yesterday. Sons of bitches, picking locations way the hell the other side of hell and gone."

"Look at those kids," Mitchum said. Three or four kids had parked their motorcycles at an intersection and were sitting backward on the seats, in the drizzle, watching traffic. "Kids hanging around street corners," Mitchum said wonderingly, as if that were a sight he didn't see much anymore. "Oogling, drooling . . ."

"Drooling," Tim said.

"Oogling," Mitchum said. "What do we gotta shoot this afternoon? We gotta jam our asses into those little cells again?"

"Those are the smallest cells I've ever seen," Tim said. "Can you imagine pulling solitary in one of those?"

"I did five days of solitary once, when I was a kid," Mitchum said. "In Texas. Of course, in Texas you might as well be in as out."

"You did solitary?" Tim said.

"I liked it," Mitchum said. "You read about Alvin Karpis, up in Canada? They finally let him out after forty years or something. Son of a bitch walks outside, and the guy who put him in is still sitting there. J. Edgar. Son of a bitch does forty years, the least we could do for him is not have J. Edgar still sitting there when he gets out a lifetime later."

"Karpis?" Tim said.

"I guess he was a real mean mother at one time," Mitchum said.

The wipers beat back and forth against the windshield, and on the sidewalks people put their heads down and made short dashes between dry places. We were in Pittsburgh, now, and the smoke and fog brought visibility down to maybe a couple of blocks.

"I'm glad we're shooting inside today," Tim said.

Mitchum whistled under his breath, and then began to sing softly to himself: "Seventy-six trombones led the big parade . . ."

"With a hundred-and-ten cornets in the rear," Tim sang, banging time against the steering wheel.

"A hundred and ten? Is that right?" Tim said after awhile.

"All I know is the seventy-six trombones," Mitchum said. "I don't have time to keep pace with all the latest developments."

So how long you been in Pittsburgh? I asked.

"I was born here," Mitchum said, "and I intend to make it my home long after U.S. Steel has died and been forgotten. I intend to remain after steel itself has been forgotten. I shall remain, here on the banks of the Yakahoopee River, a grayed eminence . . . I used to come through here during the Depression. I don't think the place has ever really and truly recovered."

He reached in his pocket for a pipe, filled it carefully and lit up. "I find myself talking to the kids," he said. "And they say . . ."

He broke off as a Mustang with two girls in it pulled up next to the Mercury at a stoplight. Through the window at his side, he mouthed a warm suggestion. "Hey, baby, you want to . . ."

The Mustang pulled away.

"They don't have lip-readers worth a damn in this town," Mitchum said.

"But the kids. I was talking about the kids. They say they figure they owe the community about two more years, and then they're pulling out before they're flung headlong into despair."

"I don't think we went through a tunnel yesterday," Tim said.

"Well, we're going through a tunnel now," Mitchum said.

"Are you sure we're supposed to be on 79 and not 76?" Tim said.

"I think I'm sure," Mitchum said. "We were either supposed to sing 'Seventy-six Trombones' to remind us to take 76 or to remind us not to. I'm not sure which."

"You're not leading me down the garden path, are you, Bob?" Tim said.

"Route 79," Mitchum said. "Maybe it was 76. Or . . . Route 30?"

"This is the goddamn airport road," Tim said. "Look there."

"Steubenville, Ohio," Mitchum said. "Jesus Christ, Tim, we're going to Steubenville, Ohio. Maybe it's just as well. Make a left turn at Steubenville and come back in on the Pennsylvania Turnpike . . ."

"Ohio's around here somewhere," Tim said.

"I've always wanted to make a picture in Ohio," Mitchum said. "Maybe I have. I was bitten by a rowboat once in Columbus."

There were three lanes of traffic in both directions, and Tim held grimly to the wheel, trying to spot a sign or an exit or a clue.

"The Vesuvius Crucible," Mitchum said. "Pull off here, and we'll ask at the Vesuvius Crucible. If anybody ought to know where they are, the Vesuvius Crucible ought to."

Tim took the next exit and drove into the parking lot of the Vesuvius Crucible. Mitchum rolled down the window on his side and called to a man inside the office: "Hey, can you tell us how to get to the Allegheny County Workhouse?"

"The what?" the man said.

"The Allegheny County Workhouse," Mitchum said.

"Hell, they closed that down back here six months ago," the man said. "It's empty now."

"We just want to visit," Mitchum said. "Old times' sake."

The man came out into the yard, scratching himself thoughtfully. "The Allegheny County Workhouse," he repeated. "Well, buster, you're real lost. You turn around here and go right back to downtown Pittsburgh. Take the underpass. When you get to downtown Pittsburgh, ask for directions there."

"How wide are we of the mark?" Mitchum said.

"Buster," the man said, "you're thirty-eight or forty miles away from where you should be."

"Holy shit," Mitchum said.

"I'm telling you," the man said, "they shut the workhouse down back here six, seven months ago. You won't find anybody there."

"Thanks just the same," Mitchum said.

Tim drove back up to the expressway overpass and came down pointed toward Pittsburgh. "We should have taken Route 8," he said.

"Sorry about that," Mitchum said. "There's the road to Monroeville. Ohio's around here somewhere."

"Nice countryside," Tim said. "You ought to buy it and build yourself a ranch."

"I could be the biggest rancher in Pittsburgh," Mitchum said. "Get up in the morning and eat ham and eggs in my embroidered pajamas. Some girl broke into the motel; did you hear about that? With a pair of embroidered PJs?"

"Embroidered?"

"A great big red heart right over the rosette area," Mitchum said. "I've got an idea. Maybe we should hire a cab and have it lead us to the Allegheny County Workhouse."

"I don't even think we're in Allegheny County," Tim said.

Mitchum hummed "Seventy-six Trombones" under his breath and filled his pipe again.

This is your first picture since *Ryan's Daughter,* right? I asked him. The picture is *Going Home,* and Mitchum plays a man who murdered his wife years ago, gets out of prison and is confronted by his son.

"There's a funny thing about that," Mitchum said. "At the same time I was reading this script, I was also reading a script about a jazz musician in San Francisco.

"So I ask myself, do I want to play a jazz musician in San Francisco, or do I want to go out on location in some god-forsaken corner of McKeesport, Pa., and live in a motel for two months? No way. No way. So these two guys come in, and we have a drink or two, and I sign the contract. On their way out, I say I'll see them in San Francisco. I thought they looked a little funny. Do you know what I did? I signed up for the wrong fucking movie!"

"Here's Route 8 right now," Tim said.

"That's Exit 8, not Route 8," Mitchum said.

"We're going to be real late," Tim said. "Real late."

"They can rehearse," Mitchum said. "They can practice falling off stairs, tripping over lights, and shouting at each other in the middle of a take."

The car was back in the tunnel again now, headed the other way. Tim came down through a series of cloverleafs and found himself back on Route 79, headed for the airport.

"I'm lost," he said. "Baby, I am lost."

In desperation, he made a U-turn across six lanes of traffic and found himself on an up-ramp going in the opposite direction with a cop walking slowly across the street toward him.

Mitchum rolled down his window. "Roll down your window," he told Tim. "Let's get a breeze in here." He shouted to the cop: "Hey, chief! We're lost! We been forty miles out in the country, and here we are headed right back the same way again."

"'What are you doing making a U-turn against all that traffic?" the cop said. "You could go to jail for that."

"Hell, chief," Mitchum said, "that's where we're trying to go. We been looking for the Allegheny County Workhouse for the last two hours."

"They closed that down back here six months ago," the policeman said.

"We're shooting a movie out there," Mitchum said.

"Hey, you're Robert Mitchum, aren't you?" the cop said.

Mitchum pulled his dark glasses down on his nose so the cop could see more of his face and said: "We are so lost."

"I tell you what you do, Bob," the cop said. "You take this underpass and follow the road that curves off on your left before you get to the bridge."

"Thanks, chief," Mitchum said.

Tim drove onto the underpass, followed the road that curved off on the left before he got to the bridge and groaned.

"We're back on Route 79 heading for the airport," he said.

"Jesus Christ," Mitchum said. "Screw that cop. Screw that cop and the boat that brought him."

"Now we gotta go back through the tunnel," Tim said. "I'm upset. I am really upset."

On the other side of the tunnel, Tim pulled over next to a state highway department parking lot and backed into it down the exit ramp. A state employee came slowly out of a shed, wiping his hands on a rag and watching Tim's unorthodox entry.

"Ask that guy," Mitchum said. "Offer him a certain amount to lead us there with a snowplow."

Tim got out and got some instructions from the state employee. The instructions required a great deal of pointing and arm waving, and their essence seemed to be: Go back that way.

Tim tried it again, back through the tunnel, across the bridge, down the overpass to a red light where a police squad car was stopped in front of the Mercury. Mitchum jumped out of the car and hurried up to the squad for instructions. He got back just as the light turned green.

"You'll see a sign up here that says Blaunox," he said. "That's what we need. Blaunox."

"I'm out of gas," Tim said.

"I got a letter from John Brison today," Mitchum said. "John's in Dingle, in Ireland. Where we shot *Ryan's Daughter.*"

"I am really upset," Tim said.

"According to John," Mitchum said, "they've formed a Robert Mitchum Fan Club in Dingle. The membership is largely composed of unwed mothers and their brothers."

"Where the hell are we?" said Tim.

"That's what happens when you shoot on location," Mitchum said. "It's nothing but a pain in the ass."

He began to whistle "Seventy-six Trombones" again, softly, but not too softly.

Mitch and Jimmy: Some Thoughts

JULY 9, 1997

All week people have been asking me who I liked better—Jimmy Stewart or Robert Mitchum. I wouldn't play the game. They were both one of a kind. Each had a style, a grace, a bearing, a voice, a face, a walk, that was unmistakable and irreplaceable. To be forced to choose between them simply because of the unhappy coincidence of their deaths is meaningless. Who would you choose: John Wayne, or Jimmy Cagney? Bette Davis, or Marilyn Monroe. See what I mean?

And yet, when the obituaries had been written and the tributes had been televised and the AMC cable channel had devoted one day to Mitch's movies and the next day to Jimmy's, I confess I felt a certain sadness that Mitchum's death was to some degree overshadowed by Stewart's. Here's how I read the general reaction: When Mitch died, we lost a legendary old movie star. When Jimmy died, we lost a national treasure. Both of these "opinions" are of course judgments made in an instant by newspeople who—let's face it—may not have ever seen most of the films either man made. In the last week I've been amazed at how many people knew who they were but had forgotten, or never knew, what they'd done.

"What was his best movie?" people have asked me. With Mitchum, I answered *Night of the Hunter,* or maybe *Out of the Past.* With Stewart, I answered firmly: *Vertigo.* And then I paused for a reaction, and got none. They hadn't seen any of them.

The one movie they'd all seen was *It's a Wonderful Life,* which on Christmas Eve seems to play on every channel not solely devoted to selling zirconium necklaces. James Stewart, in that one film, passed beyond the kind of fame you get as a movie star, and became a kind of cultural icon, a saint of our secular church. For Stewart to die was for George Bailey to die, and the ending of the film provided the perfect curtain for his life: one

21

more star in heaven, and one more angel. In her words at Stewart's memorial service, his daughter, Dr. Kelly Harcourt, evoked the character and the film by calling him "the richest man in town."

That was the James Stewart that the news shows and the newspaper editorials eulogized—the actor who appeared in a movie that has become one of the few things we all seem to share in our fragmented society.

He also appeared in darker and more difficult roles, including above all *Vertigo* but also *Rope, Winchester 73, Rear Window, Anatomy of a Murder,* and *The Naked Spur.* And in lighthearted comedies (*Philadelphia Story*), and superb adventure films (*Flight of the Phoenix*), and romantic biographies (*The Glenn Miller Story*) and in countless other fine movies. But those are what movie fans would remember. *It's a Wonderful Life* is remembered by everyone.

Robert Mitchum never made a picture like that. Perhaps he couldn't have. He embodied a completely different kind of character on the screen: harder, wiser, darker. No matter what your age was, Mitchum always seemed older than you were, just as Stewart always seemed boyish. Stewart smoked in roles, and you felt it was because the character smoked. Mitchum smoked, and it was because he needed to. And when he drank in a movie, the way he picked up the glass let you know he wasn't keeping count.

Robert Mitchum was my favorite movie star because he represented, for me, the impenetrable mystery of the movies. He knew the inside story. With his deep, laconic voice and his long face and those famous weary eyes, he was the kind of guy you'd picture in a saloon at closing time, waiting for someone to walk in through the door and break his heart.

Mitchum was the soul of film noir. And film noir is one of the three uniquely American movie genres (the others are Westerns and musicals). The way he wore a fedora, the way he let a cigarette dangle from his lip, the way he handled himself in a fight, was manly, tough, and cynical. The model for that kind of character was Bogart, but Mitchum refined it, and made it modern.

When he was in a fight in a movie, you felt like you were watching a fight. Not a skillful exercise in choreography, constructed out of pseudo-karate and special effects and stunt men. But a fight, in which one guy's fist hits another guy's gut, and it hurts, and is surprising and definitive, and is over in a flash.

Mitchum made probably the best of all film noirs, *Out of the Past,* and a lot of others. He made that distinctive American art film *Night of the Hunter,* directed by Charles Laughton, which combined a nightmarish story with the most delicate of visual whimsy (remember the animals along the river bank as the children float to safety?). To look at the span of his work, from *The Sundowners* to *The Friends of Eddie Coyle,* from *Farewell, My Lovely* to *The Lusty Men* to *The Yakuza* to *Pursued,* is to see a professional at home in many genres, periods, and accents. You can never catch him cheating, coasting, or looking phony.

When a great star or director dies, critics all over the world haul down David Thomson's big *Biographical Dictionary of Film,* because it does the best job in the fewest words of capturing the essence of its hundreds of subjects. Some of them may have been surprised by what he wrote about Mitchum:

"How can I offer this hunk as one of the best actors in the movies? There is an intriguing ambiguity in Mitchum's work, the idea of a man thinking and feeling beneath a calm exterior so that there is no need to put 'acting' on the surface. And for a big man, he is immensely agile, capable of unsmiling humor, menace, stoicism, and above all, of watching other people as if he were waiting to make up his mind."

And then Thomson added: "Since the war, no American actor has made more first-class films, in so many different moods."

I was lucky enough to meet both James Stewart and Robert Mitchum several times. Stewart was one of the nicest movie actors I ever met. He was patient, humorous, modest, smart. There was an edge to him—no one could fly twenty-two combat missions over Germany and be merely a nice guy—but he liked people and liked himself, and you felt good around him.

Mitchum was another story. He was known as the hardest interview in the business. I thought he was the best. I learned early how to talk to him. It was a rain-swept night in 1968, in a little cottage on the Dingle Peninsula in Ireland, where he drank whisky and listened to Jim Reeves records and told stories. He was making *Ryan's Daughter* and was beginning to think he should have been making something else. I was awestruck. He didn't simply fill a room, he wore it like a T-shirt.

My questions sounded inane: "What it is like, working with Mr. Lean?" His answers turned and coiled upon themselves, following paths of invention and whimsy. I realized that he had a technique for not getting bored during interviews. His technique was to free-associate about whatever he damn well pleased, and to invent stories if the real ones weren't entertaining enough.

When we met the next time, I just let him talk. I was an audience, not an interviewer. Once in McKeesport, Pennsylvania, he dismissed his driver and announced that he and I would be driven to the movie location by his friend and stand-in. We spent four hours being lost. At one point, we had left Pennsylvania altogether and were in Steubenville, Ohio, with Mitchum wondering if a snowplow operator could be bribed to lead us back to town. And all the time he talked, free-associating. I don't know if he was the best conversationalist in the movies, but he might have been the best monologist.

The last time I saw him was at the Virginia Festival of American Film, in Charlottesville, four years ago. They did a tribute to film noir and I interviewed Mitchum onstage after the screening of *Out of the Past*. He'd gone out to dinner rather than see the film again ("I don't know if I've ever seen it") and at dinner he smiled at his wife of fifty years, Dorothy, and told this story:

"Once there were a lot of fans under my hotel room window. I turned to Dorothy and asked her, 'Why do they make such a big deal? You've been married to me for years, and you're certainly not impressed. And Dorothy said to me, 'Bob, when you're up there on the screen, they're smaller than your nostril.'"

There's a truth there that applies to every movie star. But not many of them would have told the story.

So, Mitchum or Stewart? I cannot chose. I cannot do without either one of them. They are among the immortals. But when Stewart died, the entire nation went into mourning, and the president issued a statement, which he had not been moved to do the day before, when Mitchum died. And I thought, yes, all honor to Jimmy. But let us also love and remember Mitch. And I put on my laser disc of *Night of the Hunter,* and listened to Mitchum's voice coiling from the screen ("Chil . . . dren?"). And I thought, Stewart was the heart, and Mitchum was the soul.

Lee Marvin

INTRODUCTION

I interviewed Lee Marvin the first time in 1968, on the set of *Paint Your Wagon*. I went back to the Hollywood Roosevelt Hotel, wrote the interview immediately, and submitted it to the Sunday *New York Times*. It was my first appearance in the newspaper (which agreed to run it the same day as the *Sun-Times*). He was drinking Heineken's that day, too. We began in the Paramount commissary, where he observed of John Wayne, "Look. He wears his gun to lunch." We ended hours later at a lounge named the Playboy's Buffet, outside the studio gates. His director, Josh Logan, took the whole day to set up a shot and the actors were never called.

Despite the things I quoted Marvin as saying in 1968, he spoke to me again for the interview below. Despite what I wrote in this piece, he spoke to me again in 1983. Like Mitchum, he didn't give a damn about image, or perhaps knew that no matter what he said it would simply make him more perfectly Lee Marvin. By 1983 he had split up with Michelle Triola and was living in the desert outside Tucson with his wife, Pam, who had been his childhood sweetheart. She prepared lunch, and Marvin broke out the Diet Coke.

"You're not drinking so much these days?" I said.

"If I were," he said, "I'd be dead."

NOVEMBER 1970

MALIBU, 1970—The door flew open from inside, revealing Lee Marvin in a torrid embrace, bent over Michelle Triola, a fond hand on her rump. "Love!" he said. "It's all love in this house. Nothing but love. *All you need is love . . .*"

Michelle smiled as if to say, well . . .

"What's this?" Marvin cried. He snatched the *Los Angeles Times* from

25

his doormat and threw it at the front gate. LaBoo went careening after it, barking crazily.

"You bring that paper back here and I'll kill you," Marvin told La-Boo. He snarled at LaBoo and walked down the hallway and into the living room. LaBoo charged past him and jumped onto a chair. "LaBoo, you son of a bitch, I'm gonna kill you," Marvin said.

"Hello, LaBoo," Michelle said tenderly.

LaBoo wagged his tail.

"I need a beer," Marvin said. "Who's gonna get me a beer? *I'm* gonna get me a beer? I *feel* like a beer. Hell, I need a beer. Where are my glasses?" He peered around him. "Ever read this book? I got it for Christmas or some goddamn thing. A history of the West. Look here. All these cowboys are wearing chaps. Workingmen, see. Look here. Bronco Billy dressed up in the East's conception of the Western hero. See. From a dime novel. That's how authentic a Western we made when we made *Monte Walsh*. Where's that beer? That author, he knows what it was *really* like. Get me a beer."

"Finish your coffee," Michelle said.

"I said get me a *beer*."

Marvin paged through the book of Western lore, stopping to inspect an occasional page. When he stopped, he would pause for a moment and then whistle, moving on. Then silence. Only the pages turning. Now and again, a whistle.

"Where's that fucking beer, baby?" He dropped the book on the rug. "Look, if I want to develop an image, I'll do it my own fucking way."

Michelle went into the kitchen to get a beer.

"Anne . . . she seemed to be a nice girl," Marvin said. "This was when I was in London for the Royal Command Performance of *Paint Your Wagon*. Nice enough girl, Anne. Lord somebody or other kept pounding me on the back. I told him I'd already made other arrangements." Marvin whistled. "He kept poking me. Lord somebody or other, never did catch his name. I advised him to fuck off." A pause. A whistle. "If that's swinging, I'll bring them back to Malibu. Maybe to commit suicide . . ."

A record, "Victory at Sea," dropped on the stereo changer. "'Victory at Sea,'" Marvin said. "Well, thousands of ships went under, right? Tells you something."

Michelle returned with a bottle of Heineken. Marvin drank from the bottle, a long, deep drink, and then he smiled at her. "You gonna take off your clothes and jump on him now? Or later?" He smiled again. "Michelle, she's a good sport."

"Lee!" Michelle said.

"Where the hell are my glasses?" Marvin said. He took another drink from the bottle and looked on the floor around his chair.

"He took the lenses out of his glasses," Michelle said. "Last night. He said he didn't want to read any more scripts."

"Not another single goddamned script," Marvin said.

"So he took the lenses out of his glasses."

"I want simply to be the real Lee. The *real* Lee. The real Kirk Lee."

"You left the real Lee in London."

"Now I'm Kirk Lee. Not Lee Lee. Kirk Lee. I flew back from London with Sir Cary. I told him, I said, *Sir Cary, that's a nice watch you have.*" Marvin pointed his finger like a gun and made a noise that began with a whistle and ended with a pop. "*A real nice watch, Sir Cary,* I said." Whistle-pop. On the pop, his thumb came down.

"Cary has the same watch you have," Michelle said.

"No," Marvin said, "*he* has the same watch *I* have. If I saw his watch in a photograph, I could identify it anywhere. But, who gives a shit?" Whistle-pop. "Going back to the old neighborhood. This was London. What was it? Bulgaria? No, *Belgravia*. Well it was only seven-thirty in the morning. *Don't you want to stay up and watch the junkies jet in?*" Whistle. "Fuck you, pal, I'm getting some sleep."

A moment's silence for symbolic sleep. Marvin closed his eyes and threw his head back against his chair. There was a door at the other end of the living room, opening onto a porch that overlooked the beach. Through the door you could hear the waves hitting the beach, *crush, crush,* and at this moment, while Marvin pretended to sleep, the morning resolved itself as a melancholy foggy Saturday.

"Have another anchovy, sweetheart," Marvin said, rousing himself at last. He drained the Heineken. "I love them," Michelle said.

"She's been eating nothing but anchovies for the past day and a half," Marvin said. "You know why you like anchovies so much all of a sudden? You're knocked up. You're gonna have a little Lee Marvin."

"Lee!" Michelle said. "You can't say that."

"Why not?" he said. "Put it down: Michelle's knocked up. If you make it good enough, they'll never print it. And if they do print it, and come around and ask me, *Did you really say that?* I'll say, *Sure, I said it.* I need another beer."

Michelle got up and went into the kitchen.

"She's not *really* knocked up," Marvin said.

He threw a leg over the arm of the chair. "I got a haircut before I went to London," he said. "I mean, it got a little ridiculous there after a while. I didn't get my hair cut for two movies, and it got a little long. I'm going back to a . . . not a crew cut. Back to, oh, about a Presbyterian length. I'm tired of all this horseshit about hair." Marvin sighed, got up, and walked out to the porch. The air was heavy with fog.

"That goddamn buoy," he said. Just down from his stretch of beach, a buoy stood in the sand. "It floated in one morning and they stuck it up there. It's on their property. Christ, I hate the sight of it, but I can't do anything about it. It looks like a phallic symbol. Hell, it *is* a phallic symbol. You get up in the morning and come out here and there's that goddamn *buoy* staring you in the face."

He yawned. Down on the beach, a setter ran howling at a flock of birds. There was a chill this Saturday morning, and sounds were curiously muffled. Marvin peered out to sea. "Is that Jennifer Jones coming in on the surf?" he said. "No? Good."

Michelle came up behind him with a Heineken. "Thanks, sweetheart." He walked back into the living room and sat down. "What was that we saw? *Bob and Carol and Bill and Ted*? What a piece of shit that was. Good performances, but what a piece of shit."

"I loved it," Michelle said.

"You go for all that touch-me-feel-me bullshit anyway," Marvin said. "Esalen. They take your money and teach you to put one hand on two nipples. Big fucking deal, baby."

"It's about *love*," Michelle said. "It's *looking* at people. Look at me with love, Lee."

"Take off your clothes, baby." Whistle. "Who takes the Pill for us now?" Pop! "LaBoo, come in here, you mean black prince." LaBoo came in from the porch and settled down on the rug with resignation and a sigh.

"And *still* she wants to marry me," Marvin said. "It used to be, we'd check into a hotel, it was Mr. Marvin and Miss Triola. So she changed her name to Marvin, to save all that embarrassment. Now it's Mr. Marvin and Miss Marvin . . ."

He yawned and took a pull of Heineken. Michelle excused herself and wandered down the hallway. Silence. The waves. "I never did read that interview in *Playboy*," Marvin said. "I read excerpts. It was all a lot of shit. They sent some guy to interview me. I sucked him in so bad. I even gave him the garbage-man story. *How do you feel about violence in films,* he says. *I'll throw you the fuck out of here if you ask me that again,* I say."

Michelle wandered back into the room. "You took some pills?" Marvin said. "How many did you take? Should I call the doctor?"

Michelle smiled. LaBoo, on the carpet, sighed deeply.

"LaBoo," Michelle said, "you're supposed to stand around and pose in a movie star's home. That's what a poodle is for."

"He stands around and shits, that's what kind of star I am," Marvin said. "It's not everybody gets a Jap lighter from Hugh Hefner. *Gee, thanks, Hef.*" Whistle. Pop. "Well, the royal family *seemed* to like the movie, anyway. Lord somebody said he liked Jean Seberg. That was something."

"Jean has good insides."

"What?"

"I said Jean Seberg has good insides," Michelle said.

"Jesus Christ, I'm living with a dyke!" Marvin said. Whistle! Pop! "My ex-wife had something about *Playboy* when I read it."

"*Playboy* exploits women," Michelle said. "Women's liberation is against *Playboy*."

"Against *Playboy*?" Marvin said. "Whyever more?"

"It exploits women," Michelle said. "It presents women as sex objects."

"Why not?" Marvin said. "Take a snatch away from a broad and what's she got left?" Marvin spread his legs and breathed deeply. "*Oh me oh my, why must I be a sex symbol? Why won't they let me act?*"

LaBoo snorted in his sleep, waking himself. He stood up, made a circle, lay down again and closed his eyes.

The telephone rang. LaBoo growled with his eyes closed. Michelle went to answer it.

"Who's calling?" Marvin said.

"Meyer Mishkin."

"Tell him nothing for you today, Meyer, but call back tomorrow." Marvin finished his Heineken, turned it upside down, watched a single drop fall out. "My agent," he said. "He keeps wanting to know if I've read any more scripts. Fuck scripts. You spend the first forty years of your life trying to get in this fucking business, and the next forty years trying to get out. And then when you're making the bread, who needs it?

"Newman has it all worked out. I get a million. He gets a million two, but that includes $200,000 expenses. So, if that's the game . . ." Marvin shrugged. "I never talked to Newman in my life. No, I talked to him on Park Avenue once. Only to give him a piece of advice. This fifteen-year-old girl wanted his autograph. He told her he didn't give autographs, but he'd buy her a beer. *Paul,* I said, *She's only fifteen. I don't give a shit,* he said."

Marvin whistled. "I think it shows," he said. "With Newman, it shows. Cut to an old broad in Miami Beach looking at his picture in *Life* magazine. *A Gary Cooper he ain't.*"

Marvin took another beer from Michelle. "I'm waiting for some young guy to come along and knock me off so I can go to the old actors' home and talk about how great we were in nineteen-you-know. Am I waiting for him? I'd hire guys to knock *him* off. Something the other day really brought it home . . ."

He rummaged in a stack of magazines and papers next to his chair.

"I lost it."

Michelle held up a book.

"No," he said, "the other one. Yeah, here it is. *The United States Marine Corps in World War II.* Wake Island. Let's see." He produced a pair of glasses and put them on. "This cat in command. Let's see here . . ." He paged through the book, looking for something. "This cat—yeah, here it is. He was defending the island. When the brass asked the defender of the island if there was anything to be done for them, the cat wired back. *Yes. Send us more Japs.*"

Marvin whistled and squinted down at the page in wonder.

"*Send us more Japs.* Well, Japs were the last thing we needed at the time. Cut to John Wayne: *Yes, send us more Japs!* The bitch of it is, not until years later did it come out that it's the decoder's job to pad messages at the beginning and the end. So all the world was applauding this bastard's nerve, and what the world took as a gesture of defiant heroism was merely padding."

Marvin got up and went into the kitchen. "Something good about the Duke, I gotta admit," he called back over his shoulder. "When he's on, he's on. *Send us more Japs.*"

There was a rattle of bottles from the kitchen. "You stole all the beer! Michelle? You drank it all?"

"We're out," Michelle said.

"Make the call," Marvin said, coming back into the living room.

"It'll take them two hours to get here," Michelle said.

"Make the call. Make the call, or I may have to switch to the big stuff."

"I have other plans for you this afternoon."

"No—not that!" Marvin fell back in his chair. "Anything but that!" Horrified.

"It's such a foggy, gray old day," Michelle said. "We ought to just sit in front of the fire and drink Pernod. I like foggy, gray days . . ."

"Can the dog drink Pernod?" Marvin asked. "Now why the hell did I ask that? The dog gets no Pernod in this house." He stood up and looked through the window at the surf, his hands in his pockets. "I mean she really could have hurt herself, Jennifer. Came floating in on a wave . . . What's the number of the liquor store, honey?"

"Oh, nine four six six something. *You* ought to know."

Marvin went into the kitchen to make the call. "Yeah, hi. Listen, this is Lee Marvin down at 21404." Pause. "Heh, heh. You did, huh? Yeah, well this is me again." Pause. "Heh, heh. Yeah, pal, get anything cold down here. Beer. Yeah. What? Whaddaya mean, light or dark? The green one." He hung up.

"Didn't you order any anchovies?" Michelle said. "It goes back to my Sicilian grandmother."

Another record dropped on the turntable: faint, ghostly harp music. Marvin whirled wildly, looking up into the shadows of the far corners of the room. "Jesus, mother," he said, "will you *please* stay out of the room? I asked you to come only at night." He hit the reject button. "I studied violin when I was very young," he said. "You think I'm a dummy, right? I'm only *in* dummies. *The Dirty Dozen* was a dummy moneymaker, and baby, if you want a moneymaker, get a dummy."

By now he was rummaging around in the bedroom.

"Lee," Michelle said, "you're not going to put it on and parade around in it again? Are you?"

"Where is it?" Marvin said.

"I think it's in your second drawer," Michelle said. "His cap and gown. He got an honorary degree."

Marvin came out of the bedroom with a pair of binoculars. "Look what I found," he said. He went out on the porch and peered into the mist at a thin line of birds floating beyond the surf. "What are they? Coots, or . . . are they ducks?"

Marvin's son, Chris, walked into the living room. "Hi, Chris," Marvin said. "Are these coots, or . . . ducks?" Chris went out onto the porch and had a look through the binoculars. "Hard to say," Chris said. He put a leash on LaBoo and took him down to the beach for a walk. Marvin fell back into his chair. The grayness of the day settled down again. On the stereo, Johnny Cash was singing "Greensleeves." The beautiful music of "Greensleeves."

"Do you realize," Marvin said, "that he gets three million a year for singing that shit? *I walk the line, I keep my eyes wide open all the time.* I met him in Nashville. He said, *You haven't heard my other stuff? No,* I said, *I haven't.* He sent us his complete twenty-seven fucking albums. Jesus, Johnny, I like your stuff, but for Christ's sake . . ."

Marvin got down on his knees and pulled twenty-seven Johnny Cash albums off a shelf.

"He's embarrassed," Marvin said, "I'm embarrassed. We have nothing to say, really. So he sends me all his albums. I tried to listen to all of them. It took me two weeks."

"How old is Cher?" Michelle said.

"Cher?"

"Yeah."

"We don't know yet," Marvin said. "These glasses are no goddamned good. Where are my glasses?"

"He went out on the porch and stepped on his other glasses," Michelle said. "They didn't break, and he said it was an act of God, telling him not to read any more scripts. So he took the lenses and scaled them into the ocean. Now he can't see."

"Why," Marvin said, "does it take sixty-seven percent of my income to pay the publicist? He says I should take some broad to lunch, right? It costs me thirty-seven dollars to get out of the joint, and then she knocks me. You know what I asked her? *I'll bet you've never had an orgasm, have you?* I asked her."

"Lee, you didn't say that? Really?"

"I never said anything like that in my life."

Another record dropped on the stereo. "When it comes to 'Clair de Lune,'" he said, "I have to go pass water. Tinkle, is the expression. Oh, sweetheart, do you think this day will soon be o'er? I have a hangover. We had fun last night. Went up to the corner, had a few drinks, told a few lies."

He disappeared down the hallway. Chris, a good-looking kid of sixteen or seventeen, came back with LaBoo, who was banished to the porch to dry out. LaBoo squinted in through the window, wet and forlorn. "Poor LaBoo," Michelle said. "It's the second time he's been rejected today."

Marvin returned. "So what have you decided on?" he asked Chris.

"I was looking at a four-door 1956 Mercedes," Chris said.

"Hitler's car?" Marvin said. Whistle. Pop! "Kid, you deserve the best because you're the son of a star. Why don't you get a job?"

"Chris is working at a record store," Michelle said. "He's working for free right now, until the owner of the store makes enough money to pay his employees."

"Jesus Christ," Marvin said.

"I was looking at a BMW," Chris said "It's $2,100. New, it would be three thousand."

"Why not get new?" Marvin said.

"I don't have three thousand."

"But big daddy does."

"Let's order pizza," Michelle said. She picked up the phone and ordered three pizzas, one with anchovies.

"You're pregnant," Marvin said. "She's got to be. Christopher, you're going to be a grandfather."

LaBoo, who had edged into the house through a crack in the door, walked out of the bedroom now with a pair of women's panties in his mouth.

"Christ, LaBoo, keep those *panties* out of sight," Marvin said. "Last night, she says, *Where'd you get these panties? I dunno,* I say. She says, *Well they're not mine.* I say, *Honey, I sure as hell didn't wear them home.*" Marvin sighed and held his hands palms up in resignation. "The only way to solve a situation with a girl," he said, "is just jump on her and things will work out."

He took the panties from LaBoo and threw them back into the bedroom. "So what do you think?" he asked Chris.

"The BMW has fantastic cornering, Dad," Chris said. "It has really fantastic quality."

Marvin paused at the door to look out at the surf. "Don't be deceived by quality," he said. "Get something you like now, and trade it in later. The car may turn out to have such fantastic quality you'll puke seeing it around so long."

He sighed and sat down in his chair again.

LaBoo jumped into his lap.

"LaBoo, you mean black prince," Marvin said, rubbing the dog's head carelessly.

Ingmar Bergman

INTRODUCTION

In 1974, I was supposed to join a small group that would fly from Stockholm to the island of Faro and watch Bergman at work on the island where he lived. Because of a ticketing error, I arrived in Stockholm a day late, and missed the opportunity. Bergman had a publicist named Ernie Anderson, who worked through his agent, Paul Kohner. Ernie had only two clients: Bergman and Charles Bronson. Ernie arranged for this visit to the set of *Face to Face* in 1975, where I finally met Bergman and his professional family: he used the same crew members year after year, from the cinematographer Sven Nykvist to the woman who prepared tea every afternoon. I love what Bergman has to say here about the human face.

Some years later, Bergman had a disagreement with the Swedish tax authorities and left the country. He flew to Los Angeles and asked his agent Kohner to arrange a visit to a Hollywood set.

"Ernie is working on the new Charles Bronson film," Kohner told him. "You want to see that?"

He did. Ingmar Bergman, the high priest of cinematic art, visited the set of *Breakheart Pass,* a Charles Bronson Western.

"Please explain to me what you are doing," he said to Bronson.

"Well," said Bronson, "this is a scene where I get shot. So I'm wearing these squibs with fake blood under my shirt, and—but you know all this stuff. You're a director."

"No, no, please continue," Bergman said. "This is all new to me."

"You mean you don't use guns in your pictures?"

1975

STOCKHOLM—When he is in Stockholm, Ingmar Bergman lives in a new apartment complex called Karlapan. It's comfortable, not ostentatious; Bergman doesn't often have friends in because he considers it not a home but a dormitory to sleep in while he's making a film. His wife Ingrid prepares meals there, but if the Bergmans entertain it is more likely to be at his customary table in the Theater Grill, a stately restaurant directly across the street from the back door of the Royal Dramatic Theater. The table is not easily found, or seen; it is behind a large mirrored post, so that Bergman, who can see everyone in the room, is all but invisible.

During the eight or ten weeks it takes him to direct a film, Bergman awakens at a reasonable hour, around eight, and drives to Film House in a little maroon car. Film House is a large modern structure twenty-five minutes' walk from the center of Stockholm, and it houses not only film and television production facilities but also the theater, film, and dance faculties of the University of Stockholm. The building is always filled with discussion and activity, much of it centered around the bar of the Laurel and Hardy Pub on the second level, but when Bergman is in residence to make a film, a certain self-consciousness seems to descend on Film House: it's the same, I was told, as when the pope is in the Vatican.

Bergman parks in a reserved space near the side door of Film House and joins his actors and technicians for breakfast. It is served in a cluttered little room presided over by the hostess for this picture; for every film he makes, Bergman hires a hostess, and lists her in the credits. Her job is to make coffee and serve afternoon tea and fuss over people in a motherly sort of way. When you are making a picture about the silence of God, or metaphysical anguish, or suicide—as Bergman usually is—it helps if everyone feels right at home and there's a pot of coffee brewing.

The film he is working on today will be called *Face to Face,* and it is about an attempted suicide by a self-tormented psychiatrist, who will be played by Liv Ullmann. "For some time now," Bergman wrote in a letter to his cast and crew, just before production began, "I have been living with an anxiety which has had no tangible cause." His attempt to work it out led to the screenplay for *Face to Face,* in which the woman will face her terrible dread (common enough in Bergman), will attempt to surrender to it (also nothing new), but then will transcend it, will have a small victory over her darker nature (this hopefulness has only started to emerge in Bergman's work in the past three or four years, since *Cries and Whispers,* and it is the cause of much speculation among his friends).

Face to Face will be Bergman's thirty-sixth film and it comes in his thirtieth year as a director. His career falls out into a certain pleasing symmetry: after early screenplays, he began directing in 1945 as a very provincial Swedish imitator of the Italian neorealists; he had his first international success in 1955, with *Smiles of a Summer Night;* in 1965 he began work on *Persona,* that most profound of modern films; today, he is considered one of the greatest living filmmakers. For *Face to Face,* he has gathered around him once again, as he does almost every spring and early summer, his basic crew and a group of actors he has used time and again. Only occasionally will there be a new face.

Now they join him for coffee. Liv Ullmann is dressed in an old cotton shirt and a full blue denim skirt; she wears no makeup and her hair is tossed back from her forehead as if to make the declaration that she's been asleep until fifteen minutes ago. Bergman first met her on a street corner talking to her friend Bibi Andersson, just at the moment he was casting *Persona.* He liked the way they fit together, and cast them together, on the spot. She has since become one of the most important actresses in the world, but here in Film House she is friendly and plain-spoken, more like a den mother than a star. This is her seventh film for Bergman.

Gunnar Bjornstrand, tall and stately in his seventies, gravely considers the room and leafs through his script. He was the squire in *The Seventh Seal* and the father in *Through a Glass Darkly,* and is one of the most familiar figures in Bergman's repertory company. He has been ill recently, but he came out of retirement to play Ullmann's grandfather in the new film, and has responded to the work so well that Bergman has expanded the role for him. This is his sixteenth film for Bergman.

Katinka Farago, a robust woman in her thirties, hardly has time for coffee; she wants a moment to speak with Bergman about the next week's production schedule, and he listens and nods as she explains, urgently, her problems. It is the duty of a production manager to have problems; no one has ever met one who did not. Katinka came to Stockholm from Hungary in 1956, a refugee, and got a job as Bergman's script girl. He made her production manager a few years ago, in charge of all the logistics of time, space, and money. This is her seventeenth film with Bergman.

Sven Nykvist photographs Bergman's films. He is a tall, strong, fifty-one, with a beard and a quick smile. He is usually better-dressed than

Bergman, but then almost everyone is; "Ingmar," a friend says, "does not spend a hundred dollars a year for personal haberdashery." Nykvist first worked for Bergman on *The Naked Night* in 1953, and has been with him steadily since *The Virgin Spring* in 1959. This will be his nineteenth title for Bergman, and the two of them together engineered Bergman's long-delayed transition from black and white to color, unhappily in *All These Women* and then triumphantly in *A Passion of Anna* and *Cries and Whispers*.

Nykvist is in demand all over the world, and commands one of the half-dozen highest salaries among cinematographers, but he always leaves his schedule open for Bergman. "We've already discussed the new film the year before," he says, "and then Ingmar goes to his island and writes the screenplay. The next year, we shoot—usually about the fifteenth of April. Usually we are the same eighteen people working with him, year after year, one film a year."

At the Cannes Film Festival one year, he said, Bergman was talking with David Lean, the director of *Lawrence of Arabia* and *Dr. Zhivago*. "What kind of crew do you use?" Lean asked. "I make my films with eighteen good friends," Bergman said. "That's interesting," said Lean. "I make mine with 150 enemies."

It is very rare for Bergman to invite visitors—the word "outsiders" almost seems to apply—to one of his sets. It is much more common, during a difficult scene, for him to send one technician after another out to wait in the hall, until the actors are alone with Bergman, Nykvist, a sound man, an electrician, and the demands of the scene.

"When we were making *Cries and Whispers*," Liv Ullmann recalls, "none of the rest of us really knew what Harriet Andersson was doing in those scenes of suffering and death. Ingmar would send away everyone except just those few who *must* be there, and Harriet. When we saw the completed film, we were overwhelmed. It was almost as if those great scenes had been Harriet's secret—which, in a way, they were supposed to be, since in the film she died so much alone."

Liv is sitting in her dressing room, waiting to be called for the next scene. It will be a difficult one; she must explain to her child in the film why she tries to kill herself.

"They say Ingmar has changed," she says, "and he has. He doesn't look the same when he walks on the set. He's mellowed, in a nice way. He's sweeter. We've all been through some hard times with him—fights on the set—but he seems more tolerant now."

Perhaps, she said, Bergman has worked through the problem of death which haunted so many of his films. "He's faced it as a reality, and accepted it, and suddenly there's almost a sense of relief: in *Cries and Whispers* and *Scenes from a Marriage* there's a kind of acceptance at the end that wasn't there before. And in this film. He's been saying for years he's going to make a film of *The Merry Widow*. Well, now I really think he will. It may not be *The Merry Widow,* but it will be something warm and sunny. He is the most adult director in the world, making serious films for adults, but now if he could really let the child inside of him come out . . . and I think he's reached the point where he can."

She lowers her voice. There is movement down the corridor, and it may be Bergman. She isn't supposed to be giving an interview; Bergman is very concerned about the scene coming up, and he wants her to think about nothing else. Ullmann smiles; it will help her, she says, to think of anything *but* the scene. Every actress approaches these things in her own way.

Elsewhere in Film House, people seem able to think and speak of nothing else but Bergman. He is the greatest Swedish artist, they agree— an artist of world importance. And yet he was not much loved until recently in his native land. His two best markets are the United States and France. In Sweden, he was accused of dealing only with the bourgeoisie, of not facing social problems, of being concerned only with himself and not with society. These are charges he more or less agrees with, but they do not bother him.

In the bar of Film House, drinking aquavit and a beer, the Finnish director Jorn Donner waits to talk to Bergman about a documentary he's making for television: *Three Scenes with Ingmar Bergman.* Donner elaborates on Bergman's problem. "He is known all over the world, and yet he can't afford a single failure," he says. "Up until *Cries and Whispers,* each film was paying off the debts of the last. For *Cries and Whispers,* there was so little money that the actors were asked to work for three thousand dollars each and ten percent of the profits. He gave ten percent to Liv, Harriet, Sven, Ingrid Thulin, and thirty percent for himself—and this was a film totally produced himself!

"Harriet asked me if she should work for three thousand dollars. I said, certainly, to work for Ingmar—and if that's all the money there is. After the film was made, it was turned down by every major distributor. And then look what an enormous success it was! And followed by a bigger success, *Scenes from a Marriage*. And now *The Magic Flute*. But no one suspects how close he came to not being able to raise the money for *Cries and Whispers*."

It's true; until *Cries and Whispers* in 1973, Bergman hadn't had a financial success since *Persona,* released in 1966. There were great pictures— *A Passion of Anna* and *Shame*—and interesting failures like *Hour of the Wolf* and a movie that no one liked much, *The Touch,* with Elliot Gould, but they all lost money.

Then the tide turned. Not since the days of *Smiles of a Summer Night, Wild Strawberries,* and *The Seventh Seal,* in the late 1950s, has Bergman found more success with audiences than in the last few years. And *Scenes from a Marriage* found him an audience, at last, in Scandinavia, too: his neighbors on the Baltic island of Faro, where he lives as much of the year as possible, saw it on television and understood at last what it was that he did. Then Bergman's version of Mozart's *The Magic Flute* played on Swedish television on the first day of 1975, and one of every three Swedes saw it. "It's as if he's in harmony with himself," says Bengt Forslund, a Swedish producer. "All those years of films about suffering and death, and suddenly Ingmar's found all of this joy to draw on."

The red light is still on over the door to Bergman's soundstage. When it goes off, that means Bergman is not actually shooting—but entry is still forbidden except to the favored, like his wife, Ingrid. She slips through the door with some letters that need to be answered. And then it's time for the afternoon tea break. The hostess has set up tea and cakes and Bergman at last acknowledges the interviewer.

He has a little room, long, dim, and cool, like a monk's cell. It's across from the soundstage and down the way from the dressing rooms, and is furnished simply, with two chairs, a cot, and a table (on which rest two apples, a banana, a box of Danish chocolates, and a copy of the script). When he is concerned about the direction a scene is taking, he will declare a break, come into this room, lock the door, and lie down on the cot until the scene is clear in his head.

"So it is thirty years since I directed my first picture," he said. "It's strange, you know, because suddenly you have the feeling there was no time in between. The feeling when you wake up, got to the studio, see the rushes, is still exactly the same. Of course, in 1945, I was more scared, more insecure—but the tension and the passion, and the feeling of surprise every day—that's the same. I solved the problems, or didn't solve them in exactly the same way.

"The artistic problems are already solved when you write the script. But then there are the technical problems. The shooting schedule, the lab, a sick actor . . . and it has to do with your *own* conditions, too. If you feel well, or depressed—you are not a machine. And yet you must be on top of things for nine or ten weeks—if you've not slept well, or you're suffering from lust . . . I call those technical problems."

English is not his best language, but he speaks it well enough. Growing up before the Second World War, he was taught German, like all Swedish schoolchildren. As he speaks, he seems to have it all clear inside, what he wants to say. He accepts questions gravely but without a great deal of interest. It's less of an interview than an opportunity to share in his thought process. I asked him about the recent change in the direction of his work, away from despair and a little toward affirmation.

"Well," he said, "you mature. You grow up mentally, emotionally, and it's not a straight line, it's more like the growing of a tree. On the island where I live, the trees always have a strong wind from the northeast, blowing so hard that they grow almost flat against the ground. It's that way with people. You think you're in control, but really you're being changed every day by everything around you.

"Perhaps, someday, I'll stop growing. But I hope that I'll understand it myself, and, in that moment, stop making films. You know, filming and directing on the stage are both the same in the sense that you try to get in touch with other human beings. There's always that hope. But if you have the feeling you have nothing more to tell, to say—it's wise to stop making pictures. You can still work in the theater, because there you're working with big men—Shakespeare, Strindberg, Molière—so if you're old and tired and sick, at least you still have your experience to share with other actors, you can help them put across the play. To make a film is something else. If you have nothing to say, it's time to stop, because the film is you."

You talk about getting in touch with other people, I said. In so many of your films, that seems to be the subject—people trying to make contact.

"That is exactly right. If I believe in anything, I believe in the sudden relationship, the sudden contact between two human beings. When we grow up, we suddenly feel we are completely alone. We find substitutes for loneliness—but this feeling of a certain contact, a certain instant understanding between two people, that's the best thing in life. It has nothing to do with sex, by the way."

And so, at the end of *Scenes from a Marriage,* when the man and woman have been divorced for years, you have them holding each other "in a cottage in the middle of the night somewhere in the world."

He nodded. "You know," he said, "I was very surprised by the success of that film, because I wrote it only from my own experience. It took three months to make, but a lifetime to experience. Very strange.

"I was on my island with my wife, and I was preparing a stage production, and just for fun I started to write some dialogues about marriage. I started with the scene where he tells her he will go away. Well, I always write by hand, and I asked my wife, who is the only person in the world who can read my handwriting, to type it up. She found it amusing. Then I wrote the fifth scene—even more amusing!—and then the first. I could have written twenty-four more.

"But I had no idea of what would happen. No feeling of what to do with these scenes. Perhaps I could make some sort of program for television. I asked my friends Liv and Erland Josephson to read it, and they were interested. Well, everything happened just like that. It was the biggest success in the history of Swedish television—and all over Scandinavia. At last, my neighbors on the island had seen something of mine they could relate to."

Scenes from a Marriage was shot in sixteen-millimeter, unlike his previous work, which had all been in the standard thirty-five-millimeter. That was fine for television, but now Sven Nykvist was telling him that the new sixteen-millimeter Kodak color film was so good that features could be shot in it, too, with little difference in quality, a great advance in flexibility, and for a lot less money. Bergman was dubious, but agreed to shoot Mozart's *The Magic Flute* in sixteen-millimeter.

It was a project commissioned by Swedish television, and he decided to film it as it might have been performed in a little eighteenth-century theater like the Drottingholm Court Theater, perfectly preserved for two hundred years in a royal park outside Stockholm. The theater's interiors and its ingenious stage machinery—good for making thunder and lightning and waves—were duplicated in Film House, and the opera was shot in sixteen-millimeter.

After its Swedish television premiere, Nykvist and Bergman screened a thirty-five-millimeter theatrical print blown up from sixteen-millimeter, and were happy with the quality; Bergman agreed with Nykvist that the image was clear and subtle even by their demanding standards, and they decided to shoot in sixteen-millimeter from then on. *Face to Face* was being shot in sixteen-millimeter—although that was one of the few things regarding it Bergman seemed to be absolutely sure of.

"It's a little difficult to talk about right now," he said, "because we're in the middle of things and often it's not until I take the film back to my island and begin to edit it that it becomes clear to me. Of course I can say, yes, it's about a woman who tries to commit suicide, and the picture is sort of an investigation of why she does that, but—honestly, I don't know. I wrote it, but when I shoot a film I never think of it as my own script, because then I couldn't shoot a single scene. It's very personal, and yet I have to be cold, analytical, about it. Sometimes I read what I've written—dialogue that was written with emotion, and then I try to understand intellectually what a character means, and sometimes I make very strange mistakes.

"The problem is that film is the best way to the emotional center of human beings, but it's very hard to be intellectual about it. There's some sort of strange emotional logic in film that has nothing to do with the meaning. If you're the director, you have to be very careful about what you reach for, because the emotions may make you find something else altogether. But, even then, that's all right, if it makes others feel something . . . what makes me unhappy is when the audience is indifferent."

I asked him about *Persona,* the story of an actress who one day decides to stop talking, and about her relationship with the naïve young nurse who's assigned to spend the summer in the country with her. The film created a great deal of critical confusion and debate in 1966, and has continued to reveal levels of emotion; it has the ability to make audiences feel it when they don't really understand it.

"Now there's an example of what I mean," he said. "I have no theories about it. If you asked me to explain it, I couldn't. But I know that *Per-*

sona literally saved my life at the time I was writing it. I was very ill. I hadn't lost my mental balance, but I'd lost my physical balance. I had an ear disease . . . I couldn't stand up or even move my head without nausea. So I started to write down some lines every day, just a few lines, just for the discipline of going from the bed to the table without falling over. As a filmmaker, I could not work if I could not move. Now here was a story about an actress who stopped working one day, surrendered her ability to talk, and the young nurse who admired her, who wanted to understand her, but was treated badly by her . . . there's something there, but I can't explain it."

Persona contains one of Bergman's most famous shots, the faces of Liv Ullmann and Bibi Andersson photographed in such a way that the features of the two women seem to blend. They seem about to become one another, which, in a way, is what happens in the film. They seem capable of exchanging or sharing personalities. I asked Bergman about this shot, and also about his frequent use of two-shots to show characters who are in the same frame but not looking at each other or communicating.

"The two-shot, and the closeup, too, are marvelous, because . . . well, you don't have them in the theater. They give you the eyes, the skin, the mouth, and that's fascinating. And when you cut it, rehearse it, edit it, two people talking, now in closeup, now brought together into the two-shot, you can work out a wonderful rhythm, a sort of breathing, and it's beautiful.

"And the most beautiful of all is that you're close to the human face, which is the most fascinating subject possible for the camera. On TV a few days ago, I saw a little of Antonioni's new picture, *The Passenger*. And, you know, I am an admirer of Antonioni, I've learned so much from him, but I was struck by the moment they cut from his film to a closeup of Antonioni himself, for the interview.

"And as he was sitting there, here was his face, so normal, so beautiful and so human—and I didn't hear a word of what he was saying, because I was looking so closely at his face, at his eyes." Bergman held out his hands as if to compose the memory for the camera. "The ten minutes he was on the screen were more fascinating than any of his, or my, work. It told you a novel about his whole life. With my actors, with their faces . . . that is what we can sometimes do."

Now it was time to go back onto the soundstage and finish the day's

shooting. People were waiting for him in the hallway: a secretary said he
had been chosen to receive the Donatello Award of the Italian Republic;
could he come to Florence if a private jet were sent? Bibi Andersson had
stopped by for a visit, she was accompanying the Swedish prime minister,
Olaf Palme, on a state visit to South America, and then she'd go to Warsaw
in Bergman's production of *Twelfth Night*.

Bergman was quiet, friendly, dictating a reply to Rome and another
one to his producer, Dino De Laurentiis, explaining why he could not
oblige Dino's old friend, the countess in charge of the Donatello Award.
He kissed Bibi and said he would come to see her in Warsaw if he could.
And then he went back behind the big soundproof doors and the red light
blinked on. Some tourists being taken through Film House had not recognized the ordinary-looking man of fifty-seven, with his thinning brown
hair, his frayed blue jacket, his carpet slippers.

The rhythm of the seasons has been set for seven or eight years now,
ever since Bergman moved to Faro, which close inspection of the map reveals as a tiny unnamed blue dot north of the island of Gotland, in the
Baltic Sea. It is the last speck of Sweden, a wild bird preserve inhabited by
nine hundred shepherds and fishermen, and foreigners are not allowed there
because of a nineteenth-century military agreement with Russia. Bergman
found his island by accident, as a ferry stop north of Gotland, while looking for a place to shoot *Through the Glass Darkly*.

He built a house there, sturdy and spacious, and after waiting for
three years for the permit, he built an editing facility and the simple studio
in which he did the interiors for *A Passion of Anna* and parts of *Shame*. He
would return to Faro in a month or so, and spend the autumn editing *Face
to Face*. This winter, he will direct something for the Royal Dramatic Theater—he thinks perhaps something by Shaw this year. When the production has opened, he'll return to Faro, finish with *Face to Face,* and begin
work on next year's screenplay.

Copies will go out soon to Sven and Katinka and the others of the
eighteen friends, and to the actors he has chosen to use this time. The female lead will probably be played by Liv, although Bibi was in *The Touch*
and Ingrid and Harriet joined Liv in *Cries and Whispers*. The male lead may
be Erland, although Max von Sydow, who has been in eleven of Bergman's
films, is said to be eager to return to Stockholm again after several pictures

overseas. Shooting will begin in the late spring and early summer, and editing will follow in the fall.

"I think I have ten years left," Bergman had said at the close of the interview.

"There's a deal, sort of," Katinka Farago had said, speaking of Bergman's relationship with the people he makes films with. "One may get offers to work on other pictures . . . but one doesn't take another picture without asking Ingmar first. He pays what the others pay; it's not a question of money. But there is no one else like him."

Martin Scorsese and Paul Schrader

INTRODUCTION

Martin Scorsese and Paul Schrader come from different backgrounds, Scorsese from Catholicism and Little Italy, Schrader from Grand Rapids and the Dutch Reformed church. Both have highly developed ideas of sin and guilt. "Movies were forbidden," Schrader told me. "I saw my first movie when I was seventeen years old. It was *The Million Dollar Duck*. I walked out and thought, I can make a better movie than that."

I was the first person to review a Scorsese film in print. That was *I Call First*, later retitled *Who's That Knocking at My Door*, at the 1967 Chicago Film Festival. He telephoned me, and when I was in New York we hung out. I mention those early meetings in the introduction to this book. I consider him one of the greatest filmmakers of his generation. He is unequaled in his fascination with film itself, which he views without ceasing, restores, and studies; he has made documentaries about the American and Italian film heritage. I mentioned Renoir's *The River* to him after viewing his personal print at the Virginia Film Festival. "I watch it three times a year," he said. "At least three times."

One of my great experiences, also at Virginia, was doing a shot-by-shot analysis of *Raging Bull* with Thelma Schoonmaker, his lifelong editor (and Michael Powell's widow). You might think you could learn all about a film by viewing it shot by shot with its director, but having had that experience with Schoonmaker, and having done shot-by-shot analysis at the Hawaii festival with the cinematographers Owen Roizman, Allen Daviau, Haskell Wexler, and Hiro Narita, I know that the editors and cinematographers know where the bodies are buried.

MARCH 7, 1976

I met Martin Scorsese for the first time in 1969, when he was an editor on *Woodstock*. He was one of the most intense people I'd ever known—a compact, nervous kid out of New York's Little Italy who'd made one feature film and had dreams of becoming a big-time director one day. It would take him five years.

The first feature was *Who's That Knocking at My Door,* the major discovery of the 1967 Chicago Film Festival. It was the semiautobiographical story of an Italian American youth coming of age; it won praise and prizes for Scorsese, but didn't do any business, and he supported himself with editing, teaching, and odd jobs. The night I met him, we went to Little Italy and drank Bardolino wine and he talked about projects he was being offered.

He finally took one of them—a Roger Corman exploitation picture called *Boxcar Bertha*—because he needed to direct again. "Corman thinks it's an exploitation picture," Scorsese told me, "but I think it'll be something else." He was right; his talent made the film, which starred Barbara Hershey and David Carradine, better than it had to be.

The movie got him more work. In 1973, on a small budget but with total artistic freedom, he made *Mean Streets,* a sequel to *Who's That Knocking*. It was a ferocious, painful, deeply felt masterpiece. In 1974 he made his big critical and box office success, *Alice Doesn't Live Here Anymore,* for which Ellen Burstyn won an Oscar. Scorsese was established, was "bankable."

His new film, which opens here Friday at the McClurg Court, Lincoln Village, and five suburban theaters, is *Taxi Driver* with Robert De Niro—a violent and frightening return to the New York of *Mean Streets*. It looks like another hit.

Scorsese and I met for lunch during his visit last week to Chicago and were joined by Paul Schrader, who wrote the screenplay for *Taxi Driver*. They were a study in opposites: Schrader, a midwestern Protestant in pullover sweater and tie, and Scorsese, a New York Italian American, in jeans and a beard. But they'd been working together on this screenplay since 1972.

SCORSESE: Because there's a lot of violence to this picture, some of the New York reviews are calling it an exploitation film. Jesus! I went flat broke making this film. My films haven't made a lot of money. Right now, I'm living off my next film.

SCHRADER: If it's an exploitation film, I wish we had a dollar for every time we were told it would never be a success at all. This screenplay was turned down by everybody.

SCORSESE: We showed it to some New York media educators, and I thought we'd get lynched. And we showed it to some student editors . . . there was one wise guy there I recognized from a screening we had of *Alice*. He asks whether, after all my success, I'm about ready to fall on my ass. I've hardly gotten started!

SCHRADER: We get almost no valid reactions immediately after the screenings. The immediate response is usually very visceral and angry. But if this film weren't controversial, there'd be something wrong with the country.

EBERT: What you give us is this guy, De Niro, who comes from nowhere—we get hardly any background—and drives a cab in New York and eventually we realize he's seething inside, he's got all this violence bottled up . . .

SCORSESE: And he goes back again and again to where the violence is. One of the reviewers, I think it was Andrew Sarris, said how many times can you use 42nd Street as a metaphor for hell? But that's the thing about hell—it goes on and on. And he couldn't get out of it. But you're right that we don't tell you where he comes from, or what his story is. Obviously, he comes from somewhere and he picked up these problems along the way.

SCHRADER: I wrote it that way after thinking about the way they handled *In Cold Blood*. They tell you all about Perry Smith's background, how he developed his problems, and immediately it becomes less interesting because his problems aren't your problems, but his symptoms are your symptoms.

EBERT: Pauline Kael has said that Scorsese, Robert Altman, and Francis Ford Coppola are the three most interesting directors in the country right now—and that it might be due to their Catholicism, that after Watergate, the nation feels a sort of guilt and needs to make a form of reparation, and that Catholics understand guilt in a way that others don't, that they were brought up on it.

SCORSESE: Guilt. There's nothing you can tell me about guilt.

SCHRADER: I've got a lot of Protestant guilt.

SCORSESE: You can't make movies any more in which the whole country seems to make sense. After Vietnam, after Watergate, it's not just a temporary thing; it's a permanent thing the country's going through. All the things we held sacred—the whole Time-Life empire . . . whoosh! Well, *Time*'s still left.

EBERT: In a lot of your movies, there's this ambivalent attitude toward women. The men are fascinated by women, but they don't quite know how to relate to them . . .

SCORSESE: The goddess-whore complex. You're raised to worship women, but you don't know how to approach them on a human level, on a sexual level. That's the thing with Travis, the De Niro character—the taxi driver. The girl he falls for, the Cybill Shepherd character—it's really important that she's blond, a blue-eyed goddess.

SCHRADER: He goes from a goddess to a child goddess. The twelve-and-a-half-year-old prostitute he's trying to rescue—she's unapproachable, too, for him.

SCORSESE: She has the candles burning in her bedroom, she's like a saint to him. He can't imagine these pimps treating her the way they do. Before he goes to avenge her, it's almost like he cleanses himself, like in *The Virgin Spring* when Max von Sydow scourges himself with the branches before he goes out to avenge his daughter's death.

SCHRADER: We actually had that shot in the movie, and we took it out. Travis whips himself with a towel before he goes out with his guns. We took it out because it looked a little forced and unnatural.

SCORSESE: But the Catholic thing? I suppose there are a lot of Catholic references in the film, even if they're only my own personal references. Like the moment when he burns the flowers before he goes out to kill. And when he's buying the guns and the dealer lays them out one at a time on the velvet, like arranging the altar during Mass.

Schrader left for another interview, and Scorsese and I continued our conversation in his hotel room, which was furnished with two reminders of home: a large box of cookies from Cafe Roma in Little Italy ("My mother sent them, she knew I'd be homesick") and a stack of the latest issues of film magazines. Scorsese got married recently to a freelance writer named Julia

Cameron, from Libertyville, and he was planning to have dinner with his new in-laws that night. He thought he'd bring along the cookies.

EBERT: You talked about living off your next film.

SCORSESE: It'll be called *New York, New York*. it takes place in the 1940s and 1950s, it's about the big bands. Liza Minnelli plays a singer and De Niro will be her husband. It's not a musical; it's a film with music. I got that definition from Billy Wilder, who said you can't call it a musical unless the people sing in situations where you don't expect them to. It'll be about their marriage breaking up, about their problems in relating to one another . . .

EBERT: Will it take a feminist position? A lot of people embraced *Alice Doesn't Live Here Anymore* as feminist.

SCORSESE: Well, it'll be about the problems of a career marriage. I don't know if it's feminist. Actually, not *Alice,* but *Taxi Driver*—this is my feminist film. Who says a feminist movie has to be about women? Alice was never intended as a feminist tract. At the end, she's making the same mistakes. The first shot of her in Kris Kristofferson's house shows her washing the dishes. A big close-up.

EBERT: And *Taxi Driver,* where the hero can't relate to women at all, is . . .

SCORSESE: Feminist. Because it takes macho to its logical conclusion. The better man is the man who can kill you. This one shows that kind of thinking, shows the kinds of problems some men have, bouncing back and forth between the goddesses and whores. The whole movie is based, visually, on one shot where the guy is being turned down on the telephone by the girl, and the camera actually pans away from him. It's too painful to see that rejection.

EBERT: The film is dedicated to Bernard Herrmann, the great movie composer. He died just after he finished the score.

SCORSESE: God, that was terrible. Immediately after. He was so happy, he was back in Hollywood, he had a full orchestra, people were getting down on their knees to him. He was doing some jazz passages, and he insisted on finishing that day. I told him we should do it next week, because he looked tired, "No," he said, "let's do it now." That was on December 23. The next morning, the day of Christmas Eve, he was found dead. That Sunday, Julia and I flew to Chicago to get married . . .

EBERT: I wanted to ask about the violent scenes, the scenes where Travis freaks out and starts shooting.

SCORSESE: We shot those in slow motion. In forty-eight frames to the second, which is twice the ordinary twenty-four frames—and, of course, if you shoot it twice as fast and project it at the regular speed, it comes out half as fast . . .

EBERT: Which is what everyone gets backwards about slow motion.

SCORSESE: Right. And in the scenes of the killing, the slow motion and De Niro's arms . . . we wanted him to look almost like a monster, a robot, King Kong coming to save Fay Wray. Another thing: All of the close-ups of De Niro where he isn't talking were shot forty-eight frames to the second—to draw out and exaggerate his reactions. What an actor, to look so great up against a technique like that! I shot all those shots myself, to see for myself what kind of reaction we were getting.

EBERT: The whole movie's very stylized, expressionistic . . . you fragment scenes into very striking details, you control your colors to get a certain feel, there's the garish lighting . . .

SCORSESE: And then I read that I'm a realist, a naturalist! Somebody compared the picture to *Shoeshine*! Really! I'm not interested in a realistic look—not at all, not ever. Every film should look the way I feel.

EBERT: I read that De Niro really drove a cab to prepare for this role.

SCORSESE: Yeah. I drove with him several nights. He got a strange feeling when he was hacking. He was totally anonymous. People would say anything, do anything in the backseat—it was like he didn't exist. Finally a guy gets in, a former actor, who recognizes his name on the license. "Jesus," he says, "last year you won the Oscar and now you're driving a cab again." De Niro said he was only doing research. "Yeah, Bobby," says the actor. "I know. I been there, too."

After *Mean Streets* was released, I wrote a review saying that Scorsese had a chance to become the American Fellini in ten years or so. The next time we met after the review appeared, Marty looked serious and concerned: "Do you really think it's going to take ten years?"

Robert Altman

I think I've interviewed Robert Altman more often than anybody else in the movie business. That has something to do with his method of making a movie, which is to assemble large groups of people and set them all in motion at once. There are always visitors on the set. Altman presides as an impresario or host. He likes to introduce people. I wonder if he dislikes being alone. Kathryn, his wife of forty years, is always somewhere nearby, a coconspirator.

Once we both found ourselves at a film festival in Iowa City that was held only once. We both thought Pauline Kael was going to be there, which was why we'd agreed to come. Pauline later said she'd never been invited. Bob and I sat on a desk in a classroom and discussed the delicately moody *Thieves Like Us,* one of his most neglected films. Other times, I visited the sets of *Health, A Wedding,* and *Gosford Park,* and watched him rehearse the Lyric Opera adaptation of *A Wedding* years later.

He marched to his own drummer. After the Sundance premiere of his *Gingerbread Man,* he sat at a reception for a thousand people in Salt Lake City, contentedly smoking a joint. In his screening room at his original Lions Gate in Westwood, he screened rough cuts for just about anyone who wanted to come. Twice Chaz and I joined the Altmans for dinner in Chicago with mayor Richard M. and Maggie Daley; the mayor likes movies and can talk about them, and the two men had an easy rapport. Entering the restaurant on a winter night after he'd wrapped *The Company,* Robert swept in with him the snowy air and the aroma of marijuana. Daley looked at me and lifted an eyebrow not more than an eighth of an inch, and smiled so slyly you had to be looking for it.

Altman told me once he didn't mind a bad review, "because without them, what does a good review mean?" He added that in my case all of my negative reviews of his work had been mistaken.

JUNE 12, 1977

CANNES, FRANCE—Yes, it was very pleasant. We sat on the stern of Robert Altman's rented yacht in the Cannes harbor, and looked across at the city and the flags and the hills. There was a scotch and soda with lots of ice, and an efficient young man dressed all in white who came on quiet shoes to fill the glasses when it was necessary.

Altman wore a knit sport shirt with the legend of the Chicago Bears over the left pocket: a souvenir, no doubt, from his trips to Chicago to scout locations for *A Wedding*. He was in a benign mood, and it was a day to savor. The night before, his film *3 Women* had played as an official entry in the Cannes festival, and had received a genuinely warm standing ovation, the most enthusiastic of the festival.

Because his *M*A*S*H* had won the Palme d'Or in 1970, Altman could have shown this film out of competition. But he wasn't having any: "If you don't want to be in competition," he was saying, "that means you're either too arrogant, or too scared. So you might lose? I've lost before; there's nothing wrong with losing."

He was, as it turned out, only being halfway prophetic: three days later the jury would award the Palme d'Or to an Italian film, giving *3 Women* the best actress award for Shelley Duvall's performance. But on this afternoon it was still possible to speculate about the grand prize, with the boat rocking gently and nothing on the immediate horizon except, of course, the necessity to be in Chicago in June to begin a $4 million movie with forty-eight actors, most of whom would be on the set every day for two months.

"I'd be back supervising the preparation," Altman said, "except I'm lazy. Also, my staff knows what I want better than I do. If I'm there, they feel like they have to check with me, and that only slows them down."

Lauren Hutton drifted down from the upper deck. She'll play a wedding photographer making a sixteen-millimeter documentary film-within-a-film in *A Wedding,* and Altman's counting on her character to help keep the other characters straight. "With forty-eight people at the wedding party, we have to be sure the audience can tell them apart. The bridesmaids will all be dressed the same, for example. So Lauren will be armed with a book of Polaroids of everybody, as a guide for herself, and we can fall back on her confusion when we think the audience might be confused."

Fresh drinks arrived. Altman sipped his and found it good. His wife, Kathryn, returning from a tour of the yacht harbor, walked up the gangplank and said she had some calls to make. Altman sipped again.

"It's lovely sitting on this yacht," he said after a moment. "Beats any hotel in town."

The boat is called *Pakcha*? I asked.

"Yeah," said Altman. "Outta South Hampton. It's been around the world twice. Got its name in one of those South Sea Islands. *Pakcha* is a Pacific dialect word for 'traveling white businessman.'"

He shrugged, as if to say, how can I deny it? He sipped his drink again, and I asked if that story was really true about how he got the idea for *A Wedding*.

"Yeah, that's how it came about, all right. We were shooting *3 Women* out in the desert, and it was a really hot day and we were in a hotel room that was like a furnace, and I wasn't feeling too well on account of having felt too well the night before, and this girl was down from L.A. to do some in-depth gossip and asked me what my next movie was going to be. At that moment, I didn't even feel like doing this movie, so I told her I was gonna shoot a wedding next. A wedding? Yeah, a wedding.

"So a few moments later my production assistant comes up and she says, 'Bob, did you hear yourself just then?' Yeah, I say, I did. 'That's not a bad idea, is it?' She says. Not a bad idea at all, I say; and that night we started on the outline."

3 Women itself had an equally unlikely genesis, Altman recalled: "I dreamed it. I dreamed of the desert, and these three women, and I remember every once in a while I'd dream that I was waking up and sending out people to scout locations and cast the thing. And when I woke up in the morning, it was like I'd done the picture. What's more, I liked it. So, what the hell, I decided to do it."

The movie is about . . . well, it's about whatever you think it's about. Two of the women, the main characters, seem to undergo a mysterious personality transfer in the film's center, and then they fuse with the third woman to form a new personality altogether. Some viewers have found it to be an Altman statement on women's liberation, but he doesn't see it that way:

"For women's lib or against? Don't ask me. If I sat here and said the film was about X, Y, and Z, that restricts the audience to finding the film within my boundaries. I want them to go outside to bring themselves to the film. What they find there will be at least as interesting as what I did . . .

"And I kept on discovering things in the film right up to the final edit. The film begins, for example, with Sissy Spacek wandering in out of the desert and meeting Shelley Duvall and getting the job in the rehabilitation center. And when I was looking at the end of the film during the editing process, it occurred to me that when you see that final exterior shot of the house, and the dialogue asks the Sissy Spacek character to get the sewing basket—well, she could just walk right out of the house and go to California and walk in at the beginning of the movie, and it would be perfectly circular and even make sense that way. But that's only one way to read it."

Altman said he's constantly amazed by the things he reads about his films in reviews. "Sometimes," he said, "I think the critics take their lead from the statements directors themselves make about their films. There was an astonishing review in *Newsweek* by Jack Kroll, for example, of Fellini's *Casanova*. It made no sense at all, in terms of the film itself. But then I read something Fellini had said about the film, and I think Kroll was simply finding in the film what Fellini said he put there.

"With *3 Women,* now, a lot of the reviews go on and on about the supposed Jungian implications of the relationships. If you ask me to give a child's simplified difference between Jung and Freud, I couldn't. It's just a field I know nothing about. But the name of Jung turns up in the production notes that were written for the press kit, and there you are."

The problem, he said, is that people insist on getting everything straight. On having movies make sense, and on being provided with a key for unlocking complex movies.

"It's the weirdest thing. We're willing to accept anything, absolutely anything, in real life. But we demand order from our fantasies. Instead of just going along with them and saying, yeah, that's right, it's a fantasy and it doesn't make sense. Once you figure out a fantasy, it may be more satisfying but it's less fun."

For reasons having something to do with that, he said, he likes to take chances on his films: "Every film should be different, and get into a different area, and have its own look. I'd hate to start repeating myself. I have this thing I call a fear quotient. The more afraid I am, going in, the better the picture is likely to be." A pause. "And on that basis, *A Wedding* is going to be my best picture yet.

"I like to allow for accidents, for happy occurrences, and mistakes. That's why I don't plan too carefully, and why we're going to use two cameras and shoot 500,000 feet of film on *A Wedding*. Sometimes you don't know yourself what's going to work. I think a problem with some of the younger directors, who were all but raised on film, is that their film grammar has become too rigid. Their work is inspired more by other films than by life.

"That happened to Godard, and to Friedkin it may be happening. To Bogdanovich without any doubt. He has all these millions of dollars and all these great technicians, and he tells them what he wants and they give it to him. Problem is, maybe when he gets it, it turns out he didn't really want it after all, but he's stuck with it."

Altman has rarely had budgets large enough to afford such freedom, if freedom's the word. Although he's had only one smash hit, *M*A*S*H,* he keeps working and remains prolific because his films are budgeted reasonably and brought in on time. For example, *3 Women* is a challenging film that may not find enormous audiences, but at $1.6 million it will likely turn a profit.

"I made a deal with the studio," he said, "if we go over budget, I pay the difference. If we stay under, I keep the change. On that one, we came in about $100,000 under budget, which certainly wasn't enough to meet much of the overhead of keeping this whole organization going . . . but then of course you hope the film goes into profit."

He always makes a film believing it will be enormously profitable, he said: "When I'm finished, I can't see any way that millions of people won't want to see what I've done. With *The Long Goodbye,* for example, we thought we had a monster hit on our hands. With *Nashville,* my second biggest grossing film, we did have a hit, but it was oversold. Paramount was so convinced they were going through the sky on that film that they spent so damned much money promoting it that they may never break even. It grossed $16 million, which was very good considering its budget, but they thought it would top $40 million, and they were wrong."

But, of course, *A Wedding* will be a monster hit?

"I really hope so. If things work out the way I anticipate they will, it will certainly be my funniest film. I mean really funny. But then funny things happen every day."

The man in white came on quiet shoes, and there was another scotch and soda where the old one had been. Altman obviously had a funny example in mind.

"I had this lady interviewer following me around," he said. "More of that in-depth crap. She was convinced that life with Altman was a never-ending round of orgies and excess. She was even snooping around in my hotel bathroom, for Christ's sake, and she found this jar of funny white powder in the medicine cabinet. Aha! she thinks. Cocaine! So she snorts some. Unfortunately, what she didn't know was that I'm allergic to commercial toothpaste because the dentine in it makes me break out in a rash. So my wife mixes up baking soda and salt for me, and—poor girl."

He lifted his glass and toasted her, and Cannes, and whatever.

Werner Herzog

INTRODUCTION

I met Werner Herzog right at the beginning, at the 1967 New York Film Festival, in a party at the apartment of Bob Shaye, who was about to found New Line Cinema. Herzog is one of my heroes, because over forty years in fifty features and documentaries he has never compromised himself, has always defended his radical artistic vision, his mission to provide us with new images, that we may not die or despair (that's how he thinks).

At the Walker Art Center in Minneapolis one year, after a retrospective of his work, we sat onstage and talked for three hours and he was not eager to stop. No one left. He is one of those speakers, like Buckminster Fuller, whom you want to listen to indefinitely. We had two other long public discussions, at Facets Multimedia in Chicago in the 1970s and at my Overlooked Film Festival in 2003, and both ran until the small hours of the morning. He does not repeat himself, cannot bore, will not compromise, leads a life of ceaseless curiosity.

Once he told me that as a youth he walked around Albania. Why Albania? "At that time, they would not admit you to Albania."

MAY 1982

CANNES, FRANCE—On the day after *Fitzcarraldo* had its world premiere at the Cannes Film Festival, I sat and had tea with Werner Herzog, the West German who directed it. Werner Herzog is a strange, deep, visionary man. With other directors, I have an interview. With Herzog, I have an audience.

He does not speak of small matters. He would not say so, but he obviously sees himself as one of the most important artists of his time—and so, to tell the truth, do I. He makes films that exist outside the usual categories. He takes enormous risks to make them. In a widely discussed article in the *New Republic*, Stanley Kauffmann wondered if it is an item of Herzog's faith that he must risk his life with every movie he makes.

It is a logical question. Herzog makes movies about people who have larger dreams and take greater risks than ordinary men. Herzog does the same. He once went with a small crew to an island where a volcano was about to explode. He wanted to interview a man who had decided to stay behind and die. Herzog has also made movies in the middle of the Sahara, and twice he has risked his life and the lives of his associates on risky film projects in the Amazon rain jungles.

His *Aguirre: The Wrath of God* (1973) told the story of one of Pizarro's mad followers who pressed on relentlessly into the jungle in a doomed quest for El Dorado. Now there is *Fitzcarraldo*, based on the true story of an Irishman who tried to haul a whole steamship over dry land from one Amazonian river system to another.

As nearly everybody must know by now, Werner Herzog did the same thing in filming *Fitzcarraldo*. But Herzog's historical inspiration (who was named Fitzgerald) had the good sense to disassemble *his* steamship before hauling it overland; Herzog used winches and pulleys to haul an entire boat overland *intact*. And that afternoon over tea at Cannes, he was not modest about his feat: "*Apocalypse Now* was only a kindergarten compared to what we went through," he said.

At forty, he is a thin, strongly built man of average height, with hair swept back from a broad forehead. He usually wears a neat mustache. He spent an undergraduate year at a university in Pennsylvania and speaks excellent English; he once made a movie, *Stroszek*, on location in northern Wisconsin, and it included a striking image of the lost American Dream, as his hero, Bruno, looked in despair as the bank repossessed his mobile home and left him contemplating the frozen prairie.

I had seen *Fitzcarraldo* the day before. I also had seen Les Blank's *Burden of Dreams*, an unblinking, unsentimental documentary about the making of *Fitzcarraldo*. It is good to see the two films together, because Blank's documentary paints a portrait of Herzog seemingly going mad under the strain of making his impossible movie. I asked Herzog about that: did he really crack up during his months in the rain jungle and his legendary problems with civil wars, disease, Indian attacks, and defecting cast and crew members?

"Sanity?" he said. "For that you don't have to fear. I am quite sane."
He somehow sounded like the vampire hero of his *Nosferatu*. He sipped tea.
"I make sense. I don't push myself to the edge." Having said that, he pro-
ceeded to contradict it: "It is only the project that counts. If the nature of
the project makes it necessary for me to go very far, I would go anywhere.
How much you have to suffer, how little sleep you get. . . . I am the last one
to look for a situation like that, but the last one to back out if it is necessary."

He looked out over the veranda of the hotel, at the palm trees in the
spring sunshine.

"I would go down in hell and wrestle a film away from the devil if it
was necessary," said the man who had just told me he didn't push himself
to the edge.

Do you feel you have a personal mission to fulfill? I asked. Other directors sign up Goldie Hawn and shoot in Los Angeles. You sign up Klaus
Kinski and disappear into the rain forest.

"If you say 'mission,' it sounds a little heavy," he said. "I would say
'duty' or 'purpose.' When I start a new film, I am a good soldier. I do not
complain, I will hold the outpost even if it is already given up. Of course I
want to win the battle. I see each film more like a high duty that I have."

Is your duty to the film, I asked, or does the film itself fulfill a duty
to mankind? Even as I asked the question, I realized that it sounded grandiose, but Herzog nodded solemnly. He said his duty was to help mankind
find new images, and, indeed, in his films there are many great and vivid
images: a man standing on a drifting raft, surrounded by gibbering mon-
keys; a ski-jumper so good that he overjumps a landing area; men deaf and
blind from birth, feeling the mystery of a tree; a man asleep on the side of
a volcano; midgets chasing runaway automobiles; a man standing on an
outcropping rock in the middle of a barren sea; a man hauling a ship up the
side of a mountain.

"We do not have adequate images for our kind of civilization," Herzog said. "What are we to look at? The ads at the travel agent's of the Grand
Canyon? We are surrounded by images that are worn out, and I believe that
unless we discover new images, we will die out. Die like the dinosaurs. And
I mean it physically."

He leaned forward, speaking intensely, as if time were running out.
"Frogs do not apparently need images, and cows do not need them, either.

But we do. Michelangelo in the Sistine Chapel for the first time articulated human pathos in a new way that was adequate to the understanding of his time. I am not looking to make films in which actors stand around and say words that some screenwriter has thought were clever. That is why I use midgets, and a man who spent twenty-four years in prisons and asylums (Bruno S., the hero of *Stroszek*) and the deaf and blind, and why I shoot with actors who are under hypnosis, for example. I am trying to make something that has not been made before."

I said *Fitzcarraldo* almost seemed to be about itself: a film about a man who hauled a ship up a hill, made by a man who hauled a real ship up a real hill to make a film.

"It was not planned like that," Herzog said. "It was not planned to be as difficult as it was. It came to a point where the purpose of the film, the making of the film, the goals of the film, and how to make the film all became one and the same thing: to get that ship up the hill. When Jason Robards fell ill and returned to America, before I replaced him with Klaus Kinski, I thought about playing Fitzcarraldo myself. I came very close."

Why did you have to use a real boat?

"There was never any question in my mind about that. All those trashy special effects and miniatures that you see in Hollywood movies have caused audiences to lose trust in their eyes. Here, in my film, they are given back trust in their own eyes. When the boat goes up the mountain, people look at the screen, looking for something to tell them it's a trick, but it's no trick. Instinctively, they sense it. An image like that gives you courage for your own dreams."

He smiled, a little grimly. "It's a film," he said, "that will not have a remake. That man who is going to make this film again has to be born first." He paused for thought. "The mad King Ludwig II of Bavaria," he said, "could have made this film."

I observed that in *Burden of Dreams* there seemed to be some controversy over the safety and practicality of hauling the ship up the hill.

"I had engineers," Herzog said, "and I disposed of them. I had the basic idea of winches and pulleys, of a chain of combined winches. In prehistory, you can see that perhaps man did that same thing. In Brittany, there are huge boulders of rock that may have been moved two miles up ramps, with an artificial hill and a crater at the end. Whether that is how they moved those rocks or not, I fantasized about it. I saw them on a long walk I took across France and Germany. If *Fitzcarraldo* has a passport and we must list its place of birth, I would list Carnac, in Brittany, where those boulders are one of the miracles of the world. That ass Erich von Däniken, who writes of the ancient astronauts, cannot believe man is capable of such a feat, but I say give me two years and two thousand men and I will do it all over again for you."

But when you were pulling that ship up the hill, I asked, did you ever question your purpose? Did you wonder if it was all just a little ludicrous?

"There were always low points and lower, and points below the lowest," he said. "I did not allow myself private feelings. I had not the privilege of despair, anxiety, pain. I never paused, I never lost faith, and I have faith enough for fifteen more films."

Fifteen more films like this one?

"I doubt if I or anyone else can make a film like this again," he said. "Film history has shown that this profession of filmmaker has destroyed almost everyone. You can be a cello player until the age of ninety-five. You can be a poet until you die, but the life span of a filmmaker is fifteen years, of making good things. Then they crumble into ashes. I am more than twenty years already. Of course, it has to do with physical strength. For my next project, instead of a film project, I will set out after this film festival is over and walk twenty-five hundred miles on foot."

Where will you go?

He shrugged.

Meryl Streep

INTRODUCTION

The story about Meryl Streep is that there is really no story. She is a great actress, probably the best of her generation, and has given one wonderful performance after another. The rest of the time she is an admirable wife and mother, utterly free of gossip, scandal, and even anecdote. Those stories that are told about her, even the funny ones, are essentially about how gifted she is, and how much people like her. That's it.

DECEMBER 14, 1983

How does an actress go about preparing to play another human being? And what if the other person's friends are standing by to see what you do? Meryl Streep has played realistic characters before, but they were creations of the filmmakers. Her new role is Karen Silkwood, who really lived and breathed and died a controversial death, and whose lover was standing by to tell Streep what he remembered and suspected about her.

"I didn't try to turn myself into Karen. I just tried to look at what she did," Streep said the other afternoon, slowly and thoughtfully. "I put together every piece of information I could find about her, all the legal hearings and depositions and appeals. I talked a lot with Drew Stephens, who was her lover. I met with her dad. And basically what I figured out is that everybody has a different impression of you. Your lover, mother, coworker, all have these varying and contradictory impressions, and what you get is not the portrait of one person, but of three or four.

"What I finally did was look at the events in her life, and try to understand her from the inside. She worked here, she saw this, here's what she did about it—concentrating on her experiences instead of whatever was going on in her mind. For example, Drew told me she smoked a lot. So do I, in the movie. I decided that for Karen, smoking was real important.

There are times in the movie when she feels all alone and smoking is instant gratification. Once when she goes to visit her kids in Texas and she's unhappy, she reaches for that cigarette with a sort of desperation."

Streep's fingers reached for an imaginary cigarette. She was curled up in the corner of a sofa in a Chicago hotel suite. She had decided to come to the Midwest to promote her new movie, *Silkwood,* because she thought it might appeal more directly to the people out here. It's not so much the story of a controversial nuclear worker, she said, as about a working-class woman and what happened to her when she decided to make trouble.

"Karen Silkwood has come to stand for so many things to so many people that I had to start all over again in trying to play her as a person, not a symbol. I really don't think we can know much about people after they're not there to tell us. All their real, real secrets die with them. At the end of this whole experience of making this movie, I thought about those minutes before Karen's car went off the road, and I missed her. What a waste of life."

But you didn't want to "become" Karen Silkwood, in the sense that a Method actor tries to inhabit a role?

"Not really. But three weeks ago, when I saw the whole movie put together for the first time, I had a sort of a chill. At moments it really felt as if she were walking through the movie. And at the end, that last shot of Karen's gravestone? That's really hers. It's not a fake put up by the prop department. Originally there was some discussion with Mike Nichols, the director, as to whether that might be 'too much.' But this was her life, and that was her stone."

After Karen Silkwood died in 1974, there was a national controversy over the circumstances of her death. She was killed in a single-car accident while driving to meet a reporter for the *New York Times.* She was expected to hand over some documents revealing serious gaps in the safety measures at a Kerr-McGee nuclear factory in Oklahoma. The documents were not found in her car. Supporters of Silkwood suggest her death was not accidental. The company and an investigating state policeman cite the presence of tranquilizers and alcohol in her bloodstream, and call the death an accident.

I asked Streep if she had an opinion about Karen Silkwood's death. "Yes."

About whether she was murdered?

"Yes, I have a definite opinion."

Which is?

"But I'm not going to tell you. I think I'd better keep it to myself. There are a lot of legal complications involved with this movie. For example, whenever the movie says that the Kerr-McGee Company did something, it's based on a matter of public record. Otherwise we would have had to change the name of the company, the characters, everything."

One of the surprising things about the movie, I said, is that it seems so real, so convincing, in an unforced way. It records the speech and the energies, the rhythms and humors of Oklahoma working-class life in a way that never seems processed through a Hollywood formula.

Streep said she had a theory about that. "It's the difference between boldface and regular type," she said. "The words are the same, but in boldface they stand out more, and you can see that somebody's making a point of calling your attention to them. A lot of so-called real life in the movies is boldface. The actors are underlining the 'reality.' What we were trying to do here was just give the regular body type. In other words, there's nothing especially sensational about the lives these people lead."

In the movie, Streep lives in a sort of shabby, run-down house with some other people, including her boyfriend (played by Kurt Russell) and another friend, played by Cher, who turns out to be a lesbian. One night Cher brings home a girlfriend (Diana Scarwid), and the next morning, Streep and Russell meet her: She's a beautician at the local mortuary.

"Now see, a detail like that, it's so bizarre you might be tempted to leave it out," Streep said. "But people do have jobs like that, and why leave it out? Why not just accept it, along with everything else in life that's unexpected?"

One of the more unexpected things in the movie, I said, was the performance by Cher, which is so good and so natural I had to keep reminding myself that this really was Cher, of Sonny and Cher—although I already know from her performance last year in Robert Altman's *Come Back to the 5 and Dime, Jimmy Dean, Jimmy Dean,* that Cher has emerged as a genuine dramatic talent.

"It's surprising, not that she can perform, but that she's as good as she is," Streep said. "Here's a women who's been performing for twenty years. She's intelligent, of course she can act. But she's so wonderful in this role that's nothing like her!"

Was there any initial awkwardness on the set between the two of you?

"On both sides. We had to get used to each other. Accept each other. On my side, I was thinking, Cher! You know, from 'I Got You Babe' and all those other records I bought. She, on the other hand, apparently had an image of me as sitting at the right hand of Dame Edith Sitwell. I think she was intimidated by my rep.

"Also, of course, she was conscious of her appearance. She likes to be seen in public with her makeup on. That's very understandable to any woman. Once they took all her makeup away, and made her into the character, there was just all this emotion and truth there. The scene where we sit on the porch swing and hold each other . . . by the time we got to that scene, we were both on the same wavelength."

There was a cry from the next room, and Streep got up. She was traveling with her new baby, a four-month-old daughter, and it was nursing time.

"Who was Karen Silkwood, and how did I relate to her? Actually, I think Karen is more like I really am than any other part I've been able to play. I grew up in small towns, I worked for a living, I lived for a while in a commune in Vermont where nobody had any money and nobody knew whose things were whose—just like in Karen's household. I felt we were a lot alike. And another thing that's the same. If I die, nobody will know what I was really like, and that's the truth."

Woody Allen

INTRODUCTION

For years I talked with Woody Allen before almost every picture, and each interview came with one proviso: if it was syndicated, New York had to be embargoed. I don't know why, but there you are.

We would meet in the Upper East Side penthouse where he filmed the opening shots of *Manhattan,* or in his editing and screening room, or once in a pizzeria in the Village. He was unfailingly serious and analytical, and often gloomy ("none of my films have ever played below the Mason-Dixon line").

Because he worked unceasingly, a film a year, I think in a way critics grew tired of his work. Altman worked as much, but in such different styles that he didn't seem to repeat. Allen's unchanging title typography and use of period jazz gave a consistency to his pictures that some critics grew impatient with, but I continued to find his work a source of intelligence and conversation, not to mention humor and sometimes deep sadness. I was heartened that with *Melinda and Melinda* (2004) and *Match Point* (2005) he made two of his best pictures.

There was a table at Elaine's restaurant that was always understood to be Woody's. Often it stood empty in the event that he might arrive. Late one night, Elaine gave the table to Chaz and me, observing that Woody was apparently not coming in. Twenty minutes later, he arrived, and was seated at the table across from us. We nodded and smiled and Chaz said, "Oh, my God." Two days later, the incident made page six of the *New York Post*. It was as if I'd tried out the queen's throne. Woody never mentioned the incident. Six months later, the publicist and Elaine's regular Bobby Zarem told me, "I was surprised that the earth did not open up and swallow you whole."

OCTOBER 4, 1989

NEW YORK—In the course of Woody Allen's new movie, a man gets away with murder and is much happier afterward. A bright young woman rejects the dedicated documentary filmmaker who loves her, and marries a half-wit who produces successful sitcoms. A kind rabbi goes blind, a wise philosopher jumps out the window, and we laugh, that we may not cry. This is the most despairing of Allen's films, and, the more you think about it, the funniest.

What Allen is doing is questioning the veneer of faith and hope that lets us believe we live in a civilized world. Take the question of murder, for example. Most of us believe we could not live with the guilt if we committed such a crime. In Allen's movie, a respected eye doctor asks his hoodlum brother to knock off the mistress who is making his life miserable. After the murder takes place, the doctor is appalled and conscience-stricken—for a time. But you know what? In the long run, he feels better, his marriage becomes stronger, and he grows closer to his children.

That is the pattern throughout Allen's *Crimes and Misdemeanors,* in which virtue is consistently punished and wrongdoing is rewarded. It is a radical film right down to the marrow in its bones; it is bleak and cynical and angry (and funny), and yet when he discusses it, Allen prefers to use the word "realistic."

"I'd hate to think of it as cynical," he was saying the other morning, looking almost wounded that anyone could hold such an idea. We were talking in his apartment on Fifth Avenue, high above Central Park. "If you ask me," he said, "I'd say realistic because I think in real life, when you get away from all the idealistic rhetoric, that's the way things happen. You can quote Anne Frank's line about how people are so good, or Will Rogers, who said he never met a man he didn't like, but these things don't really ring true in real life. When you strip away these Pollyannish kinds of superficial things, the truth is, life is hard going, it's tough, it's Darwinian, it's dog eat dog. You have nothing to guide you except your own sense of morality, and if you lose that compass, it's a terrible existence."

Allen has thought these things before, and even expressed them in his films (his last movie, *Another Woman,* was about a woman who finds that almost everything she believed about her life and relationships was false). But never before has he found such a confident tone, such a sure way of dealing with his doubts and fears within a movie that still, somehow, works as a comedy—a tragicomedy. To see *Crimes and Misdemeanors* is to understand where the other recent Allen films have been heading—all of them, from *Hannah and Her Sisters* and *Radio Days* to *September* and *Another Woman*. This is it, at last: a world in which God is silent and a few people hold ethical values, and the bastards usually win over the good guys because they aren't afraid to fight dirty and they don't make the mistake of thinking idealistically.

"When I originally conceived the movie," Allen said, "there were two themes that interested me. One was that in our culture, nobody pays off on high aspirations. Nobody cares about that. It's the guy who can deliver who wins, and not some jerk who is spending his life trying to do nice things. That was one theme, and the other was a man who commits murder and is plagued by guilt from it, and then as time passes, realizes that nothing happens. In fact, he prospers and everything goes fine."

The result is Allen's version of *Crime and Punishment,* in which a character sees himself as above the common morality, and feels that he has the right to kill someone because he is somehow more deserving of happiness than his victim. The hero of *Crimes and Misdemeanors* is a wealthy ophthalmologist, played by Martin Landau as a citizen who is universally respected even while he cheats on his wife and manipulates the funds in the charities he administers. In a sense, it is his unblemished reputation that leads him to arrange the murder of his mistress (Anjelica Huston). He would rather be a secret murderer than be known as an adulterer and embezzler. This is the sin of pride, but in the Allen universe it goeth not before a fall.

Talking about the film with Allen, while the sun came slanting in through the windows of his book-cluttered penthouse, I began to understand more fully how the movie expresses his deepest fears. Here is a man who should be happy. Who has made the funniest comedies in recent movie history and some of the best dramas. Who has been blessed in his early fifties with children and a woman he loves. Who is one of only two or three American film directors who makes all of his films on his own terms, in his own way. And yet coexisting with this happiness is a deep dread that the rug can be pulled out from under everything, at any moment, by a universe that doesn't give a damn.

Allen has said that hardly a day passes when he doesn't seriously consider suicide—not out of despair, but simply as a choice. He works all the time, he told me, because if he stopped he might never start again. He would like to treat himself to such pleasures as reading mystery novels, but would feel guilty of taking time away from something more serious. The serenity of nature has been a consolation for even the most despairing of philosophers, but not for Woody Allen:

"I was watching *Cinderella* and *Sleeping Beauty* the other day on television with my little daughter," he said, "and you know the way Disney draws these chipmunks running around, and you could lay down in the grass, and it's all very lovely, but what you don't see are the creeping, crawling things in life. Just this morning I read in the paper that a woman died of a spider bite. A spider crawled into her bed and bit her in the head and she died. A spider the size of your thumbnail."

He looked at his thumbnail, and he looked worried.

Yes, I said, but that was a *city* spider. You could die even in the city of a spider bite.

"In my mind, it was the country. And there's more than spiders in the country. When I go to visit Mia Farrow in Connecticut, I'm always mindful of the fact that lurking in the woods is Lyme disease. When she sees the little fawns come up to the front of the house, which they do, the kids gather suddenly and say it's so beautiful. And yes, it's pretty, but boring, and it does carry Lyme ticks on it. So there are no rural consolations for me."

And the grandeur of the seashore?

"I do love the beach, but after two hours of that, after the waves are crashing and it's beautiful, and you've had your clams or whatever, then you want to go home. I want to go home and get back to the typewriter and get back to the higher achievements of the human race."

And yet the higher achievements are the ones Allen calls most into question in *Crimes and Misdemeanors*—asking if they are really or simply an expression of man's hope that the world is a good and not hostile place.

"The truth of the matter is," he said, "that this movie doesn't give you an out. When I was first screening it for some friends, there would always be one or two people who would come to me afterward and say, 'The doctor is plagued by guilt at the end, isn't he?' Or, 'I noticed at that wedding he had two champagnes in his hand, does that mean he was turning into a drunkard?' But the truth is . . . no! He isn't plagued by guilt, and he doesn't turn to drink. You can commit murder and get away with it, if that's the kind of person you want to be. People do as bad every day. The only thing that stands in your way is your own sense of right and wrong. That's why we can't make any progress with social problems, racial problems, or crack problems, because it has to come from the people involved. It can't be externally imposed. You'll never get rid of all the terrible social evils that plague people until it emanates from inside each individual himself.

"What happens is the doctor talks to his brother and he has this thing done, and he's not bothered by it. There's a slight suggestion of repudiation that's pooh-poohed in the picture, when my character says to him that he has to give himself up—because in the absence of a god, the individual has to assume responsibility. And he says that's not life, it's just the movies."

You know, I said, it's true that you never read in the papers about someone confessing that they put out a murder contract on a wife or a mistress or some relative they hate. You read about them getting caught, but you never read about how their conscience bothered them and they had to turn themselves in.

"No. It's very rare. Someone will occasionally be brought in by his own guilt on a much lesser charge, and will take his lumps. And people say, what a wonderful man, he cheated on his tax and then turned himself in. But when you murder someone, there's not such a tendency to turn yourself in."

In the movie, Allen plays the serious documentary filmmaker who is hired to make a film about his hateful brother-in-law (Alan Alda), who is a shallow, ignorant, and spectacularly successful producer of TV sitcoms. Allen's marriage is coming apart, and he falls in love with one of his production assistants (Mia Farrow). But she has ambitions to make it in the TV industry, and can clearly see that an earnest documentarian is not her ticket to the top. So she marries the Alda character. This illustrates Allen's thesis that not only do people sometimes get away with murder, but even on an everyday level they cheerfully sell out to attain success.

"What I'm saying with the Alan Alda situation," he said, "is that nobody really cares about the aspirations of people, or that they mean well, or that they aim high. They want to go with the winners. They rationalize afterward. They get on the success bandwagon and rationalize. They teach courses in college about *I Love Lucy* and things like that, just because it was so successful. The same thing happened originally with the Beatles. They came on the scene, they were criticized very much, but when their success became overwhelming, they were taken seriously. It's the same with megahit movies. People will start trying to convince themselves that they're saying something. You get all these articles about the significance of some blockbuster, and not a word about a truly significant movie that didn't make money."

The choice in this movie is clear-cut. The Allen character has filmed four hundred thousand feet on a wise old philosopher, but cannot get anyone to finance his work. There's lots of money, however, for a film about the stupid and vain zillionaire played by Alda.

"There's a little moment in the film," Allen said, "where he cares slightly what I think about him. It does bother him, down deep. He says I've gotta learn that they don't pay off on high aspirations, because he cares a little bit down deep that I don't like him.

"Years ago, there was a very successful television show and my friend Marshall Brickman was saying to me, 'Yes, they're successful and all of that, and 99 percent of their conscious mind may be accepting that, but somewhere down deep they know there's a difference between what they're doing and what Tennessee Williams did. And in the final analysis, they would probably trade all that success to be Tennessee Williams.' He was probably right. Even the sitcom producer, if you said to him, if you give this up, we're going to give you Saul Bellow's talent, he'd probably do it, because something in him recognizes that no matter how lionized he is, Bellow is better."

But what if you're Saul Bellow, I said, and you still feel inadequate, down deep, because you're not Shakespeare?

"People have asked me at times, do I envy anyone? I would have traded everything I was to be Marlon Brando, because I so envied his talent. It was so thrilling to me."

But maybe right now Brando would trade to be you.

"Not for any rational reasons. Maybe if he wanted to lose weight, or lose some years from his age. He's older than I am, and he's heavier than I am, but he'd be crazy to trade. He'd just be crazy."

But he could be directing a movie every year, and it would be his movie, not someone else's.

"I think his thing is deeper. He was just a great genius, and I would have traded with him. There are probably other people in my lifetime I would have traded with. I would have been happy to have traded with Louie Armstrong. I don't know how Saul Bellow might have felt about Shakespeare, he may feel Shakespeare's a pretty dull writer, but there may be somebody that he may have been willing to trade with. Mozart or Rembrandt or somebody."

It was getting to be time, Allen said, for him to go to the nursery school and pick up his daughter and take her across the park to Mia's apartment, where they would all have lunch together. He seemed to brighten noticeably at the prospect, and I wondered if he would really trade with Brando unless his family was thrown in as part of the trade. As we were walking out, I could look down a corridor and see the big table with the old portable typewriter on it, the typewriter he has used to write everything he has ever written. I asked him when he was going to break down and get a computer to write his movies on.

"Yeah, that's what everyone says. But I'm happy with the typewriter. It's heavy and solid, not like these plastic typewriters they have today. I remember when my mother took me to buy it, the salesman told me, 'This typewriter will last longer than you will.' It looks like he might have been right."

Spike Lee

INTRODUCTION

A week or two before the world press premiere of his *Malcolm X,* Spike Lee said he would prefer to be interviewed by African American journalists, when possible. He never made a demand that only blacks talk to him, and he never said he wouldn't talk to whites. But most news reports gave that impression, and at least one midwestern daily pulled its white movie writer off the assignment in a huff.

Two things emerged during the press weekend itself: most of the press people who talked to Spike were indeed white, and many papers and TV stations didn't have an African American they could send.

Lee was making a point, something he does effectively. Blacks buy 25 percent of the movie tickets in America, but represent a nearly invisible minority in the entertainment press. If his request offended white editors, how do they deal with one of the sneakiest open secrets in movie journalism, the way big Hollywood stars and their publicists ask for—and get—upfront approval of writers?

Some publicists ask for preapproval of questions, making clear that certain topics are out of bounds. They even negotiate what kind of play their clients will receive; if they're not promised a color photo on the magazine cover or the front page of the feature section, their star won't talk. And then there's this smarmy old ploy: "See the movie, and if you like it, the star would really like to talk to you." In other words, if you don't like it, forget the interview.

I won't go along with scams like that, which are pulled by the representatives of even the most famous movie personalities. (On the other hand, I don't need the interview to survive. Some entertainment journalists do.) No one has ever asked me if I liked a new Spike Lee picture before arranging an interview with Lee, and I doubt if anyone ever will. No question has ever been out of bounds. Nobody has ever asked how the story will be played. When Spike Lee exercised his clout, he was doing it on behalf of others, not himself.

There is one other story to tell. Seeing *Do the Right Thing* was one of the great experiences of my life as a moviegoer. I saw it at Cannes, 8:30 in the morning, and when the two quotations rolled up at the end, my eyes filled with tears. "If this film does not win the Palme d'Or," I said, "I will never come back to this festival again." It did not. "I think the movie depended on really understanding the language of the characters," Lee said, "and some of the jury didn't speak English so well." He told me I had permission to return to the festival the next year: "After all, I'm going to be on the jury."

NOVEMBER 15, 1992

NEW YORK—It was clear, after all the years of publicity and months of controversy, that *Malcolm X* had better be a good movie or Spike Lee would go down with it. He had talked the talk, and now it was time to walk the walk.

After taking the project away from a powerful white director, after saying only an African American could tell Malcolm's story, after hearing from other blacks who thought he was too bourgeois to tell it, after conducting a running battle in the press with Warner Brothers (which didn't want the movie to be as long or as expensive as Spike thought it should be), Lee and *Malcolm X* arrived at the moment of truth last weekend. The movie was at last finished, it was shown, and it had to speak for itself.

It did so as eloquently as any filmed biography I have ever seen. Spike put up, which is just as well, because it's not in his nature to shut up. *Malcolm X* belongs on the list of the great epic films about men's lives, with *Lawrence of Arabia* and *Gandhi*. It takes the life of a man who was dismissed as a separatist cult leader in his lifetime—even by many other blacks—and shows how his uncompromising analysis of race in America undermined the conventional pieties of his time. Like all great movie biographies, it does three things at once: it entertains, it educates, and it inspires.

The man behind the movie is better than any American director except Oliver Stone at stirring up prerelease controversy over his movies. The stories hit the headlines one after another: Spike thought only a black could direct the movie. Spike said kids should skip school to see *Malcolm X*. Spike wanted to be interviewed only by African Americans. These statements were much amplified in the retelling, and Spike's actual words were more reasonable than the reports made them seem. When the dust dies down, however, it won't matter exactly what Spike Lee said; the effect was to put his movie in the papers and on the evening news night after night. Like some other great directors, he is also a great promoter of his projects.

Talking to Lee after seeing the movie, I observed he'd been out on a very long limb, and that if the film hadn't lived up to its hype he'd be in big trouble about now.

"I have confidence," he said, "so anything I say, I'm gonna back up. I would not be doing all this talk just to be wolfin' if I didn't think I had the product behind it. And Denzel's performance is the ace in the hole right there, cause he's in almost all the film, so if I'm getting a great performance from him then the film has to be good."

Which is more or less true. Denzel Washington is at the heart of *Malcolm X* with a performance that spans twenty years, that shows him moving from the West to New York to the world stage, that has him changing from a two-bit gangster to an inspirational leader, and that shows his inner odyssey from dogmatic racial separatism to a growing faith that races could learn to live together. The performance makes Washington the front-runner for this year's Academy Award.

Whether Lee will win, or be nominated, in the director's category is less certain; like *Malcolm X,* he has a genius for creating enemies by saying exactly what he thinks, whether or not it's what people want to hear. Sometimes, I suggested to him, the maelstrom of controversy must be so loud it's hard to concentrate on the work.

"What you do," he said, "is, you're just so focused that you don't let the distractions get in front of the camera. Whatever happens, that has to happen behind the camera—but between the camera and the actors, that's something different; that's sacred."

Lee is a small man with a sideways grin and trademark glasses. He doesn't at first look prepossessing, but he has a confidence and a brashness that fills every space he finds himself in. I remember seeing him for the first time in 1986 at the Cannes Film Festival, where he brought a low-budget first feature named *She's Gotta Have It*. It was clear from the start that Lee had it, that he was one of those natural filmmakers, like Martin Scorsese, for whom directing movies seemed like second nature.

Lee's great third film, *Do the Right Thing* (1989) showed a Brooklyn neighborhood that descends into racial hatred. It famously ended with two quotations on the screen. One was by Martin Luther King. The other, by Malcolm X, ended with the clarion call in which Malcolm called on African Americans to advance their cause "by any means necessary." I was in the Palais du Cinema at Cannes at the moment those words appeared, and I still remember the current that ran through the audience: Malcolm still had the power to shock and threaten, twenty-five years after his death.

Maybe it was then and there that Lee decided to make a film based on *The Autobiography of Malcolm X*. Maybe it was earlier.

"I was a convert when I read the book in junior high school, back in 1968–69," he told me. "It's the most important book I'll ever read."

What was different inside you after you'd read it?

"The book gave me courage to do what I need to do to make the types of films I want to make. It takes commitment and it takes backbone not to go along with the status quo. You could easily be sucked into smiling and grinning and going for the money. That's the route I've chosen not to go."

You played hardball with Warner Brothers over the budget.

"It came in at $34 million, which is what I thought it had to cost."

Was there ever a time when you thought you'd lose that battle?

He smiled. "No. We had access to the negative. The footage had been stashed. There was no way that film could have been completed without us."

They also wondered why you had to go to Mecca and South Africa to shoot scenes.

"In an earlier stage some executives at Warner Brothers could not understand why Nelson Mandela would be in the film at all. Once they saw the film, though, it made sense to them."

It did to me, too. Many biopics end with the death of the hero, perhaps a funeral, a shot of clouds in the sky, maybe some sad music. *Malcolm X* continues with a eulogy read over Malcolm's body (then, as now, by Ossie Davis) and then comes down to the present day, to a South African classroom where Mandela recites one of Malcolm's speeches to schoolchildren.

"It's very important to show that there's a link from Malcolm X to Mandela. Same way there's a link with Marcus Garvey [the leader of an American back-to-Africa nationalist movement] at the beginning of the film. Malcolm's father was a Garveyite. Malcolm used Pan-Africanism to show the connection between what happens in Soweto and what happens on the corner in Harlem."

Seeing the movie, I said, I understood at a gut level why you felt it had to be made by a black director. Every writing class I've ever heard about begins with the advice "write what you know," and yet when you applied that to the story of Malcolm, there was a lot of controversy.

"With some films—not every film—the director needs to come from the background. Francis Ford Coppola, being an Italian American, enhanced *The Godfather* movies. Martin Scorsese, being Italian American, grew up in Little Italy, on Elizabeth and Mott Streets, and that enhanced *Mean Streets, Raging Bull,* and *GoodFellas.* And me, being African American . . . well, I don't think a white director knows what it feels like to be an African American. You might think you know but you will never know what it means to be black in this country. Also, we did a lot of research, and the people I had to talk to would not have opened up to a white director."

The movie's title sequence sets a chilling tone for what follows. We hear one of Malcolm's speeches. We see the famous video footage of Rodney King being beaten by police. And we see an American flag which fills the screen, just like the flag at the beginning of *Patton,* but this flag catches fire and burns until the cloth that is left forms an *X.*

"We wanted to use powerful symbols for the opening sequence," Lee said. "The American flag was one; let's burn the flag until it comes to a figure *X.* And let's use the Rodney King footage, but let's *really* show it. People have seen it a million times in their homes, so let's put on an effect on it that makes it seem eerie when projected on a big giant screen. It gives it that much greater impact. And then we wanted to have a Malcolm X speech over that. And by doing this, we showed that the conditions Malcolm X talked about are still with us today. It's not a history lesson, it's not a museum piece, it's not a dinosaur, and these are not fossils. This stuff is still with us."

It's crucial that the flag does not burn up. It burns down—down to an *X.* What is left is still American, and still Malcolm.

"He always said that no other country could produce a person like him."

The perception of Malcolm has changed in thirty years. I remember that when he died, many people, including many blacks, found it hard to muster a lot of sympathy, because his ideas were out of step with the conventional wisdom of the times.

"There were a lot of black folks who felt he was a maniac. A lot of people been changing their stories about how they felt about Malcolm."

You use documentary footage of Martin Luther King commenting on Malcolm's assassination, and King sounds very measured, very controlled, not overcome by grief.

"I think that's the way Martin Luther King probably felt. Do you think it was cruel to use that sound bite? It seems like he's describing the weather, doesn't it?"

King was a politician; they were fighting for the same constituency.

"Exactly. Fighting for the same people."

There is a stunning composition in the film that shows Malcolm X addressing a Black Muslim rally, while standing in front of a gigantic portrait of the Honorable Elijah Muhammad, the founder of the movement and a man Malcolm first revered, then broke from in disenchantment. The movie suggests that Malcolm may have been assassinated by followers of Elijah, perhaps also with the complicity of the FBI and CIA, which both had him under surveillance and conceivably knew of the murder plot. In the scene, Lee moves his camera closer to Malcolm, and Elijah's eyes grow gigantic, burning behind him, bracketing him. How, I asked, have Elijah Muhammad's present-day followers, led by the Rev. Louis Farrakhan, accepted the film?

"Bet we'll be hearing from Mr. Farrakhan soon, I think," Lee said.

Has he seen the film?

"Not yet. I flew to Chicago and sat down with the minister before I started shooting. We sat for four hours and he told me right off, 'You can do what you want to Malcolm but my major concern is how you treat and how you portray the Honorable Elijah Muhammad."

And he may not be too happy.

"He may not."

What about audiences in general? This is a film over three hours long, about a man who has been dead nearly thirty years and was not popular when he was alive. How will audiences respond to it? Have you tested or sneaked it?

Lee looked pleased by what he was about to say. "That's one thing I refused to do. I refused to test-market this film. I am not one of these directors who likes some marketing genius to say, 'Well, Spike, it says here 39 percent of the people liked this and 42 percent liked that.' This film, I was going with my gut. I've done test-marketing on my other films but there's too much riding at stake on this one and I don't want to be subjected to any marketing research bullshit."

The more you had riding on the film, the less you wanted research.

"Exactly. That's definitely what I felt. Denzel and me, our necks were literally on the line. And if we gotta go down, let it be because it's our vision on the screen, not some committee."

Tom Hanks

It is useful to remember what an impact *Forrest Gump* had when it was first released. It was a film that audiences simply loved. It vaulted over the head of the teenage audience directly into the hearts of adults who might go to the movies once or twice a year, but had heard they must see this one.

I was asked by *Playboy* to do a profile about Tom Hanks, and wrote it without interviewing the actor. I had interviewed him before and would again; he is the most affable and decent of men, amused, civilized, funny, but for this piece I didn't want to ask him questions. I just wanted to write about him.

SUMMER 1994

On a Saturday afternoon in August, six weeks into the run of *Forrest Gump,* every seat in the movie theater was filled—filled with the ordinary people of Michigan City, Indiana, who were like the movie audiences of my youth: not loud, not restless, not talking to the screen, not filled with bloodlust, but quite happily absorbed in the picture. At times some of them were crying. Looking around, I saw that many of those crying were men. I did not know what to make of this.

I had come to see *Forrest Gump* again because people would not stop talking to me about it. As a professional movie critic, I am like a lightning rod for anyone who has just seen a movie: they tell me if they liked it or not, as if I'd made it myself. Not in twenty-seven years on the job has a movie created more conversation among ordinary people, among the folks who only go to two or three movies a year. They just plain love it. More, they are moved by it, and they get a funny smile on their face when they talk about it, because they do not know why they are moved. The film doesn't deliver in any conventional way, and they are not quite sure what it's about. But it gets to them.

And then they mention Tom Hanks, who plays Forrest Gump, and they ask me if I thought it was a good performance, because, well, they add, "it really wasn't a performance, was it?" They don't think Hanks *is* Forrest Gump, not exactly, but they can't catch him acting in the movie. They know he got to them somehow, but they couldn't capture him in the act of doing it, and so now, thinking back, they wonder if what he did should qualify as "acting," or whether it was (they finish with a relieved nod) "just good casting."

Tom Hanks, who in the minds of some of these people might as well be Forrest Gump, is certain to get an Academy Award nomination for his performance in the movie. He may even win the Oscar for best actor, which would make it two in a row, after his award in April 1994 for *Philadelphia,* the 1993 film where he played a man dying of AIDS. In the summer of 1993, he had another big audience success with *Sleepless in Seattle,* as a lonely widower who meets a woman through a talk show, and is almost prevented from finding his future with her, while the audience, which knows everything, desperately wants him to be happy. The summer before that, in 1992, Hanks played the manager of an all-girl baseball team in *A League of Their Own,* and there, too, the audience was on his side, hoping his character would overcome his alcoholism and make a new start to his career.

For an actor, the odds against making a truly good movie are discouraging in Hollywood, which uses formulas and deals and habit patterns to push even the most original projects into narrow channels. The odds against making four in a row, four movies where the audience truly and deeply cares about your character, are so awesome that even a Spencer Tracy or a James Stewart would have thought himself blessed at the end of such a run. Hanks has done it.

Tom Hanks right now is in the unique position of being the best-loved movie actor in America, and the strange thing is, America hardly knows what to make of that, because Hanks is so hard to pin down. In some of my conversations about *Forrest Gump,* I ask people what they like the most about Tom Hanks in the movie, and they come to a dead stop. There is nothing they *particularly* like about Hanks in the movie because there was nothing they particularly noticed about him. It is the ultimate tribute to an actor, when an audience leaves the theater remembering only the character he played.

Is there even, for that matter, a character that can be described as a "Tom Hanks type"? Hanks has rarely in his career played ordinary, realistic, three-dimensional human beings. There is usually an edge of fantasy, magic, winsome humor, or otherworldly detachment about his most successful roles. The major exception, his full-hearted excursion into straight realism, is in *Philadelphia,* where AIDS is fighting his character for possession of his body, and where, in scenes like the luminous sickbed conversation with his mother (Joanne Woodward), he touches notes that everyone can identify with. He's also living in the real world in *Nothing in Common* (1987), as a cynical, fast-talking ad man who's too busy for family values, until he learns his dad (Jackie Gleason) is sick; then he discovers what's really important in life. In his upcoming film *Apollo 13,* he plays James Lovell, the astronaut whose moon mission was aborted when an oxygen tank exploded, and whose emergency return to earth was a global nail-biter. The movie is being directed by Ron Howard, who likes to go for an everyday-life feel, and is likely to be pretty realistic.

Still, despite such performances, you can't easily imagine Hanks playing the kinds of slice-of-life roles that Al Pacino, Dustin Hoffman, or De Niro specialize in. Tom Hanks is not and never could be Travis Bickle. More often, the Hanks character in a movie is like the characters played by Buster Keaton or Jacques Tati—universal figures in which some attributes are so exaggerated that the ordinary repertory of human tics and impulses is overlooked. In a silent film, many of the characters played by Hanks would be introduced with a card reading simply, *The Young Man.* To a surprising extent, most of his successful movie roles are in fantasies.

In *Splash* (1984), his first big role, he costars with a mermaid. He is a bachelor who runs a business in Manhattan, and might be mistaken for an ordinary guy, if it weren't for the mermaid, and for a certain dreamy quality that the producers must have seen when they cast him: he's the kind of guy you can somehow imagine in love with a mermaid.

In *Dragnet* (1987), he is sergeant Joe Friday's partner, whose great responsibility is to pretend that Friday's robotic PoliceSpeak makes sense. Like Jack Webb and Harry Morgan in the original TV series, Dan Aykroyd and Hanks, in the movie, are too weird, too stylized, to ever be mistaken for *real* cops. Webb's TV series was a satire of itself, with every scene ending in a punch line and the *Dragnet* theme, and in the movie you can sense Hanks subtly stiffening himself into a parody.

Big (1988) has one of his best performances, as a child who is granted his wish of inhabiting an adult's body. In *The Burbs* (1989), he's a goofy suburbanite who skips his vacation to stay home and spy on his bizarre neighbors. In the magical and overlooked *Joe vs. the Volcano* (1990), he is the central figure in a fable: A victim of overwork in a factory dungeon, told he has six months to live because of a "brain cloud," who sails to the South Seas to offer himself as a human sacrifice to be hurled into a volcano.

It might appear that Hanks plays a more realistic character in *Sleepless in Seattle,* but consider: his widower in that movie quits his Chicago job and takes his young son and moves to a houseboat in Seattle, where he spends most of the movie trapped in a plot only the audience understands—a plot that manipulates him so that he becomes the hostage of fate. His real role in the movie is to represent all of us on our blind quest for the happiness we sense is just beyond our grasp. His character's philosophy in that movie could be borrowed from Forrest Gump's mother: "Life is like a box of chocolates; you never know what you're gonna get."

Tom Hanks in his key roles plays a sort of Everyman, a put-upon, misunderstood, overworked, middle-class guy, basically nice, who means well, tries hard, wants to please and be pleased, and is tossed about by the winds of chance. "I don't know if we each have a destiny," Forrest Gump says, "or if we're floating and accidental, like on a breeze, but I think like maybe it's both—both happening at the same time." And the film's famous opening and closing shots of a feather, at the mercy of the wind, is the right image to go with that thought.

If there is a common theme to a Hanks character, an element that draws him to certain roles, it may be the element of fable. Fables teach a lesson in mythical terms, and there is something of the moral and the myth lurking beneath the surfaces of his key films: *Splash, Big, Nothing in Common, Joe vs. the Volcano, Sleepless in Seattle,* and of course *Forrest Gump.* It is even there in *The Bonfire of the Vanities,* which is among other things a sermon against greed.

Traditional movie stars are larger than life. Robert Mitchum once told me that he asked his wife: "Dorothy, why do they think I'm such a big deal? You know me as well as anyone, and you don't give a shit. So why do they care?" And his wife replied, "Mitch, it's because when you're up there on the screen, they're smaller than your nostril." The big screen makes some actors into gods, into personalities so large and overwhelming that they enter our dreams and fashion our ideas about what men and women should be. Not everyone can model for that role, and the great stars do have something magical, but the screen itself plays an important role in the process. (That is why we never care as deeply about TV stars as about movie stars.)

There is a smaller category, however, of actors who are not "bigger than life," but somehow just like life—people we feel we know and understand, and are comfortable with. We sense that these actors embody not our fantasies, but our lives. Watching them we feel congratulated, because we are watching ourselves. They reassure us that in our ordinariness we also have a kind of importance. The actors who can do that—Buster Keaton, Spencer Tracy, James Stewart, Henry Fonda, Robert Duvall, Gene Hackman, and Tom Hanks—occupy a special category. We do not value them as highly as such performers as James Cagney, Mitchum, James Dean, Robert De Niro, Al Pacino, Tom Cruise, or Sean Penn, because it seems to us they aren't "acting," but embodying qualities which must not be very special to possess, since, after all, we possess them ourselves.

The central triumph of Tom Hanks as a movie actor is that, most of the time, we believe he thinks a lot like us, and does more or less what we would do, but that he somehow does it on a larger or more ennobling scale. It is the James Stewart quality. But few actors can obtain it; with most, you see their egos peeking through, or you catch them trying too hard. The camera is a lie detector, and Hanks must be a fundamentally good person to play such roles—either that, or he is an even better actor than we think.

I've met Hanks several times, in interview situations and on sets. I don't have any idea what he's really like. These are artificial situations, where he gets to choose how he presents himself, and what he chooses is to be very level-headed and smart, with a strong element of the wry. He's much the same in one of his favorite extracurricular roles, as a talk-show guest. On Letterman and Leno, he's very quick and articulate, a natural comedian, comfortable inside his body. He never seems to search for a word or strive for a laugh; in that he's like Cary Grant. Letterman is the best bullshit detector among the TV talk hosts, but Hanks, who as a big movie star should be a ripe target, finesses him with understatement, directness, and irony. It is all done so well that we realize only later we learned nothing at all about "Tom."

The real Tom Hanks was born thirty-eight years ago in Oakland, California, and attended California State College in Sacramento, where he took drama classes, acted in Ibsen, and met a man named Vincent Dowling, who was director of the Great Lakes Shakespeare Festival in Cleveland. Dowling invited Hanks to Cleveland, where he appeared in a lot of Shakespeare (even winning a local critics' award for his work in *Two Gentlemen of Verona*). The great British actors often begin their careers at Stratford; it is somehow just like the man who would play Forrest Gump that he began in Shakespeare, too, but in Cleveland.

After time on the stage in New York, Hanks moved to Los Angeles, and was cast in *Bosom Buddies* on ABC during the 1981–82 season. He already seemed like a seasoned comedy pro, comfortable in his persona, as a Catholic school-bus driver who gets engaged in the underrated *Bachelor Party* (1984), his first role of any consequence. And later the same year he played the lead in *Splash*. There was no long period of bit roles and starvation; he was a star at twenty-eight.

I still feel he was cast incorrectly in *Splash,* the comedy where he fell in love with a mermaid played by Daryl Hannah. His brother in the film was the fat and genial John Candy, who spent his days composing inflamed letters to sex magazines, and I thought it would have been funnier if the mermaid (who had never seen a human male before) chose Candy instead of Hanks. That would have been a better use of Candy, and a better use of Hanks, too, whose best roles have him as an island of curiosity in a sea of mystery. He is never at his best in movies where he's the one who has the answers.

Look at him instead in *Big,* where in the early scenes he plays a pint-sized adolescent. (If you think this is easy, see how Martin Short handled it in *Clifford*.) He is at just that age when all of the girls in his class shoot up into Amazons, while the boys remain short and squeaky-voiced. At an amusement park, he is in line next to the girl of his dreams, and hopes to sit next to her on a thrill ride, but the ride operator won't let him on board because he's too short. Hanks's face is a study in tragedy here; he portrays his humiliation so completely that it sets up the rest of the film, as his thirteen-year-old mind is magically transported into a thirty-year-old body, and he finds his true calling—working for a toy company. His secret is that he is the only one at the company who really loves to play with the toys, and Hanks finds a childlike body language for shots like the one where he hops, skips, and jumps through the company's lobby.

Joe vs. the Volcano, which was written and directed by John Patrick Shanley (the author of *Moonstruck*) has been written off as a critical and commercial flop. I think it is one of the most original comedies of recent years, and it contains a performance by Hanks that works as an island of calm and sanity in the middle of the plot's madness. From the film's opening shots of the loathsome factory—a vast block of ugliness set down in a sea of mud—the film's art design and special effects place Hanks in a world as imaginary as Oz. The notion that he will ever really sacrifice himself to the volcano is absurd, but he seems determined to go ahead with it.

The role in the hands of another actor would have been impossible, because there is never a moment when the character can find an anchor to reality. Hanks does not need one. The key to his performance here is acceptance: without fuss, without blinking, he accepts the film's bizarre reality, and because he never fights it we can relax and accept it too.

It is that same matter-of-fact quality, of making himself at home in a world not his own, that underlies Hanks's work in *A League of Their Own* and, especially, *Forrest Gump.* In the baseball picture, he is a man who has always played in a man's game, and when he finds himself coaching a team of women, his strategy is to simply keep on doing what he knows. He doesn't try to fight it, he doesn't figure it out, he simply coaches.

In *Philadelphia,* as a dying man determined to be treated correctly by the law firm which has fired him, the Hanks character has two major characteristics: pride, and anger. Either of these is an easy excuse for overacting, but Hanks understands here, as he did in the very different *A League of Their Own,* that the audience understands the situation and doesn't need to be told about it through "acting." It is always better if a film can make you understand how a character feels without the character having to do very much, externally, to explain his emotions.

Hanks's most memorable scene in *Philadelphia* is the one where he plays a recording of an aria from the opera *Andrea Chénier* for his lawyer

(Denzel Washington), and while it's playing, provides a heartbreaking running commentary. The aria is sung to her lover by a French noblewoman at the time of the Revolution, and describes the death of her mother at the hands of a mob. It is an interesting choice of aria because it does *not* exactly parallel the condition of Hanks's own character. Instead, by explaining it to his lawyer, what the dying man is saying is: if you can understand the feelings of this woman, who exists in a world unfamiliar to you, you can understand the feelings of anyone—even my own, in the gay world which you are also so apart from. It is the kind of virtuoso scene that pleads to be overacted (the character, after all, is talking *over* Maria Callas). Hanks does not compete with Callas, however. He adopts the note of a teacher; he wants to share something that he knows. That is the feeling I sense beneath a lot of his performances; he chooses characters who can teach us something, often in the form of a fable.

Much was made of Hanks's decision to star in *Philadelphia* because he thus became, in a phrase that became much-used, the first major box office star to portray a homosexual. More daring, in my opinion, was his willingness to portray himself as so desperately sick: the character is sympathetic enough that many straight actors might have happily played him, but would they have been willing to reduce themselves, through weight loss and makeup, to the stark specter of skin and bones and Kaposi's Sarcoma which Hanks occupied in the final scenes?

In accepting the Academy Award for *Philadelphia,* Hanks made a speech which will rank among Oscar's odder moments. Some, listening to it at the time, were moved by his tribute to those who had died from AIDS, and who the movie sought to remember. Others, including those who read it in transcript, were frankly unable to make much sense of it. I was reminded of Laurence Olivier's famous acceptance speech after they gave him an honorary Oscar. The audience greeted it with a standing ovation, but the next day, when Olivier called Michael Caine and asked him what *he* thought of it, Caine told him that, frankly, he hadn't understood a word. "Quite so," Olivier said, confessing that his mind had gone blank and, as a seasoned stage veteran, he had fallen back on pseudo-Shakespearean folderol.

Hanks was filming *Forrest Gump* at the time he made his speech, and perhaps that fact makes it a little more understandable. Like *Gump,* the speech contained the right sentiments if not always complete lucidity, and it placed feeling above sense. His ability to do that convincingly is one of the reasons Hanks is able to made Forrest a human being and not a case study.

Still, *Forrest Gump* is one of the most mysterious acting jobs I have ever seen. Looking at the movie again on that summer afternoon in Indiana, surrounded by the snuffling audience, I began with the hypothesis that Hanks's secret was to do, as nearly as possible, nothing. The secret of the performance, I told myself, is that he does what Dustin Hoffman did in *Rain Man:* he finds precisely the right note, and holds it. Playing a man with an IQ of seventy-five and a limited vocal range, he sits or stands impassively, usually wearing that uniform of a blue shirt buttoned at the collar, and speaks dispassionately, unaware that he has somehow been placed at the center of all of the key events of recent American history.

Looking at the film, I found that my theory would not hold. What on a first viewing looked like a one-note performance was revealed, during this later viewing, as wide-ranging but so enormously subtle that the range is there almost without our realizing it. One of the reasons the movie has such an emotional impact may be that Hanks, by not seeming to reach for an effect, catches our hearts unprotected.

His physical performance is minimalist. He is usually sitting or standing impassively, and even in the scenes where he runs and runs (from bullies, on the football field, in Vietnam, and then across America), his face seems set. The closest Hanks comes to physical acting is in the miraculous special-effects scenes, where director Robert Zemeckis and his technicians place Hanks in the same video frames with JFK, John Lennon, LBJ, and George Wallace. Here he does a perfect job of affecting the slight stiffness and formality that people adopt in the presence of the famous, as if standing at attention.

To understanding the soul of Hanks's performance in the movie, what you have to do is listen to his voice. There are a lot of lines people remember from the film; his momma's sayings, of course, and his own philosophical insights ("You do the best with what God gave you"). But listen to the line he uses on the night he proposes marriage to Jenny (Robin Wright): "I'm not a smart man, but I know what love is." It seems at first to be delivered in a monotone, but listen carefully, and you hear that he subtly but firmly emphasizes the beats of both *love* and *is,* making them absolutely equal, and a little more stressed that the rest of the sentence. Not what *love* is, and not what love *is*, which are the ways an ordinary actor would try to sell the sentence, but what *love is*. The delivery prevents the line from sounding like pleading. It is a statement of fact, and by the quiet emphasis he puts on it, we sense how very strongly he feels.

Or listen to what he says on his wedding day, when Lieutenant Dan (Gary Sinise) arrives, walking on artificial legs, and introduces Forrest to his fiancée. The line is simply, "Lieutenant Dan!" Two words, but invested with affection, a teasing quality, and relief that Lieutenant Dan has escaped his demons. After the movie I tried to imitate the way Hanks said the name, and I failed. I could never get more than one note in at a time.

Forrest's voice is what carries the movie. He narrates it, he speaks in it, he quotes others. Some of the dialogue would tempt another actor to go for the punch line. When Forrest "invents" the bumper sticker "Shit Happens," for example, that's obviously a laugh line, but Hanks knows the laugh is there anyway, and so he doesn't go for it. To punch the line would imply that Forrest knows it is funny, and of course that would be a mistake—a mistake Hanks is too good to make.

Any successful movie invites nay-saying, and I've read criticism of the film as an insult to the mentally retarded, as a right-wing vision of America disguised in liberal clothing, and as a free ride on the coattails of our nostalgia. One critic thought it was all too significant that the microphone malfunctions during the peace rally, and we never hear what Forrest says to the crowd. But of course the point was not what he said, it was that he was there. Forrest is a Witness, careening from one historical milestone to another, just as all of us are. If he has no control over the events in his society, neither do we. It isn't true, as some critics say, that the movie simplifies our time by providing Forrest's simple homilies ("Death is just a part of life") and self-forgiving formulas ("Stupid is as stupid does"), thereby congratulating the audience on its own supposed ignorance. What the movie does is show how touching, how human, it is to carry on in the face of war, assassination, disaster, and disease, clinging to these lifelines that make us human.

Tom Hanks is at the top of his game right now, with four films in a row that have gone straight into the hearts of the audience, making him (dare I say of a man still young?) beloved. That is partly because he has had good luck in his choice of roles, and partly because he was ready to play them. It is also because there is something within Tom Hanks that audiences respond to positively. The movies are kind of a truth machine, allowing us to sit in the dark and stare as closely as we like at every nuance of an actor's manner and personality. (When, in real life, do we ever get to look at anyone that closely?)

Bad guys can become stars, and good guys can come across as jerks, but when a star is sensed to have the rare qualities of the characters he plays, and when those characters strike a chord in the audience's imagination, then there is the possibility that a myth will be born, that a Stewart, a Bogart, a Monroe, will be created.

Tom Hanks right now seems to be in the process of such a myth-creation. Actors are always at the mercy of their material, their directors, their costars, and even the social atmosphere at the time a movie is released. (Certainly the twenty-fifth anniversary summer of *Woodstock* was the perfect time for *Forrest Gump* to be playing.) My notion is that when an actor does something good, he probably deserves praise, but when he does something bad, he may not deserve blame—because in the movies, nobody can fake the genuine, but everybody can screw it up. Maybe Hanks has simply been lucky, with these four films. Maybe he has developed some kind of gift for being able to look at such unlikely material as *Forrest Gump* (or even *Joe vs. the Volcano*) and seeing through the goofiness to the promise. Whatever it is, he has found a way to play a certain kind of character on the screen, in such a way that when the audience leaves the theater, they do not think of Tom Hanks or even of Forrest Gump so much as they think of themselves, as if they have just been through something mysterious and important.

Errol Morris

INTRODUCTION

There is something of the mad inventor about Errol Morris. I have been present at several demonstrations of his Interrotron, a device that uses a pair of teleprompter screens so that he and his interview subject can look each other in the eye while they are talking. He believes this creates the sense of immediate address between subject and audience.

In his first film, however, there is a scene where his subject repeatedly looks off camera. She is Florence Rasmussen, the old woman sitting in the doorway in *Gates of Heaven,* a documentary about pet cemeteries in Northern California and one of the most mysterious and inexplicably moving films ever made.

Morris told me he found her sitting there in the doorway, and started filming. The result was a monologue any playwright would have been amazed to have written. In the course of a rambling review and complaint about her life, she darkly hints that someone is killing the neighborhood cats, that her son is ungrateful, and that she is in terrible shape but gets around pretty well. Having watched the film countless times, I eventually realized that in one way or another she flatly contradicts every single statement she makes.

NOVEMBER 9, 1997

Errol Morris is a truly odd man. I say this because he wears a disguise of normality. I have never seen him without a sport coat and a tie, his hair neatly cut, a briefcase nearby. He talks soberly and with precision, almost as if students are taking notes. And then he invents a device called the Interrotron and uses it to interview lion tamers and experts on the naked mole rat.

His new film is *Fast, Cheap, and Out of Control*. It is endlessly fascinating, the kind of film you are compelled to discuss afterward. It is about people who have chosen strange career avenues: a gardener who makes animals out of plants, a designer of robots, an animal trainer, and a man who spends a good deal of time trying to figure out where and how naked mole rats prefer to defecate.

This film is by the same man who made films about a possibly innocent man on death row in Texas, and about Stephen Hawking, the man almost trapped inside his own brain, and about a parrot who was the only witness to a murder (could the court believe that it was repeatedly squawking out the killer's name?). The Interrotron is an invention that allows his subjects to stare straight into the camera while simultaneously making direct eye contact with him.

I met Errol Morris long before I was ever in the same room with him. I met him in 1978 when I was watching his first film, *Gates of Heaven*. I met him by inference, because of what he put on the screen and what he left off. His selection process gave me a sense of the man.

By choosing to make a film about two pet cemeteries, he staked his claim to the sidelines of the American mainstream. By making the film in such a challenging way, he refused to commit himself: you could see it as cruel or caring, as satirical or pokerfaced, as cynical or deeply spiritual. Watching it, I knew that when I finally laid eyes on Morris, he would be wearing a quizzical grin.

He was. I met him in the 1980s at Facets, the video and repertory shrine in Chicago, where they showed *Gates of Heaven* in a tribute to Morris. It so happens that the theater at Facets begins with a flat floor, and then abruptly tilts upward. I sat at the dividing line, and noticed that those in front of me were silent, while those behind were laughing.

Of course they were, Morris explained. It is best to look up at drama, and down at comedy. We need to feel above comedy. Drama needs to feel above us. *Gates of Heaven* was so finely balanced between comedy and drama that the altitude of the seats determined the reaction of the audience members. Was he serious? I couldn't tell. Years later, Buddy Hackett told me he turned down big bucks in Vegas rather than play a room where the stage was higher than the audience. "They won't laugh unless they're looking down at you," he explained.

Having made *Fast, Cheap, and Out of Control,* Morris is now touring the country to flog it. It has no stars and no big ad budget, and cannot be explained in a snappy line of advertising copy. If I had to describe it, I'd say it's about people who are trying to control things—to take upon themselves the mantle of God.

"There is a Frankenstein element," Morris said. "They're all involved in some very odd inquiry about life. It sounds horribly pretentious laid out that way, but there's something mysterious in each of the stories, something melancholy as well as funny. And there's an edge of mortality. For the end of the movie I showed the gardener clipping the top of his camel, clipping in a heavenly light, and then walking away in the rain. You know that this garden is not going to last much longer than the gardener's lifetime."

The gardener's name is George Mendonca. He makes topiaries— gardens like you see at Disney World, where shrubs have been trimmed to look like camels or giraffes. He circulates endlessly in the private garden of a rich woman, trimming and waiting and trimming. A good storm will blow everything away. When he dies, the shrubs will grow out and destroy his work in a season.

Then there is Ray Mendez, the naked mole rat expert. Mole rats live in Africa and were only discovered a few years ago; they are hairless mammals whose society is organized along insect lines.

"Ray tells you," Morris said, "that he's seeking some kind of connection with 'the other,' which he defines as that which exists completely independent of ourselves. And then he talks about looking into the eye of a naked mole rat and thinking, *I know you are, you know I am.* It occurred to me that all of my movies are about language. About how language reveals secrets about people. It's a way into of their heads."

That was true right from the start, I said. *Gates of Heaven* is filled with lines that could not possibly have been written. As when that woman says, "Death is for the living and not for the dead so much."

"I like to transcribe my own interviews," Morris said. "I'm really fascinated by how people speak. And there are so many strange lines that I've heard over the years. There's this idea that documentary filmmaking is a kind of journalism. So *Gates of Heaven* becomes a movie about pet cemeteries. It's about something different altogether. There's this sense of having one foot in the real world and another foot in some dreamscape."

Did you know *Fast, Cheap, and Out of Control* was going to be about these four people, or did you find the film shaping itself?

"Well, Dave Hoover, the lion tamer—I filmed his act in 1985, in Texas. There was this money from PBS to make a movie about Dr. James Gregson, the so-called death-row doctor [who could always be counted on to testify that a killer would kill again]. And I thought, I'll bet there's a similarity between theories of how to control wild animals and theories about how to deal with violent criminals. There was. There are all these different schools of wild animal training; there's a touchy-feely school, there's a 'I'm OK, You're OK' school, transactional analysis . . ."

But then you show that young woman who takes over as the animal trainer, and she seems to be more the master of her beasts than the older man. Her lions look better; they don't look all ratty and shopworn, and she puts her head in their mouths, and cuffs them around . . ."

"Although as Dave points out, these are tigers, not lions."

Admittedly a good point, I said.

"There's supposedly a big difference. He says anybody can do that with a tiger. I asked him, I said, 'Dave, how come the head in the mouth thing, why aren't you doing that?' He said, 'A, it's a tiger, not a lion, and, B, he wouldn't have anything to do with that sort of thing because there's a problem with halitosis. Their breath's real bad.' Dave lives in this universe of his own devising. When he talks about what goes on inside a lion's head when it's facing him in the ring—well, is that what's really going on in the lion's brain, or is it Dave Hoover's crazy dreamscape?"

His lions look a little mangy.

"Periodontal difficulties, mange, gout . . ."

Maybe they won't bite him because it would hurt their gums.

"It's his world. It's his crazy universe and he says, *Outside the cage is the cage.* And I have that shot of him at the very end of the movie, exiting the cage and firing his gun into the night, as if outside was the enemy. I like all four of the characters a lot."

I do, too.

"There was a review in *Entertainment Weekly* where I was taken to task for ridiculing these four. I certainly understood the criticism. A lot people said *Gates of Heaven* was poking fun of the people. I think it's far more complicated than that. I love those people. They're all such wonderful characters in their own right."

So you shot Dave in 1985. He must have acted as a magnetic attraction which drew the other three.

"The strange attractor."

He was trying to control that which in its nature is not to be controlled. They all are. But they're all very happy people, aren't they? The gardener is a little melancholy that his work will come to an end, but they're all absorbed in what they do.

"They're committed; that's how I would describe them. They're obsessed; they're involved. To me all of the stories are sad. In two of the stories there's a world coming to an end: the topiary garden, and the lion taming. In the other stories there's a glimpse into a future which excludes us. Ray Mendez talks about the mole rat's world as the ultimate kibbutz, depending on the expandability of the individual. It's the insect-mammal future. And with Rodney Brooks, the robot designer, it's a world without us altogether, without carbon-based life. Just thinking machines."

Have you got another film in the works?

"I'm preparing a film," he said, "about an electric chair repairman."

Steven Spielberg

He tells the story about how he sneaked onto the Universal lot by taking the tour, jumping off the bus, and walking into offices and asking people what they were doing. He directed his first short when he was thirteen, *Duel* when he was twenty-five. He is the compleat filmmaker: he can go wide (*Raiders of the Lost Ark*), he can go deep (*Schindler's List*), he can do both at once (*The Color Purple, Minority Report*). With *Jaws* he took a premise that could with no trouble at all have become a dreadful movie, and made a benchmark: an enormous hit that was literate and contained superb acting and had a visual strategy that made the shark archetypal by hardly ever showing it, and was scary as hell. More than anyone since the silent clowns, he makes movies that everyone wants to see. His *Jurassic Park* is no less honorable than *Amistad,* because both exist at the intersection of craft and passion.

I've talked to him a lot over the years. Often the conversations grow technical; he likes to talk about the how and why, the tools and the jobs involved. Sometimes during an interview you have the impression that your subject is "doing publicity for the movie." When I talk to Spielberg, it's like he has something amazing he wants to tell me. He is delighted, he is fascinated, by making movies. Talking about them doesn't get old for him because he is not "promoting" them; he is engaged in the process of understanding how his new movie came to be.

DECEMBER 18, 1997

Steven Spielberg celebrates his fiftieth birthday today. If he never directed another film, his place in movie history would be secure. It is likely that when all of the movies of the twentieth century are seen at a great distance in the future—as if through the wrong end of a telescope—his best will be in the handful that endure and are remembered.

No other director has been more successful at the box office. Few other directors have placed more titles on various lists of the greatest films. How many other directors have bridged the gap between popular and critical success? Not many; one thinks of Charlie Chaplin and Buster Keaton, John Ford and Alfred Hitchcock, John Huston and Cecil B. DeMille, and although the list could go on, the important thing is to establish the company that Spielberg finds himself in.

Now he owns his own studio, DreamWorks. A few other directors have grown so powerful that they could call their own shots: in the silent days, D. W. Griffith, Chaplin, DeMille, and Rex Ingram. Since then, not many, and those who have founded studios, like Francis Coppola, have lived to regret their entry into the world of finance. But Spielberg's success has been so consistent for so many years that even the mysteries of money (in some ways, so much more perplexing than the challenge of making a good film) seem open to him.

Consider some of his titles (Spielberg has made a dozen films known to virtually everyone): *E. T.*, *Jaws*, *Close Encounters of the Third Kind*, *Raiders of the Lost Ark*, *Indiana Jones and the Temple of Doom*, *Indiana Jones and the Last Crusade*, *The Color Purple*, the two *Jurassic Park*s, and his 1993 Oscar winner for best picture, *Schindler's List*. Consider his current release, *Amistad*, concerning a trial about the moral and legal basis of slavery; he has used his success to buy the independence to make films that might not otherwise seem bankable.

If Spielberg had never directed a single film, however, he would still qualify as one of Hollywood's most successful producers. Look at these titles: *Who Framed Roger Rabbit*, the three *Back to the Future* movies, *An American Tail*, *Gremlins*, *Twister*, and many more. Yes, he's had failures (*1941*, *Always*, *Hook*) but more often than not when Spielberg makes a movie it finds one of the year's largest audiences.

To make a good movie is very difficult. To make a popular movie is not easy. To make both, time after time, is the holy grail which Hollywood seeks with the same fervor that Indy Jones devoted to the original grail. Talking to Spielberg over the years, and particularly during a four-hour conversation in the spring of 1996, I got the feeling that his success is based on his ability to stay in touch with the sense of wonder he had as a teenager—about the world, and about movies.

"I'm greedy about trying to please as many people, all in the same tent, at the same time," he told me. "I've just always wanted to please, more than I've wanted to create controversy and exclude people. And yet, when I made *E.T.*, I really thought I was making it, not for everybody in the world, but for kids. I actually told George Lucas that parents would drop their kids off at *E.T.* And the parents would go off and see another movie playing a block away."

And yet he made a movie that more people have seen, perhaps, than any other. What deeper need did it fill than simple entertainment? Why does the story of a little boy and a goofy-looking extraterrestrial make people cry who never cry at the movies?

"From the very beginning," Spielberg said, "*E.T.* was a movie about my childhood—about my parents' divorce, although people haven't often seen that it's about divorce. My parents split up when I was fifteen or sixteen years old, and I needed a special friend, and had to use my imagination to take me to places that felt good—that helped me move beyond the problems my parents were having, and that ended our family as a whole. And thinking about that time, I thought, an extraterrestrial character would be the perfect springboard to purge the pain of your parents splitting up."

It's that deeper impulse, that need, that operates under the surface of *E.T.*, making it more emotionally complex than the story itself might suggest. And in the third Indiana Jones movie, there's that bond between Indy (Harrison Ford) and his father (Sean Connery). In *Close Encounters,* the hope that alien visitors might be benign, not fearsome as they always were in science fiction movies. And in *The Color Purple,* again the impulse to heal a broken family.

Spielberg may begin with a promising idea, but in his best films he doesn't proceed with it unless there is also a connection to his heart. That may be why his Holocaust film, *Schindler's List,* is not only about horror, but about help, about man's better nature even in the worst times.

Spielberg told me that he got into the movies by sneaking onto the lot at Universal. He'd buy a ticket on the tour bus, jump off the bus, and hang around. After awhile the guards had seen him so often (always dressed in his bar mitzvah suit, not T-shirt and jeans, so that he didn't look so much like a kid) they waved him through.

By then he had already made a lot of movies. His first involved his Lionel train set. "The trains went around and around, and after a while that got boring, and I had this eight-millimeter camera, and I staged a train wreck and filmed it. That was hard on the trains, but then I could cut the film a lot of different ways, and look at it over and over again."

And what boy wouldn't rather make a movie than have a train set?

PART 2

The Best

INTRODUCTION

Movie critics are required by unwritten law to create a list of the ten best films of every year, and although I avoid "best" lists whenever possible, this is a duty I fulfill. Because ranking films is silly and pointless, but gathering a list of good ones is useful, I wish it were possible to make the lists alphabetical. Well, actually, it is, but doesn't it seem like cheating?

Looking over my lists of the best films in the appendix to this volume, I find an occasional tendency to place what I now consider the year's best film in second place, perhaps because I was trying to make some kind of point with my top pick. For example: In 1968, I should have ranked *2001* above *The Battle of Algiers*. In 1971, *McCabe and Mrs. Miller* was better than *The Last Picture Show*. In 1974, *Chinatown* was probably better, in a different way, than *Scenes from a Marriage*. In 1976, how could I rank *Small Change* above *Taxi Driver?* In 1978, I would put *Days of Heaven* above *An Unmarried Woman*. And in 1980, of course, *Raging Bull* was a better film than *The Black Stallion*.

That I always ranked those years' best films second, instead of plac-ing them further down the list, is curious; it's as if I knew they were best, but had some perverse reason for not admitting it. Trying to remember my reasoning, I think that in 1968, a year of political upheaval. *Battle of Algiers* seemed more urgent than *2001* (which after all is timeless). *The Last Picture Show* was so emotionally involving and felt so new that I undervalued what I now see as the perfection of *McCabe*. *Small Change* was a heart-warmer, but I completely fail to understand why I thought it outranked *Taxi Dri-ver*. And although I later chose *Raging Bull* as the best film of the entire decade of the 1980s, it was only the second-best film of 1980.

Readers often ask, "Do you ever change your mind about a film?" Yes. The question itself is pointless. Am I the same person I was in 1968, 1971, or 1980? I hope not. Have I learned something in the meantime? I hope so. But to read what I wrote then, rather than what I might write today, provides a reflection of the way the movies and the years reflected each other.

Bonnie and Clyde

SEPTEMBER 25, 1967

1967 *Bonnie and Clyde* is a milestone in the history of American movies, a work of truth and brilliance. It is also pitilessly cruel, filled with sympathy, nauseating, funny, heartbreaking, and astonishingly beautiful. If it does not seem that those words should be strung together, perhaps that is because movies do not very often reflect the full range of human life.

The lives in this case belonged, briefly, to Clyde Barrow and Bonnie Parker. They were two nobodies who got their pictures in the paper by robbing banks and killing people. They weren't very good at the bank robbery part of it, but they were fairly good at killing people and absolutely first-class at getting their pictures in the paper.

Bonnie was a gum-chewing waitress and Clyde was a two-bit hood out on parole. But from the beginning, they both seemed to have the knack of entertaining people. Bonnie wrote ballads and mailed them in with pictures Clyde took with his Kodak. They seemed to consider themselves public servants, bringing a little sparkle to the poverty and despair of the Dust Bowl during the early Depression years.

"Good afternoon," Clyde would say when they walked into a bank. "This is the Barrow Gang." In a way Bonnie and Clyde were pioneers, consolidating the vein of violence in American history and exploiting it, for the first time in the mass media.

Under Arthur Penn's direction, this is a film aimed squarely and unforgivingly at the time we are living in. It is intended, horrifyingly, as entertainment. And so it will be taken. The kids on dates will go to see this one, just like they went to see *Dirty Dozen* and *Born Losers* and *Hells Angels on Wheels*.

But this time, maybe, they'll get more than they counted on. The violence in most American movies is of a curiously bloodless quality. People are shot and they die, but they do not suffer. The murders are something to be gotten over with, so the audience will have its money's worth; the same is true of the sex. Both are like the toy in a Cracker Jack box: worthless, but you feel cheated if it's not there.

In *Bonnie and Clyde,* however, real people die. Before they die they suffer, horribly. Before they suffer they laugh, and play checkers, and make love, or try to. These become people we know, and when they die it is not at all pleasant to be in the audience. When people are shot in *Bonnie and Clyde,* they are literally blown to bits. Perhaps that seems shocking. But perhaps at this time, it is useful to be reminded that bullets really do tear skin and bone, and that they don't make nice round little holes like the Swiss cheese effect with Fearless Fosdick.

We are living in a period when newscasts refer casually to "waves" of mass murders, Richard Speck's photograph is sold on posters in Old Town, and snipers in Newark pose for *Life* magazine (perhaps they are busy now getting their ballads to rhyme.) Violence takes on an unreal quality. The Barrow Gang reads its press clippings aloud for fun. When C. W. Moss takes the wounded Bonnie and Clyde to his father's home, the old man snorts: "What'd they ever do for you boy? Didn't even get your name in the paper." Is that a funny line, or a tragic one?

The performances throughout are flawless. Warren Beatty and Faye Dunaway, in the title roles, surpass anything they have done on the screen before and establish themselves (somewhat to my surprise) as major actors.

Michael J. Pollard, as C. W. Moss, the driver and mechanic for the gang, achieves a mixture of moronic good humor and genuine pathos that is unforgettable. When Bonnie tells him, "We rob banks," and asks him to come along, he says nothing. But the expression on his face and the movements of his body create a perfect, delightful moment.

Gene Hackman and Estelle Parsons play Buck and Blanche Barrow, the other members of the gang, as inarticulate, simple, even good-willed. When Buck is reunited with his kid brother, they howl with glee and punch each other to disguise the truth that they have nothing to say. After the gang has shot its way out of a police trap and Buck is mortally wounded, Blanche's high, mindless scream in the getaway car provides, for me, a very adequate vision of hell.

This is pretty clearly the best American film of the year. It is also a landmark. Years from now it is quite possible that *Bonnie and Clyde* will be seen as the definitive film of the 1960s, showing with sadness, humor, and unforgiving detail what one society had come to. The fact that the story is set thirty-five years ago doesn't mean a thing. It had to be set sometime. But it was made now and it's about us.

The Battle of Algiers

MAY 30, 1968

1968 At the height of the street fighting in Algiers, the French stage a press conference for a captured FLN leader. "Tell me, general," a Parisian journalist asks the revolutionary, "do you not consider it cowardly to send your women carrying bombs in their handbags, to blow up civilians?" The rebel replies in a flat tone of voice, "And do you not think it cowardly to bomb our people with napalm?" A pause. "Give us your airplanes and we will give you our women and their handbags."

The Battle of Algiers, a great film by the young Italian director Gillo Pontecorvo, exists at this level of bitter reality. It may be a deeper film experience than many audiences can withstand: too cynical, too true, too cruel, and too heartbreaking. It is about the Algerian war, but those not interested in Algeria may substitute another war; *The Battle of Algiers* has a universal frame of reference.

Pontecorvo announces at the outset that there is "not one foot" of documentary or newsreel footage in his two hours of film. The announcement is necessary, because the film looks, feels, and tastes as real as Peter Watkins's *The War Game.* Pontecorvo used available light, newsreel film stock, and actual locations to reconstruct the events in Algiers. He is after actuality, the feeling that you are there, and he succeeds magnificently; the film won the Venice Film Festival and nine other festivals, and was chosen to open the New York Film Festival last November.

Some mental quirk reminded me of *The Lost Command,* Mark Robson's dreadful 1965 film in which George Segal was the Algerian rebel and Anthony Quinn somehow won for the French. Compared to *The Battle of Algiers,* that film and all Hollywood "war movies" are empty, gaudy balloons.

Pontecorvo has taken his stance somewhere between the FLN and the French, although his sympathies are on the side of the Nationalists. He is aware that innocent civilians die and are tortured on both sides, that bombs cannot choose their victims, that both armies have heroes and that everyone fighting a war can supply rational arguments to prove he is on the side of morality.

His protagonists are a French colonel (Jean Martin), who respects his opponents but believes (correctly, no doubt) that ruthless methods are necessary, and Ali (Brahim Haggiag), a petty criminal who becomes an FLN leader. But there are other characters: an old man beaten by soldiers; a small Arab boy attacked by French civilians who have narrowly escaped bombing; a cool young Arab girl who plants a bomb in a cafe and then looks compassionately at her victims, and many more.

The strength of the film, I think, comes because it is both passionate and neutral, concerned with both sides. The French colonel (himself a veteran of the anti-Nazi resistance), learns that Sartre supports the FLN. "Why are the liberals always on the other side?" he asks. "Why don't they believe France belongs in Algeria?" But there was a time when he did not need to ask himself why the Nazis did not belong in France.

Note: This review is curiously brief, perhaps because of space constraints. I wrote about *The Battle of Algiers* at greater length in the *Great Movies* series.

Z

1969 There are some things that refuse to be covered over. It would be more convenient, yes, and easier for everyone if the official version were believed. But then the facts begin to trip over one another, and contradictions emerge, and an "accident" is revealed as a crime.

The film *Z* is about one of these things: about the assassination, six years ago, of a leader of the political opposition in Greece. It is also about all the rest of them. For Americans, it is about the My Lai massacre, the killing of Fred Hampton, the Bay of Pigs. It is no more about Greece than *The Battle of Algiers* was about Algeria. It is a film of our time. It is about how even moral victories are corrupted. It will make you weep and will make you angry. It will tear your guts out.

It is told simply, and it is based on fact. On May 22, 1963, Gregorios Lambrakis was fatally injured in a "traffic accident." He was a deputy of the opposition party in Greece. The accident theory smelled, and the government appointed an investigator to look into the affair.

His tacit duty was to reaffirm the official version of the death, but his investigation convinced him that Lambrakis had, indeed, been assassinated by a clandestine right-wing organization. High-ranking army and police officials were implicated. The plot was unmasked in court and sentences were handed down—stiff sentences to the little guys (dupes, really) who had carried out the murder, and acquittal for the influential officials who had ordered it.

But the story was not over. When the Army junta staged its coup in 1967, the right-wing generals and the police chief were cleared of all charges and "rehabilitated." Those responsible for unmasking the assassination now became political criminals.

These would seem to be completely political events, but the young director Costa-Gravas has told them in a style that is almost unbearably exciting. *Z* is at the same time a political cry of rage and a brilliant suspense thriller. It even ends in a chase: not through the streets but through a maze of facts, alibis, and official corruption.

Like Gillo Pontecorvo, who directed *Battle of Algiers,* Costa-Gravas maintains a point of view above the level of the events he photographs. His protagonist changes during the film, as he leads us from an initial personal involvement to the indictment of an entire political system. At first, we are interested in Yves Montand, the wise and gentle political leader who is slain. Then our attention is directed to the widow (Irene Papas) and to the opposition leaders who will carry on (Charles Denner and Bernard Fresson).

And then, in the masterful last third of the film, we follow the stubborn investigator (Jean-Louis Trintignant) as he resists official pressure to conceal the scandal. He puts together his evidence almost reluctantly; he has no desire to bring down the government, but he must see justice done if he can. His sympathies are neutral, and a truly neutral judge is the most fearsome thing the Establishment can imagine. What good is justice if it can be dealt out to the state as well as to the people? (The implications here for Chicago's conspiracy trial are obvious.)

The movie at first seems to end with triumph. The rotten core of the government is exposed. The military men and the police chief are indicted for murder, official misconduct, obstructing justice. One of the assassinated leader's young followers races to bring the widow the good news. He finds her waiting by the seashore. He is triumphant; justice will be done; the government will fall. Irene Papas hears his news silently and then turns and looks out to sea. Her face reflects no triumph; only suffering and despair. What is really left for her to say?

Nothing, as we know now. The right wing won in the long run and controls Greece today. This film's director, writer, composer, and Miss Papas are all banned in Greece ("banned"—that terrible word we heard from Russia and South Africa, and now from Greece). Even the letter *Z* (which means "he is alive") is banned in Greece.

When this film was shown at the San Francisco Film Festival, it was attacked in some quarters as being anti-American, But does it not tell the simple truth? We do support the Greek junta. We do recognize the government that murdered Lambrakis. We did permit the junta to prevent free elections in Greece. And in Vietnam, the candidate who placed second in the "free elections" we sponsored sits in a Saigon jail today. His name is also banned.

Five Easy Pieces

OCTOBER 23, 1970

1970 The title of *Five Easy Pieces* refers not to the women its hero makes along the road, for there are only three, but to a book of piano exercises he owned as a child. The film, one of the best American films, is about the distance between that boy, practicing to become a concert pianist, and the need he feels twenty years later to disguise himself as an oil-field rigger. When we sense the boy, tormented and insecure, trapped inside the adult man, *Five Easy Pieces* becomes a masterpiece of heartbreaking intensity.

At the outset, we meet only the man—played by Jack Nicholson with the same miraculous offhandedness that brought *Easy Rider* to life. He's an irresponsible roustabout, making his way through the oil fields, sleeping with a waitress (Karen Black) whose every daydreaming moment is filled with admiration for Miss Tammy Wynette. The man's name is Robert Eroica Dupea. He was named after Beethoven's Third Symphony and he spends his evenings bowling and his nights wearily agreeing that, yes, his girl sings *Stand By Your Man* just like Tammy.

In these first marvelous scenes, director Bob Rafelson calls our attention to the grimy life textures and the shabby hopes of these decent middle Americans. They live in a landscape of motels, highways, TV dinners, dust, and jealousy, and so do we all, but they seem to have nothing else. Dupea's friends are arrested at the mental and emotional level of about age seventeen; he isn't, but thinks or hopes he is.

Dupea discovers his girl is pregnant (his friend Elton breaks the news out in the field, suggesting maybe it would be good to marry her and settle down). He walks out on her in a rage, has a meaningless little affair with a slut from the bowling alley, and then discovers more or less by accident that his father is dying. His father, we discover, is a musical genius who

113

moved his family to an island and tried to raise them as Socrates might have. Dupea feels himself to be the only failure.

The movie bares its heart in the scenes on the island, where Dupea makes an awkward effort to communicate with his dying father. The island is peopled with eccentrics, mostly Dupea's own family, but including a few strays. Among their number is a beautiful young girl who's come to the island to study piano with Dupea's supercilious brother. Dupea seduces this girl, who apparently suggests the early life he has abandoned. He does it by playing the piano; but when she says she's moved, he says he isn't— that he played better as a child and that the piece was easy anyway.

This is possibly the moment when his nerve fails and he condemns himself, consciously, to a life of self-defined failure. The movie ends, after several more scenes, on a note of ambiguity; he is either freeing himself from the waitress or, on the other hand, he is setting off on a journey even deeper into anonymity. It's impossible to say, and it doesn't matter much. What matters is the character during the time covered by the film: a time when Dupea tentatively reapproaches his past and then rejects it, not out of pride, but out of fear.

The movie is joyously alive to the road life of its hero. We follow him through bars and bowling alleys, motels and mobile homes, and we find him rebelling against lower-middle-class values even as he embraces them. In one magical scene, he leaps from his car in a traffic jam and starts playing the piano on the truck in front of him; the scene sounds forced, described this way, but Rafelson and Nicholson never force anything, and never have to. Robert Eroica Dupea is one of the most unforgettable characters in American movies.

The Last Picture Show

DECEMBER 21, 1971

1971 There was something about going to the movies in the 1950s that will never be the same again. It was the decade of the last gasp of the great American moviegoing habit, and before my eyes in the middle 1950s the Saturday kiddie matinee died a lingering death at the Princess Theater on Main Street in Urbana. For five or six years of my life (the years between when I was old enough to go alone, and when TV came to town) Saturday afternoon at the Princess was a descent into a dark magical cave that smelled of Jujubes, melted Dreamsicles, and Crisco in the popcorn machine. It was probably on one of those Saturday afternoons that I formed my first critical opinion, deciding vaguely that there was something about John Wayne that set him apart from ordinary cowboys. The Princess was jammed to the walls with kids every Saturday afternoon, as it had been for years, but then TV came to town and within a year the Princess was no longer an institution. It survived into the early 1960s and then closed, to be reborn a few years later as the Cinema. The metallic taste of that word, "cinema," explains what happened when you put it alongside the name "Princess."

Peter Bogdanovich's *The Last Picture Show* uses the closing of another theater on another Main Street as a motif to frame a great many things that happened to America in the early 1950s. The theater is the Royal, and along with the pool hall and the all-night cafe it supplies what little excitement and community survives in a little West Texas crossroads named Anarene.

All three are owned by Sam the Lion, who is just about the only self-sufficient and self-satisfied man in town. The others are infected by a general malaise, and engage in sexual infidelities partly to remind themselves they are alive. There isn't much else to do in Anarene, no dreams worth dreaming, no new faces, not even a football team that can tackle worth a damn. The nourishing myth of the Western (*Wagon Master* and *Red River* are among the last offerings at the Royal) is being replaced by nervously hilarious TV programs out of the East, and defeated housewives are reassured they're part of the *Strike It Rich* audience with a heart of gold.

Against this background, we meet two high school seniors named Sonny and Duane, who are the cocaptains of the shameful football squad. We learn next to nothing about their home lives, but we hardly notice the omission because their real lives are lived in a pickup truck and a used Mercury. That was the way it was in high school in the 1950s, and probably always will be: a car was a mobile refuge from adults, frustration, and boredom. When people in their thirties say today that sexual liberation is pale compared to a little prayerful groping in the front seat, they are onto something.

During the year of the film's action, the two boys more or less survive coming-of-age. They both fall in love with the school's only beauty, a calculating charmer named Jacy who twists every boy in town around her little finger before taking this skill away with her to Dallas. Sonny breaks up with his gum-chewing girlfriend and has an unresolved affair with the coach's wife, and Duane goes off to fight the Korean War. There are two deaths during the film's year, but no babies are born, and Bogdanovich's final pan shot along Main Street curiously seems to turn it from a real location (which it is) into a half-remembered backdrop from an old movie. *The Last Picture Show* is a great deal more complex than it might at first seem, and this shot suggests something of its buried structure. Every detail of clothing, behavior, background music, and decor is exactly right for 1951—but that still doesn't explain the movie's mystery.

Mike Nichols's *Carnal Knowledge* began with 1949, and yet felt modern. Bogdanovich has been infinitely more subtle in giving his film not only the decor of 1951, but the visual style of a movie that might have been shot in 1951. The montage of cutaway shots at the Christmas dance; the use of an insert of Sonny's foot on the accelerator; the lighting and black-and-white photography of real locations as if they were sets—everything forms a stylistic whole that works. It isn't just a matter of putting in Jo Stafford and Hank Williams.

The Last Picture Show has been described as an evocation of the classic Hollywood narrative film. It is more than that; it is a belated entry in that age—the best film of 1951, you might say. Using period songs and decor to create nostalgia is familiar enough, but to tunnel down to the visual level and get that right, too, and in a way that will affect audiences even if they aren't aware how, is one hell of a directing accomplishment. Movies create our dreams as well as reflect them, and when we lose the movies we lose the dreams. I wonder if Bogdanovich's film doesn't at last explain what it was that Pauline Kael, and a lot of the rest of us, lost at the movies.

The Godfather

MARCH 23, 1972

1972 We know from Gay Talese's book *Honor Thy Father* that being a professional mobster isn't all sunshine and roses. More often, it's the boredom of stuffy rooms and a bad diet of carryout food, punctuated by brief, terrible bursts of violence. This is exactly the feel of *The Godfather,* which brushes aside the flashy glamour of the traditional gangster picture and gives us what's left: fierce tribal loyalties, deadly little neighborhood quarrels in Brooklyn, and a form of vengeance to match every affront.

The remarkable thing about Mario Puzo's novel was the way it seemed to be told from the inside out; he didn't give us a world of international intrigue, but a private club as constricted as the seventh grade. Everybody knew everybody else and had a pretty shrewd hunch what they were up to.

The movie (based on a script labored over for some time by Puzo and then finally given form, I suspect, by director Francis Ford Coppola) gets the same feel. We tend to identify with Don Corleone's family not because we dig gang wars, but because we have been with them from the beginning, watching them wait for battle while sitting at the kitchen table and eating chow mein out of paper cartons.

The Godfather himself is not even the central character in the drama. That position goes to the youngest, brightest son, Michael, who understands the nature of his father's position while revising his old-fashioned ways. The Godfather's role in the family enterprise is described by his name; he stands outside the next generation which will carry on and, hopefully, angle the family into legitimate enterprises.

Those who have read the novel may be surprised to find Michael at the center of the movie, instead of Don Corleone. In fact, this is simply an economical way for Coppola to get at the heart of the Puzo story, which dealt with the transfer of power within the family. Marlon Brando, who plays the Godfather as a shrewd, unbreakable old man, actually has the character lead in the movie; Al Pacino, with a brilliantly developed performance as Michael, is the lead.

But Brando's performance is a skillful throwaway. His voice is wheezy and whispery, and his physical movements deliberately lack precision; the effect is of a man so accustomed to power that he no longer needs to remind others. Brando does look the part of old Don Corleone, mostly because of acting and partly because of the makeup, although he seems to have stuffed a little too much cotton into his jowls, making his lower face immobile.

The rest of the actors supply one example after another of inspired casting. Although *The Godfather* is a long, minutely detailed movie of some three hours, there naturally isn't time to go into the backgrounds and identities of such characters as Clemenza, the family lieutenant; Jack Woltz, the movie czar; Luca Brasi, the loyal professional killer; McCluskey, the crooked cop; and the rest. Coppola and producer Al Ruddy skirt this problem with understated typecasting. As the Irish cop, for example, they simply slide in Sterling Hayden and let the character go about his business. Richard Castellano is an unshakable Clemenza. John Marley makes a perfectly hateful Hollywood mogul (and, yes, he still wakes up to find he'll have to cancel his day at the races).

The success of *The Godfather* as a novel was largely due to a series of unforgettable scenes. Puzo is a good storyteller, but no great shakes as a writer. The movie gives almost everything in the novel except the gynecological repair job. It doesn't miss a single killing; it opens with the wedding of Don Corleone's daughter (and attendant upstairs activity); and there are the right number of auto bombs, double crosses, and garrotings.

Coppola has found a style and a visual look for all this material so *The Godfather* becomes something of a rarity: a really good movie squeezed from a bestseller. The decision to shoot everything in period decor (the middle and late 1940s) was crucial; if they'd tried to save money as they originally planned, by bringing everything up to date, the movie simply wouldn't have worked. But it's uncannily successful as a period piece, filled with sleek, bulging limousines and postwar fedoras. Coppola and his cinematographer, Gordon Willis, also do some interesting things with the color photography. The earlier scenes have a reddish-brown tint, slightly overexposed and feeling like nothing so much as a 1946 newspaper rotogravure supplement.

Although the movie is three hours long, it absorbs us so effectively it never has to hurry. There is something in the measured passage of time as Don Corleone hands over his reins of power that would have made a shorter, faster-moving film unseemly. Even at this length, there are characters in relationships you can't quite understand unless you've read the novel. Or perhaps you can, just by the way the characters look at each other.

Cries and Whispers

1973 *Cries and Whispers* is like no movie I've seen before, and like no movie Ingmar Bergman has made before; although we are all likely to see many films in our lives, there will be few like this one. It is hypnotic, disturbing, frightening.

It envelops us in a red membrane of passion and fear, and in some way that I do not fully understand it employs taboos and ancient superstitions to make its effect. We slip lower in our seats, feeling claustrophobia and sexual disquiet, realizing that we have been surrounded by the vision of a filmmaker who has absolute mastery of his art. *Cries and Whispers* is about dying, love, sexual passion, hatred, and death—in that order.

The film inhabits a manor house set on a vast country estate. The rooms of the house open out from each other like passages in the human body; with the exception of one moment when Agnes, the dying woman, opens her window and looks at the dawn, the house offers no views. It looks in upon itself.

Three women stay in the house with Agnes (Harriet Andersson), waiting for her to die. She is in the final stages of cancer, and in great pain. The women are Karin and Maria, her sisters, and Anna, the stout, round-cheeked servant. In elliptical flashbacks (intended to give us emotional information, not to tell a story), we learn that the three sisters have made little of their lives.

Karin (Ingrid Thulin) is married to a diplomat she despises. Maria (Liv Ullmann) is married to a cuckold, and so she cuckolds him (what is one to do?). Agnes, who never married, gave birth to a few third-rate watercolors. Now, in dying, she discovers at last some of the sweetness of life.

The sisters remember that they were close in childhood, but somehow in growing up they lost the ability to love, to touch. Only Anna, the ser-

121

vant, remembers how. When Agnes cries out in the night, in fear and agony, it is Anna who cradles her to her bosom, whispering soft endearments.

The others cannot stand to be touched. In a moment of conjured nostalgia, Maria and Karin remember their closeness as children. Now, faced with the fact of their sister's death, they deliberately try to synthesize feeling, and love. Quickly, almost frantically, they touch and caress each other's faces, but their touching is a parody and by the next day they have closed themselves off again.

These two scenes—of Anna embracing Agnes, and of Karin and Maria touching like frightened kittens—are two of the greatest Bergman has ever created. The feeling in these scenes—I should say, the way they force us to feel—constitutes the meaning of this film. It has no abstract message; it communicates with us on a level of human feeling so deep that we are afraid to invent words for the things found there.

The camera is as uneasy as we are. It stays at rest mostly, but when it moves it doesn't always follow smooth, symmetrical progressions. It darts, it falls back, is stunned. It lingers on close-ups of faces with the impassivity of God. It continues to look when we want to turn away; it is not moved. Agnes lies thrown on her deathbed, her body shuddered by horrible, deep, gasping breaths, as she fights for air, for life. The sisters turn away, and we want to, too. We know things are this bad—but we don't want to know. One girl in the audience ran up the aisle and out of the theater. Bergman's camera stays and watches.

The movie is drenched in red. Bergman has written in his screenplay that he thinks of the inside of the human soul as a membranous red. Color can be so important; in *Two English Girls,* a movie about the absence of passion, François Truffaut kept red out of his compositions until the movie's one moment of unfeigned feeling, and then he filled his screen with red.

All of *Cries and Whispers* is occupied with passion—but the passion is inside, the characters can't get it out of themselves. None of them can, except Anna (Kari Sylwan). The film descends into a netherworld of the supernatural; the dead woman speaks (or is it only that they think they hear her?). She reaches out and grasps for Karin (or does Karin move the dead arms?—Bergman's camera doesn't let us see). The movie, like all supernatural myths, like all legends and fables (and like all jokes—which are talismans to take the pain from truth) ends in a series of threes. The dead woman asks the living women to stay with her, to comfort her while she pauses within her dead body before moving into the great terrifying void. Karin will not. Maria will not. But Anna will, and makes pillows of her breasts for Agnes. Anna is the only one of them who remembers how to touch, and love. And she is the only one who believes in God.

We saw her in the morning, praying. We learned that she had lost her little daughter, but is resigned to God's will. Is there a God in Bergman's film, or is there only Anna's faith? The film ends with a scene of astonishing, jarring affirmation: we see the four women some months earlier, drenched with the golden sun, and we hear Anna reading from Agnes's diary, "I feel a great gratitude to my life, which gives me so much." And takes it away.

Scenes from a Marriage

SEPTEMBER 15, 1974

1974 They have reached a truce which they call happiness. When we first meet them, they're being interviewed for some sort of newspaper article, and they agree that after ten years of marriage, they're a truly happy couple. The husband, Johan, is most sure: he is successful in his work, in love with his wife, the father of two daughters, liked by his friends, considered on all sides to be a decent chap. His wife, Marianne, listens more tentatively. When it is her turn, she says she is happy, too, although in her work she would like to move in the direction of—but then she's interrupted for a photograph. We are never quite sure what she might have said, had she been allowed to speak as long as her husband. And, truth to tell, he doesn't seem to care much himself. Although theirs is, of course, a perfect marriage.

And so begins one of the truest, most luminous love stories ever made, Ingmar Bergman's *Scenes from a Marriage*. The marriage of Johan and Marianne will disintegrate soon after the film begins, but their love will not. They will fight and curse each other, and it will be a wicked divorce, but in some fundamental way they have touched, really touched, and the memory of that touching will be something to hold to all of their days.

Bergman has been working for years with the theme of communication between two people. At one time, he referred to it as "the agony of the couple." And who can forget the terrible recriminations and psychic bloodshed of the couples in *Winter Light* or *The Passion of Anna*? Here he seems finally to have resolved his crisis.

The years that preceded the making of this film saw a remarkable reconciliation going on within the work of this great artist. In *Cries and Whispers,* he was at last able to face the fact of death in a world where God seemed silent. And now, in this almost heartbreaking masterpiece, he has dealt with his fear that all men are, indeed, islands. The film (168 minutes, skillfully and without distraction edited down from six fifty-minute Swedish television programs) took him four months to make, he has said, but a lifetime to experience.

His married couple are Swedish upper-middle class. He is a professor, she is a lawyer specializing in family problems (for which, read divorce). They have two daughters, who remain offscreen. They are intelligent, independent. She truly believes their marriage is a happy one (although she doesn't much enjoy sex). One evening, he comes to their summer cottage and confesses that he has gone and fallen in love with someone else. There is nothing to be done about it. He must leave her.

The way in which his wife reacts to this information displays the almost infinite range of Liv Ullmann, who is a beautiful soul and a gifted performer. Her husband (Erland Josephson) has left her literally without an alternative ("You have shut me out. How can I help us?") and still she loves him. She fears that he will bring unhappiness upon himself. But he does leave, and the film's form is a sometimes harsh, sometimes gentle, ultimately romantic (in an adult and realistic way) view of the stages of this relationship. At first, their sexual attraction for each other remains, even though they bitterly resent each other because of mutual hurts and recriminations. The frustrations they feel about themselves are taken out on each other. At one point, he beats her and weeps for himself, and we've never seen such despair on the screen. But the passage of time dulls the immediate hurt and the feeling of betrayal. And at last, they are able to meet as fond friends and even to make love, as if visiting an old home they'd once been cozy in.

They drift apart, they marry other people (who also remain offscreen), they meet from time to time. Ten years after the film has opened, they find themselves in Stockholm while both their spouses are out of the country, and, as a nostalgic lark, decide to spend a weekend in their old summer cottage. But it's haunted with memories, and they go to a cottage nearby.

In the last section of the film (subtitled *In the Middle of the Night in a Dark House*), Marianne awakens screaming with a nightmare, and Johan holds her. And this is twenty years after they were married, and ten years after they were divorced, and they are in middle age now but in the night still fond and frightened lovers holding on for reassurance. And that is what Bergman has been able to accept, the source of his reconciliation: beyond love, beyond marriage, beyond the selfishness that destroys love, beyond the centrifugal force that sends egos whirling away from each other and prevents enduring relationships—beyond all these things, there still remains what we know of each other, that we care about each other, that in twenty years these people have touched and known so deeply that they still remember, and still need. Marianne and Johan are only married for the first part of this film, but the rest of it is also scenes from their marriage.

Nashville

JULY 2, 1975

1975 Robert Altman's *Nashville,* which is the best American movie since *Bonnie and Clyde,* creates in the relationships of nearly two dozen characters a microcosm of who we are and what we are up to in the 1970s. It's a film about the losers and the winners, the drifters and the stars in Nashville, and the most complete expression yet of not only the genius but also the humanity of Altman, who sees people with his camera in such a way as to enlarge our own experience. Sure, it's only a movie. But after I saw it I felt more alive, I felt I understood more about people, I felt somehow wiser. It's that good a movie.

The movie doesn't have a star. It does not, indeed, even have a lead role. Instead, Altman creates a world, a community in which some people know each other and others don't, in which people are likely to meet before they understand the ways in which their lives are related. And he does it all so easily, or seems to, that watching *Nashville* is as easy as breathing and as hard to stop. Altman is the best natural filmmaker since Fellini.

One of the funny things about Nashville is that most of the characters never have entrances. They're just sort of there. At times, we're watching an important character and don't even know, yet, why he's important, but Altman's storytelling is so clear in his own mind, his mastery of this complex wealth of material is so complete, that we're never for a moment confused or even curious. We feel secure in his hands, and apart from anything else, *Nashville* is a virtuoso display of narrative mastery.

It concerns several days and nights in the lives of a very mixed bag of Nashville locals and visitors, all of whom, like the city itself, are obsessed with country music. Tennessee is in the midst of a presidential primary, and all over Nashville, there are the posters and sound trucks of a quasi-populist candidate, Hal Philip Walker, who seems like a cross between George Wallace and George McGovern. We never meet Walker, but we meet both his local organizer and a John Lindsay-type PR man. They're trying to round up country-and-western talent for a big benefit, and their efforts provide a thread around which some of the story is loosely wound.

But there are many stories here, and in the way he sees their connections, Altman makes a subtle but shrewd comment about the ways in which we are all stuck in this thing together. There are the veteran country stars like Haven Hamilton (Henry Gibson), who wears gaudy white costumes, is self-conscious about his short stature, is painfully earnest about recording a painfully banal Bicentennial song, and who, down deep, is basically just a good old boy. There is the reigning queen of country music, Barbara Jean (Ronee Blakley), who returns in triumph to Nashville after treatment at a burn center in Atlanta for unspecified injuries incurred from a fire baton (she's met at the airport by a phalanx of girls from TIT—the Tennessee Institute of Twirling—only to collapse again). There is the corrupt, decadent rock star, played by Keith Carradine, who is so ruthless in his sexual aggression, so evil in his need to hurt women, that he telephones one woman while another is still just leaving his bed, in order to wound both of them.

But these characters are just examples of the people we meet in Nashville, not the leads. Everyone is more or less equal in this film, because Altman sees them all with a judicious and ultimately sympathetic eye. The film is filled with perfectly observed little moments: the star-struck young soldier keeping a silent vigil by the bedside of Barbara Jean; the campaign manager doing a double take when he discovers he's just shaken the hand of Elliott Gould ("a fairly well-known actor," Haven Hamilton explains, "and he used to be married to Barbra Streisand"); the awestruck BBC reporter describing America in breathless, hilarious hyperbole; the way a middle-aged mother of two deaf children (Lily Tomlin) shyly waits for an assignation with a rock singer; the birdbrained cheerfulness with which a young groupie (Shelley Duvall) comes to town to visit her dying aunt and never does see her, being distracted by every male over the age of sixteen that she meets.

The film circles around three motifs without, thankfully, ever feeling it has to make a definitive statement about any of them. Since they're all still very open subjects, that's just as well. What Altman does is suggest the ways in which we deal with them really, in unrehearsed everyday life, not thematically, as in the movies. The motifs are success, women, and politics.

Success: it can be studied most fruitfully in the carefully observed pecking order of the country-and-western performers. There are ones at the top, so successful they can afford to be generous, expansive, well-liked. There are the younger ones in the middle, jockeying for position. There are what can only be described as the professional musicians at the bottom, playing thanklessly but well in the bars and clubs where the stars come to unwind after the show. And at the very bottom, there are those who aspire to be musicians but have no talent at all, like a waitress (Gwen Welles) who comes to sing at a smoker, is forced to strip, and, in one of the film's moments of heartbreaking truthfulness, disdainfully flings at the roomful of men the sweat socks she had stuffed into her brassiere.

Women: God, but Altman cares for them while seeing their predicament so clearly. The women in *Nashville* inhabit a world largely unaffected by the feminist revolution, as most women do. They are prized for their talent, for their beauty, for their services in bed, but not once in this movie for themselves. And yet Altman suggests their complexities in ways that movies rarely have done before. The Lily Tomlin character, in particular, forces us to consider her real human needs and impulses as she goes to meet the worthless rock singer (and we remember a luminous scene during which she and her deaf son discussed his swimming class). Part of the movie's method is to establish characters in one context and then place them in another, so that we can see how personality—indeed, basic identity itself— is constant but must sometimes be concealed for the sake of survival or even simple happiness.

Politics: I won't be giving very much away by revealing that there is an attempted assassination in *Nashville*. The assassin, a loner who takes a room in a boardinghouse, is clearly telegraphed by Altman. It's not Altman's style to surprise us with plot. He'd rather surprise us by revelations of character. At this late date after November 22, 1963, and all the other days of infamy, I wouldn't have thought it possible that a film could have anything new or very interesting to say on assassination, but *Nashville* does, and the film's closing minutes, with Barbara Harris finding herself, to her astonishment, onstage and singing *It Don't Worry Me,* are unforgettable and heartbreaking. Nashville, which seems so unstructured as it begins, reveals itself in this final sequence to have had a deep and very profound structure but one of emotions, not ideas.

This is a film about America. It deals with our myths, our hungers, our ambitions, and our sense of self. It knows how we talk and how we behave, and it doesn't flatter us but it does love us.

Small Change

NOVEMBER 22, 1976

1976 There's a moment in François Truffaut's *Small Change* that remembers childhood so well we don't know whether to laugh or ache. It takes place in a classroom a few minutes before the bell at the end of the school day. The class cutup is called on. He doesn't have the answer (he never does), but as he stands up his eyes stray to a large clock outside the window. The hand stands at twenty-eight minutes past the hour. Click: twenty-nine minutes. He stalls, he grins, the teacher repeats the question. Click: thirty minutes, and the class bell rings. The kid breaks out in a triumphant grin as he joins the stampede from the room. This moment, like so many in Truffaut's magical film, has to be seen to be appreciated. He recreates childhood, and yet he sees it objectively, too: he remembers not only the funny moments but the painful ones. The agony of a first crush. The ordeal of being the only kid in class so poor he has to wear the same sweater every day. The painful earnestness that goes into the recitation of a dirty joke that neither the teller nor the listeners quite understand.

Truffaut has been over some of this ground before. His first feature, *The 400 Blows*, told the painful story of a Paris adolescent caught between his warring parents and his own better nature. In *Small Change* he returns to similar material in a sunnier mood. He tells the stories of several kids in a French provincial town, and of their parents and teachers. His method is episodic; only gradually do we begin to recognize faces, to pick the central characters out from the rest. He correctly remembers that childhood itself is episodic: each day seems separate from any other, each new experience is sharply etched, and important discoveries and revelations become great events surrounded by a void. It's the accumulation of all those separate moments that create, at last, a person.

"Children exist in a state of grace," he has a character say at one point.

131

"They pass untouched through dangers that would destroy an adult." There are several such hazards in *Small Change*. The most audacious—Truffaut at his best—involves a two-year-old child, a kitten, and an open window on the tenth floor. Truffaut milks this situation almost shamelessly before finally giving us the happiest of denouements. And he exhibits at the same time his mastery of film; the scene is timed and played to exist exactly at the border between comedy and tragedy, and from one moment to the next we don't know how we should feel. He's got the audience in his hand.

That's true, too, in a scene involving a little girl who has been made to stay at home as a punishment. She takes her father's battery-powered megaphone and announces indignantly to the neighbors around the courtyard that she is hungry, that her parents have gone out to a restaurant without her, and that she has been abandoned. The neighbors lower her food in a basket: chicken and fruit but not, after all, a bottle of red wine one of the neighbor kids wanted to put in. In the midst of these comic episodes, a more serious story is developed. It's about the kid who lives in a shack outside of town. He's abused by his parents, he lives by his wits, he steals to eat. His mistreatment is finally found out by his teachers, and leads to a concluding speech by one of them that's probably unnecessary but expresses Truffaut's thinking all the same: "If kids had the vote," the teacher declares, "the world would be a better and a safer place." I don't know; I think it's at least likely that a lot of kids would vote for war because it looks like so much fun on television. But Truffaut has his hopes, and *Small Change* is one of the year's most intensely, warmly, human films. In that, it joins so much of Truffaut's earlier work: what other contemporary filmmaker is so firmly in touch with the personal rhythms of life?

3 Women

MARCH 15, 1977

1977 Robert Altman's *3 Women* is, on the one hand, a straight-forward portrait of life in a godforsaken California desert community, and, on the other, a mysterious exploration of human personalities. Its specifics are so real you can almost touch them, and its conclusion so surreal we can supply our own.

The community exists somewhere in Southern California, that uncharted continent of discontent and restlessness. Some of its people have put themselves down in a place that contains, so far as we can see, a spa where old people take an arthritis cure, a Western-style bar with a shooting range out back, and a singles residential motel with a swimming pool that has the most unsettling murals on its bottom.

Into this outpost one day comes Pinky (Sissy Spacek), a child-woman so naive, so open, so willing to have enthusiasm, that in another century she might have been a saint, a strange one. She takes a job at the spa and is instructed in her duties by Millie (Shelley Duvall), who is fascinated by the incorrect belief that the men in town are hot for her. Millie recruits Pinky as a roommate in the motel.

This whole stretch of the film—the first hour—is a funny, satirical, and sometimes sad study of the community and its people, who have almost all failed at something else, somewhere else. The dominant male is Edgar (Robert Fortier), a onetime stuntman, now a boozer with a beer bottle permanently in his hand. He's married to Willie (Janice Rule), who never speaks, and is pregnant, and is painting the murals. It's all terrifically new to Pinky: drinking a beer (which she does as if just discovering the principle of a glass), or moving into Millie's apartment (which she solemnly declares to be the most beautiful place she's ever seen).

Then the film arrives at its center point, one of masked sexual horror, and the film moves from realism to a strange, haunted psychological

133

PART 2: THE BEST ❧ 134

landscape in which, somehow, Pinky and Millie exchange personalities. *3 Women* isn't Altman out of Freud via *Psychology Today,* and so the movie mercifully doesn't attempt to explain what's happened in logical terms (any explanation would be disappointing, I think, compared to the continuing mystery). Somehow we feel what's happened, though, even if we can't explain it in so many words.

The movie's been compared to Bergman's *Persona,* another film in which women seem to share personalities, and maybe *Persona,* also so mysterious when we first see it, helps point the way. But I believe Altman has provided his own signposts, in two important scenes, one at the beginning, one at the end, that mirror one another. Millie, teaching Pinky how to exercise the old folks' legs in the hot baths, places Pinky's feet on her stomach and moves them back and forth, just as Pinky sees the apparition of two twins on the other side of the pool. Later, when the older woman, Willie, is in labor, Millie places her legs in the same way and moves them in the same way, trying to assist the delivery. But the baby is stillborn, and so are the male-female connections in this small society. And so the women symbolically give birth to each other, around and around in a circle, just as (Altman himself suggests) the end of the picture could be seen as the moment just before its beginning.

The movie's story came to Altman during a dream, he's said, and he provides it with a dreamlike tone. The plot connections, which sometimes make little literal sense, do seem to connect emotionally, viscerally, as all things do in dreams. To act in a story like this must be a great deal more difficult than performing straightforward narrative, but Spacek and Duvall go through their changes so well that it's eerie, and unforgettable. So is the film.

An Unmarried Woman

MARCH 17, 1978

1978 It is, Erica thinks, a happy marriage, although perhaps she doesn't think about it much. It's there. Her husband is a stockbroker, she works in an art gallery, their daughter is in a private high school, they live in a high-rise and jog along the East River. In the morning there is *Swan Lake* on the FM radio, and the last sight at night is of the closing stock prices on the TV screen. Had she bargained for more?

One day, though, swiftly and cruelly, it all comes to an end: her husband breaks down in phony tears on the street and confesses he's in love with another woman. A younger woman. And so her happy marriage is over. At home, consumed by anger, grief, and uncertainty, she studies her face in the mirror. It is a good face in its middle thirties, and right now it looks plain scared.

So end the first, crucial passages of Paul Mazursky's *An Unmarried Woman*. They are crucial because we have to understand how completely Erica was a married woman if we're to join her on the journey back to being single again. It's a journey that Mazursky makes into one of the funniest, truest, sometimes most heartbreaking movies I've ever seen. And so much of what's best is because of Jill Clayburgh, whose performance is, quite simply, luminous.

We know that almost from the beginning. There's a moment of silence in the morning, right after Erica's husband and daughter have left the house. *Swan Lake* is playing. She's still in bed. She's just made love. She speaks from her imagination: "The ballet world was thrilled last night. . . ." And then she slips out of bed and dances around the living room in her T-shirt and panties, because she's so happy, so alive . . . and at that moment the movie's got us. We're in this thing with Erica to the end.

The going is sometimes pretty rough, especially when she's trying to make sense out of things after her husband (Michael Murphy) leaves her.

She gets a lot of support and encouragement from her three best girlfriends, and some of the movie's very best scenes take place when they meet for long lunches with lots of white wine, or lie around on long Sunday mornings paging through the *Times* and idly wondering why their lives don't seem to contain the style of a Bette Davis or a Katharine Hepburn. And then there are the scenes when she talks things over with her daughter (Lisa Lucas), who's one of those bright, precocious teenagers who uses understatement and cynicism to conceal how easily she can still be hurt.

After Erica gets over the period where she drinks too much and cries too much and screams at her daughter when she doesn't mean to, she goes to a woman psychiatrist, who explains that men are the problem, yes, but they are not quite yet the enemy. And so Erica, who hasn't slept with any man but her husband for seventeen years, finds herself having lunch in Chinese restaurants with boors who shout orders at waiters and try to kiss her in the back seat of a cab. There's also the self-styled stud (Cliff Gorman) who's been hanging around the art gallery, and she finally does go up to his place warily, gingerly, but she has to find a way sometime of beginning her life again.

And then one day a British artist is hanging a show at the gallery, and he asks her if she doesn't think one side of the painting is a little low, and she says she thinks the whole painting is too low, and he doesn't even seem to have noticed her as he says, "Let's discuss it over lunch." They fall in love. Oh, yes, gloriously, in that kind of love that involves not only great sex but walking down empty streets at dawn, and talking about each other's childhood. The painter is played by Alan Bates, who is cast, well and true, as a man who is perfectly right for her and perfectly wrong for her, both at the same time.

An Unmarried Woman plays true with all three of its major movements: the marriage, the being single, the falling in love. Mazursky's films have considered the grave and funny business of sex before (most memorably in *Bob & Carol & Ted & Alice* and *Blume in Love*). But he's never before been this successful at really dealing with the complexities and following them through. I wouldn't want to tell you too much about the movie's conclusion, but believe this much: it's honest and it's right, because Mazursky and Jill Clayburgh care too much about Erica to dismiss her with a conventional happy ending.

Clayburgh takes chances in this movie. She's out on an emotional limb. She's letting us see and experience things that many actresses simply couldn't reveal. Mazursky takes chances, too. He wants *An Unmarried Woman* to be true, for starters: we have to believe at every moment that life itself is being considered here. But the movie has to be funny, too. He won't settle for less than the truth and the humor, and the wonder of *An Unmarried Woman* is that he gets it. I've been reviewing movies for a long time now without ever feeling the need to use dumb lines like "You'll laugh—you'll cry." But I did cry, and I did laugh.

Apocalypse Now

JUNE 1, 1979

1979 In his book *The Films of My Life,* the French director François Truffaut makes a curious statement. He used to believe, he says, that a successful film had to simultaneously express "an idea of the world and an idea of cinema." But now, he writes, "I demand that a film express either the joy of making cinema or the agony of making cinema. I am not at all interested in anything in between; I am not interested in all those films that do not pulse."

It may seem strange to begin a review of Francis Coppola's *Apocalypse Now* with those words, but consider them for a moment and they apply perfectly to this sprawling film. The critics who have rejected Coppola's film mostly did so on Truffaut's earlier grounds: they have arguments with the ideas about the world and the war in *Apocalypse Now,* or they disagree with the very idea of a film that cost $31 million to make and was then carted all over the world by a filmmaker still uncertain whether he had the right ending.

That *other* film on the screen—the one we debate because of its ideas, not its images—is the one that has caused so much controversy about *Apocalypse Now.* We have all read that Coppola took as his inspiration the Joseph Conrad novel *Heart of Darkness,* and that he turned Conrad's journey up the Congo into a metaphor for another journey up a jungle river, into the heart of the Vietnam War. We've all read Coppola's grandiose statements (the most memorable: "This isn't a film about Vietnam. This film is Vietnam"). We've heard that Marlon Brando was paid $1 million for his closing scenes, and that Coppola gambled his personal fortune to finish the film, and, heaven help us, we've even read a journal by the director's wife in which she discloses her husband's ravings and infidelities.

But all such considerations are far from the reasons why *Apocalypse Now* is a good and important film—a masterpiece, I believe. Years and

138

years from now, when Coppola's budget and his problems have long been forgotten, *Apocalypse* will still stand, I think, as a grand and grave and insanely inspired gesture of filmmaking—of moments that are operatic in their style and scope, and of other moments so silent we can almost hear the director thinking to himself.

I should at this moment make a confession: I am not particularly interested in the "ideas" in Coppola's film. Critics of *Apocalypse* have said that Coppola was foolish to translate *Heart of Darkness,* that Conrad's vision had nothing to do with Vietnam, and that Coppola was simply borrowing Conrad's cultural respectability to give a gloss to his own disorganized ideas. The same objection was made to the hiring of Brando: Coppola was hoping, according to this version, that the presence of Brando as an icon would distract us from the emptiness of what he's given to say.

Such criticisms are made by people who indeed are plumbing *Apocalypse Now* for its ideas, and who are as misguided as the veteran Vietnam correspondents who breathlessly reported, some months ago, that *The Deer Hunter* was not "accurate." What idea or philosophy could we expect to find in *Apocalypse Now* and what good would it really do, at this point after the Vietnam tragedy, if Brando's closing speeches did have the "answers"? Like all great works of art about war, *Apocalypse Now* essentially contains only one idea or message, the not-especially-enlightening observation that war is hell. We do not go to see Coppola's movie for that insight—something Coppola, but not some of his critics, knows well.

Coppola also well knows (and demonstrated in the *Godfather* films) that movies aren't especially good at dealing with abstract ideas—for those you'd be better off turning to the written word—but they are superb for presenting moods and feelings, the look of a battle, the expression on a face, the mood of a country. *Apocalypse Now* achieves greatness not by analyzing our "experience in Vietnam," but by re-creating, in characters and images, something of that experience.

An example: the scene in which Robert Duvall, as a crazed lieutenant colonel, leads his troops in a helicopter assault on a village is, quite simply, the best movie battle scene ever filmed. It's simultaneously numbing, depressing, and exhilarating: as the rockets jar from the helicopters and spring through the air, we're elated like kids for a half second, until the reality of the consequences sinks in. Another wrenching scene in which the crew of Martin Sheen's navy patrol boat massacres the Vietnamese peasants in a small boat happens with such sudden, fierce, senseless violence that it forces us to understand for the first time how such things could happen.

Coppola's *Apocalypse Now* is filled with moments like that, and the narrative device of the journey upriver is as convenient for him as it was for Conrad. That's really why he uses it, and not because of literary cross-references for graduate students to catalog. He takes the journey, strings episodes along it, leads us at last to Brando's awesome, stinking hideaway . . . and then finds, so we've all heard, that he doesn't have an ending.

Well, Coppola doesn't have an ending, if we or he expected the closing scenes to pull everything together and make sense of it. Nobody should have been surprised. *Apocalypse Now* doesn't tell any kind of a conventional story, doesn't have a thought-out message for us about Vietnam, has no answers, and thus needs no ending. The way the film ends now, with Brando's fuzzy, brooding monologues and the final violence, feels much more satisfactory than any conventional ending possibly could.

What's great in the film, and what will make it live for many years and speak to many audiences, is what Coppola achieves on the levels Truffaut was discussing: the moments of agony and joy in making cinema. Some of those moments come at the same time; remember again the helicopter assault and its unsettling juxtaposition of horror and exhilaration. Remember the weird beauty of the massed helicopters lifting over the trees in the long shot, and the insane power of Wagner's music, played loudly during the attack, and you feel what Coppola was getting at: those moments as common in life as art, when the whole huge grand mystery of the world, so terrible, so beautiful, seems to hang in the balance.

The Black Stallion

1980 The first half of *The Black Stallion* is so gloriously breathtaking that the second half, the half with all the conventional excitement, seems merely routine. We've seen the second half before—the story of the kid, the horse, the veteran trainer, and the big race. But the first hour of this movie belongs among the great film-going experiences. It is described as an epic, and earns the description.

The film opens at sea, somewhere in the Mediterranean, forty or so years ago, on board a ship inhabited by passengers who seem foreign and fearsome to a small boy. They drink, they gamble, they speak in foreign tongues, they wear caftans and beards and glare ferociously at anyone who comes close to their prize possession, a magnificent black stallion.

The boy and his father are on board this ship for reasons never explained. The father gambles with the foreigners and the boy roams the ship and establishes a shy rapport with the black stallion, and then a great storm sweeps over the ocean and the ship catches fire and is lost. The boy and the stallion are thrown free, into the boiling sea. The horse somehow saves the boy, and in the calm of the next morning they both find themselves thrown onto a deserted island.

This sequence—the storm, the ship's sinking, the ordeal at sea—is a triumphant use of special effects, miniature models, back projection, editing, and all the tricks of craft that go into the filming of a fantasy. The director, Carroll Ballard, used the big water tank at Cinecittà Studios in Rome for the storm sequences; a model ship, looking totally real, burns and sinks headfirst, its propellers churning slowly in the air, while the horse and boy struggle in the foreground.

The horse in this film (its name is Cass-ole) is required to perform as few movie horses ever have. But its finest scene is the quietest one, and takes place on the island a few days after the shipwreck. Ballard and his cin-

141

ematographer, Caleb Deschanel, have already established the mood of the place, with gigantic, quiet, natural panoramas. The boy tries to spear a fish. The horse roams restlessly from the beaches to the cliffs. And then, in a single shot that is held for a long time, Ballard shows us the boy inviting the horse to eat out of his hand.

It is crucial here that this action be seen in a single shot; lots of short cuts, edited together, would simply be the filmmakers at work. But the one uninterrupted shot, with the horse at one edge of the screen and the boy at the other, and the boy's slow approach, and the horse's skittish advances and retreats, shows us a rapport between the human and the animal that's strangely moving.

All these scenes of the boy and horse on the island are to be treasured, especially a montage photographed underwater and showing the legs of the two as they splash in the surf. There are also wonderfully scary sequences, such as one in which the boy awakens to find a poisonous snake a few feet away from him on the sand. This scene exploits the hatred and fear horses have for snakes, and is cut together into a terrifically exciting climax.

But then, as all good things must, the idyll on the island comes to an end. The boy and the horse are rescued. And it's here that the film, while still keeping our interest, becomes more routine. The earlier passages of the film were amazing to look at (they were shot, with great difficulty and beauty, on Sardinia). Now we're back to earth again, with scenes shot around an old racetrack in Toronto.

And we've seen the melodramatic materials of the movie's second half many times before. The boy is reunited with his mother, the horse returns home with him, and the boy meets a wise old horse trainer who admits that, yes, that Arabian can run like the wind but the fool thing doesn't have any papers. The presence of Mickey Rooney, who plays the trainer, is welcome but perhaps too familiar. Rooney has played this sort of role so often before (most unforgettably in *National Velvet*) that he almost seems to be visiting from another movie.

Still, the melodrama is effective. Everything depends on the outcome of the big race at the film's end. The young boy, of course, is the jockey (the Elizabeth Taylor role, so to speak). Ballard and Deschanel are still gifted at finding a special, epic look for the movie; one especially good scene has the stallion racing against time, in the dark before dawn, in the rain.

The Black Stallion is a wonderful experience at the movies. The possibility remains, though, that in these cynical times it may be avoided by some viewers because it has a G rating and G movies are sometimes dismissed as being too innocuous. That's sure not the case with this film, which is rated G simply because it has no nudity, profanity, or violence, but it does have terrific energy, beauty, and excitement. It's not a children's movie; it's for adults and for kids.

My Dinner with Andre

DECEMBER 11, 1981

1981 The idea is astonishing in its audacity: a film of two friends talking, just simply talking—but with passion, wit, scandal, whimsy, vision, hope, and despair—for 110 minutes. It sounds at first like one of those underground films of the 1960s, in which great length and minimal content somehow interacted in the dope-addled brains of the audience to provide the impression of deep if somehow elusive profundity. *My Dinner with Andre* is not like that. It doesn't use all of those words as a stunt. They are alive on the screen, breathing, pulsing, reminding us of endless, impassioned conversations we've had with those few friends worth talking with for hours and hours. Underneath all the other fascinating things in this film beats the tide of friendship, of two people with a genuine interest in one another.

The two people are André Gregory and Wallace Shawn. Those are their real names, and also their names in the movie. I suppose they are playing themselves. As the film opens, Shawn travels across New York City to meet Gregory for dinner, and his thoughts provide us with background: his friend Gregory is a New York theater director, well known into the 1970s, who dropped out for five years and traveled around the world. Now Gregory has returned, with wondrous tales of strange experiences. Shawn has spent the same years in New York, finding uncertain success as an author and playwright. They sit down for dinner in an elegant restaurant. We do not see the other customers. The bartender is a wraith in the background, the waiter is the sort of presence they were waiting for in *Waiting for Godot*. The friends order dinner, and then, as it is served and they eat and drink, they talk.

What conversation! Gregory does most of the talking, and he is a spellbinding conversationalist, able to weave mental images not only out of his experiences, but also out of his ideas. He explains that he had become dissatisfied with life, restless, filled with anomie and discontent. He accepted an invitation to join an experimental theater group in Poland. It was very strange, tending toward rituals in the woods under the full moon.

From Poland, he traveled around the world, meeting a series of people who were seriously and creatively exploring the ways in which they could experience the material world. They (and Gregory) literally believed in mind over matter, and as Gregory describes a monk who was able to stand his entire body weight on his fingertips, we visualize that man and in some strange way (so hypnotic is the tale) we share the experience.

One of the gifts of *My Dinner with Andre* is that we share so many of the experiences. Although most of the movie literally consists of two men talking, here's a strange thing: we do not spend the movie just passively listening to them talk. At first, director Louis Malle's sedate series of images (close-ups, two-shots, reaction shots) calls attention to itself, but as Gregory continues to talk, the very simplicity of the visual style renders it invisible. And like the listeners at the feet of a master storyteller, we find ourselves visualizing what Gregory describes, until this film is as filled with visual images as a radio play—more filled, perhaps, than a conventional feature film.

What Gregory and Shawn talk about is, quite simply, many of the things on our minds these days. We've passed through Tom Wolfe's Me Decade and find ourselves in a decade during which there will apparently be less for everybody. The two friends talk about inner journeys—not in the mystical, vague terms of magazines you don't want to be seen reading on the bus, but in terms of trying to live better lives, of learning to listen to what others are really saying, of breaking the shackles of conventional ideas about our bodies and allowing them to more fully sense the outer world.

The movie is not ponderous, annoyingly profound, or abstract. It is about living, and Gregory seems to have lived fully in his five years of dropping out. Shawn is the character who seems more like us. He listens, he nods eagerly, he is willing to learn, but—something holds him back. Pragmatic questions keep asking themselves. He can't buy Gregory's vision, not all the way. He'd like to, but this is a real world we have to live in, after all, and if we all danced with the druids in the forests of Poland, what would happen to the market for fortune cookies?

The film's end is beautiful and inexplicably moving. Shawn returns home by taxi through the midnight streets of New York. Having spent hours with Gregory on a wild conversational flight, he is now reminded of scenes from his childhood. In that store, his father bought him shoes. In that one, he bought ice cream with a girlfriend. The utter simplicity of his memories acts to dramatize the fragility and great preciousness of life. He has learned his friend's lesson.

Sophie's Choice

DECEMBER 10, 1982

1982 Sometimes when you've read the novel, it gets in the way of the images on the screen. You keep remembering how you imagined things. That didn't happen with me during *Sophie's Choice,* because the movie is so perfectly cast and well-imagined that it just takes over and happens to you. It's quite an experience.

The movie stars Meryl Streep as Sophie, a Polish Catholic woman, who was caught by the Nazis with a contraband ham, was sentenced to a concentration camp, lost her two children there, and then was somehow spared to immigrate to Brooklyn, USA, and to the arms of an eccentric charmer named Nathan. Sophie and Nathan move into an old boarding-house, and the rooms just below them are taken by Stingo, a jug-eared kid from the South who wants to be a great novelist. As the two lovers play out their doomed, romantic destiny, Stingo falls in love with several things: with his image of himself as a writer, with his idealized vision of Sophie and Nathan's romance, and, inevitably, with Sophie herself.

The movie, like the book, is told with two narrators. One is Stingo, who remembers these people from that summer in Brooklyn, and who also remembers himself at that much earlier age. The other narrator, contained within Stingo's story, is Sophie herself, who remembers what happened to her during World War II, and shares her memories with Stingo in a long confessional. Both the book and the movie have long central flash-backs, and neither the book nor the movie is damaged by those diversions, because Sophie's story is so indispensable to Stingo's own growth, from an adolescent dreamer to an artist who can begin to understand human suffering. The book and movie have something else in common. Despite the fact that Sophie's story, her choices, and her fate are all sad, sad stories, there is a lot of exuberance and joy in the telling of them. *Sophie's Choice* begins as a young southerner's odyssey to the unimaginable North—to that strange land celebrated by his hero, Thomas Wolfe, who took the all-night train to New York with its riches, its women, and its romance. Stingo is absolutely entranced by this plump, blond Polish woman who moves so winningly into his life, and by her intense, brilliant, mad lover.

We almost don't notice, at first, as Stingo's odyssey into adulthood is replaced, in the film, by Sophie's journey back into the painful memories of her past. The movie becomes an act of discovery, as the naive young American, his mind filled with notions of love, death, and honor, becomes the friend of a woman who has seen so much hate, death, and dishonor that the only way she can continue is by blotting out the past, and drinking and loving her way into temporary oblivion. It's basically a three-character movie, and the casting, as I suggested, is just right. Meryl Streep is a wonder as Sophie. She does not quite look or sound or feel like the Meryl Streep we have seen before in *The Deer Hunter* or *Manhattan* or *The French Lieutenant's Woman*. There is something juicier about her this time; she is merrier and sexier, more playful and cheerful in the scenes before she begins to tell Stingo the truth about her past. Streep plays the Brooklyn scenes with an enchanting Polish American accent (she has the first accent I've ever wanted to hug), and she plays the flashbacks in subtitled German and Polish. There is hardly an emotion that Streep doesn't touch in this movie, and yet we're never aware of her straining. This is one of the most astonishing and yet one of the most unaffected and natural performances I can imagine.

Kevin Kline plays Nathan, the crazy romantic who convinces everyone he's on the brink of finding the cure for polio and who wavers uncertainly between anger and manic exhilaration. Peter MacNicol is Stingo, the kid who is left at the end to tell the story. Kline, MacNicol, and Streep make such good friends in this movie—despite all the suffering they go through—that we really do believe the kid when he refuses to act on an unhappy revelation, insisting, "These are my friends. I love them!"

Sophie's Choice is a fine, absorbing, wonderfully acted, heartbreaking movie. It is about three people who are faced with a series of choices, some frivolous, some tragic. As they flounder in the bewilderment of being human in an age of madness, they become our friends, and we love them.

The Right Stuff

OCTOBER 1, 1983

1983 At the beginning of *The Right Stuff,* a cowboy reins in his horse and regards a strange sight in the middle of the desert: the X-1 rocket plane, built to break the sound barrier. At the end of the film, the seven Mercury astronauts are cheered in the Houston Astrodome at a Texas barbecue thrown by Lyndon B. Johnson. The contrast between those two images contains the message of *The Right Stuff,* I think, and the message is that Americans still have the right stuff, but we've changed our idea of what it is.

The original American heroes were loners. The cowboy is the perfect example. He was silhouetted against the horizon and he rode into town by himself and if he had a sidekick, the sidekick's job was to admire him. The new American heroes are team players. No wonder Westerns aren't made anymore; cowboys don't play on teams.

The cowboy at the beginning of *The Right Stuff* is Chuck Yeager, the legendary lone-wolf test pilot who survived the horrifying death rate among early test pilots (more than sixty were killed in a single month) and did fly the X-1 faster than the speed of sound. The movie begins with that victory, and then moves on another ten years to the day when the Russians sent up Sputnik, and the Eisenhower administration hustled to get back into the space race.

The astronauts who eventually rode the first Mercury capsules into space may not have been that much different from Chuck Yeager. As they're portrayed in the movie, anyway, Gus Grissom, Scott Carpenter, and Gordon Cooper seem to have some of the same stuff as Yeager. But the astronauts were more than pilots; they were a public-relations image, and the movie shows sincere, smooth-talking John Glenn becoming their unofficial spokesman. The X-1 flew in secrecy, but the Mercury flights were telecast, and we were entering a whole new era, the selling of space.

There was a lot going on, and there's a lot going on in the movie, too. *The Right Stuff* is an adventure film, a special-effects film, a social commentary, and a satire. That the writer-director, Philip Kaufman, is able to get so much into a little more than three hours is impressive. That he also has organized this material into one of the best recent American movies is astonishing. *The Right Stuff* gives itself the freedom to move around in moods and styles, from a broadly based lampoon of government functionaries to Yeager's spare, taciturn manner and Glenn's wonderment at the sights outside his capsule window. *The Right Stuff* is likely to be a landmark movie in a lot of careers. It announces Kaufman's arrival in the ranks of major directors. It contains uniformly interesting performances by a whole list of unknown or little-known actors, including Ed Harris (Glenn), Scott Glenn (Alan Shepard), Fred Ward (Grissom) and Dennis Quaid (Cooper). It confirms the strong and sometimes almost mystical screen presence of playwright Sam Shepard, who plays Yeager. And it joins a short list of recent American movies that might be called experimental epics: movies that have an ambitious reach through time and subject matter, that spend freely for locations or special effects, but that consider each scene as intently as an art film. *The Right Stuff* goes on that list with *The Godfather, Nashville, Apocalypse Now,* and maybe *Patton* and *Close Encounters*. It's a great film.

Amadeus

SEPTEMBER 18, 1984

1984 Milos Forman's *Amadeus* is one of the riskiest gambles a filmmaker has taken in a long time—a lavish movie about Mozart that dares to be anarchic and saucy, and yet still earns the importance of tragedy. This movie is nothing like the dreary educational portraits we're used to seeing about the Great Composers, who come across as cobwebbed profundities weighed down with the burden of genius. This is Mozart as an eighteenth-century Bruce Springsteen, and yet (here is the genius of the movie) there is nothing cheap or unworthy about the approach. *Amadeus* is not only about as much fun as you're likely to have with a movie, it is also disturbingly true. The truth enters in the character of Salieri, who tells the story. He is not a great composer, but he is a good enough composer to know greatness when he hears it, and that is why the music of Mozart breaks his heart. He knows how good it is, he sees how easily Mozart seems to compose it, and he knows that his own work looks pale and silly beside it.

The movie begins with the suggestion that Salieri might have murdered Mozart. The movie examines the ways in which this possibility might be true, and by the end of the film we feel a certain kinship with the weak and jealous Salieri—for few of us can identify with divine genius, but many of us probably have had dark moments of urgent self-contempt in the face of those whose effortless existence illustrates our own inadequacies. Salieri, played with burning intensity by F. Murray Abraham, sits hunched in a madhouse confessing to a priest. The movie flashes back to his memories of Wolfgang Amadeus Mozart, the child genius who composed melodies of startling originality and who grew up to become a prolific, driven artist.

One of the movie's wisest decisions is to cast Mozart not as a charismatic demigod, not as a tortured superman, but as a goofy, immature, likable kid with a ridiculous laugh. The character is played by Tom Hulce, and if you saw *Animal House,* you may remember him as the fraternity brother who tried to seduce the mayor's daughter, while an angel and a devil whispered in his ears. Hulce would seem all wrong for Mozart, but he is absolutely right, as an unaffected young man filled with delight at his own gifts, unaware of how easily he wounds Salieri and others, tortured only by the guilt of having offended his religious and domineering father.

The film is constructed in wonderfully well-written and acted scenes—scenes so carefully made, unfolding with such delight, that they play as perfect compositions of words. Most of them will be unfamiliar to those who have seen Peter Shaffer's brooding play, on which this film is based; Shaffer and Forman have brought light, life, and laughter to the material, and it plays with grace and ease. It's more human than the play; the characters are people, not throbbing packages of meaning. It centers on the relationships in Mozart's life: with his father, his wife, and Salieri. The father never can be pleased, and that creates an undercurrent affecting all of Mozart's success. The wife, played by delightful, buxom Elizabeth Berridge, contains in one person the qualities of a jolly wench and a loving partner: she likes to loll in bed all day, but also gives Mozart good, sound advice and is a forceful person in her own right. The patrons, especially Joseph II, the Austro-Hungarian emperor, are connoisseurs and dilettantes, slow to take to Mozart's new music but enchanted by the audacity with which he defends it. And then there is Salieri (F. Murray Abraham), the gaunt court composer whose special torture is to understand better than anybody else how inadequate he is, and how great Mozart is.

The movie was shot on location in Forman's native Czechoslovakia, and it looks exactly right; it fits its period comfortably, perhaps because Prague still contains so many streets and squares and buildings that could be directly from the Vienna of Mozart's day. Perhaps his confidence in his locations gave Forman the freedom to make Mozart slightly out of period. Forman directed the film version of *Hair,* and Mozart in this movie seems to share a spirit with some of the characters from *Hair.* Mozart's wigs do not look like everybody else's. They have just the slightest suggestion of punk, just the smallest shading of pink. Mozart seems more a child of the 1960s than of any other age, and this interpretation of his personality—he was an irreverent proto-hippie who trusted, if you will, his own vibes—sounds risky, but works.

I have not mentioned the music. There's probably no need to. The music provides the understructure of the film, strong, confident, above all clear, in a way that Salieri's simple muddles only serve to illustrate. There are times when Mozart speaks the words of a child, but then the music says the same things in the language of the gods, and all is clear.

Amadeus is a magnificent film, full and tender and funny and charming—and, at the end, sad and angry, too, because in the character of Salieri it has given us a way to understand not only greatness, but our own lack of it. This movie's fundamental question, I think, is whether we can learn to be grateful for the happiness of others, and that, of course, is a test for sainthood. How many movies ask such questions and succeed in being fun, as well?

The Color Purple

1985 There is a moment in Steven Spielberg's *The Color Purple* when a woman named Celie smiles and smiles and smiles. That was the moment when I knew this movie was going to be as good as it seemed, was going to keep the promise it made by daring to tell Celie's story. It is not a story that would seem easily suited to the movies.

Celie is a black woman who grows up in the rural South in the early decades of this century, in a world that surrounds her with cruelty. When we first see her, she is a child, running through fields of purple flowers with her sister. But then she comes into clear view, and we see that she is pregnant, and we learn that her father has made her pregnant, and will give away the child as he did with a previous baby.

By the time Celie is married—to a cruel, distant charmer she calls only "Mister"—she will have lost both her children and the ability to bear children, will have been separated from the sister who is the only person on earth who loves her, and will be living in servitude to a man who flaunts his love for another woman. And yet this woman will endure, and in the end she will prevail. *The Color Purple* is not the story of her suffering but of her victory, and by the end of her story this film had moved me and lifted me up as few films have. It is a great, warm, hard, unforgiving, triumphant movie, and there is not a scene that does not shine with the love of the people who made it.

The film is based on the novel by Alice Walker, who told Celie's story through a series of letters, some never sent, many never received, most addressed to God. The letters are her way of maintaining sanity in a world where few others ever cared to listen to her. The turning point in the book, and in the movie, comes after Celie's husband brings home the fancy woman he has been crazy about for years—a pathetic, alcoholic juke-joint

154

singer named Shug Avery, who has been ravaged by life yet still has an indestructible beauty.

Shug's first words to Celie are "You sho is ugly!" But as Shug moves into the house and Celie obediently caters to her husband's lover, Shug begins to see the beauty in Celie, and there is a scene where they kiss, and Celie learns for the first time that sex can include tenderness, that she can dare to love herself. A little later, Celie looks in Shug's eyes and allows herself to smile, and we know that Celie didn't think she had a pretty smile until Shug told her so. That is the central moment in the movie.

The relationship between Shug and Celie is a good deal toned down from the book, which deals in great detail with sexual matters. Steven Spielberg, who made the movie, is more concerned with the whole world of Celie's life than he is with her erotic education. We meet many members of the rural black community that surrounds Celie. We meet a few of the local whites, too, but they are bit players in this drama.

Much more important are people like Sofia (Oprah Winfrey), an indomitable force of nature who is determined to marry Harpo, Mister's son by a first marriage. When we first see Sofia, hurrying down the road with everyone trying to keep up, she looks like someone who could never be stopped. But she is stopped, after she tells the local white mayor to go to hell, and the saddest story in the movie is the way her spirit is forever dampened by the beating and jailing she receives. Sofia is counterpoint to Celie: she is wounded by life, Celie is healed.

Shug Avery is another fascinating character, played by Margaret Avery as a sweet-faced, weary woman who sings a little like Billie Holiday and has long since lost all of her illusions about men and everything else. Her contact with Celie redeems her; by giving her somebody to be nice to, it allows her to get in touch with what is still nice inside herself.

Mister, whose real name is Albert, is played by Danny Glover, who was the field hand in *Places in the Heart*. He is an evil man, his evil tempered to some extent by his ignorance; perhaps he does not fully understand how cruel he is to Celie. Certainly he seems outwardly pleasant. He smiles and jokes and sings, and then hurts Celie to the quick—not so much with his physical blows as when he refuses to let her see the letters she hopes are coming from her long-lost sister.

And then, at the center of the movie, Celie is played by Whoopi Goldberg in one of the most amazing debut performances in movie history. Here is this year's winner of the Academy Award for best actress. Goldberg has a fearsomely difficult job to do, enlisting our sympathy for a woman who is rarely allowed to speak, to dream, to interact with the lives around her. Spielberg breaks down the wall of silence around her, however, by giving her narrative monologues in which she talks about her life and reads the letters she composes.

The wonderful performances in this movie are contained in a screenplay that may take some of the shocking edges off Walker's novel, but keeps all the depth and dimension. The world of Celie and the others is created so forcibly in this movie that their corner of the South becomes one of those movie places—like Oz, like Tara, like Casablanca—that lay claim to their own geography in our imaginations. The affirmation at the end of the film is so joyous that this is one of the few movies in a long time that inspires tears of happiness, and earns them. *The Color Purple* is the year's best film.

Platoon

1986 It was François Truffaut who said that it's not possible to make an antiwar movie, because all war movies, with their energy and sense of adventure, end up making combat look like fun. If Truffaut had lived to see *Platoon,* the best film of 1986, he might have wanted to modify his opinion. Here is a movie that regards combat from ground level, from the infantryman's point of view, and it does not make war look like fun.

The movie was written and directed by Oliver Stone, who fought in Vietnam and who has tried to make a movie about the war that is not fantasy, not legend, not metaphor, not message, but simply a memory of what it seemed like at the time to him. The movie is narrated by a young soldier (Charlie Sheen) based on Stone himself. He is a middle-class college student who volunteers for the war because he considers it his patriotic duty, and who is told, soon after he arrives in the combat zone, "You don't belong here." He believes it.

There are no false heroics in this movie, and no standard heroes; the narrator is quickly at the point of physical collapse, bedeviled by long marches, no sleep, ants, snakes, cuts, bruises, and constant, gnawing fear. In a scene near the beginning of the film, he is on guard duty when he clearly sees enemy troops approaching his position, and he freezes. He will only gradually, unknowingly, become an adequate soldier.

The movie is told in a style that rushes headlong into incidents. There is no carefully mapped plot to lead us from point to point; instead, like the characters, we are usually disoriented. Anything is likely to happen, usually without warning. From the crowded canvas, large figures emerge: Barnes (Tom Berenger), the veteran sergeant with the scarred face, the survivor of so many hits that his men believe he cannot be killed. Elias (Willem Dafoe), another good fighter, but a man who tries to escape from the reality through drugs. Bunny (Kevin Dillon), the scared kid, who has become dangerous because that seems like a way to protect himself.

There is rarely a clear, unequivocal shot of an enemy soldier. They are wraiths, half-seen in the foliage, their presence scented on jungle paths, evidence of their passage unearthed in ammo dumps buried beneath villages. Instead, there is the clear sense of danger all around, and the presence of civilians who sometimes enrage the troops just by standing there and looking confused and helpless.

There is a scene in the movie that seems inspired by My Lai, although it does not develop into a massacre. As we share the suspicion that these villagers may, in fact, be harboring enemy forces, we share the fear that turns to anger, and we understand the anger that turns to violence. Some of the men in *Platoon* have lost their bearings, are willing to kill almost anyone on the slightest pretext. Others still retain some measure of the morality of the situation. Since their own lives also may be at stake in their arguments, there is a great sense of danger when they disagree. We see Americans shooting other Americans, and we can understand why.

After seeing *Platoon,* I fell to wondering why Stone was able to make such an effective movie without falling into the trap Truffaut spoke about— how he made the movie riveting without making it exhilarating. Here's how I think he did it. He abandoned the choreography that is standard in almost all war movies. He abandoned any attempt to make it clear where the various forces were in relation to each other, so that we never know where "our" side stands and where "they" are. Instead of battle scenes in which lines are clearly drawn, his combat scenes involve 360 degrees: any shot might be aimed at friend or enemy, and in the desperate rush of combat, many of his soldiers never have a clear idea of exactly who they are shooting at, or why.

Traditional movies impose a sense of order upon combat. Identifying with the soldiers, we feel that if we duck behind this tree or jump into this ditch, we will be safe from the fire that is coming from over there. In *Platoon,* there is the constant fear that any movement offers a 50-50 chance between a safe place or an exposed one. Stone sets up his shots to deny us the feeling that combat makes sense.

The Vietnam War is the central moral and political issue of the last quarter century, for Americans. It has inspired some of the greatest recent

American films: *Apocalypse Now, The Deer Hunter, Coming Home, The Killing Fields*. Now here is the film that, in a curious way, should have been made before any of the others. A film that says—as the Vietnam Memorial in Washington says—that before you can make any vast, sweeping statements about Vietnam, you have to begin by understanding the bottom line, which is that a lot of people went over there and got killed, dead, and that is what the war meant for them.

House of Games

OCTOBER 16, 1987

1987 This movie is awake. I have seen so many films that were sleepwalking through the debris of old plots and secondhand ideas that it was a constant pleasure to watch *House of Games,* a movie about con men that succeeds not only in conning the audience, but also in creating a series of characters who seem imprisoned by the need to con, or be conned.

The film stars Lindsay Crouse as a psychiatrist who specializes in addictive behavior, possibly as a way of dealing with her own compulsions. One of her patients is a gambler who fears he will be murdered over a bad debt. Crouse walks through lonely night streets to the neon signs of the House of Games, a bar where she thinks she can find the gambler who has terrorized her client. She wants to talk him out of enforcing the debt.

The gambler (Joe Mantegna) has never heard anything like this before. But he offers her a deal: if she will help him fleece a high-roller Texan in a big-stakes poker game, he will tear up the marker. She does so. She also becomes fascinated by the backroom reality of these gamblers who have reduced life to a knowledge of the odds. She comes back the next day, looking for Mantegna. She tells him she wants to learn more about gamblers and con men, about the kind of man that he is. By the end of this movie, does she ever.

House of Games was written and directed by David Mamet, the playwright (*Glengarry Glen Ross*) and screenwriter (*The Untouchables*), and it is his directorial debut. Originally it was intended as a big-budget movie with an established director and major stars, but Mamet took the reins himself, cast his wife in the lead and old acting friends in the other important roles, and shot it on the rainy streets of Seattle. Usually the screenwriter is insane to think he can direct a movie. Not this time. *House of*

Games never steps wrong from beginning to end, and it is one of this year's best films.

The plotting is diabolical and impeccable, and I will not spoil the delight of its unfolding by mentioning the crucial details. What I can mention are the performances, the dialogue, and the setting. When Crouse enters the House of Games, she enters a world occupied by characters who have known each other so long and so well, in so many different ways, that everything they say is a kind of shorthand. At first we don't fully realize that, and there is a strange savor to the words they use.

They speak, of course, in Mamet's distinctive dialogue style, an almost musical rhythm of stopping, backing up, starting again, repeating, emphasizing, all of the time with the hint of deeper meanings below the surfaces of the words. The leading actors, Chicagoans Mantegna and Mike Nussbaum, have appeared in countless performances of Mamet plays over the years, and they know his dialogue the way other actors grow into Beckett or Shakespeare. They speak it as it is meant to be spoken, with a sort of aggressive, almost insulting directness. Mantegna has a scene where he "reads" Crouse—where he tells her about her "tells," those small giveaway looks and gestures that poker players use to read the minds of their opponents. The way he talks to her is so incisive and unadorned it is sexual.

These characters and others live in a city that looks, as the Seattle of *Trouble in Mind* did, like a place on a parallel time track. It is a modern American city, but none we have quite seen before; it seems to have been modeled on the paintings of Edward Hopper, where lonely people wait in empty public places for their destinies to intercept them. Crouse is portrayed as an alien in this world, a successful, best-selling author who has never dreamed that men like this exist, and the movie is insidious in the way it shows her willingness to be corrupted.

There is in all of us a fascination for the inside dope, for the methods of the confidence game, for the secrets of a magic trick. But there is an eternal gulf between the shark and the mark, between the con man and his victim. And there is a code to protect the secrets. There are moments in *House of Games* when Mantegna instructs Crouse in the methods and lore of the con game, but inside every con is another one.

I met a woman once who was divorced from a professional magician.

She hated this man with a passion. She used to appear with him in a baffling trick where they exchanged places, handcuffed and manacled, in a locked cabinet. I asked her how it was done. The divorce and her feelings meant nothing compared to her loyalty to the magical profession. She looked at me coldly and said, "The trick is told when the trick is sold." The ultimate question in *House of Games* is, who's buying?

Mississippi Burning

DECEMBER 10, 1988

1988 Movies often take place in towns, but they rarely seem to live in them. Alan Parker's *Mississippi Burning* feels like a movie made from the inside out, a movie that knows the ways and people of its small southern city so intimately that, having seen it, I know the place I'd go for a cup of coffee and the place I'd steer clear from. This acute sense of time and place—rural Mississippi, 1964—is the lifeblood of the film. More than any other film I've seen, this one gets inside the passion of race relations in America.

The film is based on a true story, the disappearance of Chaney, Goodman, and Schwerner, three young civil rights workers who were part of a voter registration drive in Mississippi. When their murdered bodies were finally discovered, their corpses were irrefutable testimony against the officials who had complained that the whole case was a publicity stunt, dreamed up by northern liberals and outside agitators. The case became one of the milestones, like the day Rosa Parks took her seat on the bus or the day Martin Luther King marched into Montgomery, on the long march toward racial justice in this country.

But *Mississippi Burning* is not a documentary, nor does it strain to present a story based on the facts. This movie is a gritty police drama, bloody, passionate, and sometimes surprisingly funny, about the efforts of two FBI men to lead an investigation into the disappearances. Few men could be more opposite than these two agents: Anderson (Gene Hackman), the good old boy who used to be a sheriff in a town a lot like this one, and Ward (Willem Dafoe), one of Bobby Kennedy's bright young men from the justice department. Anderson believes in keeping a low profile, hanging around the barber shop, sort of smelling out the likely perpetrators. Ward believes in a show of force, and calls in hundreds of federal agents and even the National Guard to search for the missing workers.

Anderson and Ward do not like each other very much. Both men feel they should be in charge of the operation. As they go their separate paths, we meet some of the people in the town. The mayor, a slick country-club type, who lectures against rabble-rousing outsiders. The sheriff, who thinks he can intimidate the FBI men. And Pell (Brad Dourif), a shifty-eyed deputy who has an alibi for the time the three men disappeared, and it's a good alibi—except why would he have an alibi so good, for precisely that time, unless he needed one?

The alibi depends on the word of Pell's wife (Frances McDormand), a woman who has taken a lot over the years from this self-hating racist, who needs a gun on his belt by day and a hood over his head by night, just to gather the courage to stand and walk. Anderson, the Hackman character, singles her out immediately as the key to the case. He believes the sheriff's department delivered the three men over to the local Klan, which murdered them. If he can get the wife to talk, the whole house of cards crashes down.

So he starts hanging around. Makes small talk. Shifts on his feet in her living room like a bashful boy. Lets his voice trail off, so that in the silence she can imagine that he was about to say what a pretty woman she was, still. Anderson plays this woman like a piano. And she wants to be played. Because Gene Hackman is such a subtle actor, it takes us a while to realize that he has really fallen for her. He would like to rescue her from the scum she's married to, and wrap her up in his arms.

This relationship is counterpoint to the main current of the film, which involves good police work, interrogations, searches, and—mostly—hoping for tips. There is reason to believe that the local black community has a good idea of who committed the murders, but the Klan trashes and burns the home of one family with a son who might talk, and there is terror in the air in the black neighborhood.

Parker, the director, doesn't use melodrama to show how terrified the local blacks are of reprisals; he uses realism. We see what can happen to people who are not "good nigras." The Dafoe character approaches a black man in a segregated luncheonette and asks him questions. The black refuses to talk to him—and *still* gets beaten by the Klan. Sometimes keeping your mouth shut can be sound common sense. Parker has dealt with intimidating bullies before in his work, most notably in *Midnight Express,* but what makes this film so particular is the way he understates the evil in it. There are no great villains and sadistic torturers in this film, only banal little racists with a vicious streak.

By the end of the film, the bodies have been found, the murderers have been identified, and the wheels of justice have started to grind. We knew the outcome of this case when we walked into the theater. What we may have forgotten, or never known, is exactly what kinds of currents were in the air in 1964. The civil rights movement of the early 1960s was the finest hour of modern American history, because it was the painful hour in which we determined to improve ourselves, instead of others. We grew. The South grew, the whole nation grew, more comfortable with the radical idea that all men were created equal and endowed with certain inalienable rights, among them life, liberty, and the pursuit of happiness.

What *Mississippi Burning* evokes more clearly than anything else is how recently in our past those rights were routinely and *legally* denied to blacks, particularly in the South. In a time so recent that its cars are still on the road and its newspapers have not started to yellow, large parts of America were a police state in which the crime was to be black. Things are not great for blacks today, but at least official racism is no longer on the law books anywhere. And no other movie I've seen captures so forcefully the look, the feel, the very smell, of racism. We can feel how sexy their hatred feels to the racists in this movie, how it replaces other entertainments, how it compensates for their sense of worthlessness. And we can feel something breaking free, the fresh air rushing in, when the back of that racism is broken.

Mississippi Burning is the best American film of 1988, and a likely candidate for the Academy Award as the year's best picture. Apart from its pure entertainment value—this is the best American crime movie in years—it is an important statement about a time and a condition that should not be forgotten. The Academy loves to honor prestigious movies in which long-ago crimes are rectified in far-away places. Here is a nominee with the ink still wet on its pages.

The major players—Hackman and Dafoe—are likely Oscar nominees, but I hope attention is paid to Frances McDormand, who could have turned her role into a flashy showboat performance, but chose instead to show us a woman who had been raised and trained and beaten into accepting her man as her master, and who finally rejects that role simply because with her own eyes she can see that it's wrong to treat black people the way her husband does. The woman McDormand plays is quiet and shy and fearful, but in the moral decision she makes, she represents a generation that finally said, hey, what's going on here is simply not fair.

Do the Right Thing

1989 Spike Lee's *Do the Right Thing* is the most controversial film of the year, and it only opens today. Thousands of people have already seen it at preview screenings, and everywhere I go, people are discussing it. Some of them are bothered by it—they think it will cause trouble. Others feel the message is confused. Some find it too militant, others find it the work of a middle-class director who is trying to play street-smart. All of those reactions, I think, are simply different ways of avoiding the central fact of this film, which is that it comes closer to reflecting the current state of race relations in America than any other movie of our time.

Of course it is confused. Of course it wavers between middle-class values and street values. Of course it is not sure whether it believes in liberal pieties, or militancy. Of course some of the characters are sympathetic and others are hateful—and of course some of the likeable characters do bad things. Isn't that the way it is in America today? Anyone who walks into this film expecting answers is a dreamer or a fool. But anyone who leaves the movie with more intolerance than they walked in with wasn't paying attention.

The movie takes place during one long, hot day in the Bedford-Stuyvesant neighborhood of Brooklyn. But this is not the typical urban cityscape we've seen in countless action movies about violence and guns and drugs. People live here. It's a neighborhood like those city neighborhoods in the urban movies of the Depression—people know each other, and accept each other, and although there are problems there is also a sense of community.

The neighborhood is black, but two of the businesses aren't. Sal's Famous Pizzeria has been on the same corner since before the neighborhood changed, and Sal (Danny Aiello) boasts that "these people have grown up on my pizza." And in a nearby storefront that had been boarded up for years, a Korean family has opened a fruit and vegetable stand. Nobody seems to quite know the Koreans, but Sal and his sons are neighborhood fixtures—they know everybody, and everybody knows them.

Sal is a tough, no-nonsense guy who basically wants to get along and tend to business. One of his sons is a vocal racist—in private, of course. The other is more open toward blacks. Sal's ambassador to the community is a likeable local youth named Mookie (Spike Lee), who delivers pizzas and also acts as a messenger of news and gossip. Mookie is good at his job, but his heart isn't in it; he knows there's no future in delivering pizzas.

We meet other people in the neighborhood. There's Da Mayor (Ossie Davis), a kind of everyman who knows everybody. Buggin' Out (Giancarlo Esposito), a vocal militant. Radio Raheem (Bill Nunn), whose boom box defines his life and provides a musical cocoon to insulate him from the world. Mother Sister (Ruby Dee), who is sort of the neighborhood witch. And there's the local disk jockey, whose program provides a running commentary, and a retarded street person who wanders around selling photos of Martin Luther King and Malcolm X, and then there are three old guys on the corner who comment on developments, slowly and at length.

This looks like a good enough neighborhood—like the kind of urban stage the proletarian dramas of the 1930s liked to start with. And for a long time during *Do the Right Thing,* Spike Lee treats it like a backdrop for a Saroyanesque slice of life. But things are happening under the surface. Tensions are building. Old hurts are being remembered. And finally the movie explodes in racial violence.

The exact nature of that violence has been described in many of the articles about the film—including two I wrote after the movie's tumultuous premiere at the Cannes Film Festival—but in this review I think I will not outline the actual events. At Cannes, I walked into the movie cold, and its ending had a shattering effect precisely because I was not expecting it. There will be time, in the extended discussions this movie will inspire, to discuss in detail who does what, and why. But for now I would like you to have the experience for yourself, and think about it for yourself. Since Spike Lee does not tell you what to think about it, and deliberately provides surprising twists for some of the characters, this movie is more open-ended than most. It requires you to decide what you think about it.

Do the Right Thing is not filled with brotherly love, but it is not filled with hate, either. It comes out of a weary urban cynicism that has settled down around us in recent years. The good feelings and many of the hopes of the 1960s have evaporated, and today it would no longer be accurate to make a movie about how the races in America are all going to love one another. I wish we could see such love, but instead we have deepening class divisions in which the middle classes of all races flee from what's happening in the inner city, while a series of national administrations provides no hope for the poor. *Do the Right Thing* tells an honest, unsentimental story about those who are left behind.

It is a very well made film, beautifully photographed by Ernest Dickerson, and well acted by an ensemble cast. Danny Aiello has the pivotal role, as Sal, and he suggests all of the difficult nuances of his situation. In the movie's final scene, Sal's conversation with Mookie holds out little hope, but it holds out at least the possibility that something has been learned from the tragedy, and the way Aiello plays this scene is quietly brilliant. Lee's writing and direction are masterful throughout the movie; he knows exactly where he is taking us, and how to get there, but he holds his cards close to his heart, and so the movie is hard to predict, hard to anticipate. After we get to the end, however, we understand how, and why, everything has happened.

Some of the advance articles about this movie have suggested that it is an incitement to racial violence. Those articles say more about their authors than about the movie. I believe that any good-hearted person, white or black, will come out of this movie with sympathy for all of the characters. Lee does not ask us to forgive them, or even to understand everything they do, but he wants us to identify with their fears and frustrations. *Do the Right Thing* doesn't ask its audiences to choose sides; it is scrupulously fair to both sides, in a story where it is our society itself which is not fair.

GoodFellas

SEPTEMBER 21, 1990

1990 There really are guys like this. I've seen them across restaurants and I've met them on movie sets, where they carefully explain that they are retired and are acting as technical consultants. They make their living as criminals, and often the service they provide is that they will not hurt you if you pay them. These days there is a certain guarded nostalgia for their brand of organized crime, because at least the mob would make a deal with you for your life, and not just kill you casually, out of impatience or a need for drugs.

Martin Scorsese's *GoodFellas* is a movie based on the true story of a mid-level professional criminal named Henry Hill, whose only ambition, from childhood on, was to be a member of the outfit. We see him with his face at the window, looking across the street at the neighborhood mafioso, who drove the big cars and got the good-looking women and never had to worry about the cops when they decided to hold a party late at night. One day the kid goes across the street and volunteers to help out, and before long he's selling stolen cigarettes at a factory gate and not long after that the doorman at the Copacabana knows his name.

For many years, it was not a bad life. The rewards were great. The only thing you could complain about was the work. There is a strange, confused evening in Hill's life when some kidding around in a bar leads to a murder, and the guy who gets killed is a "made man"—a man you do not touch lightly, because he has the mob behind him—and the body needs to be hidden quickly, and then later it needs to be moved, messily. This kind of work is bothersome. It fills the soul with guilt and the heart with dread, and before long Henry Hill is walking around as if there's a lead weight in his stomach.

But the movie takes its time to get to that point, and I have never seen a crime movie that seems so sure of its subject matter. There must have been a lot of retired technical consultants hanging around. Henry Hill, who is now an anonymous refugee within the federal government's witness protection program, told this life story to the journalist Nicholas Pileggi, who put it into the best seller *Wiseguy,* and now Pileggi and Scorsese have written the screenplay, which also benefits from Scorsese's first-hand observations of the Mafia while he was a kid in Little Italy with his face in the window, watching the guys across the street.

Scorsese is in love with the details of his story, including the Mafia don who never, ever talked on the telephone, and held all of his business meetings in the open air. Or the way some guys with a body in the car trunk stop by to borrow a carving knife from one of their mothers, who feeds them pasta and believes them when they explain that they got blood on their suits when their car hit a deer. Everything in this movie reverberates with familiarity; the actors even inhabit the scenes as if nobody had to explain anything to them.

GoodFellas is an epic on the scale of *The Godfather,* and it uses its expansive running time to develop a real feeling for the way a lifetime develops almost by chance at first, and then sets its fateful course. Because we see mostly through the eyes of Henry Hill (Ray Liotta), characters swim in and out of focus; the character of Jimmy Conway (Robert De Niro), for example, is shadowy in the earlier passages of the film, and then takes on a central importance. And then there's Tommy DeVito (Joe Pesci), always on the outside looking in, glorying in his fleeting moments of power, laughing too loudly, slapping backs with too much familiarity, pursued by the demon of a raging anger that can flash out of control in a second. His final scene in this movie is one of the greatest moments of sudden realization I have ever seen; the development, the buildup and the payoff are handled by Scorsese with the skill of a great tragedian.

GoodFellas isn't a mythmaking movie, like *The Godfather.* It's about ordinary people who get trapped inside the hermetic world of the mob, whose values get worn away because they never meet anyone to disagree with them. One of the most interesting characters in the movie is Henry Hills's wife, Karen (Lorraine Bracco), who is Jewish and comes from outside his world. He's an outsider himself—he's half Irish, half Italian, and so will never truly be allowed on the inside—but she's so far outside that at first she doesn't even realize what she's in for. She doesn't even seem to know what Henry does for a living, and when she finds out, she doesn't want to deal with it. She is the conarrator of the film, as if it were a documentary, and she talks about how she never goes anywhere or does anything except in the company of other mob wives. Finally she gets to the point where she's proud of her husband for being willing to go out and steal to support his family, instead of just sitting around like a lot of guys.

The parabola of *GoodFellas* is from the era of "good crimes" like stealing cigarettes and booze and running prostitution and making book, to bad crimes involving dope. *The Godfather* in the movie (Paul Sorvino) warns Henry Hill about getting involved with dope, but it's not because he disapproves of narcotics (like Brando's Don Corleone); it's because he seems to sense that dope will spell trouble for the mob, will unleash street anarchy and bring in an undisciplined element. What eventually happens is that Hill makes a lot of money with cocaine but gets hooked on it as well, and eventually spirals down into the exhausted paranoia that proves to be his undoing.

Throbbing beneath the surface of *GoodFellas,* providing the magnet that pulls the plot along, are the great emotions in Hill's makeup: a lust for recognition, and a fear of powerlessness and guilt. He loves it when the headwaiters know his name, but he doesn't really have the stuff to be a great villain—he isn't brave or heartless enough—and so when he does bad things, he feels bad afterward. He begins to hate himself. And yet he cannot hate the things he covets. He wants the prizes, but he doesn't want to pay for the tickets.

And it is there, on the crux of that paradox, that the movie becomes Scorsese's metaphor for so many modern lives. He doesn't parallel the mob with corporations, or turn it into some kind of grotesque underworld version of yuppie culture. Nothing is that simple. He simply uses organized crime as an arena for a story about a man who likes material things so much that he sells his own soul to buy them—compromises his principles, betrays his friends, abandons his family, and finally even loses contact with himself. And the horror of the film is that, at the end, the man's principal regret is that he doesn't have any more soul to sell.

JFK

DECEMBER 20, 1991

1991 Oliver Stone's *JFK* builds up an overwhelming head of urgency that all comes rushing out at the end of the film, in a tumbling, angry, almost piteous monologue—the whole obsessive weight of Jim Garrison's conviction that there was a conspiracy to assassinate John F. Kennedy. With the words come images, faces, names, snatches of dialogue, flashbacks to the evidence, all marshaled to support his conclusion that the murder of JFK was not the work of one man.

Well, do you know anyone who believes Lee Harvey Oswald acted all by himself in killing Kennedy? I don't. I've been reading the books and articles for the last twenty-five years, and I've not found a single convincing defense of the Warren Commission report, which arrived at that reassuring conclusion. It's impossible to believe the Warren report because the physical evidence makes its key conclusion impossible: one man with one rifle could not physically have caused what happened on November 22, 1963, in Dallas. If one man could not have, then there must have been two. Therefore, there was a conspiracy.

Oliver Stone's new movie *JFK* has been attacked, in the weeks before its release, by those who believe Stone has backed the wrong horse in the Kennedy assassination sweepstakes—by those who believe the hero of this film, former New Orleans state's attorney Jim Garrison, was a loose cannon who attracted crackpot conspiracy theories the way a dog draws fleas.

The important point to make about *JFK* is that Stone does not subscribe to all of Garrison's theories, and indeed rewrites history to supply his Garrison character with material he could not have possessed at the time of these events. He uses Garrison as the symbolic center of his film because Garrison, in all the United States in all the years since 1963, is the only man who has attempted to bring anyone into court in connection with the fishiest political murder of our time.

Stone's film is truly hypnotically watchable. Leaving aside all of its drama and emotion, it is a masterpiece of film assembly. The writing, the editing, the music, the photography, are all used here in a film of enormous complexity to weave a persuasive tapestry out of an overwhelming mountain of evidence and testimony. Film students will examine this film in wonder in the years to come, astonished at how much information it contains, how many characters, how many interlocking flashbacks, what skillful interweaving of documentary and fictional footage. The film hurtles for 188 minutes through a sea of information and conjecture, and never falters and never confuses us.

That is not to say that we are quite sure, when it is over and we try to reconstruct the experience in our minds, exactly what Stone's final conclusions are. *JFK* does not unmask the secrets of the Kennedy assassination. Instead, it uses the Garrison character as a seeker for truth who finds that the murder could not have happened according to the official version. Could not. Those faded and trembling images we are all so familiar with, the home movie Abraham Zapruder took of the shooting of Kennedy, have made it forever clear that the Oswald theory is impossible—and that at least one of the shots *must* have come from in front of Kennedy, not from the Texas Schoolbook Depository behind him.

Look at me, italicizing the word *must*. The film stirs up that kind of urgency and anger. The CIA and FBI reports on the Kennedy assassination are sealed until after most of us will be long dead, and for what reason? Why can't we read the information our government gathered for us on the death of our president? If Garrison's investigation was so pitiful—and indeed it was flawed, underfunded, and sabotaged—then where are the better investigations by Stone's attackers? A U.S. Senate select committee found in 1979 that Kennedy's assassination was probably a conspiracy. Why, twelve years later, has the case not been reopened?

Stone's film shows, through documentary footage and reconstruction, most of the key elements of those 1963 events. The shooting. The flight of *Air Force One* to Washington. Jack Ruby's murder of Oswald. And it shows Garrison, in New Orleans, watching the same TV reports we watched, and then stumbling, hesitantly at first, into a morass of evidence suggesting that various fringe groups in New Orleans, pro and anti-Castro, may have somehow been mixed up with the CIA and various self-appointed soldiers of fortune in a conspiracy to kill JFK.

His investigation leads him to Clay Shaw, respected businessman, who is linked by various witnesses with Lee Harvey Oswald and other possible conspirators. Some of those witnesses die suspiciously. Eventually Garrison is able to bring Shaw to trial, and although he loses his case, there is the conviction that he was onto something. He feels Shaw perjured himself, and in 1979, five years after Shaw's death and ten years after the trial, Richard Helms of the CIA admits that Shaw, despite his sworn denials, was indeed an employee of the CIA.

Most people today, I imagine, think of Garrison as an irresponsible, publicity-seeking hothead who destroyed the reputation of an innocent man. Few know Shaw perjured himself. Was Garrison the target of the same kind of paid misinformation floated in defense of Michael Milken? A good PR campaign can do a better job of destroying a reputation than any Louisiana DA. Stone certainly gives Garrison a greater measure of credibility than he has had for years, but the point is not whether Garrison's theories are right or wrong—what the film supports is simply his seeking for a greater truth.

As Garrison, Kevin Costner gives a measured yet passionate performance. "You're as stubborn as a mule," one of his investigators shouts at him. Like a man who has hold of an idea he cannot let go, he forges ahead, insisting that there is more to the assassination than meets the eye. Stone has surrounded him with an astonishing cast, able to give us the uncanny impression that we are seeing historical figures. There is Joe Pesci, squirming and hyperkinetic as David Ferrie, the alleged getaway pilot. Tommy Lee Jones as Clay Shaw, hiding behind an impenetrable wall of bemusement. Gary Oldman as Lee Harvey Oswald. Donald Sutherland as X (actually Fletcher Prouty), the high-placed Pentagon official who thinks he knows why JFK was killed. Sissy Spacek, in the somewhat thankless role of Garrison's wife, who fears for her family and marriage. And dozens of others, including Jack Lemmon, Ed Asner, Walter Matthau, and Kevin Bacon in small, key roles, their faces vaguely familiar behind the facades of their characters.

Stone and his editors, Joe Hutshing and Pietro Scalia, have somehow triumphed over the tumult of material here and made it work—made it grip and disturb us. The achievement of the film is not that it answers the mystery of the Kennedy assassination, because it does not, or even that it vindicates Garrison, who is seen here as a man often whistling in the dark. Its achievement is that it tries to marshal the anger which ever since 1963 has been gnawing away on some dark shelf of the national psyche. John F. Kennedy was murdered. Lee Harvey Oswald could not have acted alone. Who acted with him? Who knew?

Malcolm X

NOVEMBER 18, 1992

1992 Spike Lee's *Malcolm X* is one of the great screen biographies, celebrating the whole sweep of an American life that began in sorrow and bottomed out on the streets and in prison, before its hero reinvented himself. Watching the film, I understood more clearly how we do have the power to change our own lives, how fate doesn't deal all of the cards. The film is inspirational and educational—and it is also entertaining, as movies must be before they can be anything else.

Its hero was born Malcolm Little. His father was a minister who preached the beliefs of Marcus Garvey, the African American leader who taught that white America would never accept black people, and that their best hope lay in returning to Africa. Years later, Malcolm would also become a minister and teach a variation on this theme, but first he had to go through a series of identities and conversions and hard lessons of life.

His father was murdered, probably by the Klan, which had earlier burned down the family house. His mother was unable to support her children, and Malcolm was parceled out to a foster home. He was the brightest student in his classes, but was steered away from ambitious career choices by white teachers who told him that, as a Negro, he should look for something where he could "work with his hands." One of his early jobs was as a Pullman porter, and then, in Harlem, he became a numbers runner and small-time gangster.

During that stage of his life, in the late 1940s, he was known as "Detroit Red," and ran with a fast crowd including white women who joined him for sex and burglaries. Arrested and convicted, he was sentenced to prison; the movie quotes him that he got one year for the burglaries and seven years for associating with white women while committing them. Prison was the best thing that happened to Detroit Red, who fell into the orbit of the Black Muslim movement of Elijah Muhammad, and learned self-respect.

The movie then follows Malcolm as he sheds his last name—the legacy, the Muslims preached, of slave-owners—and becomes a fiery street-corner preacher who quickly rises until he is the most charismatic figure in the Black Muslims, teaching that whites are the devil and that blacks had to become independent and self-sufficient. But there was still another conversion ahead; during a pilgrimage to Mecca, he was embraced by Muslims of many colors, and returned to America convinced that there were good people of peace in all races. Not long after, in 1965, he was assassinated—probably by members of the Muslim sect he had broken with.

This is an extraordinary life, and Spike Lee has told it in an extraordinary film. Like *Gandhi,* the movie gains force as it moves along; the early scenes could come from the lives of many men, but the later scenes show a great original personality coming into focus. To understand the stages of Malcolm's life is to walk for a time in the steps of many African Americans, and to glimpse where the journey might lead.

Denzel Washington stands at the center of the film, in a performance of enormous breadth. He never seems to be trying for an effect, and yet he is always convincing; he seems as natural in an early scene, clowning through a railroad club car with ham sandwiches, as in a later one, holding audiences spellbound on street corners, in churches, on television, and at Harvard. He is as persuasive early in the film, wearing a zoot suit and prowling the nightclubs of Harlem, as later, disappearing into a throng of pilgrims to Mecca. Washington is a congenial, attractive actor, and so it is especially effective to see how he shows the anger in Malcolm, the unbending dogmatic side, especially in the early Muslim years.

Lee tells his story against an epic background of settings and supporting characters (the movie is a gallery of the memorable people in Malcolm's life). Working with cinematographer Ernest Dickerson, Lee paints the early Harlem scenes in warm, sensuous colors, and then uses cold, institutional lighting for the scenes in prison. In many of the key moments in Malcolm's life as a public figure, the color photography is intercut with a black-and-white, quasi-documentary style that suggests how Malcolm's public image was being shaped and fixed.

That image, at the time of his death, was of a man widely considered racist and dogmatic—a hate-monger, some said. It is revealing that even Martin Luther King, seen in documentary footage making a statement about Malcolm's death, hardly seems overcome with grief. The liberal orthodoxy of the mid-1960s taught that racism in America could be cured by legislation, that somehow the hopeful words in the folk songs would all come true. Malcolm doubted it would be that simple.

Yet he was not the monolithic ideologue of his public image, and one of the important achievements of Lee's film is the way he brings us along with Malcolm, so that anyone, black or white, will be able to understand the progression of his thinking. Lee's films always have an underlying fairness, an objectivity that is sometimes overlooked. A revealing scene in *Malcolm X* shows Malcolm on the campus of Columbia University, where a young white girl tells him her heart is in the right place, and she supports his struggle. "What can I do to help?" she asks. "Nothing," Malcolm says coldly, and walks on. His single word could have been the punch line for the scene, but Lee sees more deeply, and ends the scene with the hurt on the young woman's face. There will be a time, later in Malcolm's life, when he will have a different answer to her question.

Romantic relationships are not Lee's strongest suit, but he has a warm, important one in *Malcolm X*, between Malcolm and his wife, Betty (Angela Bassett), who reminds her future husband that even revolutionary leaders must occasionally pause to eat and sleep. Her sweetness and support help him to find the gentleness that got lost in Harlem and prison.

Al Freeman, Jr., is quietly amazing as Elijah Muhammad, looking and sounding like the man himself, and walking the screenplay's tightrope between his character's importance and his flaws. Albert Hall is also effective, as the tough Muslim leader who lectures Malcolm on his self-image, who leads him by the hand into self-awareness, and then later grows jealous of Malcolm's power within the movement. And there is a powerful two-part performance by Delroy Lindo, as West Indian Archie, the numbers czar who first impresses Malcolm with his power, and later moves him with his weakness.

Walking into *Malcolm X,* I expected an angrier film than Spike Lee has made. This film is not an assault but an explanation, and it is not exclusionary; it deliberately addresses all races in its audience. White people, going into the film, may expect to meet a Malcolm X who will attack them, but they will find a Malcolm X whose experiences and motives make him understandable and finally heroic. A reasonable viewer is likely to conclude that, having gone through similar experiences, he might also have arrived at the same place. Black viewers will not be surprised by Malcolm's experiences and the racism he lived through, but they may be surprised to find that he was less one-dimensional than his image, that he was capable of self-criticism and was developing his ideas right up until the day he died.

Spike Lee is not only one of the best filmmakers in America, but one of the most crucially important, because his films address the central subject of race. He doesn't use sentimentality or political cliches, but shows how his characters live, and why. Empathy has been in short supply in our nation recently. Our leaders are quick to congratulate us on our own feelings, slow to ask us to wonder how others feel. But maybe times are changing. Every Lee film is an exercise in empathy. He is not interested in congratulating the black people in his audience, or condemning the white ones. He puts human beings on the screen, and asks his audience to walk a little while in their shoes.

Schindler's List

1993 Oskar Schindler would have been an easier man to understand if he'd been a conventional hero, fighting for his beliefs. The fact that he was flawed—a drinker, a gambler, a womanizer, driven by greed and a lust for high living—makes his life an enigma. Here is a man who saw his chance at the beginning of World War II, and moved to Nazi-occupied Poland to open a factory and employ Jews at starvation wages. His goal was to become a millionaire. By the end of the war, he had risked his life and spent his fortune to save those Jews, and had defrauded the Nazis for months with a munitions factory that never produced a single usable shell.

Why did he change? What happened to turn him from a victimizer into a humanitarian? It is to the great credit of Steven Spielberg that his film *Schindler's List* does not even attempt to answer that question. Any possible answer would be too simple, an insult to the mystery of Schindler's life. The Holocaust was a vast, evil engine set whirling by racism and madness. Schindler outsmarted it, in his own little corner of the war, but he seems to have had no plan, to have improvised out of impulses that remained unclear even to himself. In this movie, the best he has ever made, Spielberg treats the fact of the Holocaust and the miracle of Schindler's feat without the easy formulas of fiction.

The movie is 184 minutes long, and like all great movies, it seems too short. It begins with Schindler (Liam Neeson), a tall, strong man with an intimidating physical presence. He dresses expensively and frequents nightclubs, buying caviar and champagne for Nazi officers and their girls, and he likes to get his picture taken with the top brass. He wears a Nazi party emblem proudly in his buttonhole. He has impeccable black market contacts, and is always able to find nylons, cigarettes, brandy: he is the right man to know. The authorities are happy to help him open a factory to build enameled cooking utensils which army kitchens can use. He is happy to hire Jews because their wages are lower, and Schindler will get richer that way.

Schindler's genius is in bribing, scheming, conning. He knows nothing about running a factory, and finds Itzhak Stern (Ben Kingsley), a Jewish accountant, to handle that side of things. Stern moves through the streets of Krakow, hiring Jews for Schindler. Because the factory is a protected war industry, a job there may be a guarantee of a longer life. The relationship between Schindler and Stern is developed by Spielberg with enormous subtlety. At the beginning of the war, Schindler wants only to make money, and at the end he wants only to save "his" Jews. We know that Stern understands this. But there is no moment when Schindler and Stern bluntly state what is happening, perhaps because to say certain things aloud could result in death.

This subtlety is Spielberg's strength all through the film. His screenplay, by Steven Zaillian, based on the novel by Thomas Keneally, isn't based on contrived melodrama. Instead, Spielberg relies on a series of incidents, seen clearly and without artificial manipulation, and by witnessing those incidents we understand what little can be known about Schindler and his scheme.

We also see the Holocaust in a vivid and terrible way. Spielberg gives us a Nazi prison camp commandant named Goeth (Ralph Fiennes), who is a study in the stupidity of evil. From the veranda of his "villa," overlooking the prison yard, he shoots Jews for target practice. (Schindler is able to talk him out of this custom with an appeal to his vanity so obvious it is almost an insult.)

Goeth is one of those weak hypocrites who upholds an ideal but makes himself an exception to it; he preaches the death of the Jews, and then chooses a pretty one named Helen Hirsch (Embeth Davidtz) to be his maid, and falls in love with her. He does not find it monstrous that her people are being exterminated, and she spared on his affectionate whim. He sees his personal needs as more important than right or wrong, life or death. Studying him, we realize that Nazism depended on people able to think like Jeffrey Dahmer.

Shooting in black and white on many of the actual locations of the events in the story (including Schindler's original factory and even the gates of Auschwitz), Spielberg shows Schindler dealing with the madness of the Nazi system. He bribes, he wheedles, he bluffs, he escapes discovery by the skin of his teeth. In the movie's most audacious sequence, when a trainload of his employees is mistakenly routed to Auschwitz, he walks into the death camp himself and brazenly talks the authorities out of their victims, snatching them from death and putting them back on the train to his factory.

What is most amazing about this film is how completely Spielberg serves his story. The movie is brilliantly acted, written, directed, and seen. Individual scenes are masterpieces of art direction, cinematography, special effects, crowd control. Yet Spielberg, the stylist whose films have often gloried in shots we are intended to notice and remember, disappears into his work. Neeson, Kingsley, and the other actors are devoid of acting flourishes. There is a single-mindedness to the enterprise that is awesome.

At the end of the film, there is a sequence of overwhelming emotional impact, involving the actual people who were saved by Schindler. We learn than "Schindler's Jews" and their descendants today number some 6,000, and that the Jewish population of Poland is 4,000. The obvious lesson would seem to be that Schindler did more than a whole nation to spare its Jews. That would be too simple. The film's message is that one man did *something,* while in the face of the Holocaust, others were paralyzed. Perhaps it took a Schindler, enigmatic and reckless, without a plan, heedless of risk, a con man, to do what he did. No rational man with a sensible plan would have gotten as far.

The French author Flaubert once wrote that he disliked *Uncle Tom's Cabin* because the author was constantly preaching against slavery. "Does one have to make observations about slavery?" he asked. "Depict it; that's enough." And then he added, "An author in his book must be like God in the universe, present everywhere and visible nowhere." That would describe Spielberg, the author of this film. He depicts the evil of the Holocaust, and he tells an incredible story of how it was robbed of some of its intended victims. He does so without the tricks of his trade, the directorial and dramatic contrivances that would inspire the usual melodramatic payoffs. Spielberg is not visible in this film. But his restraint and passion are present in every shot.

Hoop Dreams

OCTOBER 21, 1994

1994 A film like *Hoop Dreams* is what the movies are for. It takes us, shakes us, and makes us think in new ways about the world around us. It gives us the impression of having touched life itself.

Hoop Dreams is, on one level, a documentary about two black kids named William Gates and Arthur Agee, from Chicago's inner city, who are gifted basketball players and dream of someday starring in the NBA. On another level, it is about much larger subjects: About ambition, competition, race, and class in our society. About our value structures. And about the daily lives of people like the Agee and Gates families, who are usually invisible in the mass media, but have a determination and resiliency that is a cause for hope.

The movie spans six years in the lives of William and Arthur, starting when they are in the eighth grade, and continuing through the first year of college. It was intended originally to be a thirty-minute short, but as the filmmakers followed their two subjects, they realized this was a much larger, and longer, story. And so we are allowed to watch the subjects grow up during the movie, and this palpable sense of the passage of time is like walking for a time in their shoes.

They're spotted during playground games by a scout for St. Joseph's High School in suburban Westchester, a basketball powerhouse. Attending classes there will mean a long daily commute to a school with few other black faces, but there's never an instant when William or Arthur, or their families, doubt the wisdom of this opportunity: St. Joseph's, we hear time and again, is the school where another inner-city kid, Isiah Thomas, started his climb to NBA stardom.

One image from the film: Gates, who lives in the Cabrini Green project, and Agee, who lives on Chicago's South Side, get up before dawn on

184

cold winter days to begin their daily ninety-minute commute to West-chester. The street lights reflect off the hard winter ice, and we realize what a long road—what plain hard work—is involved in trying to get to the top of the professional sports pyramid. Other high school students may go to "career counselors," who steer them into likely professions. Arthur and William are working harder, perhaps, than anyone else in their school—for jobs which, we are told, they have only a .00005 percent chance of winning.

We know all about the dream. We watch Michael Jordan and Isiah Thomas and the others on television, and we understand why any kid with talent would hope to be out on the same courts someday. But *Hoop Dreams* is not simply about basketball. It is about the texture and reality of daily existence in a big American city. And as the film follows Agee and Gates through high school and into their first year of college, we understand all of the human dimensions behind the easy media images of life in the "ghetto."

We learn, for example, of how their extended families pull together to help give kids a chance. How if one family member is going through a period of trouble (Arthur's father is fighting a drug problem), others seem to rise to periods of strength. How if some family members are unemployed, or if the lights get turned off, there is also somehow an uncle with a big back yard, just right for a family celebration. We see how the strong black church structure provides support and encouragement—how it is rooted in reality, accepts people as they are, and believes in redemption.

And how some people never give up. Arthur's mother asks the film-makers, "Do you ever ask yourself how I get by on $268 a month and keep this house and feed these children? Do you ever ask yourself that question?" Yes, frankly, we do. But another question is how she finds such determination and hope that by the end of the film, miraculously, she has completed her education as a nursing assistant. *Hoop Dreams* contains more actual information about life as it is lived in poor black city neighborhoods than any other film I have ever seen. Because we see where William and Arthur come from, we understand how deeply they hope to transcend—to use their gifts to become pro athletes. We follow their steps along the path that will lead, they hope, from grade school to the NBA.

The people at St. Joseph's High School are not pleased with the way they appear in the film, and have filed suit, saying among other things that they were told the film would be a nonprofit project to be aired on PBS, not a commercial venture. The filmmakers respond that they, too, thought it would—that the amazing response which has found it a theatrical release is a surprise to them. The movie simply turned out to be a masterpiece, and its intended noncommercial slot was not big enough to hold it. The St. Joseph suit reveals understandable sensitivity, because not all of the St. Joseph people come out looking like heroes.

It is as clear as night and day that the only reason Arthur Agee and William Gates are offered scholarships to St. Joseph's in the first place is because they are gifted basketball players. They are hired as athletes as surely as if they were free agents in pro ball; suburban high schools do not often send scouts to the inner city to find future scientists or teachers.

Both sets of parents are required to pay a small part of the tuition costs. When William's family cannot pay, a member of the booster club pays for him—because he seems destined to be a high school all-American. Arthur at first does not seem as talented. And when he has to drop out of the school because his parents have both lost their jobs, there is no sponsor for him. Instead, there's a telling scene where the school refuses to release his transcripts until the parents have paid their share of his tuition.

The morality here is clear: St. Joseph's wanted Arthur, recruited him, and would have found tuition funds for him if he had played up to expectations. When he did not, the school held the boy's future as hostage for a debt his parents clearly would never have contracted if the school's recruiters had not come scouting grade school playgrounds for the boy. No wonder St. Joseph's feels uncomfortable. Its behavior seems like something out of Dickens. The name Scrooge comes to mind.

Gene Pingatore, the coach at St. Joseph's, is a party to the suit (which actually finds a way to plug the Isiah Thomas connection). He feels he's seen in an unattractive light. I thought he came across fairly well. Like all coaches, he believes athletics are a great deal more important than they really are, and there is a moment when he leaves a decision to Gates that Gates is clearly not well-prepared to make. But it isn't Pingatore, but the whole system, that is brought into question: what does it say about the values involved, when the pro sports machine reaches right down to eighth-grade playgrounds?

But the film is not only, or mostly, about such issues. It is about the ebb and flow of life over several years, as the careers of the two boys go through changes so amazing that, if this were fiction, we would say it was unbelievable. The filmmakers (Steve James, Frederick Marx, and Peter Gilbert) shot miles of film, 250 hours in all, and that means they were there for several of the dramatic turning points in the lives of the two young men. For both, there are reversals of fortune—life seems bleak, and then is redeemed by hope and even sometimes triumph. I was caught up in their destinies as I rarely am in a fiction thriller, because real life can be a cliff-hanger, too.

Many filmgoers are reluctant to see documentaries, for reasons I've never understood; the good ones are frequently more absorbing and entertaining than fiction. *Hoop Dreams,* however, is not only a documentary. It is also poetry and prose, muckraking and expose, journalism and polemic. It is one of the great moviegoing experiences of my lifetime.

Leaving Las Vegas

1995 Oh, this movie is so sad! It is sad not because of the tragic lives of its characters, but because of their goodness and their charity. What moves me the most in movies is not when something bad happens, but when characters act unselfishly. In *Leaving Las Vegas,* a man loses his family and begins to drink himself to death. He goes to Vegas, and there on the street he meets a prostitute, who takes him in and cares for him, and he calls her his angel. But he doesn't stop drinking.

The man's name is Ben (Nicolas Cage). The woman's name is Sera (Elisabeth Shue). You will not see two better performances this year. Midway in the film someone offers Ben the insight that his drinking is a way of killing himself. He smiles lopsidedly and offers a correction: "Killing myself is a way of drinking." At one point, after it is clear that Sera really cares for him, he tells her, "You can never, ever, ask me to stop drinking, do you understand?" She replies in a little voice: "I do, I really do." In a sense, it is a marriage vow.

The movie is not really about alcoholism. It is about great sad passion, of the sort celebrated in operas like *La Bohème.* It takes place in bars and dreary rented rooms and the kind of Vegas poverty that includes a parking space and the use of the pool. The practical details are not quite realistic—it would be hard to drink as much as Ben drinks and remain conscious, and it is unlikely an intelligent prostitute would allow him into her life. We brush those objections aside, because they have nothing to do with the real subject of this movie, which is that we must pity one another, and be gentle.

Ben was a movie executive. Something bad happened in his life, and his wife and son are gone. Is he divorced? Are they dead? It is never made clear. "I'm not sure if I lost my family because of my drinking, or if I'm drinking because I lost my family," he muses. The details would not help, because this is not a case history but a sad love song. Cage, a resourceful and daring actor, has never been better.

Consider an opening scene where Ben attempts to make jokey small talk with some former colleagues who have long since written him off as a lost cause. He desperately needs money because he needs a drink—"now, right now!" He is shaking. He may go into convulsions. Yet he manufactures desperately inane chatter, dropping famous names. Finally one of the former friends takes him aside, gives him some money, and says, "I think it would be best if you didn't contact me again." Minutes later, brought back to life by alcohol, he is trying to pick up a woman at a bar: "You smell good," he says. She catches a whiff of his breath: "You've been drinking all day."

What could possibly attract Sera, the prostitute, to this wounded man? We learn a little about her, in close-ups where she talks about her life to an invisible therapist. She is proud of the way she controls her clients and sets the scenarios. She is adamant that none of them is ever really allowed to know her. She has an abusive relationship with a pimp (Julian Sands), and we can guess that she probably also had an abusive father; it usually works out that way. The pimp is soon out of the picture, and *Leaving Las Vegas* becomes simply the story of two people. Perhaps she likes Ben because he is so desperate and honest. She takes him in as she might take in a wet puppy.

It is unclear to what extent he fully understands his circumstances. At times he hallucinates. He calls her his "angel" fancifully, but there are moments when she literally seems to be an angel. He hears voices behind the walls. He shakes uncontrollably. He asks her, "How did our evening go?" There is a curious, effective scene in which he tries to get a check cashed, and his hands shake too much to sign his name. He goes off to drink himself into steadiness, and then it seems he returns and makes obscene suggestions to the teller, but they all take place in his head.

Mike Figgis, who wrote, directed, and composed the music, is a filmmaker attracted to the far shores of behavior. Here he began with a novel by a man named John O'Brien, whose autobiographical sources can be guessed by the information that he killed himself two weeks after selling the book rights. To be sure this project wasn't compromised, Figgis shot it as an independent film, using Super 16 cameras to grab Las Vegas locations. The outdoor scenes feel unrehearsed and real.

The movie works as a love story, but really romance is not the point here, any more than sex is. The story is about two wounded, desperate, marginal people, and how they create for each other a measure of grace. One scene after another finds the right note. If there are two unplayable roles in the stock repertory, they are the drunk and the whore with a heart of gold. Cage and Shue make these two cliches into unforgettable people. Cage's drunkenness is inspired in part by a performance he studied, Albert Finney's alcoholic consul in *Under the Volcano*. You sense an observant intelligence peering out from inside the drunken man and seeing everything, clearly and sadly.

Shue's prostitute is however the crucial role, because Sera is the one with a choice. She sees Ben clearly, and decides to stick with him for the rest of the ride. When he lets her down badly, toward the end of the movie, she goes out and does something that no hooker should do—gets herself into a motel room with a crowd of drunken college boys—and we see how she needed Ben because she desperately needed to do something good for somebody. He was her redemption, and when it seems he scorns her gift, she punishes herself.

Leaving Las Vegas is one of the best films of the year, deserving of many Academy Award nominations. That such a film gets made is a miracle: one can see how this material could have been softened and compromised, and how that would have been wrong. It is a pure, grand gesture. That he is an alcoholic and she works the streets are simply the turnings they have taken. Beneath their occupations are their souls. And because Ben has essentially given up on his, the film becomes Sera's story, about how even in the face of certain defeat we can, at least, insist on loving, and trying.

Hookers often give themselves street names. Sera's makes me think of "Que Sera, Sera"—what will be, will be.

Fargo

1996 *Fargo* begins with an absolutely dead-on familiarity with small-town life in the frigid winter landscape of Minnesota and North Dakota. Then it rotates its story through satire, comedy, suspense, and violence, until it emerges as one of the best films I've seen. To watch it is to experience steadily mounting delight, as you realize the filmmakers have taken enormous risks, gotten away with them, and made a movie that is completely original, and as familiar as an old shoe—or a rubber-soled hunting boot from L.L. Bean, more likely.

The film is "based on a true story" that took place in Minnesota in 1987.* It has been filmed on location, there and in North Dakota, by the Coen brothers, Ethan and Joel, who grew up in St. Louis Park, a suburb of Minneapolis, and went on to make good movies like *Blood Simple, Miller's Crossing,* and *Barton Fink,* but never before a film as wonderful as this one, shot in their own backyard.

To describe the plot is to risk spoiling its surprises. I will tread carefully. A car salesman named Jerry Lundegaard (William H. Macy) desperately needs money for a business deal—a parking lot scheme that can save him from bankruptcy. He is under the thumb of his rich father-in-law (Harve Presnell), who owns the car agency, and treats him like a loser. Jerry hires a couple of scrawny lowlifes named Showalter and Grimsrud (Steve Buscemi and Peter Stormare) to kidnap his wife (Kristin Rudrüd), and promises to split an $80,000 ransom with them. Simple enough, except that everything goes wrong in completely unanticipated ways, as the plot twists and turns and makes a mockery of all of Jerry's best thinking.

Showalter is nervous, sweaty, talkative, mousy. Grimsrud is a sullen

---

*The Coen Brothers later explained that the story was completely fictional, and that the use of the opening line about it being based on a true story was a "stylistic device."

slug of few words. During the course of the kidnaping, he unexpectedly kills some people ("Oh, Daddy!" says Showalter, terrified). The bodies are found the next morning, frozen beside the highway, in the barren lands between Minneapolis and Brainerd , North Dakota, which is, as we are reminded every time we see the hulking statue outside town, the home of Paul Bunyan.

Brainerd's police chief is a pregnant woman named Marge Gunderson (Frances McDormand). She talks like one of the McKenzie Brothers, in a Canadian American Scandinavian accent that's strong on cheerful folksiness. Everybody in the movie talks like that, with lines like "You're dern tootin'." When she gets to the big city, she starts looking for a place with a good buffet. Marge Gunderson needs a jump to get her patrol car started in the morning. But she is a gifted cop, and soon after visiting the murder site, she reconstructs the crime—correctly. Eyewitnesses place two suspects in a brown Sierra. She traces it back to Jerry Lundegaard's lot. "I'm a police officer from up Brainerd," she tells him, "investigating some malfeasance."

Jerry, brilliantly played by Macy, is a man weighed down by the insoluble complexities of the situation he has fumbled himself into. He is so incompetent at crime that, when the kidnaping becomes unnecessary, he can't call off the kidnapers, because he doesn't know their phone number. He's being pestered with persistent calls from GMAC, inquiring about the illegible serial number on the paperwork for the same missing brown Sierra. He tries sending faxes in which the number is smudged. GMAC isn't fooled. Macy creates the unbearable agony of a man who needs to think fast, and whose brain is scrambled with fear, guilt, and the crazy illusion that he can somehow still pull this thing off.

Fargo is filled with dozens of small moments that make us nod with recognition. When the two low-rent hoods stop for the night at a truck stop, for example, they hire hookers. Cut to a shot of bored mercenary sex. Cut to the next shot: they're all sitting up in bed, watching the *Tonight Show* on TV. William H. Macy, who has played salesmen and con men before (he's a veteran of David Mamet's plays), finds just the right note in his scenes in the auto showroom. It's fascinating to watch him in action, trying to worm out of a lie involving an extra charge for rust-proofing.

Small roles seem bigger because they're so well written and observed.

Kristin Rudrüd has few scenes as Jerry's wife, but creates a character out of them, always chopping or stirring something furiously in the kitchen. Their teenage son, who excuses himself from the table to go to McDonald's, helps establish the milieu of the film with a bedroom that has a poster on its wall for the Accordion King. Marge, discussing a hypothetical killer who has littered the highway with bodies, observes matter-of-factly, "I doubt he's from Brainerd." Harve Presnell is a typical self-made million-aire in his insistence on delivering the ransom money himself: he earned it, and by God if anyone is going to hand it over, it'll be him. He wants his money's worth. And on the way to the violent and unexpected climax, Marge has a drink in her hotel buffet with an old high school chum who obviously still lusts after her, even though she's married and pregnant. He explains, in a statement filled with the wistfulness of the downsizable, "I'm working for Honeywell. If you're an engineer, you could do a lot worse."

Frances McDormand has a lock on an Academy Award nomination with this performance, which is true in every individual moment, and yet slyly, quietly, over the top in its cumulative effect. The screenplay is by Ethan and Joel Coen (Joel directed, Ethan produced), and although I have no doubt that events something like this really did take place in Minnesota in 1987, they have elevated reality into a human comedy—into the kind of movie that makes us hug ourselves with the way it pulls off one improb-able scene after another. Films like *Fargo* are why I love the movies.

Eve's Bayou

> Memory is a selection of images, some elusive,
> others printed indelibly on the brain. The summer
> I killed my father, I was 10 years old.

1997 With those opening words, *Eve's Bayou* coils back into the past, into the memories of a child who grew up in a family both gifted and flawed, and tried to find her own way to the truth. The words explain the method of the film. This will not be a simple-minded story that breathlessly races from A to B. It is a selection of memories, filtered through the eyes of a young girl who doesn't understand everything she sees—and filtered, too, through the eyes of her older sister, and through the eyes of an aunt who can foretell everyone's future except for her own.

As these images unfold, we are drawn into the same process Eve has gone through: we, too, are trying to understand what happened in that summer of 1962, when Eve's handsome, dashing father—a doctor and womanizer—took one chance too many. And we want to understand what happened late one night between the father and Eve's older sister, in a moment that was over before it began. We want to know because the film makes it perfectly possible that there is more than one explanation; *Eve's Bayou* studies the way that dangerous emotions can build up until something happens that no one is responsible for and that can never be taken back.

All of these moments unfold in a film of astonishing maturity and confidence; *Eve's Bayou,* one of the very best films of the year, is the debut of its writer and director, Kasi Lemmons. She sets her story in southern Gothic country, in the bayous and old Louisiana traditions that Tennessee

Williams might have been familiar with, but in tone and style she earns comparison with the family dramas of Ingmar Bergman. That Lemmons can make a film this good on the first try is like a rebuke to established filmmakers.

The story is told through the eyes of Eve Batiste, played with fierce truthfulness by Jurnee Smollett. Her family is descended from a slave, also named Eve, who saved her master's life and was rewarded with her freedom and with sixteen children. In 1962, the Batistes are the premiere family in their district, living in a big old mansion surrounded by rivers and swampland. Eve's father Louis (Samuel L. Jackson) is the local doctor. Her mother Roz (Lynn Whitfield) is "the most beautiful woman I ever have seen." Her sister Cisely (Meagan Good) is on the brink of adolescence, and the apple of her father's eye; Eve watches unhappily at a party, and afterward asks her father, "Daddy, why don't you ever dance with me?" Living with them is an aunt, Mozelle (Debbi Morgan), who has lost three husbands, "is not unfamiliar with the inside of a mental hospital," and has the gift of telling fortunes.

Dr. Batiste is often away from home on house calls—some of them legitimate, some excuses for his philandering. He is a weak but not a bad man, and not lacking in insight: "To a certain type of woman, I am a hero," he says. "I need to be a hero." On the night that her father did not dance with her, Eve steals away to a barn and falls asleep, only to awaken and see her father apparently making love with another man's wife. Eve tells Cisely, who says she was mistaken, and the doubt over this incident will echo later, on another night when much depends on whether Cisely was mistaken.

Lemmons surrounds her characters with a rich setting. There is a marketplace, dominated by the stalls of farmers and fisherman, and by the presence of a voodoo woman (Diahann Carroll) whose magic may or may not be real. Certainly Aunt Mozelle's gift is real; her prophecies have a terrifying accuracy, as when she tells a woman her missing son will be found in a Detroit hospital on Tuesday. But Mozelle cannot foresee her own life: "I looked at each of my husbands," she says, "and never saw a thing." All three died. So when a handsome painter (Vondie Curtis-Hall) comes into the neighborhood and Mozelle knows she has found true love at last, she is afraid to marry him, because it has been prophesied that any man who marries her will die.

The film has been photographed by Amy Vincent in shadows and rich textures, where even a sunny day contains dark undertones; surely she looked at the Bergman films photographed by Sven Nykvist in preparing her approach. There is a scene of pure magic as Mozelle tells Eve the story of the death of one of her husbands, who was shot by her lover; the woman and the girl stand before a mirror, regarding the scene from the past, and then Mozelle slips out of the shot and reappears in the past.

There is also great visual precision in the scenes involving the confused night when the doctor comes home drunk, and Cisely goes downstairs to comfort him. What happened? We get two accounts and we see two versions, and the film is far too complex and thoughtful to try to reduce the episode to a simple formula like sexual abuse; what happens lasts only a second, and is charged with many possibilities of misinterpretation, all of them prepared for by what has gone before.

Eve's Bayou resonates in the memory. It called me back for a second and third viewing. If it is not nominated for Academy Awards, then the Academy is not paying attention. For the viewer, it is a reminder that sometimes films can venture into the realms of poetry and dreams.

Dark City

FEBRUARY 27, 1998

1998 *Dark City* by Alex Proyas is a great visionary achievement, a film so original and exciting it stirred my imagination like Lang's *Metropolis* or Kubrick's *2001*. If it is true, as the German director Werner Herzog believes, that we live in an age starved of new images, then *Dark City* is a film to nourish us. Not a story so much as an experience, it is a triumph of art direction, set design, cinematography, special effects—and imagination.

Like *Blade Runner,* it imagines a city of the future. But while *Blade Runner* extended existing trends, *Dark City* leaps into the unknown. Its vast noir metropolis seems to exist in an alternate time line, with elements of our present and past combined with visions from a futuristic comic book. Like the first *Batman,* it presents a city of night and shadows, but it goes far beyond *Batman* in a richness of ominous, stylized sets, streets, skylines, and cityscapes. For once a movie city is the equal of any city we could imagine from a novel; this is the city *The Fifth Element* teased us with, without coming through.

The story combines science fiction with film noir—in more ways than we realize, and more surprising ways than I will reveal. Its villains, in their homburgs and flapping overcoats, look like a nightmare inspired by the thugs in *M,* but their pale faces would look more at home in *The Cabinet of Dr. Caligari*—and, frighteningly, one of them is a child. They are the Strangers, shape-changers from another solar system, and we are told they came to earth when their own world was dying. (They create, in the process, the first space vessel since *Star Wars* that is newly conceived—not a clone of that looming mechanical vision.)

They inhabit a city of rumbling elevated streamlined trains, dank flophouses, scurrying crowds, and store windows that owe something to Edward Hopper's *Nighthawks*. In this city lives John Murdoch (Rufus

Sewell), who awakens in a strange bathtub beneath a swinging ceiling lamp, to blood, fear, and guilt. The telephone rings; it is Dr. Schreber (Kiefer Sutherland), gasping out two or three words at a time, as if the need to speak is all that gives him breath. He warns Murdoch to flee, and indeed three Strangers are at the end of the corridor and coming for him.

The film will be the story of Murdoch's flight into the mean streets, and his gradual discovery of the nature of the city and the Strangers. Like many science fiction heroes, he has a memory shattered into pieces that do not fit. But he remembers the woman he loves, or loved—his wife Emma (Jennifer Connelly), who is a torch singer with sad eyes and wounded lips. And he remembers . . . Shell Beach? Where was that? He sees it on a billboard and old longings stir.

There is a detective after him, Inspector Bumstead (William Hurt). Murdoch is wanted in connection with the murders of six prostitutes. Did he kill them? Like the hero of Kafka's *The Trial,* he feels so paranoid he hardly knows. Rufus Sewell plays Murdoch like a man caught in a pinball machine, flipped into danger every time it looks like the game is over.

The story has familiar elements made new. Even the hard-boiled detective, his eyes shaded by the brim of his fedora, seems less like a figure from film noir than like a projection of an alien idea of noir. Proyas and his coscreenwriters, Lem Dobbs and David S. Goyer, use dream logic to pursue their hero through the mystery of his own life. Along the way, Murdoch discovers that he alone, among humans, has the power of the Strangers— an ability to use his mind in order to shape the physical universe. (This power is expressed in the film as a sort of transparent shimmering projection, aimed from Murdoch's forehead into the world, and as klutzy as that sounds, I found myself enjoying its very audacity: what else would mind power look like?)

Murdoch's problem is that he has no way of knowing if his memories are real, if his past actually happened, if the women he loves ever existed. Those who offer to help him cannot be trusted. Even his enemies may not be real. The movie teasingly explores the question that babies first ask in peek-a-boo: when I can't see you, are you there? It's through that game that we learn the difference between ourselves and others. But what if *we're* not there, either?

The movie is a glorious marriage of existential dread and slam-bang action. Toward the end, there is a thrilling apocalyptic battle that nearly destroys the city, and I scribbled in my notes, "For once, a sequence where the fire and explosions really work, and don't play just as effects." Proyas and his cinematographer, Dariusz Wolski, capture the kinetic energy of great comic books; their framing and foreshortening and tilt shots and distorting lenses shake the images and splash them on the screen, and it's not "action" but more like action painting.

Proyas was the director of *The Crow* (1994), the visually inspired film that was almost doomed when its star, Brandon Lee, was killed in an accident. I called that film "the best version of a comic book universe I've seen," but *Dark City* is miles beyond it. Proyas's background was in music videos, usually an ominous sign, but not here: his film shows the obsessive concentration on visual detail that's the hallmark of directors who make films that are short and expensive. There's such a wealth on the screen, such an overflowing of imagination and energy, of sets and effects. Often in f/x movies the camera doesn't feel free because it must remain within the confines of what has been created for it to see. Here we feel there's no limit.

Is the film for teenage boys and comic book fans? Not at all, although that's the marketing pitch. It's for anyone who still has a sense of wonder and a feeling for great visual style. This is a film containing ideas and true poignance, a story that has been all thought out and has surprises right up to the end. It's romantic and exhilarating. Watching it, I thought of the last dozen films I'd seen and realized they were all essentially about people standing around and talking to one another. *Dark City* has been created and imagined as a new visual *place* for us to inhabit. It adds treasure to our notions of what can be imagined.

Being John Malkovich

OCTOBER 29, 1999

1999 What an endlessly inventive movie this is! Charlie Kaufman, the writer of *Being John Malkovich,* supplies a stream of dazzling inventions, twists, and wicked paradoxes. And the director, Spike Jonze, doesn't pounce on each one like fresh prey, but unveils it slyly, as if there's more where that came from. Rare is the movie where the last half hour surprises you just as much as the first, and in ways you're not expecting. The movie has ideas enough for half a dozen films, but Jonze and his cast handle them so surely that we never feel hard-pressed; we're enchanted by one development after the next.

John Cusack stars as Craig, a street puppeteer. His puppets are dark and neurotic creatures, and the public doesn't much like them. Craig's wife, Lotte, runs a pet store, and their home is overrun with animal boarders, most of them deeply disturbed. Lotte is played by Cameron Diaz, one of the best-looking women in movies, who here looks so dowdy we hardly recognize her; Diaz has fun with her talent by taking it incognito to strange places and making it work for a living.

The puppeteer can't make ends meet in "today's wintry job climate." He answers a help-wanted ad and finds himself on floor 7½ of a building. This floor, and how it looks, and why it was built, would be inspiration enough for an entire film or a Monty Python sketch. It makes everything that happens on it funny in an additional way, on top of why it's funny in the first place.

The film is so rich, however, that the floor is merely the backdrop for more astonishments. Craig meets a coworker named Maxine (Catherine Keener) and lusts for her. She asks, "Are you married?" He says, "Yeah, but enough about me." They go out for a drink. He says, "I'm a puppeteer." She says, "Waiter? Check, please." Keener has this way of listening with her lips slightly parted, as if eager to interrupt by deconstructing what you just said and exposing you for the fool that you are.

Behind a filing cabinet on the 7½th floor, Craig finds a small doorway. He crawls through it, and is whisked through some kind of temporalspatial portal, ending up inside the brain of the actor John Malkovich. Here he stays for exactly fifteen minutes, before falling from the sky next to the New Jersey Turnpike.

Whoa! What an experience. Maxine pressures him to turn it into a business, charging people to spend their fifteen minutes inside Malkovich. The movie handles this not as a gimmick but as the opportunity for material that is somehow funny and serious, sad and satirical, weird and touching, all at once. Malkovich himself is part of the magic. He is not playing himself here, but a version of his public image—distant, quiet, droll, as if musing about things that happened long ago and were only mildly interesting at the time. It took some courage for him to take this role, but it would have taken more courage to turn it down. It's a plum.

Why are people so eager to enter his brain? For the novelty, above all. Spend a lifetime being yourself and it would be worth money to spend fifteen minutes being almost anybody else. At one point, there's a bit of a traffic jam. Lotte finds herself inside his mind while Maxine is seducing him. Lotte enjoys this experience, and decides she wants to become a lesbian, or a man. Whatever it takes. This is hard to explain, but trust me.

The movie just keeps getting better. I don't want to steal the surprises and punch lines. Even the Charlie Sheen cameo is inspired. At one point Malkovich enters himself through his own portal, which is kind of like being pulled down into the black hole of your own personality, and that trip results in one of the most peculiar single scenes I've ever seen in the movies. Orchestrating all this, Cusack's character stays cool; to enter another man's mind is of course the ultimate puppeteering experience.

Every once in a long, long while a movie comes along that is like no other. A movie that creates a new world for us, and uses it to produce wonderful things. *Forrest Gump* was a movie like that, and so in their different ways were *M*A*S*H, This Is Spinal Tap, After Hours, Babe,* and *There's Something about Mary.* What do such films have in common? Nothing. That's the point. Each one stakes out a completely new place and colonizes it with limitless imagination. Either *Being John Malkovich* gets nominated for best picture, or the members of the Academy need portals into their brains.

Almost Famous

2000 Oh, what a lovely film. I was almost hugging myself while I watched it. *Almost Famous* is funny and touching in so many different ways. It's the story of a fifteen-year-old kid, smart and terrifyingly earnest, who through luck and pluck gets assigned by *Rolling Stone* magazine to do a profile of a rising rock band. The magazine has no idea he's fifteen. Clutching his pencil and his notebook like talismans, phoning a veteran critic for advice, he plunges into the experience that will make and shape him. It's as if Huckleberry Finn came back to life in the 1970s and instead of taking a raft down the Mississippi got on the bus with the band.

The kid is named William Miller in the movie; he's played by Patrick Fugit as a boy shaped by the fierce values of his mother, who drives him to the concert that will change his life, and drops him off with the mantra, "Don't do drugs!" The character and the story are based on the life of Cameron Crowe, the film's writer-director, who indeed was a teenage *Rolling Stone* writer, and who knows how lucky he was. Crowe grew up to write and direct *Say Anything* (1989), one of the best movies ever made about teenagers; in this movie, he surpasses himself.

The movie is not just about William Miller. It's about the time, and the band, and the early 1970s, when idealism collided with commerce. The band he hooks up with is named Stillwater. He talks his way backstage in San Diego by knowing their names and hurling accurate compliments at them as they hurry into the arena. William wins the sympathy of Russell Hammond (Billy Crudup), the guitarist, who lets him in. Backstage, he meets his guide to this new world, a girl who says her name is Penny Lane (Kate Hudson). She is not a groupie, she explains indignantly, but a Band Aide. She is of course a groupie, but has so much theory about her role it's almost like sex for her is a philosophical exercise.

William's mom, Elaine (Frances McDormand) is a college professor who believes in vegetarianism, progressive politics, and the corrupting influence of rock music. Banning the rock albums of her older daughter, Anita (Zooey Deschanel), she holds up an album cover and asks her to look at the telltale signs in Simon and Garfunkel's eyes: "Pot!" Anita, who had just played the lyrics "I walked out to look for America," leaves to become a stewardess. William walks out too, in a way. He intends to be away from school for only a few days. But as Russell and the rest of Stillwater grow accustomed to his presence, he finds himself on the bus and driving far into the Southwest. Along the way, he observes the tension between Russell and Jeff Bebe (Jason Lee), the lead singer, who thinks Russell is getting more attention than his role definition deserves: "I'm the lead singer and you're the guitarist with mystique."

William has two guardian angels to watch over him. One is Penny Lane, who is almost as young as he is, but lies about her age. William loves her, or thinks he does, but she loves Russell, or says she does, and William admires Russell, too, and Russell maintains a reserve that makes it hard to know what he thinks. He has the scowl and the facial hair of a rock star, but is still only in his early twenties, and one of the best moments in the movie comes when William's mom lectures Russell over the phone about the dangers to her son: "Do I make myself clear?" "Yes, ma'am," he says, reverting to childhood.

William's other angel is the legendary rock critic Lester Bangs (Philip Seymour Hoffman), then the editor of *Creem:* "So you're the kid who's been sending me those articles from your school paper." He ignores the kid's age, trusts his talent, and shares his credo: "Be honest, and unmerciful." During moments of crisis on the road, William calls Lester for advice.

Lester Bangs was a real person, and so are Ben Fong-Torres and Jann Wenner of *Rolling Stone,* played by look-alike actors. The movie's sense of time and place is so acute it's possible to believe Stillwater was a real band. As William watches, the band gets a hit record, a hotshot producer tries to take over from the guy who's always managed them, they switch from a bus to an airplane, and there are ego wars, not least when a T-shirt photo places Russell in the foreground and has the other band members out of focus (there's a little *Spinal Tap* here).

Almost Famous is about the world of rock, but it's not a rock film, it's a coming-of-age film, about an idealistic kid who sees the real world, witnesses its cruelties and heartbreaks, and yet finds much room for hope. The Penny Lane character is written with particular delicacy, as she tries to justify her existence and explain her values (in a milieu that seems to have none). It breaks William's heart to see how the married Russell mistreats her. But Penny denies being hurt. Kate Hudson has one scene so well acted it takes her character to another level. William tells her, "He sold you to Humble Pie for 50 bucks and a case of beer." Watch the silence, the brave smile, the tear, and the precise spin she puts on the words, "What kind of beer?" It's not an easy laugh. It's a whole world of insight.

What thrums beneath *Almost Famous* is Cameron Crowe's gratitude. His William Miller is not an alienated bore, but a kid who had the good fortune to have a wonderful brother and great sister, to meet the right rock star in Russell (there would have been wrong ones), and to have the kind of love for Penny Lane that will arm him for the future and give him a deeper understanding of the mysteries of women. Looking at William—earnestly grasping his tape recorder, trying to get an interview, desperately going to Lester for advice, terrified as Ben Fong Torres rails about deadlines, crushed when it looks like his story will be rejected—we know we're looking at a kid who has the right stuff and will go far. Someday he might even direct a movie like *Almost Famous*.

Note: Why did they give an R rating to a movie perfect for teenagers?

Monster's Ball

FEBRUARY 1, 2002

(Limited release in late 2001 for Academy Award consideration; wide release in 2002)

2001 *Monster's Ball* is about a black woman and a white man who find, for a time anyway, solace in each other for their pain. But their pain remains separate and so do they; this is not a message movie about interracial relationships, but the specific story of two desperate people whose lives are shaken by violent deaths, and how in the days right after that they turn to one another because there is no place else to turn. The movie has the complexity of great fiction, and requires our empathy as we interpret the decisions that are made—especially at the end, when the movie avoids an obligatory scene that would have been conventional, and forces us to cut straight to the point.

Billy Bob Thornton and Halle Berry star as Hank and Leticia, in two performances that are so powerful because they observe the specific natures of these two characters, and avoid the pitfalls of racial cliches. What a shock to find these two characters freed from the conventions of political correctness, and allowed to be who they are: weak, flawed, needful, with good hearts tested by lifetimes of compromise. They live in a small Georgia town, circa 1990. She works the night shift in a diner, has a fat little son, has an ex-husband on Death Row. He works as a guard on Death Row, has a mean, racist father and a browbeaten son, and will be involved in her husband's execution. ("Monster's Ball" is an old English term for a condemned man's last night on earth.)

At first Hank and Leticia do not realize the connection they have through the condemned man. For another movie that would be enough plot. We can imagine the scenes of discovery and revelation. How this movie handles that disclosure is one of its great strengths; how both characters deal with it (or don't deal with it) internally, so that the movie blessedly proceeds according to exactly who they are, what they need, what they must do, and the choices open to them.

The screenplay by Milo Addica and Will Rokos is subtle and observant; one is reminded of short fiction by Andre Dubus, William Trevor, Eudora Welty, Raymond Carver. It specifically does not tell "their" story, but focuses on two separate lives. The characters are given equal weight, and have individual story arcs, which do not intersect but simply, inevitably, meet. There is an overlay of racism in the story; Hank's father Buck (Peter Boyle) is a hateful racist, and Hank mirrors his attitudes. But the movie is not about redemption, not about how Hank overcomes his attitudes, but about how they fall away from him like a dead skin because his other feelings are so much more urgent. The movie, then, is not about overcoming prejudice, but sidestepping it because it comes to seem monstrously irrelevant.

Hank is an abused son and an abusive father. His old man Buck, confined to a wheelchair and a stroller, still exercises an iron will over the family. All three generations live under his roof, and when Hank's son Sonny (Heath Ledger) opts out of the family sickness, Buck's judgment is cruel: "He was weak." We do not learn much about Leticia's parents, but she is a bad mother, alternately smothering her son Tyrell (Coronji Calhoun) with love, and screaming at him that he's a "fat little piggy." She drinks too much, has been served with an eviction notice, sees herself as a loser. She has no affection at all for Tyrell's father Lawrence (Puffy Combs), on Death Row, and makes it clear during a visitation that she is there strictly for her son. There is no side story to paint Lawrence as a victim; "I'm a bad man," he tells Tyrell. "You're the best of me."

Leticia is all messed up. She sustains a loss that derails her, and it happens, by coincidence, that Hank is there when he can perform a service. This makes them visible to one another. It is safe to say that no one else in the community is visible, in terms of human need, to either one. Hank's shy, slow courtship is so tentative it's like he's sleepwalking toward her. Her response is dictated by the fact that she has nowhere else to turn. They have a key conversation in which the bodies of both characters are tilted away from one another, as if fearful of being any closer. And notice another conversation, when she's been drinking, and she waves her hands, and one hand keeps falling on Hank's lap; she doesn't seem to notice and, here is the point, he doesn't seem willing to.

Their intimate scenes are ordinary and simple, a contrast to Hank's cold mercenary arrangement with a local hooker. The film's only flaw is the way Marc Forster allows his camera to linger on Halle Berry's half-clothed beauty; this story is not about sex appeal, and if the camera sees her that way we are pretty sure that Hank doesn't. What he sees, what she sees, is defined not by desire but by need.

Students of screenwriting should study the way the film handles the crucial passages at the end, when she discovers some drawings and understands their meaning. Here is where a lesser movie would have supplied an obligatory confrontation. Leticia never mentions the drawings to Hank. Why not? Because it is time to move on? Because she understands why he withheld information? Because she has no alternative? Because she senses that the drawings would not exist if the artist hated his subject? Because she is too tired and this is just one more nail on the cross? Because she forgives? What?

The movie cannot say. The characters have disappeared into the mysteries of the heart. *Monster's Ball* demonstrates that to explain all its mysteries, a movie would have to limit itself to mysteries that can be explained. As for myself, as Leticia rejoined Hank in the last shot of the movie, I was thinking about her as deeply and urgently as about any movie character I can remember.

Minority Report

JUNE 21, 2002

2002 At a time when movies think they have to choose between action and ideas, Steven Spielberg's *Minority Report* is a triumph—a film that works on our minds and our emotions. It is a thriller and a human story, a movie of ideas that's also a whodunit. Here is a master filmmaker at the top of his form, working with a star, Tom Cruise, who generates complex human feelings even while playing an action hero.

I complained earlier this summer of awkward joins between live action and CGI; I felt the action sequences in *Spider-Man* looked too cartoonish, and that *Star Wars Episode II,* by using computer effects to separate the human actors from the sets and CGI characters, felt disconnected and sterile. Now here is Spielberg using every trick in the book and matching them without seams, so that no matter how he's achieving his effects, the focus is always on the story and the characters.

The movie turns out to be eerily prescient, using the term "pre-crime" to describe stopping crimes before they happen; how could Spielberg have known the government would be using the same term this summer? In his film, inspired by but much expanded from a short story by Philip K. Dick, Tom Cruise is John Anderton, chief of the Department of Pre-Crime in the District of Columbia, where there has not been a murder in six years. Soon, it appears, there will be a murder—committed by Anderton himself.

The year is 2054. Futuristic skyscrapers coexist with the famous Washington monuments and houses from the nineteenth century. Anderton presides over an operation controlling three "Pre-Cogs," precognitive humans who drift in a flotation tank, their brain waves tapped by computers. They're able to pick up thoughts of premeditated murders and warn the cops, who swoop down and arrest the would-be perpetrators before the killings can take place.

Because this is Washington, any government operation that is high-profile and successful inspires jealousy. Anderton's superior, bureau director Burgess (Max von Sydow) takes pride in him, and shields him from bureaucrats like Danny Witwer (Colin Farrell), of the Justice Department. As the Pre-Crime strategy prepares to go national, Witwer seems to have doubts about its wisdom—or he is only jealous of its success?

Spielberg establishes these characters in a dazzling future world, created by art director Alex McDowell, that is so filled with details large and small that we stop trying to figure out everything and surrender with a sigh. Some of the details: a computer interface that floats in midair, manipulated by Cruise with the gestures of a symphony conductor; advertisements that crawl up the sides of walls and address you personally; cars that whisk around town on magnetic cushions; robotic "spiders" that can search a building in minutes by performing a retinal scan on everyone in it. *Blade Runner,* also inspired by a Dick story, shows a future world in decay; *Minority Report* offers a more optimistic preview.

The plot centers on a rare glitch in the visions of the Pre-Cogs. Although "the Pre-Cogs are never wrong," we're told, "sometimes . . . they disagree." The dissenting Pre-Cog is said to have filed a minority report, and in the case of Anderton the report is crucial, because otherwise he seems a certain candidate for arrest as a precriminal. Of course, if you could outsmart the Pre-Cog system, you would have committed the perfect crime . . .

Finding himself the hunted instead of the hunter, Anderton teams up with Agatha (Samantha Morton), one of the Pre-Cogs, who seemed to be trying to warn him of his danger. Because she floats in a fluid tank, Agatha's muscles are weakened (have Pre-Cogs any rights of their own?), and Anderton has to half-drag her as they flee from the Pre-Crime police. One virtuoso sequence shows her foreseeing the immediate future and advising Anderton about what to do to elude what the cops are going to do next. The choreography, timing, and wit of this sequence make it, all by itself, worth the price of admission.

But there are other stunning sequences. Consider a scene where the "spiders" search a rooming house, and Anderton tries to elude capture by immersing himself in a tub of ice water. This sequence begins with an overhead cross section of the apartment building and several of its inhabitants, and you would swear it had to be done with a computer, but no: this is an actual physical set, and the elegant camera moves were elaborately choreographed. It's typical of Spielberg that, having devised this astonishing sequence, he propels it for dramatic purposes and doesn't simply exploit it to show off his cleverness. And watch the exquisite timing as one of the spiders, on its way out, senses something and pauses in midstep.

Tom Cruise's Anderton is an example of how a star's power can be used to add more dimension to a character than the screenplay might supply. He compels us to worry about him, and even in implausible action sequences (like falls from dizzying heights) he distracts us by making us care about the logic of the chase, not the possibility of the stunt.

Samantha Morton's character (is "Agatha" a nod to Miss Christie?) has few words and seems exhausted and frightened most of the time, providing an eerie counterpoint for Anderton's man of action. There is poignance in her helplessness, and Spielberg shows it in a virtuoso two-shot, as she hangs over Anderton's shoulder while their eyes search desperately in opposite directions. This shot has genuine mystery. It has to do with the composition and lighting and timing and breathing, and like the entire movie it furthers the cold, frightening hostility of the world Anderton finds himself in. The cinematographer, Janusz Kaminski, who has worked with Spielberg before (not least on *Schindler's List*), is able to get an effect that's powerful and yet bafflingly simple.

The plot I will avoid discussing in detail. It is as ingenious as any film noir screenplay, and plays fair better than some. It's told with such clarity that we're always sure what Spielberg wants us to think, suspect, and know. And although there is a surprise at the end, there is no cheating: the crime story holds water.

American movies are in a transition period. Some directors place their trust in technology. Spielberg, who is a master of technology, trusts only story and character, and then uses everything else as a workman uses his tools. He makes *Minority Report with* the new technology; other directors seem to be trying to make their movies *from* it. This film is such a virtuoso high-wire act, daring so much, achieving it with such grace and skill. *Minority Report* reminds us why we go to the movies in the first place.

Monster

JANUARY 1, 2004

(Limited release in late 2003 for Academy Award consideration; wide release in 2004)

2003 What Charlize Theron achieves in Patty Jenkins's *Monster* isn't a performance but an embodiment. With courage, art, and charity, she empathizes with Aileen Wuornos, a damaged woman who committed seven murders. She does not excuse the murders. She simply asks that we witness the woman's final desperate attempt to be a better person than her fate intended.

Wuornos received a lot of publicity during her arrest, trial, conviction, and 2002 execution for the Florida murders of seven men who picked her up as a prostitute (although one wanted to help her, not use her). The headlines, true as always to our compulsion to treat everything as a sporting event or an entry for the Guinness book, called her "America's first female serial killer." Her image on the news and in documentaries presented a large, beaten-down woman who did seem to be monstrous. Evidence against her was given by Selby Wall (Christina Ricci), an eighteen-year-old who became the older woman's naive lesbian lover and inspired Aileen's dream of earning enough money to set them up in a "normal" lifestyle. Robbing her clients led to murder, and each new murder seemed necessary to cover the tracks leading from the previous one.

I confess that I walked into the screening not knowing who the star was, and that I did not recognize Charlize Theron until I read her name in the closing credits. Not many others will have that surprise; she was just honored as best actress of the year by the National Society of Film Critics. I didn't recognize her—but more to the point, I hardly tried, because the performance is so focused and intense that it becomes a fact of life. Observe the way Theron controls her eyes in the film; there is not a flicker of inattention, as she urgently communicates what she is feeling and thinking. There's the uncanny sensation that Theron has forgotten the camera and the script and is directly channeling her ideas about Aileen Wuornos. She has made herself the instrument of this character.

I have already learned more than I wanted to about the techniques of disguise used by makeup artist Toni G. to transform an attractive twenty-eight-year-old into an ungainly street prostitute, snapping her cigarette butt into the night before stepping forward to talk with a faceless man who has found her in the shadows of a barren Florida highway. Watching the film, I had no sense of makeup technique; I was simply watching one of the most real people I had ever seen on the screen. Jenkins, the writer-director, has made the best film of the year. Movies like this are perfect when they get made, before they're ground down by analysis. There is a certain tone in the voices of some critics that I detest—that superior way of explaining technique in order to destroy it. They imply that because they can explain how Theron did it, she didn't do it. But she does it.

The movie opens with Aileen informing God that she is down to her last five dollars, and that if God doesn't guide her to spend it wisely she will end her life. She walks into what happens to be a lesbian bar and meets the eighteen-year-old Selby, who has been sent to live with Florida relatives and be "cured" of lesbianism. Aileen is adamant that she's had no lesbian experience, and indeed her sordid life as a bottom-rung sex worker has left her with no taste for sex at all. Selby's own sexuality functions essentially as a way to shock her parents and gratify her need to be desired. There is a stunning scene when the two women connect with raw sexual energy, but soon enough sex is unimportant compared to daydreaming, watching television, and enacting their private soap opera in cheap roadside motels.

Aileen is the protector and provider, proudly bringing home the bacon—and the keys to cars that Selby doesn't ask too many questions about. Does she know that Aileen has started to murder her clients? She does and doesn't. Aileen's murder spree becomes big news long before Selby focuses on it. The crimes themselves are triggered by Aileen's loathing for prostitution—by a lifetime's hatred for the way men have treated her since she was a child. She has only one male friend, a shattered Vietnam veteran and fellow drunk (Bruce Dern). Although she kills for the first time in self-defense, she is also lashing out against her past. Her experience of love with Selby brings revulsion uncoiling from her memories; men treat her in a cruel way and pay for their sins and those of all who went before them. The most heartbreaking scene is the death of a good man (Scott Wilson) who actually wants to help her, but has arrived so late in her life that the only way he can help is to be eliminated as a witness.

Aileen's body language is frightening and fascinating. She doesn't know how to occupy her body. Watch Theron as she goes through a repertory of little arm straightenings and body adjustments and head tosses and hair touchings, as she nervously tries to shake out her nervousness and look at ease. Observe her smoking technique; she handles her cigarettes with the self-conscious bravado of a thirteen-year-old trying to impress a kid. And note that there is only one moment in the movie where she seems relaxed and at peace with herself; you will know the scene, and it will explain itself. This is one of the greatest performances in the history of the cinema.

Christina Ricci finds the correct note for Selby Wall—so correct some critics have mistaken it for bad acting, when in fact it is sublime acting in its portrayal of a bad actor. She plays Selby as clueless, dim, in over her head, picking up cues from moment to moment, cobbling her behavior out of notions borrowed from bad movies, old songs, and barroom romances. Selby must have walked into a gay bar for the first time only a few weeks ago, and studied desperately to figure out how to present herself. Selby and Aileen are often trying to improvise the next line they think the other wants to hear.

We are told to hate the sin but not the sinner, and as I watched *Monster* I began to see it as an exercise in the theological virtue of charity. It refuses to objectify Wuornos and her crimes and refuses to exploit her story in the cynical manner of true crime sensationalism—insisting instead on seeing her as one of God's creatures worthy of our attention. She has been so cruelly twisted by life that she seems incapable of goodness, and yet when she feels love for the first time she is inspired to try to be a better person.

She is unequipped for this struggle, and lacks the gifts of intelligence and common sense. She is devoid of conventional moral standards. She is impulsive, reckless, angry, and violent, and she devastates her victims, their families, and herself. There are no excuses for what she does, but there are reasons, and the purpose of the movie is to make them visible. If life had given her anything at all to work with, we would feel no sympathy. But life has beaten her beyond redemption.

Million Dollar Baby

DECEMBER 15, 2004

2004 Clint Eastwood's *Million Dollar Baby* is a masterpiece, pure and simple, deep and true. It tells the story of an aging fight trainer and a hillbilly girl who thinks she can be a boxer. It is narrated by a former boxer who is the trainer's best friend. But it's not a boxing movie. It is a movie about a boxer. What else it is, all it is, how deep it goes, what emotional power it contains, I cannot suggest in this review, because I will not spoil the experience of following this story into the deepest secrets of life and death. This is the best film of the year.

Eastwood plays the trainer, Frankie, who runs a seedy gym in Los Angeles and reads poetry on the side. Hilary Swank plays Maggie, from southwest Missouri, who has been waitressing since she was thirteen and sees boxing as the one way she can escape waitressing for the rest of her life. Otherwise, she says, "I might as well go back home and buy a used trailer, and get a deep fryer and some Oreos." Morgan Freeman is Eddie, who Frankie managed into a title bout. Now he lives in a room at the gym and is Frankie's partner in conversations that have coiled down through the decades. When Frankie refuses to train a "girly," it's Eddie who persuades him to give Maggie a chance: "She grew up knowing one thing. She was trash."

These three characters are seen with a clarity and truth that is rare in the movies. Eastwood, who doesn't carry a spare ounce on his lean body, doesn't have any padding in his movie, either: even as the film approaches the deep emotion of its final scenes, he doesn't go for easy sentiment, but regards these people, level-eyed, as they do what they have to do.

Some directors lose focus as they grow older. Others gain it, learning how to tell a story that contains everything it needs and absolutely nothing else. *Million Dollar Baby* is Eastwood's twenty-fifth film as a director, and his best. Yes, *Mystic River* is a great film, but this one finds the simplic-

214

ity and directness of classical storytelling; it is the kind of movie where you sit very quietly in the theater and are drawn deeply into lives that you care very much about.

Morgan Freeman is the narrator, just as he was in *The Shawshank Redemption,* which this film resembles in the way the Freeman character describes a man who became his lifelong study. The voice is flat and factual: you never hear Eddie going for an effect or putting a spin on his words. He just wants to tell us what happened. He talks about how the girl walked into the gym, how she wouldn't leave, how Frankie finally agreed to train her, and what happened then. But Eddie is not merely an observer; the film gives him a life of his own when the others are offscreen. It is about all three of these people.

Hilary Swank is astonishing as Maggie. Every note is true. She reduces Maggie to a fierce intensity. Consider the scene where she and Eddie sit at a lunch counter, and Eddie tells the story of how he lost the sight in one eye, how Frankie blames himself for not throwing in the towel. It is an important scene for Freeman, but what I want you to observe is how Hilary Swank has Maggie do absolutely nothing but listen. No "reactions," no little nods, no body language except perfect stillness, deep attention, and an unwavering gaze.

There's another scene, at night driving in a car, after Frankie and Maggie have visited Maggie's family. The visit didn't go well. Maggie's mother is played by Margo Martindale as an ignorant and selfish monster. "I got nobody but you, Frankie," Maggie says. This is true, but do not make the mistake of thinking there is a romance between them. It's different and deeper than that. She tells Frankie a story involving her father, who she loved, and an old dog she loved, too.

Look at the way the cinematographer, Tom Stern, uses the light in this scene. Instead of using the usual "dashboard lights" that mysteriously seem to illuminate the whole front seat, watch how he has their faces slide in and out of shadow, how sometimes we can't see them at all, only hear them. Watch how the rhythm of this lighting matches the tone and pacing of the words, as if the visuals are caressing the conversation.

It is a dark picture overall. A lot of shadows, many scenes at night, characters who seem to be receding into their private fates. It is also a "boxing movie" in the sense that it follows Maggie's career, and there are several fight scenes. She wins right from the beginning, but that's not the point; *Million Dollar Baby* is about a woman who is determined to make something of herself, and a man who doesn't want to do anything for this woman, and will finally do everything.

The screenplay is by Paul Haggis, who has worked mostly on TV but with this work earns an Oscar nomination. Other nominations, and possibly Oscars, will go to Swank, Eastwood, Freeman, the picture, and many of the technicians—and possibly the original score composed by Eastwood, which always does what is required and never distracts. Haggis adapted the story from *Rope Burns: Stories from the Corner,* a 2000 book by Jerry Boyd, a seventy-year old fight manager who wrote it as "F. X. Toole." The dialogue is poetic but never fancy. "How much she weigh?" Maggie asks Frankie about the daughter he hasn't seen in years. "Trouble in my family comes by the pound." And when Frankie sees Eddie's feet on the desk: "Where are your shoes?" Eddie: "I'm airing out my feet." The foot conversation continues for almost a minute, showing the film's freedom from plot-driven dialogue, its patience in evoking character.

Eastwood is attentive to supporting characters, who make the surrounding world seem more real. The most unexpected is a Catholic priest who is seen, simply, as a good man; the movies all seem to put a negative spin on the clergy these days. Frankie goes to Mass every morning and says his prayers every night, and Father Horvak (Brian F. O'Byrne) observes that anyone who attends daily Mass for twenty-three years tends to be carrying a lot of guilt. Frankie turns to him for advice at a crucial point, and the priest doesn't respond with church orthodoxy but with a wise insight: "If you do this thing, you'll be lost, somewhere so deep you will never find yourself." Listen, too, when Haggis has Maggie use the word "frozen," which is what an uneducated backroads girl might say, but is also the single perfect word that expresses what a thousand could not.

Movies are so often made of effects and sensation these days. This one is made out of three people and how their actions grow out of who they are and why. Nothing else. But isn't that everything?

Crash

MAY 6, 2005

2005 *Crash* tells interlocking stories of whites, blacks, Latinos, Koreans, Iranians, cops and criminals, the rich and the poor, the powerful and powerless, all defined in one way or another by racism. All are victims of it, and all are guilty of it. Sometimes, yes, they rise above it, although it is never that simple. Their negative impulses may be instinctive, their positive impulses may be dangerous, and who knows what the other person is thinking?

The result is a movie of intense fascination; we understand quickly enough who the characters are and what their lives are like, but we have no idea how they will behave, because so much depends on accident. Most movies enact rituals; we know the form and watch for variations. *Crash* is a movie with free will, and anything can happen. Because we care about the characters, the movie is uncanny in its ability to rope us in and get us involved.

Crash was directed by Paul Haggis, whose screenplay for *Million Dollar Baby* led to Academy Awards. It connects stories based on coincidence, serendipity, and luck, as the lives of the characters crash against one another other like pinballs. The movie presumes that most people feel prejudice and resentment against members of other groups, and observes the consequences of those feelings.

One thing that happens, again and again, is that peoples' assumptions prevent them from seeing the actual person standing before them. An Iranian (Shaun Toub) is thought to be an Arab, although Iranians are Persian. Both the Iranian and the white wife of the district attorney (Sandra Bullock) believe a Mexican American locksmith (Michael Pena) is a gang member and a crook, but he is a family man.

A black cop (Don Cheadle) is having an affair with his Latina partner (Jennifer Esposito), but never gets it straight which country she's from. A cop (Matt Dillon) thinks a light-skinned black woman (Thandie Newton) is white. When a white producer tells a black TV director (Terrence Dashon Howard) that a black character "doesn't sound black enough," it never occurs to him that the director doesn't "sound black," either. For that matter, neither do two young black men (Larenz Tate and Ludacris), who dress and act like college students, but have a surprise for us.

You see how it goes. Along the way, these people say exactly what they are thinking, without the filters of political correctness. The district attorney's wife is so frightened by a street encounter that she has the locks changed, then assumes the locksmith will be back with his "homies" to attack them. The white cop can't get medical care for his dying father, and accuses a black woman at his HMO with taking advantage of preferential racial treatment. The Iranian can't understand what the locksmith is trying to tell him, freaks out, and buys a gun to protect himself. The gun dealer and the Iranian get into a shouting match.

I make this sound almost like episodic TV, but Haggis writes with such directness and such a good ear for everyday speech that the characters seem real and plausible after only a few words. His cast is uniformly strong; the actors sidestep cliches and make their characters particular.

For me, the strongest performance is by Matt Dillon, as the racist cop in anguish over his father. He makes an unnecessary traffic stop when he thinks he sees the black TV director and his light-skinned wife doing something they really shouldn't be doing at the same time they're driving. True enough, but he wouldn't have stopped a black couple or a white couple. He humiliates the woman with an invasive body search, while her husband is forced to stand by powerless, because the cops have the guns—Dillon, and also an unseasoned rookie (Ryan Phillippe), who hates what he's seeing but has to back up his partner.

That traffic stop shows Dillon's cop as vile and hateful. But later we see him trying to care for his sick father, and we understand why he explodes at the HMO worker (whose race is only an excuse for his anger). He victimizes others by exercising his power, and is impotent when it comes to helping his father. Then the plot turns ironically on itself, and both of the cops find themselves, in very different ways, saving the lives of the very same TV director and his wife. Is this just manipulative storytelling? It didn't feel that way to me, because it serves a deeper purpose than mere irony: Haggis is telling parables, in which the characters learn the lessons they have earned by their behavior.

Other cross-cutting Los Angeles stories come to mind, especially Lawrence Kasdan's more optimistic *Grand Canyon* and Robert Altman's more humanistic *Short Cuts*. But *Crash* finds a way of its own. It shows the way we all leap to conclusions based on race—yes, all of us, of all races, however fair-minded we may try to be—and we pay a price for that. If there is hope in the story, it comes because as the characters crash into one another, they learn things, mostly about themselves. Almost all of them are still alive at the end, and are better people because of what has happened to them. Not happier, not calmer, not even wiser, but better. Then there are those few who kill or get killed; racism has tragedy built in.

Not many films have the possibility of making their audiences better people. I don't expect *Crash* to work any miracles, but I believe anyone seeing it is likely to be moved to have a little more sympathy for people not like themselves. The movie contains hurt, coldness, and cruelty, but is it without hope? Not at all. Stand back and consider. All of these people, superficially so different, share the city and learn that they share similar fears and hopes. Until several hundred years ago, most people everywhere on earth never saw anybody who didn't look like them. They were not racist because, as far as they knew, there was only one race. You may have to look hard to see it, but *Crash* is a film about progress.

PART 3

Foreign Films

INTRODUCTION

This is not a collection of the best foreign films of the years covered, although they are without exception great films. It's more a selection of directors, countries, styles, and purposes. It's one of the sections that makes me grateful for the hard work of the book's editors; for me to choose from hundreds of titles would have been an agony.

Most of the reviews are exactly as written at the time, even if later I revisited them in a longer *Great Movies* essay. The purpose is to capture the immediate experience. In a few cases, such as *The Music Room* and *Au Hasard Balthazar,* a *Great Movies* piece was the first review I wrote. In the case of *Belle de Jour,* we have my review of a 1996 revival.

It is so poignant to be reminded of the 1970s in particular, when every year or two would see a new film by Luis Buñuel, Fellini, Bergman, Bertolucci, Herzog, Rainer

Werner Fassbinder, Godard, Satyajit Ray, Truffaut, Kurosawa, Eric Rohmer, Claude Chabrol, not to mention the Americans.

I am right now teaching a class on Fassbinder, who would have been sixty in the year 2005. When he died at thirty-eight, we lost all of those films. He directed ten in his first year as a filmmaker. What I appreciate now more than I did at the time is that despite his unceasing activity, his speed (a three-week shoot was typical), his alarming personal lifestyle, and his pose of alienation, he was along with everything else a painstaking stylist, a perfectionist whose visual strategies, often with Robby Müller behind the camera, are elegant and considered. On the DVD of *Ali: Fear Eats the Soul,* there is an introduction by Todd Haynes (who, like Fassbinder, was influenced by Douglas Sirk). Listen to his comments on "The Look," the way the film is about how people and groups define each other by how they regard each other, and how in the film Fassbinder observes this, and his camera regards them.

Tokyo Story

OCTOBER 16, 1972

Yasujiro Ozu's *Tokyo Story* tells a tale as simple and universal as life itself. It is about a few ordinary days in the lives of some ordinary people, and then about the unanticipated death of one of them. What it tells us about the nature of life or death is not new or original—what could be?—but it is true.

Ozu's story can be summarized in a few words. An old couple make the long train trip to Tokyo to visit their children. During their stay of a week or ten days, they are treated politely but with a certain distraction; life moves quickly in the big city, and there is not always time for the parents and their courtly provincial ways. On the train journey home, the mother falls ill. The children are summoned, and all but one are at the bedside when she dies.

There is great sadness, of course, and sympathy for the old father. But life must go on. The children were casually indifferent to their parents in life. Now that the mother is dead, they speak of their regrets that they didn't do more for her; but they also maneuver quietly for some of her possessions, and within a day after the funeral they have all returned to the city, leaving the father alone.

Of all the relatives, the one who is most considerate of the father is not even a blood relative: a daughter-in-law, the widow of a son who died, was the warmest toward the old couple when they were in Tokyo, and now she is the kindest to the old man. He tells her, after his wife's funeral, that she should remarry as soon as possible. "My son is dead," he says, "and it is not right for you not to marry." He says he would feel better if she forgot his son; he does not see any irony in this attitude, so soon after his wife's funeral, and perhaps there really isn't any.

Tokyo Story was made in 1953, or at about the same period that a group of great Japanese films was beginning to make a first impression on

Western audiences. The best known are *Rashomon, Ugetsu Monogatari,* and *Gate of Hell.* But *Tokyo Story* was not imported at that time, and its current national release represents a kind of posthumous tribute to Ozu.

It is clear that *Tokyo Story* was one of the unacknowledged masterpieces of the early-1950s Japanese cinema, and that Ozu has more than a little in common with that other great director, Kenji Mizoguchi (*Ugetsu*). Both of them use their cameras as largely impassive, honest observers. Both seem reluctant to manipulate the real time in which their scenes are acted; Ozu uses very restrained editing, and Mizoguchi often shoots scenes in unbroken takes.

This objectivity creates an interesting effect; because we are not being manipulated by devices of editing and camera movement, we do not at first have any very strong reaction to *Tokyo Story.* We miss the visual cues and shorthand used by Western directors to lead us by the nose. With Ozu, it's as if the characters are living their lives unaware that a movie is being shot. And so we get to know them gradually, begin to look for personal characteristics and to understand the implications of little gestures and quiet remarks.

Tokyo Story moves quite slowly by our Western standards, and requires more patience at first than some moviegoers may be willing to supply. Its effect is cumulative, however; the pace comes to seem perfectly suited to the material. And there are scenes that will be hard to forget: the mother and father separately thanking the daughter-in-law for her kindness; the father's laborious, drunken odyssey through a night of barroom nostalgia; and his reaction when he learns that his wife will probably die.

We speak so casually of film "classics" that it is a little moving to find one that has survived twenty years of neglect, only to win Western critical acclaim nine years after the director's death.

The Music Room

JANUARY 17, 1999
(Great Movies)

Satyajit Ray's *The Music Room* (1958) has one of the most evocative opening scenes ever filmed. A middle-aged man, his face set into deep weariness, sits on the wide, flat roof of his house in an upholstered chair that has been dragged outdoors for his convenience. He stares into space. His servant, his face betraying long alarm about his master, scurries toward him with a hookah, one of those ancient water pipes smoked by the Cheshire Cat in *Alice* and by the idle in Indian films. The man observes the preparations. "What month is it?" he finally asks.

This man is named Huzur Biswambhar Roy. He lives in a crumbling palace on the banks of a wide river, in the midst of an empty plain. It is the late 1920s. He is the last in a line of landlords who flourished in Bengal in the nineteenth century; the time for landlords has passed, and his money is running out. For years he has had little to do, and only one passion, listening to concerts in his music room.

He has been long jealous of his closest neighbor, the despised moneylender Mahim Ganguly. Mahim is low-caste and vulgar, but hardworking and ambitious. From time to time sounds carried on the air inform Huzur of Mahim's doings: far-off music, or the distant putt-putt of a generator reveal that he has even brought electricity into his home. He learns that Mahim has held a party. "Was I invited?" Huzur asks his servant. He was, he learns—and Mahim was much distressed that he did not attend. "Do I ever go anywhere?" "No."

After winning worldwide fame with the first two films of his Apu Trilogy, which were the first Indian titles to aspire to, and reach, the status of art, Satyajit Ray paused before finishing his trilogy about abject poverty to make this film about genteel poverty. Newly available on video at last in a high-quality print, it is the story of a man who has been compared to

King Lear because of his pride, stubbornness, and the way he loses every-thing that matters.

Almost every scene involves Huzur, played by Chhabi Biswas, an ac-tor who was such a favorite of Ray's that when he died in 1962, Ray said he simply stopped writing important middle-aged roles. In *The Music Room* Biswas plays a man so profoundly encased in his existence that few realities can interfere. With no income and a dwindling fortune, he is nevertheless called "lord" by the shifty Mahim, and although his enormous palace is neglected and only two servants remain, he carries on, oblivious.

His life centers on music. More precisely, on giving expensive con-certs to show off his music room, or *jalsaghar,* with its shimmering chan-delier, its ornamental carpet, and its portraits of Huzur and his ancestors. He lives to flaunt what remains of his wealth. After the opening sequence on the rooftop, much of the film is told in flashback to a time years earlier, and centers around two concerts given in the room.

The first is a coming-of-age "thread ceremony" in honor of his son, Khoka. Only the best musicians will suffice, and Huzur reclines on pil-lows, flanked by his male neighbors and relatives, as the musicians and a celebrated woman singer perform. A slow camera pans the faces of the lis-teners, pausing at the vulgar Mahim, who is restless, does not enjoy Indian classical music, and reaches for a drink.

The evening is a triumph, even though Huzur's wife, waiting impa-tiently upstairs, berates him for mortgaging her jewels to pay for it. He is asleep before she finishes. Not long after, his wife and son leave for a river journey to the house of her father, and in a touching scene she bows to him as they leave, and then reveals a modern note: "Behave yourself!"

But the despised Mahim comes to see him with an invitation for a concert of his own. Ray structures the scene as a confrontation between privilege and new wealth: Huzur composes himself on a sofa and appears to be so deeply engrossed in his reading that he hardly notices Mahim. Then he counters that he, himself, is planning a concert for that very same evening! In the background, the servant, who knows the condition of their finances, looks stunned.

The second concert has disturbing undercurrents. Even the singer, a bearded man with a stricken face, seems aware of approaching doom. Huzur has sent word that his wife and son must return for the event, but they have not yet arrived, and as the chandelier sways in the wind and lightning streaks through the sky, Huzur looks down and sees an insect drowning in his glass. It is an omen of great loss.

The third concert comes at the end of the long period of withdrawal. We are back in the present. The last of the jewels will be pawned. Huzur will go out in style. He impetuously outbids Mahim for the services of a famous, even scandalous, woman singer and dancer. At the end when Mahim commits the folly of attempting to tip the woman, the crook of Huzur's walking stick comes down firmly on his hand: it is for the lord to tip in his own house. Huzur hands the woman the last of his gold coins. The great closing sequence shows Huzur in the afterglow of this reckless grand gesture. Drunk, he toasts the portraits of his ancestors, until he sees a spider crawling up the leg of his own portrait. It is dawn. The loyal retainer pulls away the draperies to admit the cold light.

Satyajit Ray (1921–1992) was an unusually tall man, handsome as a movie star, the grandson of a landlord such as Huzur's ancestors. In Calcutta in the late 1940s he was a commercial artist for an ad agency, and founded a cinema club which bought its own print of *Potemkin* and imported films from around the world. He rejected the mass-produced Bengali films of the time as so much sub-Hollywood tripe, and with *Pather Panchali* (1955), the first of his famous Apu Trilogy, he won a top prize at Cannes and established himself as the preeminent Indian filmmaker in the eyes of the world.

At the New York Film Festival in 1970, he was asked why he was now moving his camera more than in the Apu Trilogy. "Because I can afford the equipment," he smiled. In his book *Our Films, Their Films,* he recalled that he had never shot a foot of film before the first day of filming *Pather Panchali.* When his cinematographer, Subrata Mitra, visited the Hawaii Film Festival a few years ago, he told me, "We started together. I had never exposed a single foot of film before that day."

Ray made many fine films. The Apu Trilogy and *The Music Room* rank highest, I think, but there are also *The Big City* (1963), about a woman who breaks with convention and goes to work when her husband is laid off; *Days and Nights in the Forest* (1970), about office workers who take a holiday of self-discovery; *Distant Thunder* (1973), about an Indian village hearing echoes of World War II; *The Chess Players* (1977), about British attempts to seize the land of a lord who can barely bring himself to notice them; and *Home and the World* (1984), based on the Rabindranath Tagore novel about a landowner who prides himself on his modern ideas, until his wife falls in love with his friend.

The Music Room is Ray's most evocative film, and he fills it with observant details. The insect in the glass, the bliss of an elephant being bathed in the river, the joy of the servants reopening the dusty music room, the way the chandelier reflects Huzur's states of mind, the way when the servant sprinkles the guests with scent he adds an extra contemptuous shake for Mahim.

Despite the faded luxury which surrounds Huzur, the film is not ornate in any way. Perhaps as a reaction to the hundreds of overwrought Indian musical melodramas churned out annually, Ray made an austere character study—also with music. His hero deserves the comparison with King Lear, because like Lear he arouses our sympathy even while indulging his vanity and stubbornly doing all of the wrong things. Like Lear, he thinks himself a man more sinned against than sinning. Like Lear, he is wrong.

Au Hasard Balthazar

MARCH 19, 2004
(Great Movies)

Robert Bresson is one of the saints of the cinema, and *Au Hasard Balthazar* (1966) is his most heartbreaking prayer. The film follows the life of a donkey from birth to death, while all the time giving it the dignity of being itself—a dumb beast, noble in its acceptance of a life over which it has no control. Balthazar is not one of those cartoon animals that can talk and sing and is a human with four legs. Balthazar is a donkey, and it is as simple as that.

We first see Balthazar as a newborn, taking its first unsteady steps, and there is a scene that provides a clue to the rest of the film; three children sprinkle water on its head and baptize it. What Bresson may be suggesting is that although the church teaches that only humans can enter into heaven, surely there is a place at God's side for all of his creatures.

Balthazar's early life is lived on a farm in the rural French district where all the action takes place; the donkey will be owned many of the locals, and return to some of them more than once. A few of them are good, but all of them are flawed, although there is a local drunk who is not cruel or thoughtless to the animal, despite his other crimes.

Balthazar's first owner is Marie (Anne Wiazemsky), who gives him his name. Her father is the local schoolmaster, and her playmate is Jacques (Walter Green), who agrees with her that they will marry someday. Jacques' mother dies, and his grief-stricken father leaves the district, entrusting his farm to Marie's father (Philippe Asselin), in whom he has perfect trust. Marie loves Balthazar, and delights in decorating his bridle with wild flowers, but she does nothing to protect him when local boys torment the beast. The leader of this gang is Gerard (François Lafarge), and when Marie glances up to the church choir during Mass as Gerard sings, he brings evil even to the holy words.

Marie's father is a victim of the sin of pride. Although he has managed the farm with perfect honesty, he refuses to produce records or receipts to prove himself, after rumors are spread by jealous neighbors that he is stealing from the owner. To the despair of Marie's mother (Nathalie Joyaut), he follows his stubbornness straight into bankruptcy. Balthazar becomes the possession of the local baker, and is used by the baker's boy (none other than Gerard) to deliver bread. Gerard mistreats and abuses Balthazar, who eventually simply refuses to move. Gerard responds by tying a newspaper to its tail and setting it on fire. Eventually under Gerald's mistreatment the donkey collapses and there is talk of putting it down.

But the town drunk, Arnold (Jean-Claude Guilbert), saves him and brings him back to life, and then there is Balthazar's brief moment of glory when he is hired out as a circus animal—the Mathematical Donkey, who can solve multiplication tables. This life is soon brought to an end, as Balthazar becomes the property of a recluse, and then finally wanders back on its own to the stable where it began its life, and where it finds Marie's father and even Marie.

But this is not a sentimental ending. Marie is a weak girl, who rejects the sincere Jacques when he returns as a young man to say he still loves her. She prefers Gerard, who mistreats her but seems glamorous with his leather jacket and motorbike. What we see through Balthazar's eyes is a village filled with small, flawed, weak people, in a world where sweetness is uncommon and cruelty comes easily.

That is what we see—but what does Balthazar see? The genius of Bresson's approach is that he never gives us a single moment that could be described as one of Balthazar's "reaction shots." Other movie animals may roll their eyes or stomp their hooves, but Balthazar simply walks or waits, regarding everything with the clarity of a donkey who knows it is a beast of burden, and that its life consists of either bearing or not bearing, of feeling pain or not feeling pain, or even feeling pleasure. All of these things are equally beyond its control.

There is however Balthazar's bray. It is not a beautiful sound, but it is the sound a donkey can make, and when Balthazar brays it might sound to some like a harsh complaint, but to me it sounds like a beast who has been given one noise to make in the world, and gains some satisfaction by making it. It is important to note that Balthazar never brays on cue to react to specific events; that would turn him into a cartoon animal.

Although the donkey has no way of revealing its thoughts, that doesn't prevent us from supplying them—quite the contrary; we regard that white-spotted furry face and those big eyes, and we feel sympathy with every experience the donkey undergoes. That is Bresson's civilizing and even spiritual purpose in most of his films; we must go to the characters, instead of passively letting them come to us. In the vast majority of movies, everything is done for the audience. We are cued to laugh or cry, be frightened or relieved; Hitchcock called the movies a machine for causing emotions in the audience.

Bresson (and Ozu) take a different approach. They regard, and they ask us to regard along with them, and to arrive at conclusions about their characters that are our own. This is the cinema of empathy. It is worth noting that both Ozu and Bresson use severe stylistic limitations to avoid coaching our emotions. Ozu in his sound films almost never moves his camera; every shot is framed and held, and frequently it begins before the characters enter the scene and continues after they leave.

Bresson's most intriguing limitation is to forbid his actors to act. He was known to shoot the same shot ten, twenty, even fifty times, until all "acting" was drained from it, and the actors were simply performing the physical actions and speaking the words. There was no room in his cinema for De Niro or Penn. It might seem that the result would be a movie filled with zombies, but quite the contrary: by simplifying performance to the action and the word without permitting inflection or style, Bresson achieves a kind of purity that makes his movies remarkably emotional. The actors portray lives without informing us how to feel about them; forced to decide for ourselves how to feel, forced to empathize, we often have stronger feelings than if the actors were feeling them for us.

Given this philosophy, a donkey becomes the perfect Bresson character. Balthazar makes no attempt to communicate its emotions to us, and it communicates its physical feelings only in universal terms: Covered with snow, it is cold. Its tail set afire, it is frightened. Eating its dinner, it is content. Overworked, it is exhausted. Returning home, it is relieved to find a familiar place. Although some humans are kind to it and others are cruel, the motives of humans are beyond its understanding, and it accepts what they do because it must.

Now here is the essential part. Bresson suggests that we are all Balthazars. Despite our dreams, hopes, and best plans, the world will eventually do with us whatever it does. Because we can think and reason, we believe we can figure a way out, find a solution, get the answer. But intelligence gives us the ability to comprehend our fate without the power to control it. Still, Bresson does not leave us empty-handed. He offers us the suggestion of empathy. If we will extend ourselves to sympathize with how others feel, we can find the consolation of sharing human experience, instead of the loneliness of enduring it alone.

The final scene of *Au Hasard Balthazar* makes that argument in a beautiful way. The donkey is old and near death, and wanders into a herd of sheep—as, indeed, it began its life in such a herd. The other animals come and go, sometimes nuzzling up against it, taking little notice, accepting this fellow animal, sharing the meadow and the sunshine. Balthazar lies down and eventually dies, as the sheep continue about their business. He has at last found a place where the other creatures think as he does.

Belle de Jour

1967

(This was a review of the 1996 theatrical revival.)

Here now is Luis Buñuel's *Belle de Jour,* a movie from 1967, to teach us a lesson about what is erotic in the cinema. We will begin with Catherine Deneuve's face, as she listens to a taxi driver describe a famous Parisian brothel—a place where bored women might work for an afternoon or two every week, to earn some extra money. Her face is completely impassive. The camera holds on it. The taxi driver continues his description. We understand that the Deneuve character is mesmerized by what she hears, and that sooner or later she will be compelled to visit that brothel and have the experience of being a "belle de jour."

We already know something about the character, whose name is Séverine. She is married to a rich, bland, young businessman (Jean Sorel). The marriage is comfortable but uneventful. An older friend (the saturnine Michel Piccoli) makes a bold attempt to seduce her, but she does not respond. "What interests me about you is your virtue," he says. Perhaps that is why she is not interested: she desires not a man who thinks she is virtuous, but one who thinks she is not.

Here she is in the street, approaching the luxurious apartment building where Madame Anais presides over the famous brothel. The camera focuses on her feet (Buñuel was famously obsessed with shoes). She pauses, turns away. Eventually she rings the bell and enters. Madame Anais (the elegant, realistic Geneviève Page) greets her, and asks her to wait for a time in her office. Again, Deneuve's face betrays no emotion. None at all. Eventually she learns the rules of the house, and after some thought, agrees to them. She is a belle de jour.

The film will contain no sweaty, steamy, athletic sex scenes. Hardly any nudity, and that discreet. What is sexual in this movie takes place entirely within the mind of Séverine. We have to guess at her feelings. All she ever says explicitly is, "I cannot help myself." Much happens offscreen. The most famous scene in *Belle de Jour*—indeed, one of the best-remembered scenes in movie history—is the one where a client presents her with an ornate little box. He shows her what is inside the box. During his hour with Séverine, he wants to employ it. She shakes her head, no. What is in the box? We never find out.

Consider that scene. In all the years that have passed since I first saw *Belle de Jour,* I have always wondered what was in the box. Suppose the movie had been dumbed down by modern Hollywood. We would have seen what was in the box. And Séverine would have shaken her head the same way, and we would have forgotten the scene in ten minutes.

What is erotic in *Belle de Jour* is suggested, implied, hinted at. We have to complete the link in our own imagination. When we watch the shower scene between Sharon Stone and Sylvester Stallone in *The Specialist,* or the "harassment" scene between Demi Moore and Michael Douglas in *Disclosure,* nothing is left to the imagination. We see every drop of sweat, we see glistening skin, hungry lips, grappling bodies. And we are outside. We are voyeurs, watching them up there on the screen, doing something we are not involved in. It is a technical demonstration.

But in *Belle de Jour,* we are invited into the secret world of Séverine. We have to complete her thoughts, and in that process they become our thoughts. The movie understands the hypnotic intensity with which humans consider their own fantasies. When Séverine enters a room where a client is waiting, her face doesn't reflect curiosity or fear or anticipation— and least of all lust—because she is not regarding the room, she is regarding herself. What turns her on is not what she finds in the room, but that she is entering it.

Luis Buñuel, one of a small handful of true masters of the cinema, had an insight into human nature that was cynical and detached; he looked with bemusement on his characters as they became the victims of their own lusts and greeds. He also had a sympathy with them, up to a point. He understands why Séverine is drawn to the brothel, but he doesn't stop there, with her adventures in the afternoon. He pushes on, to a bizarre conclusion in which she finally gets what she *really* wants.

I will not reveal the ending. But observe, as it is unfolding, a gunfight in the street. Buñuel does not linger over it; in fact, he films it in a perfunctory fashion, as if he was in a hurry to get it out of the way. The gunplay is necessary in order to explain the next stage of the movie's plot. It has no other function. Today's directors, more fascinated by style than story, would have lingered over the gunfight—would have built it up into a big production number, to supply the film with an action climax that would have been entirely wrong. Not Buñuel.

The Wild Child

OCTOBER 16, 1970

François Truffaut's *The Wild Child* is the story of a "wolf boy" who lived like an animal in the woods, and about the doctor who adopted him and tried to civilize him. The story is essentially true, drawn from an actual case in eighteenth-century France, and Truffaut tells it simply and movingly. It becomes his most thoughtful statement on his favorite subject: the way young people grow up, explore themselves, and attempt to function creatively in the world.

This process was the subject of Truffaut's first film, *The 400 Blows,* and he returned to the same autobiographical ground with his recent *Stolen Kisses*. Now, again using Jean-Pierre Léaud as the actor, he's at work on the third film in the trilogy. In this one, reportedly, the autobiographical character survives adolescence and enters bravely into manhood.

That is a happy ending forever out of the reach of the Wild Child, who has been so traumatically affected by his forest life that he can hardly comprehend the idea of language. There's even a question, at first, as to whether he can hear. He can, but makes little connection between the sounds of words and their meanings. The doctor makes slow progress, or none, for months at a time. Then perhaps there's a small breakthrough. He records it all in his journal, and Truffaut's spoken English narration from the journal carries most of the ideas in the film.

The Wild Child is about education at its most fundamental level, about education as the process by which society takes millions of literally savage infants every year, and gradually seduces them into sharing the conventions of everybody else. There's a question, of course, as to whether "civilization" is good for man, or if he'd be happier in a natural state.

That question is at the root of *The Wild Child*. Since the boy can never function "normally" in society, should he have been left in the woods? It's a question for us, in this uncertain age; but not for the doctor, who shares the rational optimism of Jefferson and never seriously questions the worth of his efforts. He believes in the nobility of man, and detests the idea of a human being scavenging for survival in the forest.

Truffaut places his personal touch on every frame of the film. He wrote it, directed it, and plays the doctor himself. It is an understated, compassionate performance, a perfect counterpoint to Jean-Pierre Cargol's ferocity and fear. The day-to-day record of the doctor's attempts to teach the boy to walk upright, to dress himself, to eat properly, to recognize sounds and symbols, is endlessly fascinating. So often movies keep our attention by flashy tricks and cheap melodrama; it is an intellectually cleansing experience to watch this intelligent and hopeful film.

Note: Because Truffaut's narration is in English and the boy speaks hardly at all, there are very few subtitles to be read and the movie is completely accessible even to, say, third- or fourth-graders. I imagine most children would find it completely fascinating.

Claire's Knee

Now if I were to say, for example, that *Claire's Knee* is about Jerome's desire to caress the knee of Claire, you would be about a million miles from the heart of this extraordinary film. And yet, in a way, *Claire's Knee* is indeed about Jerome's feelings for Claire's knee, which is a splendid knee. Jerome encounters Claire and the other characters in the film during a month's holiday he takes on a lake between France and Switzerland. He has gone there to rest and reflect before he marries Lucinda, a woman he has loved for five years. And who should he run into but Aurora, a novelist who he's also been a little in love with for a long time.

Aurora is staying with a summer family that has two daughters: Laura, who is sixteen and very wise and falls in love with Jerome, and Claire, who is beautiful and blonde and full of figure and spirit. Jerome and Aurora enter into a teasing intellectual game, which requires Jerome to describe to Aurora whatever happens to him during his holiday. When they all become aware that Laura has fallen in love with the older man, Jerome encourages her in a friendly, platonic way. They have talks about love and the nature of life, and they grow very fond of each other, although of course the man does not take advantage of the young girl.

But then Claire joins the group, and one day while they are picking cherries, Jerome turns his head and finds that Claire has climbed a ladder and he is looking directly at her knee. Claire herself, observed playing volleyball or running, hand-in-hand, with her boyfriend, is a sleek animal, and Jerome finds himself stirring with desire. He doesn't want to run away with Claire, or seduce her, or anything like that; he plans to marry Lucinda. But he tells his friend Aurora that he has become fascinated by "Claire's knee"; that it might be the point through which she could be approached, just as another girl might respond to a caress on the neck, or the cheek, or the arm. He becomes obsessed with desire to test this theory, and one day has an opportunity to touch the knee at last.

As with all the films of Eric Rohmer, *Claire's Knee* exists at levels far removed from plot (as you might have guessed while I was describing the plot). What is really happening in this movie happens on the level of character, of thought, of the way people approach each other and then shy away. In some movies, people murder each other and the contact is casual; in a work by Eric Rohmer, small attitudes and gestures can summon up a universe of humanity.

Rohmer has an uncanny ability to make his actors seem as if they were going through the experiences they portray. The acting of Béatrice Romand, as sixteen-year-old Laura, is especially good in this respect; she isn't as pretty as her sister, but we feel somehow she'll find more enjoyment in life because she is a . . . well, a better person underneath. Jean-Claude Brialy is excellent in a difficult role. He has to relate with three women in the movie, and yet remain implicitly faithful to the unseen Lucinda. He does, and since the sexuality in his performance is suppressed, it is, of course, all the more sensuous. *Claire's Knee* is a movie for people who still read good novels, care about good films, and think occasionally.

Last Tango in Paris

OCTOBER 14, 1972

Bernardo Bertolucci's *Last Tango in Paris* is one of the great emotional experiences of our time. It's a movie that exists so resolutely on the level of emotion, indeed, that possibly only Marlon Brando, of all living actors, could have played its lead. Who else can act so brutally and imply such vulnerability and need? For the movie is about need; about the terrible hunger that its hero, Paul, feels for the touch of another human heart. He is a man whose whole existence has been reduced to a cry for help and who has been so damaged by life that he can only express that cry in acts of crude sexuality.

Bertolucci begins with a story so simple (which is to say, so stripped of any clutter of plot) that there is little room in it for anything but the emotional crisis of his hero. The events that take place in the everyday world are remote to Paul, whose attention is absorbed by the gradual breaking of his heart. The girl, Jeanne, is not a friend and is hardly even a companion; it's just that because she happens to wander into his life, he uses her as an object of his grief.

The movie begins when Jeanne, who is about to be married, goes apartment-hunting and finds Paul in one of the apartments. It is a big, empty apartment, with a lot of sunlight but curiously little cheer. Paul rapes her, if rape is not too strong a word to describe an act so casually accepted by the girl. He tells her that they will continue to meet there, in the empty apartment, and she agrees.

Why does she agree? From her point of view—which is not a terribly perceptive one—why not? One of the several things this movie is about is how one person, who may be uncommitted and indifferent, nevertheless can at a certain moment become of great importance to another. One of the movie's strengths comes from the tragic imbalance between Paul's need and Jeanne's almost unthinking participation in it. Their difference is so great that it creates tremendous dramatic tension; more, indeed, than if both characters were filled with passion.

They do continue to meet, and at Paul's insistence they do not exchange names. What has come together in the apartment is almost an elemental force, not a connection of two beings with identities in society. Still, inevitably, the man and the girl do begin to learn about each other. What began, on the man's part, as totally depersonalized sex develops into a deeper relationship almost to spite him.

We learn about them. He is an American, living in Paris these last several years with a French wife who owned a hotel that is not quite a whorehouse. On the day the movie begins, the wife has committed suicide. We are never quite sure why, although by the time the movie is over we have a few depressing clues.

The girl is young, conscious of her beauty and the developing powers of her body, and is going to marry a young and fairly inane filmmaker. He is making a movie of their life together; a camera crew follows them around as he talks to her and kisses her—for herself or for the movie, she wonders.

The banality of her "real" life has thus set her up for the urgency of the completely artificial experience that has been commanded for her by Paul. She doesn't know his name, or anything about him, but when he has sex with her it is certainly real; there is a life in that empty room that her fiancé, with all of his cinema verité, is probably incapable of imagining.

She finds it difficult, too, because she is a child. A child, because she hasn't lived long enough and lost often enough to know yet what a heartbreaker the world can be. There are moments in the film when she does actually seem to look into Paul's soul and half understand what she sees there, but she pulls back from it; pulls back, finally, all the way—and just when he had come to the point where he was willing to let life have one more chance with him.

A lot has been said about the sex in the film; in fact, *Last Tango in Paris* has become notorious because of its sex. There is a lot of sex in this film—more, probably, than in any other legitimate feature film ever made—but the sex isn't the point; it's only the medium of exchange. Paul has somehow been so brutalized by life that there are only a few ways he can still feel.

Sex is one of them, but only if it is debased and depraved—because he is so filled with guilt and self-hate that he chooses these most intimate of activities to hurt himself beyond all possibilities of mere thoughts and words. It is said in some quarters that the sex in the movie is debasing to the girl, but I don't think it is. She's almost a bystander, a witness at the scene of the accident. She hasn't suffered enough, experienced enough, to more than dimly guess at what Paul is doing to himself with her. But Paul knows, and so does Bertolucci; only an idiot would criticize this movie because the girl is so often naked but Paul never is. That's their relationship.

The movie may not contain Brando's greatest performance, but it certainly contains his most emotionally overwhelming scene. He comes back to the hotel and confronts his wife's dead body, laid out in a casket, and he speaks to her with words of absolute hatred—words which, as he says them, become one of the most moving speeches of love I can imagine.

As he weeps, as he attempts to remove her cosmetic death mask ("Look at you! You're a monument to your mother! You never wore makeup, never wore false eyelashes . . ."), he makes it absolutely clear why he is the best film actor of all time. He may be a bore, he may be a creep, he may act childish about the Academy Awards—but there is no one else who could have played that scene flat out, no holds barred, the way he did, and make it work triumphantly.

The girl, Maria Schneider, doesn't seem to act her role so much as to exude it. On the basis of this movie, indeed, it's impossible to really say whether she can act or not. That's not her fault; Bertolucci directs her that way. He wants a character who ultimately does not quite understand the situation she finds herself in; she has to be that way, among other reasons, because the movie's ending absolutely depends on it. What happens to Paul at the end must seem, in some fundamental way, ridiculous. What the girl does at the end has to seem incomprehensible—not to us; to her.

What is the movie about? What does it all mean? It is about, and means, exactly the same things that Bergman's *Cries and Whispers* was about, and meant. That's to say that no amount of analysis can extract from either film a rational message. The whole point of both films is that there is a land in the human soul that's beyond the rational—beyond, even, words to describe it.

Faced with a passage across that land, men make various kinds of accommodations. Some ignore it; some try to avoid it through temporary distractions; some are lucky enough to have the inner resources for a successful journey. But of those who do not, some turn to the most highly charged resources of the body; lacking the mental strength to face crisis and death, they turn on the sexual mechanism, which can at least be depended upon to function, usually.

That's what the sex is about in this film (and in *Cries and Whispers*). It's not sex at all (and it's a million miles from intercourse). It's just a physical function of the soul's desperation. Paul in *Last Tango in Paris* has no difficulty in achieving an erection, but the gravest difficulty in achieving a life-affirming reason for one.

THE MOVIE REVISITED, AUGUST 11, 1995

Watching Bernardo Bertolucci's *Last Tango in Paris* twenty-three years after it was first released is like revisiting the house where you used to live, and where you did wild things you don't do anymore. Wandering through the empty rooms, which are smaller than you remember them, you recall a time when you felt the whole world was right there in your reach, and all you had to do was take it.

This movie was the banner for a revolution that never happened. "The movie breakthrough has finally come," Pauline Kael wrote, in the most famous movie review ever published. "Bertolucci and Brando have altered the face of an art form." The date of the premiere, she said, would become a landmark in movie history comparable to the night in 1913 when Stravinsky's *Rites of Spring* was first performed, and ushered in modern music. *Last Tango* premiered, in case you have forgotten, on October 14, 1972. It did not quite become a landmark. It was not the beginning of something new, but the triumph of something old—the "art film," which was soon to be replaced by the complete victory of mass-marketed "event films." The shocking sexual energy of *Last Tango in Paris* and the daring of Marlon Brando and the unknown Maria Schneider did not lead to an adult art cinema. The movie frightened off imitators, and instead of being the first of many X-rated films dealing honestly with sexuality, it became almost the last. Hollywood made a quick U-turn into movies about teenagers, technology, action heroes, and special effects. And with the exception of a few isolated films like *The Unbearable Lightness of Being* and *In the Realm of the Senses,* the serious use of graphic sexuality all but disappeared from the screen.

I went to see *Last Tango of Paris* again because it is being revived at Facets Multimedia, that temple of great cinema, where the largest specialized video sales operation in the world subsidizes a little theater where people still gather to see great films projected through celluloid onto a screen. (I am reminded of the readers in Truffaut's *Fahrenheit 451,* who committed books to memory in order to save them.)

It was a good 35 mm print, and I was drawn once again into the hermetic world of these two people, Paul and Jeanne, their names unknown to each other, who meet by chance in an empty Paris apartment and make sudden, brutal, lonely sex. Paul's marriage has just ended with his wife's suicide. Jeanne's marriage is a week or two away, and will supply the conclusion for a film being made by her half-witted fiancé.

In anonymous sex they find something that apparently they both need, and Bertolucci shows us enough of their lives to guess why. Paul (Brando) wants to bury his sense of hurt and betrayal in mindless animal passion. And Jeanne (Schneider) responds to the authenticity of his emotion, however painful, because it is an antidote to the prattle of her insipid boyfriend and bourgeois mother. Obviously their "relationship," if that's what it is, cannot exist outside these walls, in the light of the real world.

The first time I saw the film there was the shock of its daring. The "butter scene" had not yet been cheapened in a million jokes, and Brando's anguished monologue over the dead body of his wife—perhaps the best acting he has ever done—had not been analyzed to pieces. It simply happened. I once had a professor who knew just about everything there was to know about *Romeo and Juliet,* and told us he would trade it all in for the opportunity to read the play for the first time. I felt the same way during the screening: I was so familiar with the film that I was making contact with the art instead of the emotion.

The look, feel, and sound of the film are evocative. The music by Gato Barbieri is sometimes counterpoint, sometimes lament, but it is never simply used to tell us how to feel. Vittorio Storaro's slow tracking shots in the apartment, across walls and the landscapes of bodies, are cold and remote; there is no attempt to heighten the emotions. The sex is joyless and efficient, and beside the point: whatever the reasons these two people have for what they do with one another, sensual pleasure is not one of them.

Brando, who can be the most mannered of actors, is here often affectless. He talks, he observes, he states things. He allows himself bursts of anger and that remarkable outpouring of grief, and then at the end he is wonderful in the way he lets all of the air out of Paul's character by turning commonplace with the speech where he says he likes her. The moment is wonderful because it releases the tension, it shows what was happening in that apartment, and we can feel the difference when it stops.

In my notes I wrote: "He is in scenes as an actor, she is in scenes as a thing." This is unfair. Maria Schneider, an unknown whose career dissipated after this film, does what she can with the role, but neither Brando nor Bertolucci was nearly as interested in Jeanne as in Paul. Because I was young in 1972, I was unable to see how young Jeanne (or Schneider) really was; the screenplay says she is twenty and Paul is forty-five, but now when I see the film she seems even younger, her open-faced lack of experience contradicting her incongruously full breasts. Both characters are enigmas, but Brando knows Paul, while Schneider is only walking in Jeanne's shoes.

The ending. The scene in the tango hall is still haunting, still part of the whole movement of the third act of the film, in which Paul, having created a searing moment out of time, now throws it away in drunken banality. The following scenes, leading to the unexpected events in the apartment of Jeanne's mother, strike me as arbitrary and contrived. But still Brando finds a way to redeem them, carefully remembering to park his gum before the most important moment of his life.

Fellini's Roma

JANUARY 12, 1973

Federico Fellini first included his name in the title of one of his movies with *Fellini Satyricon* (1969), and then for legal reasons: a quickie Italian version of the *Satyricon* was being palmed off in international film markets as the real thing. Once having savored the notion, however, Fellini found it a good one, and now we have *Fellini's Roma,* to be followed in a year or two by *Fellini's Casanova.* The name in the title doesn't seem conceited or affected, as it might from another director (*Peckinpah's Albuquerque?*). This *is* Fellini's Rome and nobody else's, just as all of his films since *La Dolce Vita* have been autobiographical musings and confessions from the most personal—and the best—director of our time. Any connection with a real city on the map of Italy is libelous. Fellini's Rome gets its suburbs trimmed when he goes for a haircut.

The movie isn't a documentary, although sometimes he lets it look like one. It's a rambling essay, meant to feel like free association. There's a very slight narrative thread, about a young man named Fellini who leaves the little town of Rimini and comes to the great city and is overwhelmed by its pleasures of body and spirit. He moves into a mad boardinghouse that would make a movie all by itself: he dines with his neighbors in great outdoor feasts when the summer heat drives everyone into the piazzas, he attends a raucous vaudeville show, and he visits his first whorehouse . . . and then his second.

This material, filmed with loving attention to period detail, exists by itself in the movie; there's no effort to link the naive young Fellini with the confident genius who appears elsewhere in the movie. It's as if Fellini, the consummate inventor of fantasies, didn't grow out of his young manhood— he created it from scratch.

The autobiographical material is worked in between pseudo-documentary scenes that contain some of the most brilliant images Fellini has ever devised. The movie opens with a monumental Roman traffic jam that, typically, becomes important because Fellini has deigned to photograph it. He swoops above it on a crane, directing his camera, his movie, and the traffic. A blinding rainstorm turns everything into a hellish apparition, and then there's a final shot, held just long enough to make its point, of the autos jammed around the Coliseum.

The image is both perfect and natural; as someone commented about Fellini's *8½*, his movies are filled with images, and they're all obvious. If Bergman is the great introvert of the movies, forever probing more and more deeply, Fellini is the joyous exponent of surfaces and excess, of letting more hang out than there is. The obviousness of his images gives his movies a curious kind of clarity; he isn't reaching for things to say, but finding ways to say the same things more memorably. The decadence of Rome has been one of his favorite subjects throughout his career, and who could forget Anita Ekberg in the fountain or the Mass procession at dawn in *La Dolce Vita*?

But in *Roma* he is even more direct, more stark: an expedition to inspect progress on the Rome subway system suddenly becomes transcendent when workmen break through to an underground crypt from pre-Christian times. The frescoes on the walls are so clear they might have been painted yesterday—until the air of the modern city touches them. Rome, the eternal city, has historically been as carnal as it has been sacred. Fellini won't settle for one or the other; he uses scenes of carnality to symbolize a blessed state, and vice versa. Nothing could be more eternal, more patient, and more resigned than Fellini's use of a weary prostitute standing beside a highway outside Rome. She is tall, huge-bosomed, garishly made up, and her feet are tired. She stands among the broken stones of the Roman Empire, expecting nothing, hoping for nothing.

The prostitute, so often used as a symbol of fleeting moments and insubstantial experiences, becomes eternal; and the church, always the symbol of the unchanging, the rock, becomes temporal. In his most audacious sequence, Fellini gives us an "ecclesiastical fashion show," with rollerskating priests and nuns whose habits are made of blinking neon lights. What is unreal, and where is the real? Fellini doesn't know, and he seems to believe that Rome has never known. Rome has simply endured, waiting in the hope of someday finding out. *Fellini's Roma* has been attacked in some circles as an example of Fellini coasting on his genius. I find this point of view completely incomprehensible. Critics who would force Fellini back into traditional narrative films are missing the point; Fellini isn't just giving us a lot of flashy scenes, he's building a narrative that has a city for its protagonist instead of a single character.

The only sly thing is that the city isn't Rome—it's Fellini, disguised in bricks, mortar, and ruins. Fellini, who cannot find his way between the flesh and the spirit, who cannot find the connection between his youth and his greatness, and whose gift is to make movies where everything is obvious and nothing is simple. That was the dilemma that the Fellini character faced in *8½*, when he couldn't make sense of his life, and it's the dilemma we all face every day, isn't it?

Stroszek

APRIL 21, 1978

Werner Herzog has subtitled *Stroszek* as "a ballad," and so it is: it's like one of those bluegrass nonsense ballads in which impossible adventures are described in every verse, and the chorus reminds us that life gets teedjus, don't it? But because Herzog has one of the most original imaginations of anyone now making movies, *Stroszek* is a haunting and hilarious ballad at the same time, an almost unbelievable mixture of lunacy, comedy, tragedy, and the simply human.

Consider. He gives us three main characters who are best friends, despite the fact that they're improbable as people and impossible as friends. There's Stroszek himself, just released from prison in Germany. He's a simple soul who plays the piano and the accordion and never quite understands why people behave as they do. There's Eva, a dim but pleasant Berlin prostitute. And there's old Sheitz, a goofy soul in his seventies who has been invited to live with his nephew in upstate Wisconsin.

This mixture is further complicated by the fact that Stroszek is played by Bruno S., the same actor Herzog used in *Kaspar Hauser*. Bruno S. is a mental patient, described by Herzog as schizophrenic, and it's a good question whether he's "acting" in this movie or simply exercising a crafty survival instinct. No matter: he comes across as saintly, sensitive, and very strange.

The three friends meet when Eva's two pimps beat her up and throw her out. She comes to live with Stroszek. The pimps (evil hoods right out of a Fassbinder gangster movie) later visit Stroszek and Eva and beat them both up, leaving Stroszek kneeling on his beloved piano with a school bell balanced on his derriere.

It is clearly time to leave Berlin, and old Scheitz has the answer: visit his relatives in America. The nephew lives on a Wisconsin farm in an incredibly barren landscape, but to the Germans it's the American Dream.

They buy an enormous mobile home, seventy feet long and fully furnished, and install a color TV in it. Eva gets a job as a waitress, and turns some tricks on the side at the truck stop. Stroszek works as a mechanic, sort of. Old Scheitz wanders about testing the "animal magnetism" of fence posts.

The Wisconsin scenes are among the weirdest I've ever seen in a movie: notice, for example, the visit Stroszek and Eva get from that supercilious little twerp from the bank, who wants to repossess their TV set and who never seems to understand that nothing he says is understood. Or notice the brisk precision with which an auctioneer disposes of the mobile home, which is then carted away, all seventy feet of it, leaving the bewildered Stroszek looking at the empty landscape it has left behind.

Stroszek gets most hypnotically bizarre as it goes along, because we understand more of the assumptions of the movie. One of them is possibly that Kaspar Hauser might have become Stroszek, had he lived for another century and studied diligently. (Hauser, you might remember, was the "wild child" kept imprisoned in the dark for nineteen years, never taught to speak, and then dumped in a village square.)

The film's closing scenes are wonderfully funny and sad, at once. Stroszek and Scheitz rob a barber shop, and then Stroszek buys a frozen turkey, and then there is an amusement park with a chicken that will not stop dancing (and a policeman reporting "The dancing chicken won't stop"), and a wrecker driving in a circle with no one at the wheel, and an Indian chief looking on impassively, and somehow Herzog has made a statement about America here that is as loony and utterly original as any ever made.

The Marriage of Maria Braun

NOVEMBER 16, 1979

ainer Werner Fassbinder has been working his way toward this film
for years, ever since he began his astonishingly prodigious output
with his first awkward but powerful films in 1969. His films are always
about sex, money, and death, and his method is often to explore those three
subjects through spectacularly incompatible couples (an elderly cleaning
woman and a young black worker, a James Dean look-alike and a thirteen-
year-old girl, a rich gay-about-town and a simple-minded young sweepstakes winner). Whatever his pairings and his cheerfully ironic conclusions,
though, there is always another subject lurking in the background of his
approximately thirty-three (!) features. He gives us what he sees as the rise
and second fall of West Germany in the three postwar decades considered
in the context of the overwhelming American influence on his country.

With the masterful epic *The Marriage of Maria Braun,* he makes his
clearest and most cynical statement of the theme, and at the same time
gives us a movie dripping with period detail, with the costumes and decor
he is famous for, with the elegant decadence his characters will sell their
souls for in a late-1940s economy without chic retail goods.

Fassbinder's film begins with a Germany torn by war and ends with
a gas explosion and a soccer game. His ending may seem arbitrary to some,
but in the context of West German society in the 1970s it may only be good
reporting. His central character, Maria Braun, is played with great style
and power by Hanna Schygulla, and Maria's odyssey from the war years to
the consumer years provides the film's framework.

The film opens as Maria marries a young soldier, who then goes off
to battle and presumably is killed. It follows her during a long period of
mourning, which is punctuated by a little amateur hooking (of which her
mother tacitly approves) and then by a tender and very carefully observed

251

liaison with a large, strong, gentle black American soldier whom she really likes—we guess.

The soldier's accidental death and her husband's return are weathered by Maria with rather disturbing aplomb, but then we begin to see that Maria's ability to feel has been atrophied by the war, and her ability to be surprised has withered away. If war makes any plans absolutely meaningless, then why should one waste time analyzing coincidences?

Fassbinder has some rather bitter fun with what happens in the aftermath of the soldier's death (the love-struck, or perhaps just shell-shocked, husband voluntarily goes to prison, and Maria rises quickly in a multinational corporation). The movie is more realistic in its treatment of characters than Fassbinder sometimes is, but the events are as arbitrary as ever (and why not—events only have the meanings we assign to them, anyway).

The mini-apocalypse at the end is a perfect conclusion (an ending with "meaning" would have been obscene for this film), and then I think we are left, if we want it, with the sum of what Fassbinder has to say about the rebuilding of Germany: we got the stores opened again, but we don't know much about the customers yet.

Wings of Desire

1988

In notes that he wrote after directing *Wings of Desire,* Wim Wenders reflected that it would be terrible to be an angel: "To live for an eternity
and to be present all the time. To live with the essence of things—not to
be able to raise a cup of coffee and drink it, or really touch somebody." In
his film, this dilemma becomes the everyday reality of two angels, who
move through Berlin observing people, listening, reflecting, caring. They
can see and hear, but are cut off from the senses of touch, taste, and smell.
Human life appears to them as if it were a movie.

The angels look like two ordinary men, with weary and kind faces.
They can move through the air free of gravity, but in all other respects they
appear to the camera to be just as present as the human characters in a scene.
Their role is a little unclear. They watch. They listen. Sometimes, when
they are moved by the plight of a human they care about, they are able to
stand close to that person and somehow exude a sense of caring or love,
which seems to be vaguely perceived by the human, to whom it can provide a moment of hope or release.

The angel we are most concerned with in the film is Damiel, played
by Bruno Ganz, that everyman of German actors whose face is expressive
because it is so lived-in, so tired. He moves slowly through the city, hearing snatches of conversation, seeing moments of lives, keenly aware of his
existence as a perpetual outsider. One day he comes across Marion (Solveig
Dommartin), a trapeze artist, and is moved by her sadness. He helps her in
the ways that he can, but eventually he realizes that he does not want to end
her suffering so much as to share it.

That is the problem with being an angel. He can live forever, but in a
sense, he can never live. To an angel, a being who exists in eternity, human
lives must seem to be over in a brief flash of time, in a wink of history, and
yet during our brief span, at least humans are really alive—to grow, to

learn, to love, to suffer, to drink a cup of coffee, while an angel can only imagine the warmth of the cup, the aroma of the coffee, the taste, the feel.

Damiel determines to renounce immortality and accept human life with all its transience and pain. And in that act of renunciation, he makes one of the most poignant and romantic of gestures. He is accepting the limitations not only of his loved one, but of life itself.

Wings of Desire was directed by Wenders (whose credits include *Paris, Texas* and *The American Friend*), and cowritten by Wenders and Peter Handke, the German novelist who also wrote and directed *The Left-Handed Woman*. They are not interested in making some kind of softhearted, sentimental Hollywood story in which harps play and everybody feels good afterward.

Their film is set in divided Berlin, most insubstantial of cities because its future always seems deferred. Most of the film is shot in black and white, the correct medium for this story, because color would be too realistic to reflect the tone of their fable. Many of the best moments in the film have no particular dramatic purpose, but are concerned only with showing us what it is like to be forever an observer. Ganz walks quietly across empty bridges. He looks into vacant windows. He sits in a library and watches people as they read. He is there, and he is not there. The sterility of his existence almost makes us understand the choice of Lucifer in renouncing heaven in order to be plunged into hell, where at least he could suffer, and therefore, feel.

This is the kind of film that needs to be seen in a meditative frame of mind. It doesn't much matter what happens in the story, but it does matter how well we are able to empathize with it, how successfully we are able to enter into the state of mind of an angel. Leaving the movie, I reflected that sometimes we are bored by life, and feel as if nothing exciting is happening. But if we had spent eternity as an angel, observing life without feeling it, and then were plunged into a human body with its physical senses, think what a roar and flood of sensations would overwhelm us! It would be almost too much to bear. It would be everyday life.

Raise the Red Lantern

MARCH 27, 1992

The fourth wife of the rich old man comes to live in his house against her will. She has been educated, and thinks herself ready for the wider world, but her mother betrays her, selling her as a concubine, and soon her world is no larger than the millionaire's vast house. Its living quarters are arrayed on either side of a courtyard. There is an apartment for each of the wives. She is quietly informed of the way things work here. A red lantern is raised each night outside the quarters of the wife who will be honored by a visit from the master.

So opens *Raise the Red Lantern,* a Chinese film of voluptuous physical beauty and angry passions, set circa 1920. It is one of this year's Academy Award nominees in the foreign category, directed by Zhang Yimou, whose *Ju Dou* was nominated last year. This film, based on the novel *Wives and Concubines* by Su Tong, can no doubt be interpreted in a number of ways— as a cry against the subjection of women in China, as an attack on feudal attitudes, as a formal exercise in storytelling—and yet it works because it is so fascinating simply on the level of melodrama.

We enter into the sealed world of the rich man's house, and see how jealousies fester in its hothouse atmosphere. Each of the four wives is treated with the greatest luxury, pampered with food and care, servants, and massages, but they are like horses in a great racing stable, cared for at the whim of the master. The new wife, whose name is Songlian, is at first furious at her fate. Then she begins to learn the routine of the house, and is drawn into its intrigues and alliances. If you are only given one game to play, it is human nature to try to win it.

Songlian is played by Gong Li, an elegant woman who also starred in quite different roles in Zhang Yimou's two previous films. In *Red Sorghum,* she was the defiant young woman, sold into marriage to a wealthy vintner, who takes over his winery after his death and makes it prosperous with the help of a sturdy peasant who has earlier saved her from rape. In *Ju Dou*, she was the young bride of a wealthy old textile merchant, who enslaved both her and his poor young nephew—with the result that she and the nephew fall in love, and the merchant comes to a colorful end in a vat of his own dyes.

Zhang Yimou is obviously attracted to the theme of the rich, impotent old man and the young wife. But in *Raise the Red Lantern,* it is the system of concubinage that he focuses on. The rich man is hardly to be seen, except in hints and shadows. He is a patriarchal offstage presence, as his four wives and the household staff scheme among themselves for his favor.

We meet the serene first wife, who reigns over the other wives and has the wisdom of longest experience in this house. Then there are the resigned second wife, and the competitive third wife, who is furious that the master has taken a bride younger and prettier than herself. The servants, including the young woman assigned to Songlian, have their own priorities. And there is Dr. Gao (Cui Zhihgang), who treats the wives, and whose medical judgments are instrumental in the politics of the house. The gossip that whirls among the wives and their servants creates the world for these people; little that happens outside ever leaks in.

Zhang Yimou's visual world here is part of the story. His master shot, which he returns to again and again, looks down the central space of the house, which is open to the sky, with the houses of the wives arrayed on either side, and the vast house of the master at the end. As the seasons pass, the courtyard is sprinkled with snow, or dripping with rain, or bathed in hot, still sunlight. The servants come and go. Up on the roof of the house is a little shed which is sometimes whispered about. It has something to do with an earlier wife, who did not adjust well.

Yimou uses the bold, bright colors of *Ju Dou* again this time; his film was shot in the classic three-strip Technicolor process, now abandoned by Hollywood, which allows a richness of reds and yellows no longer possible in American films. There is a sense in which *Raise the Red Lantern* exists solely for the eyes. Entirely apart from the plot, there is the sensuous pleasure of the architecture, the fabrics, the color contrasts, the faces of the actresses. But beneath the beauty is the cruel reality of this life, just as, beneath the comfort of the rich man's house is the sin of slavery.

The Scent of Green Papaya

MARCH 11, 1994

Here is a film so placid and filled with sweetness that watching it is like listening to soothing music. *The Scent of Green Papaya* takes place in Vietnam between the late 1940s and early 1960s, and is seen through the eyes of a poor young woman who is taken as a servant into the household of a merchant family. She observes everything around her in minute detail, and gradually, as she flowers into a beautiful woman, her simple goodness impresses her more hurried and cynical employers.

The woman, named Mui, is an orphan—a child, when she first comes to work for the family. She learns her tasks quickly and well, and performs them so unobtrusively that sometimes she seems almost like a spirit. But she is a very real person, uncomplaining, all-seeing, and the film watches her world through her eyes. For her, there is beauty in the smallest details: a drop of water trembling on a leaf, a line of busy ants, a self-important frog in a puddle left by the rain, the sunlight through the green leaves outside the window, the scent of green papaya.

We understand the workings of the household only through her eyes. We see that the father drinks, and is unfaithful, and that the mother runs the business and the family. We see unhappiness, and we also see that the mother comes to think of Mui with a special love—she is like a daughter. As Mui grows and the family's fortunes fade, the routine in the household nevertheless continues unchanged, until a day when the father is dead and the business in disarray. Then Mui is sent to work as the servant of a young man who is a friend of the family.

She has known this young man for a long time, ever since they both were children. He was the playmate of her employer's son. Now he has grown into a sleek and sophisticated man-about-town, a classical pianist, French-speaking, with an expensive mistress. Mui serves him as she served her first family, quietly and perfectly. And we see through small signs that she loves him. These signs are at first not visible to the man.

The Scent of Green Papaya, which is one of this year's Oscar nominees in the foreign language category, is first of all a film of great visual beauty; watching it is like seeing a poem for the eyes. All of the action, indoors and out, is set in Saigon in the period before the Vietnam War, but what is astonishing is that this entire film was made in Paris, on a soundstage. Everything we see is a set. There is a tradition in Asian films of sets that are obviously artificial (see *Kwaidan,* with its artificial snowfalls and forests). But the sets for *Green Papaya* are so convincing that at first we think we are occupying a small, secluded corner of a real city.

The director, Tran Anh Hung, undoubtedly found it impossible to make a film of this type in today's Vietnam, which is hardly nostalgic for the colonial era. That is one reason he recreated his period piece on a soundstage. Another reason may be that he wanted to achieve a kind of visual perfection that real life seldom approaches; every small detail of his frame is idealized in an understated but affecting way, so that Mui's physical world seduces us as much as her beauty.

Some will prefer the first two-thirds of the film to the conclusion: there is a purity to the observation of Mui's daily world that has a power of its own. Toward the end of the film, plot begins to enter, and we begin to wonder when the young pianist will notice the beautiful woman who lives under his roof, and loves him so. There is an old, old movie tradition of the scene where a man suddenly sees a woman through fresh eyes, and realizes that the love he has been looking for everywhere is standing right there in front of him. These scenes can be laughable, but they can also sometimes be moving, and when that moment arrives in *Scent of Green Papaya,* it has been so carefully prepared that there is a true joy to it.

There is another scene of great gladness, when the man begins to teach the young woman to read. So deep is the romanticism of the film that we almost question whether this is an advancement for her: her simplicity, her unity of self and world, is so deep that perhaps literacy will only be a distraction. It is one of the film's gifts to inspire questions like that.

I have seen *The Scent of Green Papaya* three times now—the first time in May 1993 at Cannes, where it was named the best film by a first time director. It is a placid, interior, contemplative film—not plot-driven, but centered on the growth of the young woman. As such, you might think it would seem "slower" on later viewings, but I found that the opposite was true: as I understood better what the movie was, I appreciated it more, because like a piece of music it was made of subtleties that only grew deeper through familiarity. This is a film to cherish.

Spirited Away

Spirited Away has been compared to *Alice in Wonderland,* and indeed it tells of a ten-year-old girl who wanders into a world of strange creatures and illogical rules. But it's enchanting and delightful in its own way, and has a good heart. It is the best animated film of recent years; the latest work by Hayao Miyazaki, the Japanese master who is a god to the Disney animators.

Because many adults have an irrational reluctance to see an animated film from Japan (or anywhere else), I begin with reassurances: it has been flawlessly dubbed into English by John Lasseter (*Toy Story*); it was cowinner of this year's Berlin Film Festival against "regular" movies; it passed *Titanic* to become the top-grossing film in Japanese history; and it is the first film ever to make more than $200 million before opening in America. I feel like I'm giving a pitch on an infomercial, but I make these points because I come bearing news: this is a wonderful film. Don't avoid it because of what you think you know about animation from Japan. And if you only go to Disney animation—well, this is being released by Disney.

Miyazaki's works (*My Neighbor Totoro, Kiki's Delivery Service, Princess Mononoke*) have a depth and complexity often missing in American animation. Not fond of computers, he draws thousand of frames himself, and there is a painterly richness in his work. He's famous for throwaway details at the edges of the screen (animation is so painstaking that few animators draw more than is necessary). And he permits himself silences and contemplation, providing punctuation for the exuberant action and the lovable or sometimes grotesque characters.

Spirited Away is told through the eyes of Chihiro (voice by Daveigh Chase), a ten-year-old girl, and is more personal, less epic, than *Princess Mononoke.* As the story opens, she's on a trip with her parents, and her father unwisely takes the family to explore a mysterious tunnel in the woods. On the other side is what he speculates is an old theme park, but the food stalls still seem to be functioning, and as Chihiro's parents settle down for a free meal, she wanders away and comes upon the film's version of wonderland, which is a towering floating bathhouse.

A boy named Haku appears as her guide, and warns her that the sorceress who runs the bathhouse, named Yu-Baaba, will try to steal her name and thus her identity. Yu-Baaba (Suzanne Pleshette) is an old crone with a huge face; she looks a little like a Toby mug, and dotes on a grotesquely huge baby named Bou. Ominously, she renames Chihiro, who wanders through the structure, which is populated, like *Totoro,* with little balls of dust that scurry and scamper underfoot.

In the innards of the structure, Chihiro comes upon the boiler room, operated by a man named Kamaji (David Ogden Stiers), who is dressed in a formal coat and has eight limbs, which he employs in a bewildering variety of ways. At first he seems as fearsome as the world he occupies, but he has a good side, is no friend of Yu-Baaba, and perceives Chihiro's goodness.

If Yu-Baaba is the scariest of the characters and Kamaji the most intriguing, Okutaresama is the one with the most urgent message. He is the spirit of the river, and his body has absorbed the junk, waste, and sludge that has been thrown into it over the years. At one point he actually yields up a discarded bicycle. I was reminded of a throwaway detail in *My Neighbor Totoro,* where a child looks into a bubbling brook, and there is a discarded bottle at the bottom. No point is made; none needs to be made.

Japanese myths often use shape-shifting, in which bodies reveal themselves as facades concealing a deeper reality. It's as if animation was invented for shape-shifting, and Miyazaki does wondrous things with the characters here. Most alarming for Chihiro, she finds that her parents have turned into pigs after gobbling up the free lunch. Okutaresama reveals its true nature after being freed of decades of sludge and discarded household items. Haku is much more than he seems. Indeed the entire bathhouse seems to be under spells affecting the appearance and nature of its inhabitants.

Miyazaki's drawing style, which descends from the classical Japanese graphic artists, is a pleasure to regard, with its subtle use of colors, clear lines, rich detail and realistic depiction of fantastical elements. He suggests not just the appearances of his characters, but their natures. Apart from the stories and dialogue, *Spirited Away* is a pleasure to regard just for itself. This is one of the year's best films.

City of God

JANUARY 24, 2003

City of God churns with furious energy as it plunges into the story of the slum gangs of Rio de Janeiro. Breathtaking and terrifying, urgently involved with its characters, it announces a new director of great gifts and passions: Fernando Meirelles. Remember the name. The film has been compared with Scorsese's *GoodFellas,* and it deserves the comparison. Scorsese's film began with a narrator who said that for as long as he could remember he wanted to be a gangster. The narrator of this film seems to have had no other choice.

The movie takes place in slums constructed by Rio to isolate the poor people from the city center. They have grown into places teeming with life, color, music, and excitement—and also with danger, for the law is absent and violent gangs rule the streets. In the virtuoso sequence opening the picture, a gang is holding a picnic for its members when a chicken escapes. Among those chasing it is Rocket (Alexandre Rodrigues), the narrator. He suddenly finds himself between two armed lines: the gang on one side, the cops on the other.

As the camera whirls around him, the background changes and Rocket shrinks from a teenager into a small boy, playing soccer in a housing development outside Rio. To understand his story, he says, we have to go back to the beginning, when he and his friends formed the Tender Trio and began their lives of what some would call crime and others would call survival.

The technique of that shot—the whirling camera, the flashback, the change in colors from the dark brightness of the slum to the dusty sunny browns of the soccer field—alert us to a movie that is visually alive and inventive as few films are. Meirelles began as a director of TV commercials, which gave him a command of technique—and, he says, trained him to work quickly, to size up a shot and get it and move on. Working with the cinematographer César Charlone, he uses quick cutting and a mobile, hand-held camera to tell his story with the haste and detail it deserves. Some-times those devices can create a film that is merely busy, but *City of God* feels like sight itself, as we look here and then there, with danger or op-portunity everywhere.

The gangs have money and guns because they sell drugs and commit robberies. But they are not very rich because their activities are limited to the City of God, where no one has much money. In an early crime, we see the stickup of a truck carrying cans of propane gas, which the crooks sell to homeowners. Later there is a raid on a bordello, where the customers are deprived of their wallets. (In a flashback, we see that raid a second time, and understand in a chilling moment why there were dead bodies at a site where there was not supposed to be any killing.)

As Rocket narrates the lore of the district he knows so well, we un-derstand that poverty has undermined all social structures in the City of God, including the family. The gangs provide structure and status. Be-cause the gang death rate is so high, even the leaders tend to be surprisingly young, and life has no value except when you are taking it. There is an as-tonishing sequence when a victorious gang leader is killed in a way he least expects, by the last person he would have expected, and we see that essen-tially he has been killed not by a person but by the culture of crime.

Yet the film is not all grim and violent. Rocket also captures some of the Dickensian flavor of the City of God, where a riot of life provides ready-made characters with nicknames, personas, and trademarks. Some like Benny (Phelipe Haagensen) are so charismatic they almost seem to tran-scend the usual rules. Others, like Knockout Ned and Little Ze, grow from kids into fearsome leaders, their words enforced by death.

The movie is based on a novel by Paolo Lins, who grew up in the City of God, somehow escaped it, and spent eight years writing his book. A note at the end says it is partly based on the life of Wilson Rodriguez, a Brazilian photographer. We watch as Rocket obtains a (stolen) camera that he treasures, and takes pictures from his privileged position as a kid on the streets. He gets a job as an assistant on a newspaper delivery truck, asks a photographer to develop his film, and is startled to see his portrait of an armed gang leader on the front page of the paper.

"This is my death sentence," he thinks, but no: the gangs are delighted by the publicity, and pose for him with their guns and girls. And during a vicious gang war, he is able to photograph the cops killing a gangster—a murder they plan to pass off as gang-related. That these events throb with immediate truth is indicated by the fact that Luiz Inácio Lula da Silva, the newly elected president of Brazil, actually reviewed and praised *City of God* as a needful call for change.

In its actual level of violence, *City of God* is less extreme than Scorsese's *Gangs of New York,* but the two films have certain parallels. In both films, there are really two cities: the city of the employed and secure, who are served by law and municipal services, and the city of the castaways, whose alliances are born of opportunity and desperation. Those who live beneath rarely have their stories told. *City of God* does not exploit or condescend, does not pump up its stories for contrived effect, does not contain silly and reassuring romantic sidebars, but simply looks, with a passionately knowing eye, at what it knows.

PART 4

Documentaries

INTRODUCTION

The greatest experience I have ever had at a documentary was when I saw *Hoop Dreams* with Gene Siskel three weeks before its Sundance premiere. Here was a film than began as a thirty-minute sports doc of modest ambition, and grew over four years into an American saga. Its ending could not have been improved upon by Hollywood. Its moments of truth were searing. We reviewed it on the TV show that very week, urging Sundance audiences to look for it. It is a scandal that it did not win an Oscar, and I wrote angry articles about the Academy Award documentary award process, one of them revealing that the jurors had turned it off after fifteen minutes. That controversy led to a reform of the Oscar procedures for nominating documentaries.

Hoop Dreams is not here, for the excellent reason that it appears elsewhere in the book, as the best film of 1994. Of the films below, *Gates of Heaven* ranks for me as the most impenetrable mystery. How can it be so wry, so implacable in its gaze, so funny, so moving? I have shown it over and over again to audiences who had no idea what to expect, and were left enchanted and mystified.

Of the others, reading them again for this book, I was reminded how often I was moved by the immediate experience of these real people on the screen. The "Up" documentaries show, as no other films have, the process by which we grow up and grow old, how in our beginnings are our ends. In the neglected *Dear America,* how uncanny when they match a letter with footage of the person who wrote it. In *Heidi Fleiss,* there is the moment I mention in which Ivan Nagy smiles helplessly at the camera, and I feel we are regarding the face of evil, the smiling serpent. As for *Shoah,* it is long, but it is deeper than it is long, and to experience it is to be informed about the Holocaust in a way not approached by any other film. All of the documentaries considered here are extraordinary in that the makers were able to obtain their footage by one difficult way or another. The popularity of home video cameras has transformed the genre; now footage is available that could not have existed decades ago, and when Werner Herzog in *Grizzly Man* tells of the life and death of Timothy Treadwell, we can see footage Treadwell himself made of himself and his bears, including the one that may have killed him.

Woodstock

MAY 3, 1970

> *Defense attorney:* Where do you live?
> *Abbie Hoffman:* I live in Woodstock nation.
> *Defense attorney:* Will you tell the court and the jury where it is?
> *Abbie Hoffman:* Yes, it is a nation of alienated young people. We carry it around with us as a state of mind, in the same way the Sioux Indians carry the Sioux nation with them. . . .

Michael Wadleigh's *Woodstock* is an archeological study of that nation, which existed for three days a year ago. Because of this movie, the Woodstock state of mind now has its own history, folklore, myth. In terms of evoking the style and feel of a mass historical event, *Woodstock* may be the best documentary ever made in America. But don't see it for that reason; see it because it is so good to see.

It has a lot of music in it, photographed in an incredible intimacy with the performers, but it's not by any means only a rock-music movie. It's a documentary about the highs and lows of the society that formed itself briefly at Woodstock before moving on. It covers that civilization completely, showing how the musicians sang to it and the Hog Farm fed it and the Port-O-San man provided it with toilet facilities.

And it shows how 400,000 young people formed the third largest city in New York State, and ran it for a weekend with no violence and no hassles, and with a spirit of informal cooperation. The spirit survived even though Woodstock was declared a "disaster area," and a thunderstorm soaked everyone to the skin, and the food ran out. But you know all that.

The remarkable thing about Wadleigh's film is that it succeeds so completely in making us feel how it must have been to be there. It does that to the limits that a movie can. One local column complained that *Woodstock* was

267

fun but didn't really recreate the actual experience. Well, that would have taken a film three days long, and an audience of 400,000, and rain showers inside the State-Lake Theater, and even then it would only have been a movie. People who go to movies looking for the "real thing" are looking for the wrong thing. They should go looking instead for a real movie.

Woodstock does what all good documentaries do. It is a bringer of news. It reports, it shows, it records, and it interprets. It gives us maybe 60 percent music and 40 percent on the people who were there, and that is a good ratio, I think. The music is very much part of the event, especially since Wadleigh and his editors have allowed each performer's set to grow and build and double back on itself without interference.

That is what rock music in concert is all about, as I understand it. Rock on records is another matter, usually, but in the free form of a concert like Woodstock, the whole point is that the performers and their audience are into a back-and-forth thing from which a totally new performance can emerge.

We get that feeling from Jimi Hendrix when he improvises a guitar arrangement of *The Star Spangled Banner,* rockets bursting in the air and all. We get it from Country Joe, poker-faced, leading the crowd through the anti-Vietnam *I Feel Like I'm Fixin' to Die Rag.* We get it in the raunchy 1950s vulgarity of Sha-Na-Na doing a tightly choreographed version of *At the Hop.* And we get it so strongly that some kind of strange sensation inhabits our spine, when Joe Cocker and everybody else in the whole Woodstock nation sings *With a Little Help from My Friends.*

This sort of participation can happen at a live concert, and often enough it does. But it is hard to get on film, harder than it looks. By way of comparison, you may want to drop in at the Festival theater this week and see the documentary *Festival,* made at Newport a couple of years ago. A lot of the same performers were there, doing some of the same things, but *Festival* is a record of their performances. You don't get the feeling that the cameramen and editor are participating.

You do in *Woodstock,* maybe because Wadleigh's crew understood the music better and had the resources to shoot 120 miles of film with sixteen cameras. This gave them miles and hours of film to throw away, but it also gave them a choice when they got into the editing room. They weren't stuck with one camera pointed at a performer; they could cut to reaction shots, to multiple images, to simultaneous close-ups when two members of a band did a mutual improvisation.

And of course they always had the option of remaining simple, even shy, when the material called for it. One of the most moving moments in the film, for me, is Joan Baez singing the old Wobbly song *Joe Hill,* and then rapping about her husband David, and then putting down the guitar and singing *Swing Low, Sweet Chariot,* with that voice which is surely the purest and sweetest of our generation. Wadleigh and company had the integrity to let her just sing it. No tricks. No fancy camera angles. Just Joan Baez all alone on an enormous, pitch-black screen.

But then when the occasion warrants it, they let everything hang out. When Santana gets into their intricate rhythm thing, Wadleigh goes to a triple screen and frames the drummer with two bongo players. All in synchronized sound (which is not anywhere near as easy as it sounds under outdoor concert conditions). And the editing rhythm follows the tense, driving Santana lead. The thing about this movie, somehow, is that the people who made it were right there, right on top of what the performers were doing.

Watch, for example, the way Richie Havens is handled. He is supposed to be more or less a folk singer—a powerful one, but still within the realm of folk and not rock. So you would think maybe he'd seem slightly less there than the hard-rock people? Not at all, because Wadleigh's crew went after the power in Havens's performance, and when they got it they stuck so close to it visually that in his second song, *Freedom,* we get moved by folk in the way we ordinarily expect to be moved by rock.

We see Havens backstage, tired, even a little down. Then he starts singing, and we don't see his face again, but his thumb on the guitar strings, punishing them. And then (in an unbroken shot) down to his foot in a sandal, pounding with the beat, and then the fingers, and then the foot, and only then the face, and now this is a totally transformed Richie Havens, and we are so close to him, we see he doesn't have any upper teeth. Not that it matters; but we don't usually get that close to anybody in a movie.

Moving along with the music, paralleling it sometimes on a split screen, are the more traditionally documentary aspects of *Woodstock.* There are the townspeople, split between those who are mean and ordinary and closed off, and those like the man who says, "Kids are hungry, you gotta feed 'em. Right?" And the farmer who makes his land available. And kids skinny-dipping, and turning on, and eating and sleeping.

Wadleigh never forces this material. His movie is curiously objective, in fact. Not neutral; he's clearly with the kids. But objective; showing what's there without getting himself in the way, so that the experience comes through directly.

With all that film to choose from in the editing room, he was able to give us dozens of tiny unrehearsed moments that sum up the Woodstock feeling. The skinny-dipping, for example, is free and unself-conscious, and we can see that. But how good it is to see that kid sitting on a stump in the water and turning to the camera and saying, "Man, a year ago I never would have believed this was the way to swim. But, man, this is the way to swim."

Some mention should be made, I suppose, of Wadleigh's use of the split screen. Multiple images became popular after Expo '67, and commercial directors tried it with rather dreary results in movies like *The Boston Strangler* and *The Thomas Crown Affair*. It didn't seem to work, maybe because the split screen is distracting in a fiction film that has to tell a story.

But in *Woodstock* it's used in other ways: as counterpoint, as ironic commentary, sometimes even just as a pleasant trip. It allows us to see the same rock group from several different points of view, for example. It allows Wadleigh to advance the narrative of his film by showing the sky clouding up on one screen, while people hold down canvas on another. This is smoother, more simultaneous, than an orthodox style of cutting back and forth.

What you're left with finally, though, are the people. I almost said the "kids," but that wouldn't include the friendly chief of police, or the farmer, or Hugh Romney from the Hog Farm ("Folks, we're planning breakfast in bed for 400,000 people"), or the Port-O-San man, or the townspeople who took carloads of food to the park.

Wadleigh and his team have recorded all the levels. The children. The dogs (who were allowed to run loose in this nation). The freaks and the straights. The people of religion (Swami Gi and three nuns giving the peace sign). The cops (eating Popsicles). The army (dropping blankets, food, and flowers from helicopters). *Woodstock* is a beautiful, complete, moving, ultimately great film, and years from now when our generation is attacked for being just as uptight as all the rest of the generations, it will be good to have this movie around to show that, just for a weekend anyway, that wasn't altogether the case.

Harlan County, U.S.A.

APRIL 3, 1976

One moment among many in *Harlan County, U.S.A.*: The striking miners are holding an all-day rally and picnic. A big tent has been pitched, and it's filled with people, some of them familiar to us by now, others new. There are speeches and songs and union battle cries, and then an old woman takes the microphone. The words she sings are familiar: "They say in Harlan County, there are no neutrals there. You'll either be a union man or a thug for Sheriff Blair." And then the whole tentful joins in the chorus: "Which side are you on?"

The woman who is leading the singing wrote the song fifty years ago, during an earlier strike in the county the miners call "Bloody Harlan." And here it is 1973, in a county where the right of workers to organize has presumably long since been won, and the song is not being sung out of nostalgia. It is being sung by striking coal miners in Harlan County, where it still applies.

That's the most uncomfortable lesson we learn in Barbara Kopple's magnificent documentary: that there are still jobs for scabs and strikebreakers, that union organizers still get shot at and sometimes get killed, and that in Harlan County, Kentucky, it still matters very much which side you're on. And so a song we know best from old Pete Seeger records suddenly proves itself still frighteningly relevant.

The movie [which won the 1976 Academy Award for best feature-length documentary] was shot over a period of eighteen months in eastern Kentucky, after the miners at the Brookside mine voted to join the United Mine Workers. The Duke Power Company refused to sign the UMW contract, fought the strike, and was fought in turn by the miners and most particularly their wives.

Barbara Kopple and her crew stayed in Harlan County during that entire time, living in the miners' homes and recording the day-by-day progress of the strike. It was a tumultuous period, especially since the mine workers' union itself was deep in the midst of the Tony Boyle–Jock Yablonski affair. But what emerges from the film is not just a document of a strike, but an affecting, unforgettable portrait of a community.

The cameras go down into the mines to show us the work, which is backbreaking, dirty, and brutal. We get to meet many of the miners, and to notice a curious thing about the older ones: they tend to talk little, as if their attentions are turned inward to the source of the determination that takes them back down the mine every day. Their wives, on the other hand, seem born to lead strikes. The film shows them setting up committees, organizing picket lines, facing (and sometimes reciprocating) violence, and becoming eloquent orators.

Kopple is a feminist, and her work includes *Year of the Women*. In *Harlan County,* though, she doesn't seem to have gone looking for examples of capable, competent, strong women: they were simply inescapable. There are talents, energies, and intelligences revealed in this film that could, if we would tap them, transform legislatures and bring wholesale quantities of common sense to public life. There are tacticians, strategists, and philosophers in *Harlan County, U.S.A.* who make the UMW theoreticians look tame and the company spokesmen look callow and inane.

The movie is a great American document, but it's also entertaining; Kopple structures her material to provide tension, brief but vivid characterizations, and dramatic confrontations (including one incredibly charged moment when the sheriff attempts to lead a caravan of scabs past the picket line). There are gunshots in the film, and a death, and also many moments of simple warmth and laughter. The many union songs on the sound track provide a historical context, and also help Kopple achieve a fluid editing rhythm. And most of all there are the people in the film, those amazing people, so proud and self-reliant and brave.

Gates of Heaven

JUNE 25, 1981

There are many invitations to laughter during this remarkable documentary, but what *Gates of Heaven* finally made me feel was an aching poignancy about its subjects. They say you can make a great documentary about almost anything, if only you see it well enough and truly, and this film proves it.

Gates of Heaven, which has no connection with the unfortunate *Heaven's Gate,* is a documentary about pet cemeteries and their owners. It was filmed in Southern California, so of course we immediately anticipate a sardonic look at peculiarities of the Moonbeam State. But then *Gates of Heaven* grows ever so much more complicated and frightening, until at the end it is about such large issues as love, immortality, failure, and the dogged elusiveness of the American Dream.

The film was made by a California filmmaker named Errol Morris, and it has been the subject of notoriety because Werner Herzog, the West German director, promised to eat his shoe if Morris ever finished it. Morris did finish it, and at the film's premiere in Berkeley, Herzog indeed boiled and ate his shoe.

Gates of Heaven is so rich and thought-provoking, it achieves so much while seeming to strain so little, that it stays in your mind for tantalizing days. It opens with a monologue by a kind-looking, somewhat heavyset paraplegic, with a slight lisp that makes him sound like a kid. His name is Floyd McClure. Ever since his pet dog was run over years ago by a Model A Ford, he has dreamed of establishing a pet cemetery. The movie develops and follows his dream, showing the forlorn, bare patch of land where he founded his cemetery at the intersection of two superhighways.

Then, with cunning drama, it gradually reveals that the cemetery went bankrupt and the remains of 450 animals had to be dug up. Various

274

people contribute to the story: one of McClure's investors, a partner, two of the women whose pets were buried in his cemetery, and an unforgettable old woman named Florence Rasmussen, who starts on the subject of pets, and switches, with considerable fire, to her no-account son.

Then the action shifts north to the Napa Valley, where a go-getter named Cal Harberts has absorbed what remained of McClure's dream (and the 450 dead pets) into his own pet cemetery, the Bubbling Well Pet Memorial Park. It is here that the movie grows heartbreaking, painting a portrait of a lifestyle that looks chillingly forlorn, and of the people who live it with relentless faith in positive thinking.

Harberts, a patriarch, runs his pet cemetery with two sons, Phil and Dan. Phil, the older one, has returned home after a period spent selling insurance in Salt Lake City. He speaks of having been overworked. Morris lets the camera stay on Phil as he solemnly explains his motivational techniques, and his method of impressing a new client by filling his office with salesmanship trophies. He has read all of Clement Stone's books on "Positive Mental Attitude," and has a framed picture of Stone on his wall. Phil looks neat, presentable, capable. He talks reassuringly of his positive approach to things, "mentally-wise."

Then we meet the younger brother, Dan, who composes songs and plays them on his guitar. In the late afternoon, when no one is at the pet cemetery, he hooks up his 100-watt speakers and blasts his songs all over the valley. He has a wispy mustache and looks like a hippie. The family hierarchy is clear. Cal, in the words of Phil, is "El Presidento." Then Dan comes next, because he has worked at the cemetery longer. Phil, the golden boy, the positive thinker, is maintaining his P.M.A. in the face of having had to leave an insurance business in Salt Lake City to return home as third in command at a pet cemetery.

The cemetery itself is bleak and barren, its markers informing us, "God is love; dog is god backwards." An American flag flies over the little graves. Floyd McClure tells us at the beginning of the film that pets are put on Earth for two reasons: to love and to be loved. At the end of this mysterious and great movie, we observe the people who guard and maintain their graves, and who themselves seem unloved and very lonely. One of the last images is of old Cal, the patriarch, wheeling past on his forklift, a collie-sized coffin in its grasp.

Say Amen, Somebody

S ay *Amen, Somebody* is the most joyful movie I've seen in a very long
time. It is also one of the best musicals and one of the most interesting documentaries. And it's also a terrific good time. The movie is about
gospel music, and it's filled with gospel music. It's sung by some of the pioneers of modern gospel, who are now in their seventies and eighties, and
it's sung by some of the rising younger stars, and it's sung by choirs of kids.
It's sung in churches and around the dining room table; with orchestras
and a cappella; by an old man named Thomas A. Dorsey in front of thousands of people, and by Dorsey standing all by himself in his own backyard. The music in *Say Amen, Somebody* is as exciting and uplifting as any
music I've ever heard on film.

The people in this movie are something, too. The filmmaker, a
young New Yorker named George T. Nierenberg, starts by introducing
us to two pioneers of modern gospel: Mother Willie May Ford Smith,
who is seventy-nine, and Professor Dorsey, who is eighty-three. She was
one of the first gospel soloists; he is known as the Father of Gospel Music.
The film opens at tributes to the two of them—Mother Smith in a St. Louis
church, Dorsey at a Houston convention—and then Nierenberg cuts back
and forth between their memories, their families, their music, and the music sung in tribute to them by younger performers.

That keeps the movie from seeming too much like the wrong kind of
documentary—the kind that feels like an educational film and is filled
with boring lists of dates and places. *Say Amen, Somebody* never stops moving, and even the dates and places are open to controversy (there's a hilarious sequence in which Dorsey and Mother Smith disagree very pointedly
over exactly which of them convened the first gospel convention).

What's amazing in all of the musical sequences is the quality of the
sound. A lot of documentaries use "available sound," picked up by micro-

phones more appropriate for the television news. This movie's concerts are miked by up to eight microphones, and the Dolby system is used to produce full stereo sound that really rocks the theater. A phenomenon during screenings of this film is the tendency of the audience to get into the act.

Willie May Ford Smith comes across in this movie as an extraordinary woman, spiritual, filled with love and power. Dorsey and his longtime business manager, Sallie Martin, come across at first as a little crusty, but then there's a remarkable scene where they sing along, softly, with one of Dorsey's old records. By the end of the film, when the ailing Dorsey insists on walking under his own steam to the front of the gospel convention in Houston, and leading the delegates in a hymn, we have come to see his strength and humanity. Just in case Smith and Dorsey seem too noble, the film uses a lot of mighty soul music as counterpoint, particularly in the scenes shot during a tribute to Mother Smith at a St. Louis Baptist church. We see Delois Barrett Campbell and the Barrett Sisters, a Chicago-based trio who have enormous musical energy; the O'Neal Twins, Edward and Edgar, whose *Jesus Dropped the Charges* is a show-stopper; Zella Jackson Price, a younger singer who turns to Mother Smith for advice; the Interfaith Choir, and lots of other singers.

Say Amen, Somebody is the kind of movie that isn't made very often, because it takes an unusual combination of skills. The filmmaker has to be able to identify and find his subjects, win their confidence, follow them around, and then also find the technical skill to really capture what makes them special.

Nierenberg's achievement here is a masterpiece of research, diligence, and direction. But his work would be meaningless if the movie didn't convey the spirit of the people in it, and *Say Amen, Somebody* does that with mighty joy. This is a great experience.

The "Up" Movies: *28 Up*

FEBRUARY 7, 1986

The child is father of the man.
—William Wordsworth

Somewhere at home are photographs taken when I was a child. A solemn, round-faced little boy gazes out at the camera, and as I look at him I know in my mind that he is me and I am him, but the idea has no reality. I cannot understand the connection, and as I think more deeply about the mystery of the passage of time, I feel a sense of awe.

Watching Michael Apted's documentary *28 Up,* I had that feeling again and again, that awe that time does pass, and that the same individual does pass through it, grows from a child to an adult, becoming someone new over the passage of years, but still containing some of the same atoms and molecules and fears and gifts that were stored in the child.

This film began twenty-one years ago as a documentary for British television. The assignment for Michael Apted was to interview several seven-year-olds from different British social classes, races, backgrounds, and parts of the country, simply talking with them about what they found important or interesting about their lives. Seven years later, when the subjects were fourteen, Apted tracked them down and interviewed them again. He repeated the process when they were twenty-one, and again when they were twenty-eight, and this film moves back and forth within that material, looking at the same people when they were children, teenagers, young adults, and now warily approaching their thirties.

We have always known that the motion picture is a time machine. John Wayne is dead, but the angle of his smile and the squint in his eye will be as familiar to our grandchildren as it is to us. Orson Welles is dead, but a hundred years from now the moment will still live when the cat rubs against his shoe in *The Third Man,* and then the light from the window catches his sardonic grin. What is remarkable about *28 Up* is not, however, that the same individuals have been captured at four different moments in their lives. We quickly grow accustomed to that. What is awesome is that we can see so clearly how the seven-year-old became the adolescent, how the teenager became the young man or woman, how the adult still contains the seeds of the child.

One sequence follows the lives of three upper-class boys who come from the right families and go to all the right schools. One of the boys is a snob, right from the beginning, and by the time he is twenty-one he is a bit of a reactionary prig. We are not surprised when he declines to be interviewed at twenty-eight; we could see it coming. We are curious, though, about whether he will check back in at thirty-five, perhaps having outlived some of his self-importance.

Another little boy is a winsome loner at seven. At fourteen, he is a dreamy idealist, at twenty-one he is defiant but discontented, and at twenty-eight—in the most unforgettable passage in the film—he is an outcast, a drifter who moves around Great Britain from place to place, sometimes living in a shabby house trailer, still a little puzzled by how he seems to have missed the boat, to never have connected with his society.

There is another little boy who dreams of growing up to be a jockey, and who is a stable boy at fourteen, and does get to be a jockey, briefly, and now drives a cab and finds in his job some of the same personal independence and freedom of movement that he once thought jockeys had. There is a determined young Cockney who is found, years later, happily married and living in Australia and doing well in the building trades. There is a young woman who at twenty-one was clearly an emotional mess, a vague, defiant, bitter, and unhappy person. At twenty-eight, married and with a family, she is a happy and self-assured young woman; the transformation is almost unbelievable.

As the film follows its subjects through the first halves of their lives, our thoughts are divided. We are fascinated by the personal progressions we see on the screen. We are distracted by wonderment about the mystery of the human personality. If we can see so clearly how these children become these adults—was it just as obvious in our own cases? Do we, even now, contain within us our own personal destinies for the next seven years? Is change possible? Is the scenario already written?

I was intending to write that certain groups would be particularly interested in this movie. Teachers, for example, would hardly be able to see *28 Up* without looking at their students in a different, more curious light. Poets and playwrights would learn from this film. So would psychiatrists. But then I realized that *28 Up* is not a film by or for experts. It is superb journalism, showing us these people passing through stages of their lives in such a way that we are challenged to look at our own lives. It is as thought-provoking as any documentary I've ever seen.

I look forward to the next edition of this film, when its subjects are thirty-five. I have hope for some, fear for others. It is almost scary to realize that this film has given me a fair chance of predicting what lies ahead for these strangers. I almost understand the motives of those who chose to drop out of the experiment.

The "Up" Movies: *35 Up*

FEBRUARY 14, 1992

35 UP is the latest installment in the most engrossing long-distance documentary project in the history of film. It began twenty-eight years ago, when a group of ordinary British citizens of various backgrounds were interviewed about their views of the world—at the age of seven. Ever since, at seven-year intervals, director Michael Apted has revisited the subjects for an update on their lives and views, and in this new film the children born in the mid-1950s are marching into middle age, for the most part with few regrets.

Before writing this review, I went back to look again at *28 Up* (1985), which has just been released on video. I wanted to freshen my memory of Neil, the loner who has become the most worrisome of Apted's subjects. When we first see him, at the age of seven, he is already clear on how he wants to spend his life: he wants to be a bus driver, choosing the route himself, telling all of his passengers what to look at out of the windows. By fourteen, Neil was a visionary with big hopes for his life, but something happened between then and twenty-one, when we found him angry and discontented. At twenty-eight, in an image that has haunted me, he was an outcast, living in a small house trailer on the shores of a bleak Scottish lake, and there was real doubt in my mind whether he would still be alive at thirty-five.

He is. He still lives alone, still harbors the view that people cannot quite be trusted to choose for themselves, still doubts he will find a wife to put up with him. Now he lives in subsidized housing on a Scottish island, where last year he directed the village pageant. He was not invited to direct it again this year, and complains morosely that if people would only have learned to follow instructions, the pageant might have turned out better.

Most of the other subjects of the film have turned out more happily. There is Tony, who at seven wanted to be a jockey and at fourteen had

281

found employment as a stable boy. In an earlier film we saw him studying "the knowledge," the year-long process by which a London cabbie must learn his city before he is granted a license, and now, at thirty-five, his children growing up nicely, he is happy to own his own taxi. He realized his dreams, he says; he was a jockey, briefly, and once got to race against Lester Piggott.

We revisit the three working-class girls of the earlier films, who gather around a pub table to assess their lives, with which they are reasonably content. And we see the progress of an upper-class boy who came across as such a snob at twenty-one that he declined to be interviewed at twenty-eight. He is back at thirty-five, somewhat amazingly involved in a relief project for Eastern Europe, and we sense that he has grown out of his class snobbery (to a degree; he cannot resist pointing out a portrait of a royal ancestor).

In my review of 28 Up, I quoted Wordsworth: "The child is father of the man." We can see that even more clearly in 35 Up. The faces gather lines and maturity, the hair sometimes is beginning to turn gray, the slenderness of youth has started to sag. But the eyes are the same. The voices are the same—deeper, but still expressing the thoughts of the same person who was already there, somehow formed, at the age of seven. And in almost every case the personality and hopes of the seven-year-old has predicted the reality of the adult life. (There is one exception, a woman who seemed depressed and aimless at twenty-one, but has undergone a remarkable transformation into cheerful adulthood; I would like her to talk frankly, sometime, about what happened to her between twenty-one and later.)

Some of the subjects complain ruefully that the project has violated their privacy. One of the working-class women says that she is well content with her life, except every seven years when Apted comes nosing around. Others have opted out of 35 Up because they no longer welcome the attention. Most have remained, apparently with the thought that since they have gone this far, they might as well stay the distance.

Somewhere in the midst of the Up project lurks the central mystery of life. How do we become who we are? How is our view of ourselves and our world fashioned? Educators and social scientists might look at these films and despair, because the essential ingredients of future life all seem to be in place at seven, formed in the home and even in the womb before school or the greater world have had much impact. Even more touchingly, in the voices and eyes of these people at thirty-five, we see human beings confronting the fact of their own mortality.

Nearly thirty years have passed since the camera first recorded them peering out at the world around them. In another seven years, most of them will be back again. None has yet died. The project will continue as long as any of them cooperate. Eventually the time will come when only two or three are still alive, and then none. And many years in the future, viewers will be able to look at this unique record, and contemplate the beauty and mystery of life. I am glad most of the subjects of this project have sacrificed their privacy to us every seven years, because in a sense they speak for us, and help us take our own measure.

The "Up" Movies: *42 Up*

APRIL 14, 2000

Give me the child until he is seven,
and I will show you the man.
—Jesuit saying

In 1964, a British television network began an intriguing experiment. They would interview a group of seven-year-olds, asking them what they wanted to do in life, and what kind of a future they envisioned. Then these same subjects would be revisited every seven years, to see how their lives were turning out. It was an intriguing experiment, using film's unique ability to act as a time machine—"the most remarkable nonfiction film project in the history of the medium," wrote Andrew Sarris.

Now here is *42 Up*, the sixth installment in the series. I have seen them all since *14 Up*, and every seven years the series measures out my own life, too. It is impossible to see the films without asking yourself the same questions—without remembering yourself as a child and a teenager, and evaluating the progress of your life.

I feel as if I know these subjects, and indeed I do know them better than many of the people I work with every day, because I know what they dreamed of at seven, their hopes at fourteen, the problems they faced in their early twenties, and their marriages, their jobs, their children, even their adulteries.

When I am asked for career advice, I tell students that they should spend more time preparing than planning. Life is so ruled by luck and chance, I say, that you may end up doing a job that doesn't even exist yet. Don't think you can map your life, but do pack for the journey. Good advice, I think, and yet I look at *42 Up* and I wonder if our fates are sealed at an early age. Many of the subjects of the series seemed to know at seven what they wanted to do and what their aptitudes were, and they were

284

mostly right. Others produced surprises, and keep on producing them right into middle age.

Michael Apted could not have predicted that his future would include a lifelong commitment to this series. He was a young man at the beginning of his career when he worked as a researcher on *7 Up,* choosing the fourteen subjects who would be followed. He became the director of *14 Up,* and has guided the series ever since, taking time off from a busy career as the director of feature films (*Coal Miner's Daughter, Gorillas in the Mist*). In his introduction to a new book about the series, he says he does not envy his subjects: "They do get notoriety and it's the worst kind of fame— without power or money. They're out in the street getting on with their lives and people stop them and say, 'Aren't you that girl?' or Don't I know you?' or 'You're the one . . . ,' and most of them hate that."

The series hasn't itself changed their lives, he believes. "They haven't got jobs or found partners because of the film, except in one case when a friendship developed with dramatic results."

That case involves Neil, who for most longtime followers of the series has emerged as the most compelling character. He was a brilliant but pensive boy, who at seven said he wanted to be a bus driver, so he could tell the passengers what to look for out the windows; he saw himself in the driver's seat, a tour guide for the lives of others. What career would you guess for him? An educator? A politician?

In later films he seemed to drift, unhappy and without direction. He fell into confusion. At twenty-eight, he was homeless in the Highlands of Scotland, and I remember him sitting outside his shabby house trailer on the rocky shore of a loch, looking forlornly across the water. He won't be around for the next film, I thought: Neil has lost his way. He survived, and at thirty-five was living in poverty on the rough Shetland Islands, where he had just been deposed as the (unpaid) director of the village pageant; he felt the pageant would be going better if he were still in charge.

The latest chapter in Neil's story is the most encouraging of all the episodes in *42 Up,* and part of the change is because of his fellow film subject Bruce, who was a boarding school boy, studied math at Oxford, and then gave up a career in the insurance industry to become a teacher in London inner city schools. Bruce has always seemed one of the happiest of the subjects. At forty, he got married. Neil moved to London at about that time, was invited to the wedding, found a job through Bruce, and today—well, I would not want to spoil your surprise when you find the unlikely turn his life has taken.

Apted says in his introduction to the book *42 Up* (The New Press, $16.95) that if he had the project to do again, he would have chosen more middle-class subjects (his sample was weighted toward the upper and working classes), and more women. He had a reason, though, for choosing high and low: the original question asked by the series was whether Britain's class system was eroding. The answer seems to be: yes, but slowly. Sarris, writing in the *New York Observer,* delivers this verdict: "At one point, I noted that the upper-class kids, who sounded like twits at 7 compared to the more spontaneous and more lovable lower-class kids, became more interesting and self-confident as they raced past their social inferiors. It was like shooting fish in a barrel. Class, wealth and social position did matter, alas, and there was no getting around it."

None of the fourteen have died yet, although three have dropped out of the project (some drop out for a film and are back for the next one). By now many have buried their parents. Forced to confront themselves at seven, fourteen, twenty-one, twenty-eight and thirty-five, they seem mostly content with the way things have turned out. Will they all live to forty-nine? Will the series continue until none are alive? This series should be sealed in a time capsule. It is on my list of the ten greatest films of all time, and is a noble use of the medium.

Shoah

NOVEMBER 24, 1985

For more than nine hours I sat and watched a film named *Shoah,* and when it was over, I sat for a while longer and simply stared into space, trying to understand my emotions. I had seen a memory of the most debased chapter in human history. But I had also seen a film that affirmed life so passionately that I did not know where to turn with my confused feelings. There is no proper response to this film. It is an enormous fact, a 550-minute howl of pain and anger in the face of genocide. It is one of the noblest films ever made.

The film's title is a Hebrew word for chaos or annihilation—for the Holocaust. The film is a documentary, but it does not contain images from the 1940s. There are no old newsreel shots, no coverage of the war crimes trials. All of the movie was photographed in the last five or six years by a man named Claude Lanzmann, who went looking for eyewitnesses to Hitler's "Final Solution." He is surprisingly successful in finding people who were there, who saw and heard what went on. Some of them, a tiny handful, are Jewish survivors of the camps. The rest are mostly old people, German and Polish, some who worked in the camps, others who were in a position to observe what happened.

They talk and talk. *Shoah* is a torrent of words, and yet the overwhelming impression, when it is over, is one of silence. Lanzmann intercuts two kinds of images. He shows the faces of his witnesses. And then he uses quiet pastoral scenes of the places where the deaths took place. Steam engines move massively through the Polish countryside, down the same tracks where trains took countless Jews, Gypsies, homosexuals and other so-called undesirables to their deaths. Cameras pan silently across pastures, while we learn that underneath the tranquility are mass graves. Sometimes the image is of a group of people, gathered in a doorway, or in front of a church, or in a restaurant kitchen.

Lanzmann is a patient interrogator. We see him in the corners of some of his shots, a tall, lanky man, informally dressed, chain-smoking. He wants to know the details. He doesn't ask large, profound questions about the meaning of the extermination of millions of people. He asks little questions. In one of the most chilling sequences in the film, he talks to Abraham Bomba, today a barber in Tel Aviv. Bomba was one of the Jewish barbers ordered to cut off the hair of Jewish women before they were killed in Treblinka. His assignment suggests the shattering question: how can a woman's hair be worth more than her life? But Lanzmann does not ask overwhelming and unanswerable questions like this. These are the sorts of questions he asks:

> You cut with what? With scissors?
> There were no mirrors?
> You said there were about sixteen barbers? You cut the hair of how many women in one batch?

The barber tries to answer. As he talks, he has a customer in his chair, and he snips at the customer's hair almost obsessively, making tiny movements with his scissors, as if trying to use the haircut as a way to avoid the questions. Their conversation finally arrives at this exchange, after he says he cannot talk any more:

> A. I can't. It's too horrible. Please.
> Q. We have to do it. You know it.
> A. I won't be able to do it.
> Q. You have to do it. I know it's very hard. I know and I apologize.
> A. Don't make me go on, please.
> Q. Please. We must go on.

Lanzmann is cruel, but he is correct. He must go on. It is necessary to make this record before all of those who were witnesses to the Holocaust have died.

His methods in obtaining the interviews were sometimes underhanded. He uses a concealed television camera to record the faces of some of the old Nazi officials whom he interviews, and we look over the shoulders of the TV technicians in a van parked outside the buildings where they live. We see the old men nonchalantly pulling down charts from the wall to explain the layout of a death camp, and we hear their voices, and at one point when a Nazi asks for reassurance that the conversation is private, Lanzmann provides it. He will go to any length to obtain this testimony.

He does not, however, make any attempt to arrange his material into a chronology, an objective, factual record of how the Final Solution began, continued, and was finally terminated by the end of the war. He uses a more poetic, mosaic approach, moving according to rhythms only he understands among the only three kinds of faces we see in this film: survivors, murderers, and bystanders. As their testimony is intercut with the scenes of train tracks, steam engines, abandoned buildings, and empty fields, we are left with enough time to think our own thoughts, to meditate, to wonder.

This is a long movie but not a slow one, and in its words it creates something of the same phenomenon I experienced while watching *My Dinner with Andre*. The words themselves create images in the imagination, as they might in a radio play. Consider the images summoned by these words, spoken by Filip Müller, a Czech Jew assigned to work at the doors of the gas chambers, a man who survived five waves of liquidations at Auschwitz:

> A. You see, once the gas was poured in, it worked like this: it rose from the ground upwards. And in the terrible struggle that followed—because it was a struggle—the lights were switched off in the gas chambers. It was dark, no one could see, so the strongest people tried to climb higher. Because they probably realized that the higher they got, the more air there was. They could breathe better. That caused the struggle. Secondly, most people tried to push their way to the door. It was psychological; they knew where the door was; maybe they could force their way out. It was instinctive, a death struggle. Which is why children and weaker people and the aged always wound up at the bottom. The strongest were on top. Because in the death struggle, a father didn't realize his son lay beneath him.
> Q. And when the doors were opened?
> A. They fell out. People fell out like blocks of stone, like rocks falling out of a truck.

The images evoked by his words are unutterably painful. What is remarkable, on reflection, is that Müller is describing an event that neither he nor anyone else now alive ever saw. I realized, at the end of his words, that a fundamental change had taken place in the way I personally visualized the gas chambers. Always before, in reading about them or hearing about them, my point of view was outside, looking in. Müller put me inside.

That is what this whole movie does, and it is probably the most important thing it does. It changes our point of view about the Holocaust. After nine hours of *Shoah,* the Holocaust is no longer a subject, a chapter of history, a phenomenon. It is an environment. It is around us. Ordinary people speak in ordinary voices of days that had become ordinary to them. A railroad engineer who drove the trains to Treblinka is asked if he could hear the screams of the people in the cars behind his locomotive.

> A. Obviously, since the locomotive was next to the cars. They screamed, asked for water. The screams from the cars closest to the locomotives could be heard very well.
> Q. Can one get used to that?
> A. No. It was extremely distressing.

He knew the people behind him were human, like him. The Germans gave him and the other workers vodka to drink. Without drinking, they couldn't have done it.

Some of the strangest passages in the film are the interviews with the officials who were actually responsible for running the camps and making the Final Solution work smoothly and efficiently. None of them, at least by their testimony, seem to have witnessed the whole picture. They only participated in a small part of it, doing their little jobs in their little corners; if they are to be believed, they didn't personally kill anybody, they just did small portions of larger tasks, and somehow all of the tasks, when added up and completed, resulted in people dying. Here is the man who scheduled the trains that took the Jews to die:

> Q. You never saw a train?
> A. No, never. We had so much work, I never left my desk. We worked day and night.

And here is a man who lived 150 feet from a church where Jews were rounded up, held, and then marched into gas vans for the trip to the crematoriums:

Q. Did you see the gas vans?

A. No . . . yes, from the outside. They shuttled back and forth. I never looked inside; I didn't see Jews in them.

What is so important about *Shoah* is that the voices are heard of people who did see, who did understand, who did comprehend, who were there, who know that the Holocaust happened, who tell us with their voices and with their eyes that genocide occurred in our time, in our civilization.

There is a tendency while watching *Shoah* to try to put a distance between yourself and the events on the screen. These things happened, after all, forty or forty-five years ago. Most people now alive have been born since they happened. Then, while I was watching the film, came a chilling moment. A name flashed on the screen in the subtitles, the name of one of the commandants at Treblinka death camp. At first I thought the name was "Ebert"—my name. Then I realized it was "Eberl." I felt a moment of relief, and then a moment of intense introspection as I realized that it made no difference what the subtitle said. The message of this film (if we believe in the brotherhood of man) is that these crimes were committed by people like us, against people like us.

But there is an even deeper message as well, and it is contained in the testimony of Filip Müller, the Jew who stood at the door of a crematorium and watched as the victims walked in to die. One day some of the victims, Czech Jews, began to sing. They sang two songs: "The Hatikvah" and the Czech national anthem. They affirmed that they were Jews and that they were Czechs. They denied Hitler, who would have them be one but not the other. Müller speaks:

A. That was happening to my countrymen, and I realized that my life had become meaningless. (His eyes fill with tears.) Why go on living? For what? So I went into the gas chamber with them, resolved to die. With them. Suddenly, some who recognized me came up to me. . . . A small group of women approached. They looked at me and said, right there in the gas chamber . . .

Q. You were inside the gas chamber?

A. Yes. One of them said, "So you want to die. But that's senseless. Your death won't give us back our lives. That's no way. You must get out of here alive, you must bear witness to our suffering and to the injustice done to us."

And that is the final message of this extraordinary film. It is not a documentary, not journalism, not propaganda, not political. It is an act of witness. In it, Claude Lanzmann celebrates the priceless gift that sets man apart from animals and makes us human, and gives us hope: the ability for one generation to tell the next what it has learned.

Dear America:
Letters Home from Vietnam

SEPTEMBER 16, 1988

Surf's up, and the Beach Boys are singing. American kids dive into the waves and come up wet and grinning, and there's a cooler of beer waiting under the palm trees. It looks like Vietnam is going to be a fun place. The opening scenes of *Dear America: Letters Home from Vietnam* are so carefree, so lighthearted, that it doesn't even seem strange that most of the soldiers look exactly like the kids they are—high school graduates drafted straight into war.

On the soundtrack, we hear the voices of these soldiers, in the words they wrote home. They speak of patriotism, of confidence, of new friendships. In their letters there is a sense of wonder at this new world they have found, a world so different from the American cities and towns they left behind. And then gradually the tone of their letters begins to change.

There have been many great movies about Vietnam. This is the one that completes the story. It has no plot except that thousands of young men went to a faraway country and had unspeakable experiences there, and many of them died or were wounded for life in body or soul.

This movie is so powerful precisely because it is so simple. The words are the words of the soldiers themselves, and the images are taken from their own home movies and from TV news footage of the war.

There are moments here that cannot be forgotten, and most of them are due to the hard work of the filmmaker, director Bill Couturié, who has not taken just any words and any old footage, but precisely the right words to go with the images. Couturié began with an anthology of letters written home by U.S. soldiers in Vietnam. Then he screened the entire archive of TV news footage shot by NBC-TV from 1967 to 1969—two million feet of film totaling 926 hours. He also gained access to footage from the Defense Department, including previously classified film of action under

293

fire. Much of the footage in this film has never been seen publicly before, and watching it, you know why.

What Couturié and his researchers have done is amazing. In many cases, they have matched up individual soldiers with their letters—we see them as we hear their words, and then we discover their fates.

"I tell you truthfully I doubt if I'll come out of this alive," a private named Raymond Griffiths writes home to his girlfriend. "In my original squad, I'm the only one left unharmed." He died in action on the Fourth of July, 1966.

There are amateur 8 mm home movies here, of GIs clowning in front of the camera, and cracking beers, and cleaning their weapons. There are frightening fire fights and unflinching shots of men in the process of dying. And there are chilling scenes, such as the one when Gen. William Westmoreland greets the survivors from a bloodbath and his words are the words of an automaton, with utterly no emotion in his voice as he "chats" with his troops. He is so false, it seems like a bad performance. If this footage had been shown on TV at the time, he might have been forced to resign.

The movie follows a chronology that roughly corresponds to a soldier's year in Vietnam. From the first days of swimming in the surf to the last exhausted days of fear and despair, it never looks away.

And the words of the soldiers have the eloquence of simple truth. One soldier writes of the bravery of men who rescued their comrades under enemy fire. Another writes of a momentary hush in a tank battle on Christmas Eve, and of hearing someone begin to sing "Silent Night" and others joining in.

The words in the letters are read by some forty different actors and actresses, whose voices you can sometimes identify, until you stop thinking in those terms. The voices include Robert De Niro, Martin and Charlie Sheen, Kathleen Turner, Tom Berenger, Brian Dennehy, Howard Rollins, Jr., Sean Penn, Matt Dillon, Michael J. Fox. The music on the soundtrack is all from the period, and then, at the end of the movie, there is a heartbreaking flash-forward to the Vietnam War Memorial in Washington, D.C., fifteen years later, and we hear Bruce Springsteen's *Born in the USA* as Ellen Burstyn reads from a letter that the mother of a dead veteran left at the foot of the wall of names:

Dear Bill, Today is Feb. 13, 1984. I came to this black wall again to see and touch your name, William R. Stocks, and as I do I wonder if anyone ever stops to realize that next to your name, on this black wall, is your mother's heart. A heart broken 15 years ago today, when you lost your life in Vietnam.

They tell me the letters I write to you and leave here at this memorial are waking others up to the fact that there is still much pain left, after all these years, from the Vietnam War.

This I know. I would rather have had you for twenty-one years, and all the pain that goes with losing you, than never to have had you at all.

Mom

Choose any film as the best movie ever made about Vietnam, and this is the other half of the same double feature. François Truffaut once wrote that it was impossible to make an "anti-war film," because any war film, no matter what its message, was sure to be exhilarating.

He did not live to see this film.

Crumb

People who have been damaged by life can make the most amazing adjustments in order to survive and find peace. Sometimes it is a toss-up whether to call them mad, or courageous. Consider the case of R. Crumb. He was the most famous comics artist of the 1960s, whose images like "Keep on Truckin'" and "Fritz the Cat" and his cover for the Janis Joplin *Cheap Thrills* album helped to fix the visual look of the decade. He was also a person hanging onto sanity by his fingernails, and it is apparently true that his art saved his life.

Crumb, which is one of the most remarkable and haunting documentaries ever made, tells the story of Robert Crumb, his brothers Max and Charles, and an American childhood which looks normal in the old family photographs but concealed deep wounds and secrets. It is the kind of film that you watch in disbelief, as layer after layer is peeled away and you begin to understand the strategies that have kept Crumb alive and made him successful, when one of his brothers became a recluse in an upstairs bedroom and the other passes his time quite literally sitting on a bed of nails.

Movies like this do not usually get made because the people who have lives like this usually are not willing to reveal them. *Crumb* was directed by Terry Zwigoff, who had two advantages: he had known Crumb well for many years, and he was himself so unhappy and suicidal during the making of the film that in a sense Crumb let him do it as a favor.

Of Crumb's importance and reputation there is not much doubt. His original illustrations and the first editions of his 1960s and 1970s underground comic books command high prices. His new work is shown in galleries, and is in important collections. No less an authority than Robert Hughes, the art critic of *Time* magazine, appears in *Crumb* to declare him "the Brueghel of the last half of the twentieth century."

But *Crumb* is not really about the art, although it will cause you to look at his familiar images with a new eye. It is about the artist, who grew up in a dysfunctional family led by a father who was an overbearing tyrant—a depressive, sadistic bully who, according to this film, beat his sons and lost few opportunities to demean them. (There were also two sisters, who declined to participate in the film.)

All three brothers retreated into fantasies in an attempt to cope with their home life. It was Charles, the oldest, who first started to draw comic strips, and then Robert began to copy him. The brothers seem to have had strong fantasy relationships with comic characters; Charles began to pretend he was Long John Silver. And while it is one thing to learn that Robert masturbated while looking at comics, especially his own, it is another to learn that his prime erotic fixation was with Bugs Bunny.

Many of the people in Crumb's life talk with great frankness about him, including his brothers, his mother, his first wife, Dana (who says he began to develop a "new vision" in 1966 after experimenting with drugs) and his present wife, Aline Kominsky, who recounts bizarre details of his lifestyle with acceptance and understanding. We learn most from Robert himself, however.

He was intensely unhappy in high school, nursed deep grudges against his contemporaries, and uses high school enemies as the models for many of the unattractive caricatures in his work. It is surprising to learn how closely autobiographical some of his drawings are; in his comics men are fixated by callipygian women, and dream of riding them piggyback, and then we see Robert doing the same thing at a gallery opening. He pages through the faces in a high school yearbook, and then we see their look-alikes in his cartoons.

If Robert was unhappy in high school, Charles found it an ordeal from which he never really recovered. In a visit to the family home, occupied by Charles and his mother, we visit the upstairs room that he rarely left, and with Robert essentially acting as the interviewer, he remembers, "I was good-looking, but there was something wrong with my personality; I was the most unpopular kid in school." On a visit to Max, we find him living as a monk, drawing a long linen tape through his body to clean his intestines, and showing recent oil paintings of considerable skill (he still has his mail-order test from the Famous Artists School).

Mrs. Crumb, interviewed while sprawled on a sofa and worrying darkly about the window shades, seems complacent about the fact that Charles never leaves the house: "At least he's not out taking illegal drugs or making some woman miserable."

Zwigoff shows us details of many Crumb comic strips which are intensely violent, sadistic, and hateful toward women. And he interviews such voices of sanity as Deirdre English, former editor of *Mother Jones,* who finds his work pornographic—"an arrested juvenile vision." So it is, and her voice expresses not puritanism but concern and simple observation. Yet as I left the film I felt that if anyone had earned the right to express Crumb's vision, it was Crumb, since his art is so clearly a coping mechanism that has allowed him to survive and deal with his pain. *Crumb* is a film that gives new meaning to the notion of art as therapy.

Heidi Fleiss, Hollywood Madam

MAY 3, 1996

> Eventually we'll never know each other.
> Probably very soon.
> —Heidi Fleiss on Ivan Nagy

Oh, the face of evil can be charming. Remember Hannibal Lecter. Or consider, in the real world, the case of Ivan Nagy. He is a sometime Hollywood movie director who was also—if you can believe his detractors—a pimp, a drug dealer, and a police informer who betrayed his lover while still sleeping with her. He has an impish little smile that he allows to play around his face, and it implicates you in his sleaze. *Come on,* the smile suggests, *who are we kidding? We're all men of the world here; we know this stuff goes on.*

Ivan Nagy was a key player in the life of Heidi Fleiss, the "Hollywood Madam," who was sentenced to three years for procuring prostitutes for an A-list of top Hollywood players and free-spending Arabs. Heidi was not an innocent when she met Nagy. At sixteen, she was already the lover of the millionaire financial swindler Bernie Cornfield. But it was Nagy who (according to the legendary Madam Alex) "sold" Heidi to Alex for $500, then used her as a mole to take over Alex's thriving call girl operation. And it was Nagy who eventually turned Heidi over to the police—again, if Madam Alex can be believed.

What is intriguing about *Heidi Fleiss, Hollywood Madam* is that no one can necessarily be believed. This is an endlessly suggestive, tantalizing documentary, in which the young life of Heidi Fleiss is reflected back at us from funhouse mirrors: now she is a clever businesswoman, now a dupe, now a cynical hooker, now an innocent wrapped around the little finger of a manipulative hustler. Watching the film, we hear several versions of the same stories. Someone is lying, yes—but is anyone telling the truth?

Nick Broomfield is an enterprising documentary filmmaker for the BBC, who tracks his prey with a lightweight camera and sound equipment that can hear around corners. This film is the record of his six months on the case of Heidi Fleiss. She might seem like an insignificant, even pathetic figure, but by the time Broomfield is finished, she has become a victim, and almost sympathetic, if only in contrast with the creatures she dealt with. She wanted to be bad, but had absolutely no idea what she was getting into. "As much bravado as she displays, to me she's still a little kid," her mother tells Broomfield.

Her *mother* participated in this documentary? Most certainly. And so did Heidi, and Nagy, and Victoria Sellers (Peter's daughter and Heidi's best friend), and Madam Alex, and former Los Angeles police chief Daryl Gates. They participated because Broomfield paid them to talk. Madam Alex counts out her cash carefully, and we see Gates pocketing $2,500 before submitting to Broomfield's questions.

What we learn is that Alex was for many years the most successful madam in Los Angeles. Arrested for tax evasion, she got off with probation after an LAPD detective testified that she was a valuable police informant. She allegedly used Nagy, a filmmaker with a respectable front, to obtain airline tickets for her, since she couldn't get a credit card. Perhaps he also located cocaine for her clients. She says Nagy "sold" her Heidi, at around the age of twenty, and that Heidi helped Nagy steal away her empire. Heidi was the front, but Nagy was always the power and the brains.

Nagy says Madam Alex was "one of the most evil women I've met in my life." He smiles. He asks Broomfield, "Do I look like I need $500?" Then he sells him a home video of himself and Heidi. In the video, he tries to get her to take off her clothes, and she observes with concern but not alarm that "some green stuff" is coming out of that part of a man's anatomy he least desires to produce green stuff. A man who would sell that video needs $500.

Broomfield finds Mike Brambles, an LAPD detective (now in jail for robbery), who says Heidi's problem was that she was a bad police informant. She didn't cooperate, and so Nagy set her up to take the fall. Heidi doesn't seem to know if this is true. She describes her business (her clients wanted "typical untouched Southern California eighteen-year-old girls next door. No high heels. Blondes, blondes, blondes"). She is realistic ("A lot of times they'd hire us just to watch them do drugs"). She confesses to always having been attracted to older men ("Over forty, they're all the right age to me").

There is talk of a shadowy Israeli named Cookie, who everyone in the film seems frightened of. If Nagy is the power behind Heidi, is Cookie behind everything? No one will say. Broomfield is tireless in poking his nose, and camera, into these lives. During one visit to Alex he finds her maid using incense to purify the apartment against evil spirits. Nagy conducts a tour of his art collection. Heidi is interviewed in front of her bookshelf, which contains a set of the Great Books of the Western World: did she buy them, or did a client trade them in?

At the end of the film, after Heidi has been found guilty and is going to prison, and she has every reason to hate Nagy, there is a remarkable scene. Nagy calls her on the phone, and lets us eavesdrop as he sweet-talks her. You can tell she still falls for him. Nagy smiles to the camera, helplessly: "There you go," he says. Charming.

Microcosmos

JANUARY 10, 1997

There are so many different insect species that there's a famous scientific quip: Essentially *all* species are insects. Their biomass—the combined weight of the creepy-crawly things—is many times greater than the combined weight of everything else that swims, flies, walks, and makes movies. Insects are the great success story on planet Earth; they were here before we arrived and will remain long after we've gone, inhabiting their worlds of mindless and intricate beauty.

Children, being built nearer to the ground and having more time on their hands, are close observers of ants and spiders, caterpillars and butterflies. Adults tune them out; bugs are things you slap, swat, step on, or spray. *Microcosmos* is an amazing film that allows us to peer deeply into the insect world and marvel at creatures we casually condemn to squishing. The makers of this film took three years to design their close-up cameras and magnifying lenses, and to photograph insects in such brilliant detail that if they were cars, we could read their city stickers.

The movie is a work of art and whimsy as much as one of science. It uses only a handful of words, but is generous with music and amplified sound effects, dramatizing the unremitting struggle of survival that goes on in a meadow in France. If a camera could somehow be transported to another planet, in order to photograph alien life forms, would the result be any more astonishing than these invasions into the private lives of snails and bees, mantises and beetles, spiders and flies?

Where did these forms come from? These legs—two, four, six, a thousand? Eyes like bombardier's turrets? Giant pincers? Honeyed secretions? Metamorphoses from a wormy crawling thing into a glorious flying thing? Grasshoppers that look like plants, and beetles that look like ants? Every one of these amazing creatures represents a successful Darwinian solution to the problem of how to reproduce and make a living. And so are we.

One beautiful creature after another takes the screen. There is a parade of caterpillars. A dung beetle, tirelessly moving his treasure. Two snails engaging in a long and very loving wet kiss. Spiders methodically capturing and immobilizing their prey (what a horrible fate; does the victim understand what has happened to it?). Ants construct lives of meticulous order and then a hungry pheasant comes along and gobbles up thousands of them. More ants construct more anthills, flawless in design and function, and then the hills are bombed by raindrops that look to them as big as beach balls.

There is a fight to the death between two beetles, and their struggle looks as gargantuan as the battling dinosaurs in *Jurassic Park*. There are tiny insects who live in, on, and for the nectar supplied by plants that are perfectly designed for them. Ladybugs seem so ill-designed to fly that every takeoff seems like a clumsy miracle; do they get sweaty palms? Overhead there is a towering canopy of jungle foliage, consisting of the grasses and flowers of the meadow.

See whatever other movies you want to this year. *Microcosmos* is in a category of its own. There is no other film like it. If the movies allow us to see places we have not visited and people we do not know, then *Microcosmos* dramatically extends the range of our vision, allowing us to see the world of the creatures who most completely and enduringly inhabit the Earth.

Sometimes the close-up cameras are almost embarrassingly intimate; should we blush, to see these beings engaged in their crucial daily acts of dining, loving, fighting, being born, and dying? You may leave this movie feeling a little like a god. Or like a big, inelegant, and energy-inefficient hunk of clunky design. Of course, we're smart and they're not. We know the insects exist, and they don't know we exist. Or need to.

PART 5

Overlooked and Underrated

INTRODUCTION

Every critic has films about which he is right and the world is wrong. Here are some of mine. A few, like *Trouble in Mind,* have been so thoroughly overlooked that its director, Alan Rudolph, told me he fears a print no longer exists. Others, like *El Norte,* are Oscar-nominated classics, but have not found the wide audiences they deserve.

In 1999 I started Roger Ebert's Overlooked Film Festival at the University of Illinois at Urbana-Champaign. We look at twelve or fourteen films over a five-day period in the magnificent old Virginia Theater. We look at overlooked formats (70 mm, Todd AO, silents), overlooked genres (musicals, documentaries, even Bollywood, which is certainly overlooked in America), and films that for one reason or another never received the recognition they deserved. What amazes me is how well they play, how the audience shares my mystification that other audiences did not embrace them. I have never heard more laughter than at the Overlooked screening of an Australian comedy named *The Castle,* which Harvey Weinstein told me they shelved at Miramax because "it didn't test well."

Thieves Like Us

1974

Like so much of his work, Robert Altman's *Thieves Like Us* has to be approached with a certain amount of imagination. Some movies are content to offer us escapist experiences and hope we'll be satisfied. But you can't sink back and simply absorb an Altman film; he's as concerned with style as subject, and his preoccupation isn't with story or character, but with how he's showing us his tale. That's the case with *Thieves Like Us,* which no doubt has all sorts of weaknesses in character and plot, but which manages a visual strategy so perfectly controlled that we get an uncanny feel for this time and this place. The movie is about a gang of fairly dumb bank robbers, and about how the youngest of them falls in love with a girl, and about how they stick up some banks and listen to the radio and drink Coke and eventually get shot at.

The outline suggests *Bonnie and Clyde,* but *Thieves Like Us* resembles it only in the most general terms of period and setting. The characters are totally different; Bonnie and Clyde were antiheroes, but this gang of Altman's has no heroism at all. Just a kind of plodding simplicity, punctuated by some of the characters with violence, and by the boy with a kind of wondering love. They play out their sad little destinies against two backdrops: one is the pastoral feeling of the southern countryside, and the other is an exactly observed series of interior scenes that recapture just what it was like to drowse through a slow, hot summer Sunday afternoon, with the radio in the background and the kids playing at pretending to do Daddy's job. If Daddy is a bank robber, so what?

The radio is constantly on in the background of *Thieves Like Us,* but it's not used as a source of music as it was in *American Graffiti* or *Mean Streets.* The old shows we hear are not supposed to be heard by Altman's characters; they're like theme music, to be repeated in the film when the same situations occur. *Gangbusters* plays when they rob a bank, for example, even though the bank would have been closed before *Gangbusters* came on. That's okay, because the radio isn't supposed to be realistic; it's Altman's wry, elegiac comment on the distance between radio fantasy and this dusty, slow-witted reality.

At the heart of the movie is a lovely relationship between the young couple, played by Keith Carradine and Shelley Duvall. They've both been in Altman movies before (just about everybody in view here is in his stock company), and it's easy to see why he likes them so. They don't look like movie stars. They share a kind of rangy grace, an ability to project shyness and uncertainty. There's a scene in bed that captures this; it's a two-shot with Keith in the foreground and Shelley, on her back, eyes to the ceiling, slowly exhaling little plumes of smoke. Nothing is said. The radio plays. Somehow we know just how this quiet, warm moment feels.

The movie's fault is that Altman, having found the perfect means for realizing his story visually, did not spend enough thought, perhaps, on the story itself. *Thieves Like Us* is not another *Bonnie and Clyde,* and yet it does end in a similar way, with a shoot-out. And by this time, we've seen too many movies that have borrowed that structure, that have counted on the bloody conclusion to lend significance to what went before. In *Thieves Like Us,* there just wasn't that much significance, and I don't think there's meant to be. These are small people in a weary time, robbing banks because that's their occupation, getting shot because that's the law's occupation.

Altman's comment on the people and time is carried out through the way he observes them; if you try to understand his intention by analyzing the story, you won't get far. Audiences have always been so plot-oriented that it's possible they'll just go ahead and think this is a bad movie, without pausing to reflect on its scene after scene of poignant observation. Altman may not tell a story better than any one, but he sees one with great clarity and tenderness.

Bring Me the Head of Alfredo Garcia

(Great Movies)

I think I can feel Sam Peckinpah's heart beating and head pounding in every frame in *Bring Me the Head of Alfredo Garcia* (1974), a film he made during a period of alcoholic fear and trembling. I believe its hero, Bennie, completes his task with the same dogged courage as Peckinpah used to complete the movie, and that Bennie's exhaustion, disgust, and despair at the end might mirror Peckinpah's own. I sense that the emotional weather on the set seeped onto the screen, haunting it with a buried level of passion. If there is anything to the auteur theory, then *Alfredo Garcia* is the most autobiographical film Peckinpah ever made.

The film was reviled when it was released. The reviews went beyond hatred into horror. It was "grotesque, sadistic, irrational, obscene, and incompetent," wrote Joy Gould Boyum in the *Wall Street Journal*. It was "a catastrophe," said Michael Sragow in *New York* magazine. "Turgid melodrama at its worst," said *Variety*. Martin Baum, the producer, recalled a sneak preview with only ten people left in the theater at the end: "They hated it! Hated it!"

I gave it four stars and called it "some kind of bizarre masterpiece." Now I approach it again after twenty-seven years, and find it extraordinary, a true and heartfelt work by a great director who endured despite, or perhaps because of, the demons that haunted him. Courage usually feels good in the movies, but it comes in many moods, and here it feels bad but necessary, giving us a hero who is heartbreakingly human—a little man determined to accomplish his mission in memory of a woman he loved, and in truth to his own defiant code.

The film stars Warren Oates (1928–1982), that sad-faced, gritty actor with the crinkled eyes, as a forlorn piano player in a Mexican brothel—an American at a dead end. When a powerful Mexican named El Jefe (Emilio Fernández) discovers that his daughter is pregnant, he commands, "Bring me the head of Alfredo Garcia," and so large is the reward he offers that two bounty hunters (Gig Young and Robert Webber) come into the brothel looking for Alfredo, and that is how Bennie finds out about the head. He knows that a prostitute named Elita (Isela Vega) was once sweet on Alfredo, and he discovers that the man is already dead.

He and Elita love each other, in the desperate fashion of two people who see no other chance of survival. He needs money to escape from the trap he is in. He will dig up the body, steal the head, deliver it to El Jefe, and then he and Elita will live happily ever after—a prospect they honor but do not believe in. During Bennie's odyssey across the dusty roads of Mexico, many will be killed, and the head, carried in a gunnysack, will develop a foul odor and attract a blanket of flies. But it represents Bennie's fortune, and he will die to defend it.

The parallels with *Treasure of the Sierra Madre* are obvious, starting with a broken-down barfly down on his luck, and when Gig Young's character says his name is "Fred C. Dobbs," the name of Bogart's character in *Treasure,* it's a wink from Peckinpah. Dobbs is finally defeated, and so is Bennie, but Bennie at least goes out on his own terms, even though his life spirals down into proof that the world is a rotten place and has no joy for Bennie.

Alfredo Garcia is a mirror image of the formula movie where the hero goes on the road on a personal mission. The very reason for wanting Alfredo Garcia's head—revenge—is moot because Garcia is already dead. By the end, Bennie identifies with the head, talks to "Al," acknowledges that Al was the true love of Elita's life, and puts the stinking head under a shower where once he sat on the floor and watched Elita, and tells it, "a friend of ours tried to take a shower in there."

The sequences do not flow together; they bang together, daily trials under the scorching sun. Of all the extraordinary scenes in the film, the best is the one where Bennie and Elita pull off the road for a picnic, and talk long and softly, tenderly, to each other. Kris Kristofferson, who plays a biker who interrupts this scene, recalled years later that it was supposed to end with Bennie confessing that he had never thought of asking Elita to marry him. "But the scene didn't stop there," he told Garner Simmons, author of *Peckinpah: A Portrait in Montage.* "She [Vega] didn't stop. She says,

'Well, ask me.' And he says, 'What?' And she says, 'To marry you.' And I swear to God, Warren just looked like every other guy who's ever been confronted like that. But he didn't break character. He says, 'Will you marry me?' And then she starts crying. And every time I saw it, it broke me up. Warren said to me: 'I just knew there was no place to hide in that scene. She had me, and I was cryin', too.'"

Then the two bikers appear, and the one played by Kristofferson intends to rape Elita. She knows Bennie has a concealed gun but the bikers are dangerous and she tells the man who has just proposed to her not to risk his life, because, as a prostitute, "I been here before and you don't know the way." It is the sad poetry of that line that expresses Peckinpah's vision, in which people find the courage to do what they must do in a world with no choices.

The film's screenplay and story, by Peckinpah, Gordon T. Dawson and Frank Kowalski, has other dialogue as simple, direct, and sad. When Elita questions the decision to cut off Garcia's head, Bennie tells her, "There's nothing sacred about a hole in the ground or the man that's in it—or you, or me." And then he says, "The church cuts off the toes and fingers and every other damn thing—they're saints. Well, Alfredo is our saint." Later, there is a hint of Shakespeare, even, in Bennie's remark to the sack: "You got jewels in your ears, diamonds up your nose."

The thing is, Oates and Vega are so tired and sweet and utterly without movie-actor affect in this film. They seem worn out and hopeless. These are holy performances. Maybe the conditions of the shoot, and the director's daily personal ordeal, wore them down, and that informed their work. David Weddle, who wrote a book on Peckinpah named *If They move . . . Kill 'Em!,* quotes Gordon Dawson as a daily witness on the location. Dawson had worked with Peckinpah many times before but refused to ever work with him again: "He really lost it on 'Alfredo.' It tore my heart right out."

Peckinpah was a tragic drunk, and booze killed him in 1984, at fifty-nine. When I visited the Durango, Mexico, set of his *Pat Garrett and Billy the Kid* (1973), he sat in a chair under an umbrella, his drink in his hand, and murmured his instructions to an assistant. "The studio screwed him so thoroughly on that picture that he got sick," Kristofferson told me. "There were days when he couldn't raise himself up from his chair." When Peckinpah visited Chicago to promote *Alfredo Garcia,* he sat in a darkened hotel room, wearing dark glasses, hung over, whispering, and I remembered that in the movie Bennie even wears his dark glasses to bed.

Booze destroyed Peckinpah's life, but in this film, I believe, it allowed him, or forced him, to escape from the mindless upbeat formulas of the male action picture, and to send Bennie down a road on which, no matter how bad a man feels, he finishes his job. Some days on the set there must not have been a dime's worth of difference between Peckinpah and Bennie.

Sam Peckinpah directed *The Wild Bunch* (1969), the best Western I have seen, and he brought in a lot of box office money in a career that included *Straw Dogs* and *The Getaway.* He came up as a writer on TV Westerns, starting with *Gunsmoke* in 1955, and in his earliest Western as a director, *Ride the High Country* (1962) he starred the old-timers Randolph Scott and Joel McCrea in a story of two professionals hired to do a job. *The Wild Bunch* was also about aging men whose loyalty was to one another and not to society.

A real director is at his best when he works with material that reflects his own life patterns. At a film festival, after *Pat Garrett* had become the latest of his films to be emasculated by a studio, he was asked if he would ever make a "pure Peckinpah" and he replied, "I did *Alfredo Garcia* and I did it exactly the way I wanted to. Good or bad, like it or not, that was my film."

Saint Jack

DECEMBER 23, 1979

S ometimes a character in a movie inhabits his world so freely, so easily, that he creates it for us as well. Ben Gazzara does that in *Saint Jack,*
as an American exile in Singapore who finds himself employed at the trade
of pimp. He sticks his cigar in his mouth and walks through the crowded
streets in his flowered sport shirts. He knows everyone, he knows all the
angles—but this isn't a smart-aleck performance, something borrowed
from Damon Runyon. It's a performance that paints the character with a
surprising tenderness and sadness, with a wisdom that does not blame
people for what they do, and thus is cheerfully willing to charge them for
doing it.

The character, Jack Flowers, is out of a book by Paul Theroux, who
took a nonfiction look at this same territory in *The Great Railway Bazaar,*
one of the best modern books of travel. The film is by Peter Bogdanovich,
and what a revelation it is, coming after three expensive flops. Bogdanovich, who began so surely in *The Last Picture Show,* seemed to lose feeling
and tone as his projects became more bloated. But here everything is right
again, even his decision to organize the narrative into an hour of atmosphere and then an hour of payoff. Everything.

Not many films are this good at taking an exotic location like Singapore and a life with the peculiarities of Jack Flowers's, and treating them
with such casual familiarity that we really feel Jack lives there—knows it
inside out. The movie is complex without being complicated. Its story line
is a narrative as straight as *Casablanca*'s (with which it has some kinship), but
its details teem with life.

We meet the scheming Chinese traders Jack sometimes works for;
the forlorn and drunken British exiles who inhabit "clubs" of small hopes
and old jokes; the whores who do not have hearts of gold or minds at all;
the odd Ceylonese girl who is Jack's match in cynicism, but not his better.

And we meet William Leigh, another remarkable fictional creation. Leigh is a British citizen out from Hong Kong on business, who looks up Jack Flowers because Jack can arrange things. To Jack's well-concealed surprise, William Leigh doesn't want a prostitute. He wants some talk, a drink, some advice about a hotel room. Jack never really gets to know Leigh, but a bond forms between them because Leigh is decent, is that rare thing, a good man.

Denholm Elliott, usually seen here in third-rate British horror films, has the role, and triumphs in it. It is a subtle triumph; the movie doesn't give Leigh noble speeches or indeed much of anything revealing to say, but Elliott exudes a kind of cheery British self-pride, mixed with fears of death, that communicates as clearly as a bell.

Jack Flowers, meanwhile, runs into trouble. Singapore hoodlums are jealous of the success of his brothel, so they kidnap him and tattoo insulting names on his arms (altogether a more diabolical and satisfactory form of gangland revenge than the concrete overcoat). Jack has the tattoos redecorated into flowers, as William Leigh gets drunk with him. Then, his Singapore business opportunities at an end, he signs up with an American CIA type (Bogdanovich) to run an army brothel near a rest and recreation center.

One of the joys of this movie is seeing how cleanly and surely Bogdanovich employs the two levels of his plot. One level is Jack's story, and leads up to an attempted blackmailing scene that's beautifully sustained. The other level is that of William Leigh, whose life is so different from Jack's, and yet whose soul makes sense to him. The levels come together in a conclusion that is inevitable, quietly noble, wonderfully satisfactory.

All of this works so well because Bogdanovich, assisted by a superb script and art direction, shows us Jack Flowers's world so confidently and because Ben Gazzara makes Jack so special. It's not just a surprise that Gazzara could find the notes and tones to make Saint Jack live. He has been a good actor for a long time. What's surprising, given the difficulties of this character, is that anyone could.

El Norte

AUGUST 1, 2004
(Great Movies)

At the dawn of the independent film movement, two of its founders made what *Variety* called its first epic. *El Norte* (1983) told the story of a Guatemalan brother and sister who fled persecution at home and journeyed north the length of Mexico with a dream of finding a new home in the United States. They were illegal aliens, but then and now, the California economy could not function without their invisible presence as cheap labor. The movie tells their story with astonishing visual beauty, with unashamed melodrama, with anger leavened by hope. It is a *Grapes of Wrath* for our time.

The movie was directed by Gregory Nava, produced by Anna Thomas, and cowritten by both of them. They were later to make *My Family/Mi Familia* (1995), which traces three generations of a Mexican American family in Los Angeles, and Nava is currently the executive producer and supervising director of the *American Family* series on PBS, about an extended Latino family in Los Angeles. But I met Nava and Thomas much earlier, in 1976 at the Chicago Film Festival with their first film, *The Confessions of Amans*. It cost $24,000 and won the prize as best first feature.

That was before Sundance, before IFC, before Miramax. They were the cofounders of the Independent Feature Project, which today holds the Indie Spirits Awards in a vast tent on the beach at Santa Monica. When they founded it, everyone at the meeting fit comfortably into their living room. And when they made *El Norte,* no film like it had been attempted.

Despite its limited budget, the movie is bursting with energy and ambition. At 139 minutes, it is told in three sections, concerning the early life of the brother and sister, their harrowing trek to *el norte,* and their life in Los Angeles. It was shot partly in Mexico, and then, after their exposed footage and an accountant were seized and held for ransom, in California.

The filmmakers tell harrowing stories of cash payoffs at gunpoint, and how Nava's parents slipped out of the country carrying some of the dailies.

But the film never reflects that backstage ordeal; it chooses, indeed, to paint its story not in the grim grays of neorealism, but with the palate of Mexico, filled with color and fantasy. An early scene involving clouds of butterflies combines local legend with magical realism, and abundant life comes into the film through the shirts, dresses, ponchos, and blankets of the characters, and through the joyous use of color in their homes and villages. Nava explained to me one reason for the Mexican love of color: "The rich browns and reds and yellows make brown skin look beautiful; American interiors are painted an eggshell white that doesn't do much for brown skin or any other kind of skin."

The movie stars two unknowns, David Villalpando as Enrique, and Zaide Silvia Gutiérrez as his sister Rosa. They have the spontaneous, unrehearsed quality of some of the actors in neorealist films like *Bicycle Thief*, and an infectious optimism and naiveté that makes us protective of them. In the opening scenes they live as their ancestors have for many generations, in a village of beauty and dignity, a true community. Meals by candlelight are followed by the evening stroll on the little local *ramblas*.

But the people spend long hours at backbreaking labor, picking coffee beans under the harsh eyes of intimidating overseers. Their father Arturo (Ernesto Gómez Cruz) is trying to organize a workers' union; he is betrayed, and everyone at a union meeting is murdered by government troops. Their mother (Alicia Del Lago) disappears. And, yes, events like this are the price we are willing to pay for our morning coffee; I confess when I order my first cup I do not much think of the Arturos and the union-busting international corporations that make their own laws.

Enrique and Rosa have hidden, and feel forced to flee. They have a good idea of America, they think, from the *Good Housekeeping* magazines treasured by their godmother Josefita (Stella Quan), who gives them her savings for the journey and describes a land where everyone—even the poorest—has a refrigerator and an indoor toilet.

Their progress through Mexico is hard enough, but crossing the border is a nightmare. They hire a *coyote,* a man expert at helping Mexicans enter America, and have the good luck to find an honest one. He suggests they crawl into America through an empty drainage pipe, and he will meet them at the other end. He gives them flashlights, they start to crawl, and they're attacked by hordes of screaming rats. The scene is horrifying, not least because it's pretty clear these are real rats. Disease-free rats purchased from a laboratory, yes, but real rats all the same, and although Zaide Silvia Gutiérrez was phobic about rats, she insisted on doing her own scenes, and her panic is real.

As they were crawling through the pipe, it occurred to me that we are fortunate to live in a country people want to enter, instead of escape. And fortunate because so many of our immigrants are the best and the brightest. It takes imagination, ambition, and courage to leave your homeland and start over again in a strange land. One reason immigrants often seem to do well here is that they were self-selected as brave and determined.

In Los Angeles, Enrique and Rosa enter the job market, Enrique as a dishwasher and busboy, Rosa first in a garment factory and then as a maid. They are undocumented, but necessary; a 2004 movie named *A Day without a Mexican* is a fantasy imagining the collapse of the California economies after all the Enriques and Rosas disappear. In Guatemala, Enrique's father told them the bosses cared nothing for a man, only for his strong arms. Now in America trucks from day-labor contractors pull into the motels where Chicanos live, and the men hopefully cluster about, showing their muscles.

The great Mexican American character actress Lupe Ontiveros makes one of her first appearances in this movie (Jennifer Lopez had her first meaningful movie role in *Mi Familia,* and became a star in Nava's 1997 *Selena*). Ontiveros plays Nacha, who becomes Rosa's confidant and protector and counsels her on how to deal with the gringos: "Just smile and say 'yes' to whatever they say." Rosa tries to smile and say "yes" when her employer confronts her with an unbelievably complicated automatic washer and dryer, but finally surrenders and, in one of the film's welcome laughs, simply spreads the laundry out on the grass, to dry in the sun.

Another of the film's many strong supporting performances is by Trinidad Silva, as the motel manager and labor broker, who defines situations by imposing his will upon them. He might have had a rich career, but was killed in a traffic accident a few years after the film was made.

The closing scenes use the power of melodrama to involve our emotions, and they succeed; the simplicity and depth of Gutiérrez's acting is heartbreaking. I've read reviews criticizing the film for its melodrama, but it occurred to me that the lives of many poor people are melodrama from birth to death. It takes a lot of money to insulate yourself in a less eventful, more controllable, life.

Seen after twenty years, *El Norte* retains its direct power to move and anger. The story needs no updating; it repeats every day. The movie really makes no statement about immigration itself, because policy questions are irrelevant to its characters. They want what we all want, better lives for themselves and their children. Their story is the same story enacted by the German, Irish, and Italian immigrants to America—by all of us, even the Native Americans, who came from Mongolia.

In the years since the film was released, the underlying reality of illegal immigration has remained essentially the same: America forbids it, yet requires it as a source of cheap labor. Someone like Cesar Chavez, who fought for the rights of Chicano farm laborers, was attacked because he revealed the nation's underlying hypocrisy on the subject.

The stories of Enrique and Rosa end sadly, but Nava returned to the subject of immigrant families in *My Family,* where they endure and prevail. A Mexican American couple walk to Los Angeles, move in with an uncle they have never met before, and by the end of their lives count among their children a nun, a lawyer, a writer, and a gang member shot dead by the police. They agree they have had wonderful lives, and that it would be wrong to ask for too much.

To Live and Die in L.A.

NOVEMBER 1, 1985

In the hierarchy of great movie chase sequences, the recent landmarks include the chases under the Brooklyn elevated tracks in *The French Connection,* down the hills of San Francisco in *Bullitt,* and through the Paris Metro in *Diva.* Those chases were not only thrilling in their own right, but they also reflected the essence of the cities where they took place. Now comes William Friedkin, director of *The French Connection,* with a new movie that contains another chase that belongs on that short list. The movie is set in Los Angeles, and so, of course, the chase centers on the freeway system.

To Live and Die in L.A. is a law-enforcement movie, sort of. It's about secret service agents who are on the trail of a counterfeiter who has eluded the law for years, and who flaunts his success. At one point, when undercover agents are negotiating a deal with the counterfeiter in his expensive health club, he boasts, "I've been coming to this gym three times a week for five years. I'm an easy guy to find. People know they can trust me." Meanwhile, he's asking for a down payment on a sale of bogus bills, and the down payment is larger than the secret service can authorize. So Richard Chance (William L. Petersen), the hot-dog special agent who's the hero of the movie, sets up a dangerous plan to steal the advance money from another crook and use it to buy the bogus paper and bust the counterfeiter.

Neat. The whole plot is neat, revolving around a few central emotions—friendship, loyalty, arrogance, anger. By the time the great chase sequence arrives, it isn't just a novelty that's tacked onto a movie where it doesn't fit. It's part of the plot. The secret service agents bungle their crime, the cops come in pursuit, and the chase unfolds in a long, dazzling ballet of timing, speed, and imagination.

The great chases are rarely just chases. They involve some kind of additional element—an unexpected vehicle, an unusual challenge, a strange

319

setting. The car-train chase in *The French Connection* was a masterstroke. In *Diva,* the courier rode his motor scooter into one subway station and out another, bouncing up and down the stairs. Or think of John Ford's sustained stagecoach chase in *Stagecoach,* or the way Buster Keaton orchestrated *The General* so that trains chased each other through a railway system.

The masterstroke in *To Live and Die in L.A.* is that the chase isn't just on a freeway. It goes the wrong way down the freeway. I don't know how Friedkin choreographed this scene, and I don't want to know. It probably took a lot of money and a lot of drivers. All I know is that there are high-angle shots of the chase during which you can look a long way ahead and see hundreds of cars across four lanes, all heading for the escape car, which is aimed at them, full speed. It is an amazing sequence.

The rest of the movie is also first-rate. The direction is the key. Friedkin has made some good movies (*The French Connection, The Exorcist, Sorcerer*) and some bad ones (*Cruising, Deal of the Century*). This is his comeback, showing the depth and skill of the early pictures. The central performance is by William L. Petersen, a Chicago stage actor who comes across as tough, wiry, and smart. He has some of the qualities of a Steve McQueen, with more complexity. Another strong performance in the movie is by Willem Dafoe as the counterfeiter, cool and professional as he discusses the realities of his business.

I like movies that teach me about something, movies that have researched their subject and contain a lot of information, casually contained in between the big dramatic scenes. *To Live and Die in L.A.* seems to know a lot about counterfeiting and also about the interior policies of the secret service. The film isn't just about cops and robbers, but about two systems of doing business, and how one of the systems finds a way to change itself in order to defeat the other.

That's interesting. So is the chase.

Trouble in Mind

MARCH 21, 1986

Here is a movie that takes place within our memories of the movies. The characters, the mysteries, and especially the doomed romances are all generated by old films, by remembered worlds of lurid neon signs and deserted areas down by the docks, of sad cafes where losers linger over a cup of coffee and lonely rooms where the lightbulb is a man's only friend. This is a world for which the saxophone was invented.

The movie begins with a man being released from prison, of course. He is dressed in black and has a beard and wears a hat, of course, and is named Hawk, of course, and the first place he goes when he arrives in town is Wanda's Cafe, where Wanda keeps a few rooms upstairs for her old lovers to mend their broken dreams.

The cafe is on a worn-out old brick street down at the wrong end of Rain City. It's the kind of place that doesn't need to advertise, because its customers are drawn there by their fates. One day, a young couple turn up in a broken-down camper. The kid is named Coop, and he knows he always gets into trouble when he comes to the city, but he needs to make some money to support his little family. His girlfriend, Georgia, looks way too young to have a baby, but there it is, bawling in her arms. She's a blond with a look in her eyes that makes Hawk's heart soar.

Coop falls into partnership with the wrong man, a black man named Solo who sits in a back booth at Wanda's and recites poems about anger and hopelessness. Before long, Coop and Solo are involved in a life of crime, and Hawk is telling Georgia she's living with a loser. Wanda stands behind the counter and watches all this happen with eyes that have seen a thousand plans go wrong. She hires Georgia as a waitress. That turns Hawk into a regular customer. Wanda knows Hawk is in love with Georgia, because Wanda and Hawk used to be in love with each other, and once you learn to hear that note in a man's voice, you hear it even when he's not singing to you.

Coop and Solo are trying to sell hot wristwatches. Hilly Blue doesn't like that. Hilly is the boss of the local rackets, and lives in a house furnished like the Museum of Modern Art. The best way to describe Hilly Blue is to say that if Sydney Greenstreet could have reproduced by parthenogenesis after radioactive damage to his chromosomes, Hilly would have been the issue.

Trouble in Mind is not a comedy, but it knows that it is funny. It is not a fantasy, and yet strange troops patrol the streets of Rain City, and as many people speak Korean as English. It does not take place in the 1940s, but its characters dress and talk and live as though it did. Could this movie have been made if there had never been any movies starring Richard Widmark, Jack Palance, or Robert Mitchum? Yes, but it wouldn't have had any style.

To really get inside the spirit of *Trouble in Mind,* it would probably help to see *Choose Me* (1984) first. Both films are the work of Alan Rudolph, who is creating a visual world as distinctive as Fellini's and as cheerful as Edward Hopper's. He does an interesting thing. He combines his stylistic excesses with a lot of emotional sincerity, so that we believe these characters are really serious about their hopes and dreams, even if they do seem to inhabit a world of imagination.

Look at it this way. In Woody Allen's *The Purple Rose of Cairo,* a character stepped out of a movie and off the screen and into the life of a woman in the audience. If that had happened in *Trouble in Mind,* the woman would have asked the character why he even bothered.

Sometimes the names of movie actors evoke so many associations that further description is not necessary. Let's see. Hawk is played by Kris Kristofferson. Coop is Keith Carradine. Wanda is Geneviève Bujold. Hilly Blue is the transvestite Divine, but he is not in drag this time, allegedly. Mix them together, light them with neon reds and greens, and add a blond child-woman (Lori Singer) and a black gangster (Joe Morton) whose shades are his warmest feature, and perhaps you can begin to understand why it never rains in Rain City.

Housekeeping

JANUARY 22, 1988

In a land where the people are narrow and suspicious, where do they draw the line between madness and sweetness? Between those who are unable to conform to society's norm, and those who simply choose not to, because their dreamy private world is more alluring? That is one of the many questions asked, and not exactly answered, in Bill Forsyth's *Housekeeping,* which is one of the strangest and best films of the year.

The movie, set some thirty or forty years ago in the Pacific Northwest, tells the story of two young girls who are taken on a sudden and puzzling motor trip by their mother, to visit a relative. Soon after they arrive, their mother commits suicide, and before long her sister, their Aunt Sylvie, arrives in town to look after them.

Sylvie, who is played by Christine Lahti as a mixture of bemusement and wry reflection, is not an ordinary type of person. She likes to sit in the dusk so much that she never turns the lights on. She likes to go for long, meandering walks. She collects enormous piles of newspapers and hundreds of tin cans—carefully washing off their labels and then polishing them and arranging them in gleaming pyramids. She is nice to everyone and generally seems cheerful, but there is an enchantment about her that some people find suspicious.

Indeed, even her two young nieces are divided. One finds her "funny," and the other loves her, and eventually the two sisters will take separate paths in life because they differ about Sylvie. At first, when they are younger, she simply represents reality to them. As they grow older and begin to attend high school, however, one of the girls wants to be "popular" and resents having a weird aunt at home, while the other girl draws herself into Sylvie's dream.

The townspeople are not evil, merely conventional and "concerned." Parties of church ladies visit, to see if they can "help." The sheriff eventually gets involved. But *Housekeeping* is not a realistic movie, not one of those disease-of-the-week docudramas with a tidy solution. It is funnier, more offbeat, and too enchanting to ever qualify on those terms.

The writer-director, Bill Forsyth, has made all of his previous films in Scotland (they make a list of whimsical, completely original comedies: *Gregory's Girl, Local Hero, Comfort and Joy, That Sinking Feeling*). For his first North American production, he began with a novel by Marilynne Robinson that embodies some of his own notions, such as that certain people grow so amused by their own conceits that they cannot be bothered to pay lip service to yours.

In Christine Lahti, he has found the right actress to embody this idea. Although she has been excellent in a number of realistic roles (she was Gary Gilmore's sister in *The Executioner's Song,* and Goldie Hawn's best friend in *Swing Shift*), there is something resolutely private about her, a sort of secret smile that is just right for Sylvie. The role requires her to find a delicate line; she must not seem too mad or willful, or the whole charm of the story will be lost. And although there are times in the film when she seems to be indifferent to her nieces, she never seems not to love them.

Forsyth has surrounded that love with some extraordinary images, which help to create the magical feeling of the film. The action takes place in a house near a lake which is crossed by a majestic, forbidding railroad bridge, and it is a local legend that one night decades ago, a passenger train slipped ever so lazily off the line and plunged down, down, into the icy waters of the frozen lake. The notion of the passengers in their warm, well-lit carriages, plunging down to their final destination, is one that Forsyth somehow turns from a tragedy into a notion of doomed beauty. And the bridge becomes important at several moments in the film, especially the last one.

The natural setting of the film (in British Columbia) and the production design by Adrienne Atkinson are also evocative; it is important that the action takes place in a small, isolated community, in a place cut off from the world where whimsies flourish and private notions can survive. At the end of the film, I was quietly astonished; I had seen a film that could perhaps be described as being about a madwoman, but I had seen a character who seemed closer to a mystic, or a saint.

The Rapture

NOVEMBER 8, 1991

> As flies to wanton boys, are we to the gods;
> They kill us for their sport.
> —Shakespeare, *King Lear*

Her life is a bleak and sinful void. She finds God, and is reborn. But then, after a period during which she finds peace through her new beliefs, her life becomes a void again—this time, on God's terms. Sharon, the woman played brilliantly and courageously by Mimi Rogers in *The Rapture,* is a character like Job, tested by God to the breaking point. Unlike Job, she finally refuses to be toyed with any longer.

Her story is told in one of the most challenging and infuriating movies I've seen—a radical, uncompromising treatment of the Christian teachings about the final judgment. Almost all movies with a religious theme are made by people who are themselves religious, or who piously pretend to be. *The Rapture,* written and directed by Michael Tolkin, is seen from a more literal, skeptical point of view: All right, he seems to be saying, if this is what the end of creation is going to be like, then we should stare unblinking at its full and terrifying implications.

As the movie opens, Sharon and her lover Vic (Patrick Bauchau) are swingers, mate-swappers who cruise the bars together, looking for likely prospects. When they find others who want to swing, they go home for sexual games which Sharon finds increasingly unrewarding. Is this all life is—partying all night, and spending her days in a tiny cubicle, working as an operator for the telephone company?

Tolkin uses Sharon's daytime job as a metaphor for modern man, who communicates more easily than ever before, but more impersonally. Sharon's job requires her to talk to hundreds of people all day long, but in a mechanical way. Her nighttime sex life is almost a reaction to the sterile existence of her days.

Then she overhears some of her coworkers talking, during a lunch break, about "the rapture," about the imminent second coming of Christ, about "the boy," who is their prophet. She is curious, and is taken to one of their meetings, and finds that all over the world some people are sharing the same dream, of the imminent end of the world. It is a dream she has herself. Torn between her sinful existence and the hope of these believers, she attempts to commit suicide, but instead experiences an overwhelming spiritual experience, and is born again.

Ah, but the movie does not lead us where we expect it to go, after her experience. She leaves Vic, she finds a partner who is spiritually healthier, she has a daughter, she leads a blameless life, and then, when the girl is about six, Sharon becomes convinced that the Second Coming is imminent. She goes out into the wilderness with her daughter, to await the moment when she expects God to gather the two of them into heaven. And she waits. And waits. And a national park policeman takes pity on them, as they stand under the merciless sun.

Sharon is guilty, I believe, of the sin of Pride. She thinks she knows when, and how, God will call her. God does not perform according to her timetable. And yet Tolkin does not cheat us with an ending in which Sharon is simply seen as deluded. God does exist in this film, and he does make judgments about individuals such as Sharon, and the world does end, with the fearsome horsemen of the apocalypse in the sky, and the bars falling from the doors of the prison-cells.

It is simply that, by the time of the judgment, Sharon has had enough. She commits a shocking action, she tries to stand firm and unflinching in her faith, but she finally comes to believe that God has asked too much of her. Her actions in the last twenty minutes of this film send audiences boiling out of the theater, engaged in fierce discussions. After decades of "religious" films which were simply sentimentalized fables, here is a film that demands its audiences to make their own peace with the rules of an inflexible deity.

Watching the film, I began to realize that I would feel cheated if Tolkin did not give us some vision of heaven—did not take Sharon to another plane, in one way or another. He does not cheat us, and the closing passages of this film are stunning in their implications. It is true that on a limited budget *The Rapture* is not able to give us sensational special effects—a state-of-the-art heaven, if you will. It doesn't matter. He gives us an idea of heaven that transcends any possible special effect, and bring us face to face with the awful, and awe-full, consequences of that day when the saints go marching in.

A Soldier's Daughter Never Cries

SEPTEMBER 25, 1998

You can sense the love of a daughter for her parents in every frame of *A Soldier's Daughter Never Cries*. It's only brought into the foreground in a couple of scenes, but it courses beneath the whole film, an underground river of gratitude for parents who were difficult and flawed, but prepared their kids for almost anything.

The movie is told through the eyes of Channe, a young girl whose father is a famous American novelist. In the 1960s, the family lives in Paris, on the Ile St. Louis in the Seine. Bill Willis (Kris Kristofferson) and his wife Marcella (Barbara Hershey) move in expatriate circles ("We're Euro-trash"), and the kids go to a school where the students come from wildly different backgrounds. At home, dad writes, but doesn't tyrannize the family with the importance of his work, which he treats as a job ("Typing is the one thing I learned in high school of any use to me"). There is a younger brother, Billy, who was adopted under quasi-legal circumstances, and a nanny, Candida, who turns down a marriage proposal to stay with the family.

All of this is somewhat inspired, I gather, by fact. The movie is based on an autobiographical novel by Kaylie Jones, whose father, James Jones, was the author of *From Here to Eternity, The Thin Red Line,* and *Whistle.* Many of the parallels are obvious: Jones lived in Paris, drank a lot, and had heart problems. Other embellishments are no doubt fiction, but what cannot be concealed is that Kaylie was sometimes almost stunned by the way both parents treated her with respect as an individual, instead of patronizing her as a child.

The overarching plot line is simple: the children become teenagers, the father's health causes concerns, the family eventually decides to move back home to North Carolina. The film's appeal is in the details. It recreates a childhood of wonderfully strange friends, eccentric visitors, a Paris which was more home for the children than for the parents, and a homecoming which was fraught for them all. The Willises are like a family sailing in a small boat to one comfortable but uncertain port after another.

The movie was directed by James Ivory and produced by Ismail Merchant, from a screenplay by their longtime collaborator, the novelist Ruth Prawer Jhabvala. She also knows about living in other people's countries, and indeed many of Ivory's films have been about expatriates and exiles (most recently another American in France, in *Jefferson in Paris*). There is a delight in the way they introduce new characters and weave them into the family's bohemian existence. This is one of their best films.

Channe and young Billy are played as teenagers by Leelee Sobieski and Jesse Bradford. We learn some of the circumstances of Billy's adoption, and there is a journal, kept by his mother at the age of fifteen, which he eventually has to decide whether to read or not. He has some anger and resentment, which his parents deal with tactfully; apart from anything else, the film is useful in the way it deals with the challenge of adoption.

Channe, at school, becomes close friends with the irrepressible Francis Fortescue (Anthony Roth Costanzo), who is the kind of one-off original the movie makes us grateful for. He is flamboyant and uninhibited, an opera fan whose clear, high voice has not yet broken, and who exuberantly serenades the night with his favorite arias. We suspect that perhaps he might grow up to discover he is gay, but the friendship takes place at a time when such possibilities are not yet relevant, and Channe and Francis become soul mates, enjoying the kind of art-besotted existence Channe's parents no doubt sought for themselves in Paris.

The film opens with a portrait of the Willises on the Paris cocktail party circuit, but North Carolina is a different story, with a big frame house and all the moods and customs of home. The kids hate it. They're called "frogs" at school. Channe responds by starting to drink and becoming promiscuous, and Billy vegetates in front of the TV set. Two of the best scenes involve a talk between father and daughter about girls who are too loose, and another, after Channe and a classmate really do fall in love, where Bill asks them if they're having sex. When he gets his answer, he suggests, sincerely, that they use the girl's bedroom: "They're gonna do it anyway; let them do it right."

A Soldier's Daughter Never Cries is not a textbook for every family. It is a story about this one. If a parent is remembered by his children only for the work he did, then he spent too much time at work. What is better is to be valued for who you really were. If the parallels between this story and the growing up of Kaylie Jones are true ones, then James Jones was not just a good writer but a good man.

The Saddest Music in the World

MAY 14, 2004

S o many movies travel the same weary roads. So few imagine entirely original worlds. Guy Maddin's *The Saddest Music in the World* exists in a time and place we have never seen before, although it claims to be set in Winnipeg in 1933. The city, we learn, has been chosen by the *London Times,* for the fourth year in a row, as "the world capital of sorrow." Here Lady Port-Huntley (Isabella Rossellini) has summoned entries for a contest which will award $25,000 "in depression-era dollars" to the performer of the saddest music.

This plot suggests no doubt some kind of camp musical, a sub–Monty Python comedy. What Maddin makes of it is a comedy, yes, but also an eerie fantasy that suggests a silent film like *Metropolis* crossed with a musical starring Nelson Eddy and Jeanette McDonald, and then left to marinate for long forgotten years in an enchanted vault. The Canadian filmmaker has devised a style that evokes old films from an alternate timeline; *The Saddest Music* is not silent and not entirely in black and white, but it looks like a long-lost classic from decades ago, grainy and sometimes faded; he shoots on 8 mm film and video and blows it up to look like a memory from cinema's distant past.

The effect is strange and delightful; somehow the style lends quasi-credibility to a story that is entirely preposterous. Because we have to focus a little more intently, we're drawn into the film, surrounded by it. There is the sensation of a new world being created around us. The screenplay is by the novelist Kazuo Ishiguro, who wrote the very different *Remains of the Day.* Here he creates, for Maddin's visual style, a fable that's *Canadian Idol* crossed with troubled dreams.

Lady Port-Huntley owns a brewery, and hopes the contest will promote sales of her beer. Played by Rossellini in a blonde wig that seems borrowed from a Viennese fairy tale, she is a woman who has lost her legs and propels herself on a little wheeled cart until being supplied with fine new glass legs, filled with her own beer.

To her contest come competitors like the American Chester Kent (Mark McKinney of *Kids in the Hall*), looking uncannily like a snake-oil salesman, and his lover Narcissa (Maria de Medeiros), who consults fortune-tellers on the advice of a telepathic tapeworm in her bowels. If you remember de Medeiros and her lovable little accent from *Pulp Fiction* (she was the lover of Bruce Willis's boxer), you will be able to imagine how enchantingly she sings "The Song Is You."

Kent's brother Roderick (Ross McMillan) is the contestant from Serbia. Their father Fyodor (David Fox) enters for Canada, singing the dirge "Red Maple Leaves." One night while drunk he caused a car crash and attempted to save his lover by amputating her crushed leg—but, alas, cut off the wrong leg, and is finally seen surrounded by legs. And that lover, dear reader, was Lady Port-Huntley.

Competitors are matched off two by two. "Red Maple Leaves" goes up against a pygmy funeral dirge. Bagpipers from Scotland compete, as does a hockey team that tries to lift the gloom by singing "I Hear Music." The winner of each round gets to slide down a chute into a vat filled with beer. As Lady Port-Huntley chooses the winners, an unruly audience cheers. Suspense is heightened with the arrival of a cellist whose identity is concealed by a long black veil.

You have never seen a film like this before, unless you have seen other films by Guy Maddin, such as *Dracula: Pages from a Virgin's Diary* (2002), or *Archangel* (1990). Although his *Tales from the Gimli Hospital* was made in 1988, his films lived on the fringes, and I first became aware of him only in 2000, when he was one of the filmmakers commissioned to make a short for the Toronto Film Festival. His *Heart of the World,* now available on DVD with *Archangel* and *Twilight of the Ice Nymphs,* was a triumph, selected by some critics as the best film in the festival. It, too, seemed to be preserved from some alternate universe of old films.

The more films you have seen, the more you may love *The Saddest Music in the World*. It plays like satirical nostalgia for a past that never existed. The actors bring that kind of earnestness to it that seems peculiar to supercharged melodrama. You can never catch them grinning, although great is the joy of Lady Port-Huntley when she poses with her sexy new beer-filled glass legs. Nor can you catch Maddin condescending to his characters; he takes them as seriously as he possibly can, considering that they occupy a mad, strange, gloomy, absurd comedy. To see this film, to enter the world of Guy Maddin, is to understand how a film can be created entirely by its style, and how its style can create a world that never existed before, and lure us, at first bemused and then astonished, into it.

PART 6

Essays and Think Pieces

INTRODUCTION

In the newspaper business we call these Thinkers, or Thumb-Suckers. The critic becomes a pundit and profoundly addresses the issues of the day. The article about *The Color Purple* was written on the airplane to Chicago, the day after the Academy Awards. The article on the A rating is one of many I've written over the years. I have also debated Jack Valenti on the subject, to no avail. My personal thought is that the movie industry and the theater owners have no desire to establish a workable rating that would actually prevent them from selling tickets. The directors' loss of freedom to make adult films is one the industry can live with.

THAT'S THE WAY IT IS

The Color Purple and the Oscars

MARCH 30, 1986

LOS ANGELES—They caught up with Quincy Jones just as he was entering Swifty Lazar's big post-Oscar bash at Spago, the chic pizza joint up above the Sunset Strip. They asked him why he thought *The Color Purple* had been so completely shut out at this year's Academy Awards, why it didn't even get one single lousy Oscar for anything, not even in one of those obscure technical categories. And Jones, who composed the music for the movie and was its coproducer, said:

"That's the way it is."

He paused. "And." He paused again, then said, "And that's the way it is. Someday we're going to have to change that." Then he went inside, where Swifty and several hundred pals were attending Hollywood's version of prom night.

That's the way it is.

A flat statement, concealing a multitude of possibilities. I cannot read Quincy Jones's mind, and so cannot tell you for sure what he meant. But I imagine he was making a quiet, almost dispassionate statement about a black film in a white society.

Nobody would say, or probably even believe, that the academy voters were being racist in their across-the-board rejection of *The Color Purple*. After all, these were the same voters who gave the movie eleven nominations. A movie has to stand or fall on its perceived merits, and not on the race of its cast or the subject of its screenplay. Perhaps, all the same, there was a small irony in the fact that the academy passed over a movie about blacks in a white land to give seven Oscars to *Out of Africa,* a film about whites in a black land.

Perhaps there was another irony in the fact that many influential black writers and leaders denounced *The Color Purple* for what they saw as a negative portrayal of black men, but none of them denounced *Out of*

Africa, with its vague portraits of tribal blacks who were trotted onscreen for a touch of authenticity.

In a Hollywood world where blacks are hardly ever made the center of major films, why attack the film that tried to say something that gave attention and love to its unforgettable characters? Was it a certain provincialism on the part of those black critics, who saw the movie in terms of how it would present blacks to white audiences, instead of seeing it as a movie about certain black characters, some of them good people, some of them bad?

This much seems true: the controversy over *The Color Purple,* which extended even to pickets outside Dorothy Chandler Pavilion on Oscar night, did nothing to help the film. The typical academy voter is hard to characterize, but there are two generalizations we can make. He or she is not young, and not black.

This typical voter possibly enjoyed *Out of Africa* because it was a reminder of an earlier, simpler time in Hollywood, when stately epics were cast with major stars and cloaked in literacy and respectability. Here was a film directed by Sydney Pollack, Hollywood's idea of a true professional (and mine, too—I am not attacking *Out of Africa,* only wondering why *The Color Purple* was snubbed). The film starred Meryl Streep, the reigning queen of great Hollywood actresses (she deserves to be), and Robert Redford, a modern leading man of mythic proportions, and Klaus Maria Brandauer, the sort of distinguished European actor Hollywood has always liked to import for a new face in a tricky role.

And then you have a film starring names that most of the academy voters had never heard before: Whoopi Goldberg, Oprah Winfrey, Margaret Avery and Danny Glover. It was directed, however, by a name they could quickly recognize, Steven Spielberg. And as we consider Spielberg more carefully, perhaps we can begin to understand some of the subtle reasons the academy turned away from *The Color Purple.*

There has never been a Hollywood director more successful than Steven Spielberg. Not Cecil B. DeMille, not John Ford, not Frank Capra or Alfred Hitchcock or George Lucas or Francis Ford Coppola or any combination of two of those names. Steven Spielberg is the man, more than any other, who in the last decade has understood the sort of films that most people want to see, and has made them, and made them well. His credits include *Jaws, Close Encounters of the Third Kind, Raiders of the Lost Ark, Indiana Jones and the Temple of Doom,* and *E.T.,* which was the largest-grossing film in history. As a producer, he has made *Gremlins, Poltergeist, Back to the Future,* and many other films, virtually every one of them successful. If a major Hollywood studio executive were to simply sign Spielberg to an exclusive contract, he would have done such a good thing for his shareholders that he could then justifiably retire on full salary.

Hollywood admires success, and it admires Spielberg's success. He is not only a great professional, but a nice man, who is not known for tantrums or egotism or controversy. After the academy voters failed to nominate him as one of the year's best directors, he steadfastly refused to be publicly angry, insisting "I am not a belly-acher," and turning up at the Oscarcast just like all the other guests.

And yet, understand this. Spielberg achieves, over and over again, what so many people in the movie industry desperately wish they could do only once. Or half of once. He has good taste, technical mastery, artistic flair, and popular charm. People kill themselves out here—literally work and worry and negotiate themselves to death—trying to turn worthless little pieces of crap into movies. Because you cannot be stupid and get far in Hollywood, the people who make bad movies are usually smart enough to know they are bad. Hollywood is such a competitive town that you need to be smart, gifted, and lucky to claw yourself up to the point where you can make bad movies. There is a lot of self-hatred involved.

Now here comes this kid who makes it look so easy. Who can't seem to fail. Who makes a movie like *E.T.* that not only grosses hundreds of millions of dollars but is just as popular all over the world as here at home, and is even acclaimed as a masterpiece of popular art. There is something unfair about it. Nobody should get all the breaks.

In Hollywood, *The Color Purple* was widely seen, rightly or wrongly, as Spielberg's bid for a different kind of acclaim. He deliberately set out (you can hear people say) to buy an important novel such as *The Color Purple* and make it into an important film, and show that he had political and social convictions to go along with his storytelling skills.

Hollywood gets perverse about situations like that. It understands very well why a man might spend a year making a movie that a thirteen-year-old would disdain as trash. But if a man blessed with great success tries to do something really wonderful, there is a tendency to slap him down. It is just too much of an affront to all the compromises and little ethical deaths that happen every day all over town.

Someday, Steven Spielberg will win his Oscar. This year he was rebuked and snubbed, and so Hollywood will provide the happy ending and give him an Oscar two or three years from now, and people will explain that it is "really" for *The Color Purple*. That's the way the Oscar game has always been played.

But what about the people who made *The Color Purple*? What about Quincy Jones, quietly saying, "That's the way it is?" Someday he will win an Oscar, too, and someday maybe Whoopi and all the others will win Oscars—you never know. But the moment has passed for *The Color Purple* and will never come again.

I don't think Jones meant, by his comment, that the movie lost for racist reasons, or that those who voted against it didn't like the black faces on the screen, the black voices on the soundtrack or the black story that was told. Here's what I think he meant: that in a society run by whites, and with white values and assumptions so deeply entrenched that sometimes they are invisible and unconscious—especially to those who hold them—*The Color Purple* got passed over for all the same old reasons of politics and jealousy and shabbiness and business as usual.

Spielberg made the first major movie in years that was entirely devoted to an aspect of the black experience in America, and the Hollywood establishment ignored the movie for reasons that had little or nothing to do with the movie itself! It's not even that the voters didn't like it. They probably did like it. But in the politics of Oscar (can't you hear them saying), "This just wasn't Steven's year." The black protests against the film did not cause it to lose, but they helped, by creating a climate in which the voters felt no obligation to honor the film.

Spielberg will get his Oscar.

Life will go on.

It will be a long time before another major, serious movie by an important director is made about black people.

That's the way it is.

LEGACY OF *STAR WARS*

MAY 28, 1987

The fans came from nowhere. How had the word spread? By early morning on the day that *Star Wars* opened, ten years ago on May 25, the movie lines were snaking down the block. By late afternoon, when the press caught up with the story, instant experts were calmly explaining that they had already seen the movie two times and were back in line to see it again. And so was launched the most influential single film of the decade. "May the Force be with you," the new star warriors chanted on TV, and an instant mythology was born.

Star Wars gave birth to at least ten trends that have fundamentally changed the way Hollywood addresses the mass audience:

1. It symbolized the box-office rebirth of science fiction, which had been moribund since the 1950s, with the exception of *2001: A Space Odyssey*.

2. It was the first major film to use emerging computer technology to create animation.

3. It reached a new plateau in special effects.

4. It announced the end of the "film generation" and its fascination with personal films by auteurs such as Godard, Antonioni, Scorsese, Altman, and Bergman, and the beginning of what we might call a "narrative generation"—audiences who simply wanted to be told a story.

5. It built on the success of *Jaws* in proving that "breakthrough films" could make hundreds of millions of dollars, rewrite the fate of a studio, and spawn whole industries to supply books, toys, posters, and other tie-in merchandise.

6. It was the first film to conclusively demonstrate that "repeaters" could change box-office history. Few of the original *Star Wars* fans saw it only once. Some saw it dozens of times.

7. It proved that the star system—the use of expensive, famous actors—could be supplanted by a story that created its own stars. Few people

341

knew who played the voices of R2-D2 (Kenny Baker) or C-3PO (Anthony Daniels), and if they knew that James Earl Jones was the voice of Darth Vader, did they know that the man inside the suit was named Dave Prouse? The costumes, not their inhabitants, were the stars.

8. The success of the movie and its sequels, which were frankly inspired by the Saturday afternoon cliff-hanging serials of the 1930s and 1940s, brought a reevaluation of those kinds of popular entertainments, spinning off such other blockbusters as *Raiders of the Lost Ark, Romancing the Stone,* and *Indiana Jones and the Temple of Doom.*

9. In the decade before 1977, young American directors were trying to make the Great American Film. Afterward, many of them were trying to make the Great American Hit. In 1976, a year before *Star Wars,* Martin Scorsese was an example of the best young American directors, and he made *Taxi Driver.* In the years after *Star Wars,* the directors after Scorsese have, by and large, stopped swinging for that particular fence, and started measuring their success by the box office.

10. It is not a trend, but it is a sign of something: like many other great movies, *Star Wars* contributed a phrase to the language, "May the Force be with you."

If I sound less than thrilled by the *Star Wars* revolution, that is not altogether fair. I loved *Star Wars.* After seeing it for the first time, I compared it to those "out-of-the-body experiences" you read about in the supermarket tabloids—where people are transported to other dimensions, and unceremoniously deposited back here, hours or days later. The movie was made with skill, craft, intelligence, and a sense of humor.

It represented a breakthrough in popular culture: the insight that big budgets need not be limited to historical epics and the film versions of turgid bestsellers, but could be applied to thrilling "kids' stories," transforming them into enormously enjoyable entertainments.

The best story I've heard about *Star Wars* involves a board meeting at Twentieth Century Fox when George Lucas was halfway through directing his saga, and was running over budget. The Fox board sat through footage of Luke Skywalker and Han Solo; then the lights went up and the board members suggested that maybe Fox should just admit it had made a mistake and stop production on the picture. Maybe the special effects could be recycled into some kind of Saturday morning kiddie TV show.

Alan Ladd, Jr., the production chief, rose to his feet. Known for his reluctance to make long speeches in public, he immediately had the room's attention: Laddie spoke so rarely that he was always listened to. There was a silence.

"Could . . . be great," he said, and sat down. The board voted the additional money.

The important thing to realize is that the Fox board was not totally out of its mind. There was no historical precedent for the success of a movie like *Star Wars,* a movie which said a cliff-hanging "children's story" could be married to breakthrough technology. When George Lucas submitted his original script to the studio, how did anyone have the imagination to envision what he had in mind? His previous credits had included *THX 1138* (1970), a futurist fantasy modeled on *1984,* and *American Graffiti* (1973), a wonderful comedy about adolescence. What did either film have to do with the Force?

Picture in your mind those thrilling sword fights with laser beams. The breath-stopping moments when the scout ships swoop low between the steel canyons of the Death Star. The amazing use of throwaway detail in the scene set in the saloon on Alderaan, the intergalactic watering hole. How could mere words on a page convey what Lucas had in mind, or inspire belief in the special-effects genius he would use to achieve it?

Star Wars was a great landmark in American movies, and the trilogy (completed by *The Empire Strikes Back* and *Return of the Jedi*) has created a group of classics that will be returned to and enjoyed for generations, like *The Wizard of Oz* (which, indeed, *Star Wars* resembled—especially in the trio of C-3PO, R2-D2, and Chewbacca, who bore unmistakable resemblances to the Scarecrow, the Tin Man, and the Cowardly Lion).

But the news is not altogether good. The news never is. In the ten years before *Star Wars,* American cinema was passing through a sort of golden age, in which a new generation of directors was looking for new directions. Inspired by the French New Wave—that early 1960s explosion of personal filmmaking by Truffaut, Godard, Resnais, Chabrol, and others—they wanted to make films that reflected how they saw the world. Look at some of the titles from that period: *Bonnie and Clyde, Easy Rider, Mean Streets, Days of Heaven, M*A*S*H, Annie Hall, Five Easy Pieces, Nashville, The Conversation,* even the original *Rocky,* which was the personal film Stallone made before selling Rocky's soul to the box office.

In the decade since *Star Wars,* there has been less emphasis on personal vision. Indeed, Hollywood production chiefs are often hostile to filmmakers who have some kind of an offbeat project, and films such as *Terms of Endearment* and even *Platoon* were turned down by dozens of executives.

What they're looking for is a new combination of old formulas. Hollywood believes it knows more or less what will sell: special effects, nonstop action, humor based on violence. Eddie Murphy's *Beverly Hills Cop II* is a textbook example of this new mentality. If Murphy, with his talent, had come up in the decade before *Star Wars,* he might have become one of the great original screen comedians of his time. In the decade since 1977, a talent like his is routinely shoehorned into bankrupt shoot-and-chase, slice-and-dice plots like *Cop II.* Hollywood believes Eddie is a genius—but could he get backing for a truly personal project, an oddball screenplay that only he could picture in his mind's eye, for a movie that would be all Murphy and no formula? Not likely.

In Hollywood the other day, at ceremonies marking the first decade of *Star Wars,* George Lucas announced that another *Star Wars* trilogy is on the drawing boards. His master plan is to eventually make nine movies in the series. The *Star Wars* saga will likely live forever—and that might even be long enough for Hollywood to outgrow it.

JOHN CASSAVETES
An Appreciation

FEBRUARY 10, 1989

They called John Cassavetes a *cinema verité* director in one of the obituaries. That's French for the "cinema of truth," the kind of documentary moviemaking where the director stands back and doesn't interfere while things happen naturally. John Cassavetes never made a *cinema verité* film in his life. He was always in there up to his neck, swimming upstream against life and shouting instructions to those in his wake. If you want a French phrase to describe his work, try *cinema désordre*—the cinema of messiness. But don't take that as a criticism. Cassavetes made films that gloriously celebrated the untidiness of life, at a time when everybody else was making neat, slick formula pictures.

Most people, if they knew him at all, knew him as a movie star. He was an army deserter in *Edge of the City,* and Mia Farrow's husband in *Rosemary's Baby,* and he got an Oscar nomination for *The Dirty Dozen,* and in *Two-Minute Warning* he was a cop trying to stop a sniper at a football game, and he was in *The Fury* and *Tempest,* always as a wry, intense actor who put a spin on every scene, who seemed to be enjoying some private irony.

But it was as a director that Cassavetes invested his heart and soul, and he told people he made the commercial movies just to raise money to make his own movies. He starred in some of them, too—most notably in *Love Streams* (1984), which could almost be viewed as his own obituary—and in others he starred his friends Ben Gazzara, Peter Falk, or Seymour Cassel. And over and over again he used his wife, Gena Rowlands, who won two Oscar nominations for her work in his films.

When Cassavetes died February 2 at the age of fifty-nine, the news did not come as a surprise. He had been gravely ill with liver disease for at least four years, and when they dedicated this year's Park City (Utah) USA Film Festival to him in late January, they already knew he wouldn't be able to attend. But in a sense he was there anyway, in spirit, because the USA

345

festival is dedicated to independent American filmmaking, and there were those who said John Cassavetes had practically invented the movement.

His first film, named *Shadows,* was released in 1961 and caused a sensation. It was shot in 16 mm on a tiny budget on the streets of New York, and it was about characters who looked and talked like real people, and whose lives were disorganized and chaotic and filled with surprises. They did not inhabit well-planned plots, and Cassavetes's camera did not regard them with meticulous camera movements. His filmmaking style in those days was spontaneous and jerky, hand-held, and if *Shadows* would look a little forced today, at the time it felt like a bombshell.

Shadows helped create the "underground" film movement. Other movies were made in the same spirit—Shirley Clarke's *The Connection,* Adolfas Mekas's *Hallelujah the Hills*—and after a flirtation with the Hollywood studio system that produced the unsuccessful *Too Late Blues* and *A Child Is Waiting* in 1963, Cassavetes went back to acting and regrouped his forces for *Faces* (1968), his great anarchic comedy about a couple (Rowlands and John Marley) trapped in a cheerless marriage, and an eccentric misfit (Cassel) who offered them freedom.

Faces was his biggest hit, and it also defined the style for the rest of his films. He would show us talkative, neurotic people trapped in unworkable situations, and watch them growing increasingly desperate as they tried to figure their way out of them. He would not enmesh them in plots. He would let them freewheel with all the craziness and spontaneity of the real world, and we would have to pay attention because they were capable of doing literally anything—like real people.

Consider, for example, *Love Streams,* in which Cassavetes plays an alcoholic writer holed up in a house in the Hollywood Hills. He writes bad novels about bad women, while hookers march through his life. He doesn't have to leave home for trouble; it finds him there, and in one extraordinary sequence his former wife turns up at the door, says "This is your son," and deposits a small boy. The Cassavetes character has no idea what to do with a small boy, but he knows what to do with a buddy, and so he pours the kid a beer, complains to him about women, and takes him to Vegas for the weekend. Later in the same movie, the writer's sister (Gena Rowlands) turns up with two horses, a goat, a duck, some chickens, a dog, and a parrot. She had, it turns out, stopped at a pet store on her way, and thought it was a shame all of those animals were being imprisoned.

Cassavetes's most conventional film with Rowlands was probably *Gloria* (1980), in which she played the former mistress of a mobster, who takes a young boy under her wing after the mob wipes out his family. They go on the run together, developing a funny, offbeat relationship along the way.

That was one of the movies Rowlands got an Oscar nomination for. The other one was *A Woman Under the Influence* (1974), which also won Cassavetes a nomination for direction. It was an intense, off-center, wacky melodrama about a construction gang boss (Peter Falk) whose wife (Rowlands) is cracking up. The movie takes place before and after she spends six months in a mental institution, and its secret is that the Falk character is at least as crazy as his wife. The movie contains the wild, impulsive scenes for which Cassavetes became famous—especially one in which the manic Falk, torn by grief and confusion, bundles his frightened children into a truck for a compulsory "day at the beach" that is an exercise in misery.

It is always a miracle when an independent production, financed by the director or by a loose consortium of investors, gets made at all. Sometimes Cassavetes was able to make films, but unable to get them released. I think one of his best films is *The Killing of a Chinese Bookie* (1976), with Ben Gazzara as the cynical operator of a strip club on Sunset Strip. He passes his time dating the strippers and playing poker, until he gets in trouble with the mob and is told that he must kill a Chinese bookie or he will be killed himself. He is not clever enough to avoid the assignment, and the question is whether he will be brave enough to perform it. This film has fallen through some kind of crack in the distribution system and is seldom seen. And another film, *Opening Night,* starred Gena Rowlands as an actress and was finished in 1978 but not seen until the 1988 New York Film Festival.

In all of Cassavetes's films there are sudden, unexpected bursts of humor—as when Cassel is discovered in bed with Rowlands in *Faces,* and flees from the bed and through the window and down the garage roof and across the lawn in one unbroken shot. Or the scene in *A Woman Under the Influence* where a construction worker somehow dumps a plate of spaghetti in his lap (and the scene is not slapstick; it has a point to it). Cassavetes made one pure comedy, however, the enchanting *Minnie and Moskowitz* (1971), with Cassel as a goofy car hiker and Rowlands as an intellectual who falls in love with him because he can make her smile.

But always there beside the humor, and sometimes contained in it, are the painful moments of truth—honest, sometimes brutal soliloquies in which the characters mercilessly dissect their own lives, and those around them. John Marley had a scene like that in *Faces,* in which he confronted the emptiness of his life, and Gazzara found a sequence in *The Killing of a Chinese Bookie* in which he confesses his mistakes to a woman who may love him. In *A Woman Under the Influence* there is an extraordinary confrontation between the husband and wife in which all of the pain and endurance of their marriage is on the screen. And in *Love Streams,* the movie during which Cassavetes first began to fall ill, there are moments in which his character seems to be looking into a mirror instead of a camera.

All of Cassavetes's films contained an exuberance of life. They were about passionate, disorganized people who had worked their way into trouble but had not lost the ability to hope or laugh. They had a certain shapelessness to them—a messiness that made them more interesting, because you could never guess (as you can with most Hollywood films) what "had" to happen next. Cassavetes must have never taken one of those deadening professional scriptwriting classes in which everything is reduced to a formula. He started with off-the-wall characters, and was curious to see what fixes they would get themselves into. This approach did not always work (I thought *Husbands,* in 1969, was a rambling and indulgent exercise in improvisation, with Cassavetes, Falk, and Gazzara allowing themselves to get away with murder). But when it did work, it was so spontaneous, so open to surprise, that it made conventional films feel like machines.

I met Cassavetes a couple of times, and then I understood his films in a better way. They were like he was, filled with energy and passion and big hopes and nagging fears, and hounded by the carping of those too small to follow in his tracks. Now that he is gone, his films will have to speak for him, and few directors have left behind work that duplicates more exactly the pleasure of being in their company.

WHY I LOVE BLACK AND WHITE

1989

> It's still the same old story,
> A fight for love and glory . . .

On the night of November 9, 1988, Ted Turner presented a colorized version of *Casablanca* on cable television. And that was one of the saddest days in the history of the movies. It was sad because it demonstrated that there is no movie which Turner would spare, no classic however great which is safe from the vulgarity of his computerized graffiti gangs.

Bergman: *Do you remember Paris?*

Bogart: *I remember every detail. The Germans wore gray. You wore blue.*

And so they knew to color her dress blue, and also her eyes, and probably the wallpaper behind her and maybe a few other items here and there. And what would Bogart wear? Brown? That wouldn't show up very well against the grays of the clothing in the original picture. Maybe he could wear blue, too. Jimmy Cagney did, in the colorized version of *Yankee Doodle Dandy*. A bright sky blue, which we all know was probably the basic color in George M. Cohan's wardrobe.

There are few issues in the area of film preservation that arouse more anger than the issue of colorization. That is because it is an issue involving taste, and, to put it bluntly, anyone who can accept the idea of the colorization of black-and-white films has bad taste. The issue involved is so clear, and the artistic sin of colorization is so fundamentally wrong, that colorization provides a pass-fail examination. If you "like" colorized movies, it is doubtful that you know why movies are made, or why you watch them.

All of this is beyond Ted Turner, who owns *Casablanca* lock, stock, and barrel, having purchased the rights to it and hundreds of other films with the money of his stockholders. Now he deems it his responsibility to colorize old black-and-white movies in order to maximize the profits of those stockholders, just as other corporations have made their stockholders happy by polluting the environment in other ways.

There is no use trying to convince Turner that colorization is evil—that he is polluting the imaginations of countless young people who will see *Casablanca* for the first time in a colorized version. You can only see a movie for the first time once. And if your first viewing is colorized, you will never be able to experience the full original impact of the real film. Turner would not understand that. Apparently he has never sat in the darkness of a movie theater and felt in his bones the perfection of black-and-white photography, its absolute appropriateness for stories like *Casablanca*. When Turner was challenged at a press conference on the issue of colorization, he said he planned to "colorize *Casablanca* just to piss everybody off." This is a statement which reflects the subtlety of his thinking on the issue.

I have no doubt there are sincere people who believe that colorization "improves" a movie, that a black-and-white movie is somehow missing something. These people are sincere, but they are not thoughtful. They have never looked inside to ask themselves what their standards are, why they enjoy what they enjoy, why certain movies work for them. Everyone has seen many black-and-white moves. Were they not enjoyable? Did they not seem appropriate in black and white? Were they missing something? Were they, for example, missing an ugly overcoat of "colors" slapped on top of the blacks and whites and grays, to provide a tarted-up imitation of color, like cosmetics on a corpse?

There are basic aesthetic issue here. Colors have emotional resonance for us. Reds have passion, yellows speak of hope, some greens are sickly, others speak of nature. On a properly controlled palette, a color movie can be a thing of wonder—although many of the earliest Technicolor movies look silly today because such an effort was made to throw in lots of bright colors to get the studio's money's worth.

Black-and-white movies present the deliberate absence of color. This makes them less realistic than color films (for the real world is in color). They are more dreamlike, more pure, composed of shapes and forms and movements and light and shadow. Color films can simply be illuminated. Black-and-white films have to be lighted. With color, you can throw light in everywhere, and the colors will help the viewer determine one shape from another, and the foreground from the background. With black and white, everything would tend toward a shapeless blur if it were not for meticulous attention to light and shadow, which can actually create a world in which the lighting indicates a hierarchy of moral values.

In Hitchcock's *Notorious,* there is a moment when Ingrid Bergman walks slowly through a doorway toward Cary Grant. He is listening to a record of secret testimony, which proves she is not a Nazi spy. At the beginning of the shot, Grant thinks she is guilty. In the middle, he does not know. At the end, he thinks she is innocent. Hitchcock begins with Bergman seen in backlit silhouette. As she steps forward, she is half light, half shadow. As the testimony clears her, she is fully lighted. The lighting makes the moral judgments. To add color to the scene would clarify nothing, would add additional emotional information which might be confusing, and would destroy the purity of the classical lighting.

Most of us do not consciously look at movies in the way that I've looked at the scene from *Notorious.* But in our subconscious, that's how we see them. In almost all serious black-and-white movies, bands of light and shadow are thrown across the faces and bodies of the characters from time to time, to involve them in a visually complex web. In *Night and the City,* Richard Widmark, as a cornered rat, seems trapped by the bars of darkness which fall on him. If you colorize the underlying image of his face and clothing, you lose the contrast of the lighting. Since the shadows are pure and the colorization is not, you get an oil and water effect, visually disturbing.

In *Casablanca,* the Bogart character is developed through the use of lighting. At the beginning of the film, he seems to be a cynical man who cares only about the profits of his nightclub. When he sees Ingrid Bergman again after a long time, he is short and cruel with her, because he thinks she betrayed him. Then he learns more about her marriage to the Paul Henreid character, the Resistance hero, and by the end of the film Bogart has turned from a cynic into an idealist.

This change in his character is mirrored by the development in his lighting. In early scenes he is often harshly lit, or lit from beneath by the light of a lamp or a match, so his facial structure looks sinister. His face is rarely completely lighted. Henreid, by contrast, is usually well-lighted. Bergman's face seems shadowed when we doubt her motives, and becomes more clearly seen as we understand her. If you slap the pinks and tans of the colorizer's paintbrush onto their faces, you add a distracting dimension and you reduce the contrasts between lighter and darker areas. You make the movie look bland, less dramatic. You wash out the drama of the lighting.

The other night I was looking once again at another great black-and-white movie, *It's a Wonderful Life*. This is the movie that Frank Capra thinks is the greatest he has ever directed, and Jimmy Stewart thinks is the best he has acted in. Stewart went to Washington to testify against the colorizing of the movie, and Capra, from his sickbed, made a plea that the film not be colorized. But because the copyrights had expired, the film was fair game—and a sickening colorized version has appeared on television and in the video stores.

The movie, once again, is about a moral transformation. In the early scenes the Stewart character is a bright young man who can't seem to stop helping people, until he becomes the moral backbone of the little town of Bedford Falls. In later scenes, after a series of setbacks, he has a long night of despair. He loses hope. He turns bitter. He stands on a bridge and considers suicide.

James Stewart's face is one of the most open and trustworthy faces in the history of the movies. In early scenes, it is fully lighted—and the light of his moral character almost seems to shine through his skin. In the shocking later scenes, as he despairs, Capra shoots him in shadow, and seems to have even used makeup to darken him, make him look more ravaged by the night after he has walked out into it. Do we need to know, as he stands on the bridge, that his face is pink and his coat is brown and heaven knows what color his shirt is?

There are two arguments here, one positive, one negative:

1. Black and white is a legitimate and beautiful artistic choice in motion pictures, creating feelings and effects that cannot be obtained any other way.

2. "Colorization" does not produce color movies, but only sad and sickening travesties of black-and-white movies, their lighting destroyed, their atmospheres polluted, their moods altered almost at random by the addition of an artificial layer of coloring that is little more than legalized vandalism.

Some small steps of progress have been made in the struggle against colorization. Recently the National Film Preservation Act was passed by Congress, in the face of expensive lobbying by Turner and the Hollywood studios. It would authorize a panel of experts to designate twenty-five films a year as "national treasures," and anyone colorizing or otherwise materially altering them would have to add a warning on the film and on any cassette boxes that their work had been done without the consent of the original filmmakers. This warning is likely to be as about effective as the health warnings on cigarette packages—but it is a step in the right direction.

Does Ted Turner care that Congress has stated that what he does to movies is a form of artistic desecration? I am sure he does, because additional legislation may someday prevent colorization altogether. In the meantime, the Film Preservation Act is a moral victory. And there is a way that you, dear reader, can share in that victory. Do not support the broadcast, the rental, or the sale of colorized films.

THE CASE FOR AN A RATING

APRIL 1990

The distinguished British actress Helen Mirren was a member of the Royal Shakespeare Company and has played most of the Bard's major women's roles. So when director Peter Greenaway called from England to ask her to testify on behalf of the movie they made together, *The Cook, the Thief, His Wife, and Her Lover,* it was partly because she would make a most respectable witness.

Greenaway's film had been denied an R rating by the movie industry's Classification and Ratings Administration, and so Mirren took the red-eye flight from Los Angeles to New York to appeal the verdict before the system's Appeals Board. At the hearing she was asked a curious question:

"What would your comfort level be if you were sitting next to a nine-year-old during this movie?"

Mirren couldn't believe her ears. "I told them a person would have to be insane to take a nine-year-old to a film like this," she told me. "It's intended for adults, not children."

But that hypothetical nine-year-old stands at the center of the current controversy over the nation's movie rating system, which—strange as it seems—has no practical way of declaring a movie for "adults only." The implication of the R rating—which says those under seventeen can be admitted with a parent or adult guardian—is that the Ratings Board must consider the possibility of underage viewers in making its decisions. They're not supposed to be there, but they might be. And without a workable "adults only" rating, the system provides no way to keep them out. No way except the discredited and disreputable X rating, which is identified in everybody's mind with hard-core pornography, and is the kiss of death for any movie seeking broad commercial distribution in the United States.

The implications of the R-rating trap are disturbing for anyone concerned with freedom of speech and artistic expression in America. Under

354

the guise of providing voluntary guidance for parents, the Motion Picture Association of America is actually operating an unofficial censorship system. The addition of an A rating for adults only would give the system flexibility and filmmakers more breathing room, but the MPAA and its longtime head, Jack Valenti, remain inflexibly and uncompromisingly opposed to the A rating.

The Cook, the Thief, His Wife, and Her Lover, which was denied an R rating by the Motion Picture Association of America's Classification and Ratings Administration, is one of many pictures to fall into the R-versus-X twilight zone in recent months. It is a shocking satire using nudity, sex, and cannibalism as its weapons. Some viewers, myself included, think it is an important work. Others do not. Almost everyone would agree that it is not a film for children. But there is no way for the MPAA to classify it for "adults only." Under the Alice in Wonderland logic of the ratings system, it either gets an R or it gets no rating at all.

The MPAA's R-rating category is theoretically intended to steer children away from certain movies. But there is a hole in it as wide as the swinging doors in a movie theater: it provides only that those under seventeen "will not be admitted without a parent or adult guardian."

Half of all the American movies made since 1968 have been rated R. And anyone who has been under seventeen during those twenty-two years knows from personal experience how easy it is to get into an R movie. The "adult guardian" can be an older brother or sister, a friend, or simply someone standing next to you in line. Many theaters, staffed by employees who are themselves teenagers, do not even bother to check.

Aware of this, the MPAA looks at R movies as if it were the theoretical adult guardian—which is why Mirren could be asked the schoolmarmish question of how she'd feel taking a nine-year-old to her movie. Isn't it clear that some movies are just plainly and simply not intended for children, no matter whom they go in with?

When Valenti's MPAA first teamed up with the National Association of Theater Owners in 1968 to install a voluntary national ratings system, there were dozens of local movie censorship boards in America. Some of them were standing jokes—like Chicago's, which provided patronage jobs for the widows of policemen. Valenti thought a voluntary industry-wide system would replace the local bluenoses and head off threatened national legislation, and he was right: "Today," he boasts, "there is only one local censorship board in the country—in Dallas."

Over the years the Classification and Ratings Administration has developed a routine for processing hundreds of movies every year. Members of the board—chosen to represent a cross-section of parents and the moviegoing public—view every film submitted in the MPAA's screening room in Los Angeles. They recommend a rating: G for general audiences, PG for movies where "parental guidance" is suggested, PG-13 for movies where parents are urged to note that some material may be unsuitable for younger viewers, and R for movies off limits to those under seventeen "without a parent or adult guardian."

The board cannot give a film an X rating, because the MPAA never copyrighted the X. But the X can be self-applied by the distributors of a film, and hard-core pornographers are cheerfully willing to label their films X, or even claim the nonexistent XX and XXX ratings.

If movie distributors don't like the rating they've been given, they can appeal. If they lose, they can make trims in hopes of qualifying for an R, they can be released "unrated," or they can self-apply the X (something no mainstream studio or director is willing to do). Several films in recent years have clashed with the guidelines of the R rating. Most of them made cuts to qualify for an R rating, including 9½ Weeks with Kim Basinger, Angel Heart with Mickey Rourke, and Crimes of Passion with Kathleen Turner. (All of these movies were later released on home video in their unedited "original" versions, although viewers were hard-pressed to tell the difference.)

In the spring of 1990, the movie ratings controversy heated up when a number of films found themselves in conflict with the MPAA at the same time. They included not only The Cook, the Thief, His Wife, and Her Lover, but also Tie Me Up! Tie Me Down! by the Spanish director Pedro Almodóvar, the shocking but brilliant Henry: Portrait of a Serial Killer, and Wild Orchid, an erotic drama starring Mickey Rourke and directed by Zalman King, who wrote 9½ Weeks.

What was beyond the pale in these movies? One morning I sat with King in his editing room, next to a moviola where he was able to show me two versions of the love scene objected to by the MPAA. It was hard to tell them apart. The scene was shot in lush fleshtones, bathed in a warm light, and showed Mickey Rourke and Carré Otis apparently making love. As is inevitably the case with R-rated movies, the genital areas of the actors were not visible.

"There!" King said at one point. "That overhead shot—they objected to that being at the end of the sequence. So I took it out at the end and moved it to the middle."

As the images flickered on the small editing screen, I saw the unclothed bodies of Rourke and Otis making what seemed to be passionate love. Later, seeing the entire movie, I understood the context: this emotional explosion came after a long buildup in which the two were attracted to each other, yet each had reasons for remaining aloof. The love scene was the payoff for the entire drama.

"I make erotic films," King told me. "That's my stock in trade. I don't have car crashes or violence. All of the drama in this film leads up to the final scene. If they don't let me have that scene, my movie loses its whole reason for existence."

Although the Ratings Board is reluctant to come right out and say what is or isn't acceptable in an R-rated love scene, the practical experience of filmmakers who have been through the ratings process suggests that the board is uncomfortable with graphic thrusting or undulating movements. That's one reason so many movie love scenes are shot from the shoulders up. To get the R rating, apparently, sexual intercourse should involve proximity more than movement.

While it might be unsettling to Rourke and Otis to learn that the intimate continuity of their onscreen lovemaking was being casually rearranged, it was just as surprising for me to see what small differences apparently separated the R rating from the hinterlands of the X. The version the board approved looked a lot like the one they turned down. What was the difference? The board has a policy of never discussing its decisions, which are held behind closed doors. Some industry insiders, however, believe you can actually "wear the board down" by appealing several times, making them sit through a movie over and over again to evaluate small changes. That's an expensive process, however, since it involves making many costly prints of a film.

If a movie like King's is denied an R rating, a director like King usually chooses to reedit it himself. If he doesn't, it may be recut by the studio, since most Hollywood contracts require directors to deliver a movie with a specified rating. Sometimes it's easier to cut than to appeal; going through the appeals process is a risky business since it takes time and may mean a movie misses its targeted opening date.

But some directors take their work so seriously that they fight through the appeals process. One movie which appealed and won was Brian De Palma's *Scarface* (1983). But most films are rejected. The appeals are held in a screening room in New York City, where movies are shown to a twenty-two-member committee—half of them from the National Association of Theater Owners, half selected by the MPAA. When filmmakers appear before the appeals board, they're asked to make a statement defending their original version, after which the MPAA's position is stated by Richard D. Heffner, head of the Classification and Ratings Administration. Then the filmmaker leaves the room, Heffner stays, and a vote is taken.

"Want to know how long they debated before they took their vote on my movie?" Helen Mirren asked me. "Thirty-five seconds."

There are, no doubt, some people who would believe that was too long, that all "dirty movies" deserve what they get. But freedom of expression is a right which movie directors should possess, just as writers, painters, and journalists do, and by creating economic penalties for films it denies an R rating, the MPAA is imposing a form of censorship. It's an irony that the MPAA board was actually started to head off censorship by allowing Hollywood to police itself. Valenti argues, and it is correct, that over the years the movie ratings system has probably prevented more censorship problems than it has created.

But this current controversy comes against the backdrop of a rising national tide of censorship and attacks on free expression. The legal difficulties of the rap group 2 Live Crew and the raging debate over flag burning are but two examples. The question is: whose standards does the MPAA uphold when it rates a movie? I believe its primary constituency is not the parents of America, as Valenti claims, but the moguls of Hollywood.

As someone who has seen virtually every Hollywood movie made over the past two decades, I've noticed that the MPAA's tolerance level for violence has grown steadily more permissive, perhaps under the unstated pressure of the Hollywood studios who pay the MPAA's bills—and who depend on heavy-duty summer action pictures to pay *their* bills.

These days, sex and nudity seem to be more offensive to the ratings board than violence and profanity. During the same season when the MPAA was throwing up its hands over the *Wild Orchid* lovemaking shot, it was supplying R ratings to Arnold Schwarzenegger's *Total Recall*, a hymn of nonstop and extreme violence; to Eddie Murphy's *Another 48 Hrs.*, with its brutal bar brawls and those trademarked Murphy riffs of four-letter words; and to *RoboCop II*, with its scene of a brain being smashed on the pavement and its twelve-year-old character who is a foul-mouthed killer for a drug kingpin.

There's even sociological evidence to back up my observation, especially as it applies to women. Social researchers Ni Yang of UCLA and Daniel Linz of the University of California at Santa Barbara found in a recent study that R-rated movies actually contain more violence against women than does hard-core pornography. The study, reported in *Variety*, reduced everything to chilling statistics indicating that women were treated violently about twice as often in R-rated movies as in X-rated ones.

Jack Valenti, the most vocal defender of the ratings system in its current form, is quick to deny charges of censorship, pointing out that the rating system is voluntary.

"If I were a director who made a movie that did not qualify for an R rating, and that movie was important to me, I would go right ahead and release it unrated," Valenti told me recently in Los Angeles.

I replied that when a filmmaker finds that thousands of theaters will not show that unrated film, and countless media outlets will not accept advertising for it—isn't he facing de facto censorship?

"The rating system is designed as an advisory for parents," Valenti said. "It does not and should not take into account anybody's economic situation."

Sometimes, in a debate like this, the critic of the ratings system finds himself defending films not to his personal liking. But that is what freedom of expression is all about.

I am the first to agree that a movie like *Wild Orchid* is a shallow, silly sex film. But if there are adult filmgoers who want to see it as King made it, that should be their right. Many people would be offended by *The Cook, the Thief, His Wife, and Her Lover*, but it was *intended* as an offensive film, and art is often intended to shock.

And what about directors of unquestioned importance, who are asked to alter their films to qualify for an R rating? In May of this year, David

Lynch's *Wild at Heart* won the Golden Palm, the top award at the Cannes Film Festival. But it will not be seen by American moviegoers in the same form that it played at Cannes; one disputed shot has been softened by the addition of a cinematic smoke screen.

Martin Scorsese is widely considered to be the greatest American director of his generation. No one would deny the power of his *Taxi Driver* (1976), and his *Raging Bull* (1980) was voted by every poll in sight as the single best film of the 1980s. But his new film, *GoodFellas*, also reportedly faced problems with the ratings board.

When Lynch and Scorsese have to take scissors to their films because the MPAA is unwilling to bend on a rating system that needs fixing, it is time for reform.

At the time the ratings system was first created in 1968, there was a category designed to indicate movies for adults only: the infamous X category. In the early years the X was not an automatic mark of shame, and such reputable pictures as *Midnight Cowboy, The Killing of Sister George, Candy, A Clockwork Orange,* and *Beyond the Valley of the Dolls* (which I wrote) carried the X rating. The early 1970s were boom years for hard-core pornography, however, and soon the X rating came to be exclusively identified with porno movies. No mainstream movie studio, director, or theater chain wanted to have anything to do with it. The last major movie released with an X rating was *Last Tango in Paris,* in 1972.

In the eighteen years since then, the United States has essentially been the only country in the Western world with no category suggesting that a film is appropriate for adults only. The X rating has become the trademark of pornography. Why didn't the MPAA copyright the X, thus ensuring its proper use as the last stop on a conventional rating scale? "We acted on the advice of lawyers," Valenti told me. "We felt we needed an open-ended system so that we could not be charged with restraint of trade. We don't give you the X. We deny you the R, and what you do then is up to you."

In practice, that means all ordinary Hollywood movies and imports must somehow squeeze into the R rating. If they don't fit, the MPAA offers two choices: release the film without any rating at all, or self-apply the X rating.

These are not practical alternatives for the reasons I've already mentioned: theater chains routinely have leases with shopping malls forbidding them to play X-rated films, and it's impossible to advertise X or un-rated movies in many cities. As a result, a movie that is released outside the ratings system stands little chance of wide distribution.

There is an obvious way out of this dilemma, one proposed by Gene Siskel and myself on our television program as long ago as 1987: create a new A-rating category, for "adults only," and position it between the R and the X. The A would specify that tickets could not be sold to anyone under seventeen. The X rating would still be self-applied, and would continue to indicate hard-core pornography, but now there would be an acceptable, enforceable rating in between for movies that are frankly intended for adults.

The movement for an A rating has picked up considerable support since Siskel and I first proposed it. Members of the National Society of Film Critics recently sent a letter to the MPAA advocating the A, and there's a resolution in the Illinois House of Representatives that would encourage the same. A court fight is also brewing over the rating system. Miramax Films, distributor of *The Cook* and *Tie Me Up!*, hired constitutional attorney William Kunstler to spearhead its suit against the MPAA. Although Miramax lost that case, it was a Pyrrhic victory for the MPAA, which was told by the judge its system was arbitrary and ripe for revision.

In his fight against the A rating, Valenti finds himself confronted by critics from both the right and left. Liberals support the A category because it provides a way for directors to express themselves without trying to squeeze their vision into the R guidelines. And conservatives, alarmed by the escalating permissiveness of R-rated movies and the ease with which children can attend them, would like an "adults only" category to isolate movies not intended for young viewers.

When I proposed an A rating during a meeting with Valenti not long ago, he flatly rejected it. "The rating system is a voluntary guide intended for parents," he said piously, "and the nation's parents believe that it works." If you've seen Valenti on a talk show, you've heard him use the same words. He discourages anybody other than himself from speaking for the ratings system, and always uses the same polished sound bites.

Valenti also suggests practical difficulties with enforcing an A rating. Using one of his favorite debating weapons—a list of perversions and deviant behavior that he rattles off like a vice cop—he told me, "How can you

draw a line between the A and the X? Between A-rated incest, child molestation, cannibalism, and sadomasochism, and X-rated incest, child molestation, cannibalism, and sadomasochism? How can you say which scenes
of child molestation are artistic, and which are pornographic? The members of the rating board are mere human beings. How can you expect them
to draw a line like that?"

A statement like that has a certain genius to it. It seems to imply that
the MPAA is holding the line against the appearance of unspeakable practices on our neighborhood movie screens, when in fact all Valenti is really
doing is sending up a smoke screen.

The answer to his question, of course, is that the same "mere human
beings" who draw the lines between the PG-13 and R ratings would also
be expected to know when the R ended and the A began. Valenti's board
members would not have to make those difficult hypothetical decisions between art and pornography because the A rating would still leave the system open-ended. If the MPAA refused a film an A rating, it would *still* be
able to go out unrated, or with a self-applied X.

But to answer his question directly: where *do* we draw the line? What
I told Valenti that day was that there was scarcely a mature person alive
who did not instinctively know the difference between A and X, between
"adults only" and pornographic, and that if they needed help, they could
use the Supreme Court's definition of pornography.

The point, in any event, is not to include pornography within the
MPAA system, but to release the pressure on the overburdened R category.
When the MPAA originally installed its ratings system, it intended the X
to perform the same function that the A is now being suggested for; Valenti
and his planners clearly did not foresee the rise of hardcore, and the preemp-
tion of the X by the pornographers.

If the A rating seems like such manifestly good common sense, why
are Valenti and his MPAA so inflexibly opposed to it? I am not a mind
reader, but I can think of an obvious possibility.

The ratings system in its current form contains no category that ad-
vises theater owners not to sell tickets under any circumstances. If an A category were introduced, exhibitors who subscribe to the voluntary MPAA
system would be required to actually refuse admission to anyone under
seventeen.

That's a requirement that conjures up a dreaded nightmare in the imagination of theater owners. It's the specter of a potential customer standing at the ticket window, being told he cannot buy a ticket. If Hollywood has to choose between the loss of artistic integrity and the loss of a ticket sale, integrity loses in a flash. Before the studios and the exhibitors allow those hypothetical underage viewers and their "adult guardian" to be turned away with dollars in their hands, they'll stretch the R category until it bursts.

WELL, *ARE* MOVIES BETTER THAN EVER?

1990

They've taken another one of those polls in which Americans declare that the movies are not as good as they used to be—and that, what's more, they're too sexy, violent, profane, and expensive. As a result, the pollsters discovered, people are watching their VCR machines more and going to the movies less.

There are a few facts that would seem to fly in the face of this national poll. For one, the national box office has never been stronger, and indeed the box office take has been setting records for the last five years. For another, moviegoers demonstrate an overwhelming desire to see movies containing sex, profanity, and violence—and stay away from G-rated films with such a vengeance that studios throw in a few four-letter words just to be sure of the PG-13 rating.

What people say and what they do are often very different things, and this is never more evident than in surveys like the wire-service poll of 1,084 Americans. On the basis of the questions asked, the answers could have been predicted without the necessity of conducting the poll. For example, the one question movie critics hear over and over again is, "Are the movies better than ever?" Or, as the pollsters asked, are they better than they were in the year of 1939—which saw such productions as *Gone with the Wind, The Wizard of Oz, Wuthering Heights,* and *Gunga Din?* The poll found, not surprisingly, that most Americans thought the movies had gotten worse in the last fifty years.

The first thing I would want to know is, how many of the respondents were over sixty-five? That would have made them fifteen years old in 1939, a reasonable age for judging the movies. Remember that the poll-

364

sters were presumably asking about the general run of movies of 1939—
not just *Gone with the Wind*. So we would want someone who had gone to
the movies frequently in that year. And who, of course, still goes to the
movies frequently today, so that they would have a basis of comparison.

My guess is that none of the 1,084 respondents of the poll would fit
the description. Instead, what the poll sample was really saying was that
Gone with the Wind and *The Wizard of Oz* were better than the movies they
had seen recently—such as, perhaps, *Weekend at Bernie's* and *Ghostbusters 2*.
We are exposed to all of the movies of the present, but remember only the
best movies of the past. People forget that it would be possible to put together a long list of 1939 movies that were even worse than *Ghostbusters 2*,
hard as that might be to believe.

The questions about sex, violence, and profanity come up in movie
polls all the time, and the answers never fail to amaze me. Without exception, Americans declare that the movies have too much nudity, violence,
sex, and profanity. And yet when they vote with their box-office dollars,
they go to violent, sexy, profane movies with great cheerfulness. This is an
example of the universal human tendency to be censorious on the behalf
of others, while retaining full freedom to sin for oneself. What the respondents are really saying is that dirty movies are OK for them, but not
for other people.

I am reminded of the Legion of Decency, which was operated by the
Catholic Church in America when I was growing up. On a designated
Sunday every year, Catholics were invited to stand up in church, put their
hands over their hearts, and take the pledge of the Legion of Decency—
which condemned lewd and immoral books and movies. The pledge was
entirely voluntary of course, but I fail to remember anyone who refused to
take it. Can you imagine the effect of someone sitting resolutely in his pew,
his heart uncrossed, during the pledge? It would have been like a public
pledge of indecency.

And yet Catholics did somehow attend about the same movies as
everybody else in those years—even such titles as *The French Line,* an un-
speakably sinful Jane Russell movie that got priceless publicity when the
Legion condemned it. Libidinous little altar boys like myself pored over
the lists of "Condemned" movies in the weekly issues of *Our Sunday Visitor,* and when its movie critic, Dale Francis, railed against the wet blouse

worn by Sophia Loren in *Boy on a Dolphin,* we tore out his articles and memorized them. Most of us wouldn't have known what to look for beneath a wet blouse if it hadn't been for his warnings.

What I'm suggesting is that ordinary moviegoers have a certain fondness for sex and violence, but don't want to admit to it. Another possibility is that those people who dislike sex and violence never go to the movies anyway—and this is borne out by the fact that wholesome, G-rated family movies rarely do significant business unless they are Disney animated cartoons. If people don't like sex and violence, why is Eddie Murphy a bigger star than Benji?

I am also curious about the wording of the wire service article when it reports that people were watching their VCRs more and attending movies less. The industry's own much more far-reaching polls indicate that VCRs have actually gotten people *more* involved in current movies. Especially in the over-thirty group, people who had stopped going out to the movies have started again, because their interest has been reawakened by the movies they see on tapes and disks. It is also true, although the wire service didn't say so, that most video rentals are of recent box office hits—so that the stay-at-homes are watching the same movies as the filmgoers.

All of this begs the question of whether "the movies" are better or worse than they were in 1939. A newsweekly did a story on the fiftieth anniversary of that great year, in which Hollywood seemed unable to do anything wrong. And indeed it was impressive to read the names of the great films of 1939, and to reflect how sadly movies had declined since then.

But think. Any good movie is a miracle, since so many forces strain to make it fail. Movies are good not because of the year they were made, but because of the people who made them, and the struggle they waged. *The Wizard of Oz* is one of the great fantasies of all time, a film with universal appeal. But recently I was watching Steven Spielberg's *E.T.* again, on Laserdisc, and I venture to say it will stand the test of time as well as *The Wizard of Oz* has. *Gunga Din* is a great melodramatic swashbuckler—but so are the *Indiana Jones* pictures. And if *Gone with the Wind* was the greatest epic of its time, the industry has produced some great epics since, including *Lawrence of Arabia, Apocalypse Now,* and *2001.*

I do not argue that the movies are "better than ever." I am concerned that Hollywood has grown better in recent years at marketing movies than at making them. American theaters are mired each summer in a handful of multimillion-dollar sequels and action productions, and if moviegoers tell the pollsters they are discouraged after seeing *Ghostbusters 2* or *RoboCop II,* I agree with them.

I also agree, to a degree, with the complaints about violence in films. I have no argument with violence itself—it is a valid subject for movies— but I am tired of the routine chase sequences which seem to substitute for third acts in so many of today's movies. And I am also rapidly tiring of the stalkings and shoot-outs that replace dialogue in many movies. (It takes a superior action picture, like Richard Donner's *Lethal Weapon 2,* to remind me that violence and sequels can still be entertaining.)

As for sex and nudity, I have news for the pollsters and the 1,084 moviegoers they polled. There is a great deal less of both in today's movies than in the movies of ten or twenty years ago. One reason is the Motion Picture Rating System, which penalizes sex more than violence, and which has lost control of the X rating—which was intended to describe "adult" pictures, but is now the exclusive terrain of hard-core pornography. A movie like *Last Tango in Paris* would not be made and distributed by the current American film industry.

Looking through the poll again, I find that Americans believe movies are priced too high, in addition to everything else. I wonder. When I started as a film critic, in 1967, first-run tickets in Chicago were $2. Today in many theaters they are $6 or $7. What else has only tripled in price in twenty-two years? Have you checked out the price of milk lately? Gasoline? Cat food?

The fact is that hundreds of movies are made every year, 1989 as well as 1939, and in the categories of pollsters, most of them are "poor" or "fair" but a lot are "good" and some are "excellent." That's why I was disappointed that the wire service didn't report one additional finding—that the 1,084 respondents were pleased with the high quality of film criticism in America today, which helped to steer them toward good movies so successfully that 60 percent enjoyed their last film. That would be a damn fine percentage, coming from a stockbroker or a weatherman. How sharper than a serpent's tooth is an ungrateful moviegoer.

A PULITZER FOR THE MOVIES

OCTOBER 29, 1997

The movies are one hundred years old in 1997, and the Pulitzer Prizes are seventy. This would be a good time for them to get together. In addition to the journalism categories, Pulitzers are awarded in the areas of music, drama, and literature—but they have never been given to the movies, where they might actually have a greater influence.

The Tonys, Emmys, Oscars, Grammys, National Book Awards, and Obies are all insider prizes, run by the industries they honor. The Pulitzers have always stood outside and a little above, convening panels of independent experts to look for the best work in a field without regard for popularity, sales, or sentiment.

A Pulitzer Prize for film would presumably go to the kind of good film that doesn't often get nominated for an Oscar. It would not be inhibited, as the Oscars are, by a tendency to select films that reflect favorably on the industry. It would consider documentaries and made-for-TV movies, as well as theatrical fiction films.

This year, for example, Pulitzer candidates might include a film like *In the Company of Men,* with its searing portrait of male corporate culture. Or Spike Lee's *4 Little Girls,* about the Birmingham church bombing. Or *Gattaca,* about a fearsome new world of genetic discrimination. Or *Eve's Bayou,* a Louisiana child's rich and tragic family memory. Or *Waco: The Rules of Engagement,* which offers a revisionist portrait of what happened in the Branch Davidian siege. Or *George Wallace,* the made-for-cable biography of the troubling politician.

The Pulitzer's board members meet at Columbia University in New York on November 3 to consider changes in the prizes. Surprisingly, it will be the first time they have seriously considered adding movies, according to Kristen McCary of Hollywood Hills, California, who is leading a campaign for the change.

One tricky question they're sure to discuss is: who would the Pulitzer Prize for Best Film go to? The Pulitzer in drama goes to the playwright, not the production. The Pulitzers in music go to the composers, not the conductors or recording artists. Literature prizes, of course, go to the authors—but who is the author of a film?

That question has occupied the movie industry almost since its inception. The Oscar for best film is presented to a film's producer, in keeping with the Hollywood tradition that studios and producers are the only true begetters. The top prizes at film festivals are generally accepted by the directors, in keeping with the ascendant *auteur* theory, which holds that the director is the ultimate author of a film. But French critics first proposed the *auteur* theory because in France until the late 1950s the screenwriter was considered the true author. And in the case of the adaptation of a great work of literature—the 1996 *Hamlet,* say—who is more the author? William Shakespeare, or Kenneth Branagh? Do not answer too hastily; Branagh won an Oscar nomination for his screenplay of *Hamlet,* even though he proudly filmed Shakespeare's uncut text.

Movies are children with many parents. It is impossible to untangle the contributions of the collaborators on a film—also including the actors, cinematographer, editor, composer, set designer, and special-effects artists. It is obvious, I think, that Pulitzer judges should consider only the excellence of a film, and not get involved in sorting out its pedigree. The Pulitzer Prize for Film should be awarded to the film itself, period, end of discussion.

Consider. The Pulitzer for drama goes to the playwright because his play is the underlying reality on which all productions must be based. The judges cannot see or imagine all productions, but they will all reflect the same text. It's the same with a musical composition.

But a film is seen everywhere in the same form. It will not feature different actors or costumes for its run in Chicago than it had on Broadway. All of the collaborators have come together once, made the film, and gone their separate ways. No matter who made what contribution to a great film, together they made this film and no other. They did not make a bad film, although they might have. The film itself should be honored, and Pulitzer's glory shine on all the contributors.

What practical good would the Pulitzer Prize for Film be? Would it be just one more award? Not at all. The Pulitzers are seen as more informed and disinterested than the honors given within each art form. They are the most prestigious awards in America. The annual debate over Pulitzer finalists would draw attention to many worthy films. The prizewinner would be booked into more theaters and win a larger audience, and its life on television and on video would be greatly enhanced.

The American film industry today straddles a great divide. On the one side are the multimillion-dollar blockbusters, the thrillers, and special-effects pictures. On the other, the renaissance in the world of independent and alternative films. The Oscars will usually be tilted toward the mainstream films—and above all toward successful films; it is easier for a film to pass through the eye of a needle than for a box office flop to win the Oscar.

The Pulitzers might help restore the balance between success and quality—might even act as an inspiration or a rebuke for the Oscar voters. It's time for America's most important honor in the arts to be extended to America's most important contribution to the arts.

CELLULOID VS. DIGITAL
The War for the Soul of the Cinema

DECEMBER 12, 1999

I have seen the future of the cinema, and it is not digital. No matter what you've read, the movie theater of the future will not use digital video projectors, and it will not beam the signal down from satellites. It will use film, and the film will be right there in the theater with you.

How can this be? How can a technology that is a century old possibly be preferable to new digital gizmos? This is a story of the limitations of video projection, and the hidden resources of light-through-celluloid. Please read carefully. The future of traditional cinema is at stake.

In recent months the *Wall Street Journal, New York Times,* and *Los Angeles Times* have carried breathless reports that Hollywood is on the brink of a digital revolution. Even *Wired* magazine, usually informed on technical matters, printed the howler that digital projection is "far better" than film. George Lucas and Texas Instruments have teamed up to showcase *The Phantom Menace* with digital projection in theaters on both coasts. Disney is now preparing digital theatrical demos; its *Bicentennial Man* will open in digital Friday at the AMC South Barrington.

These custom installations, we are told, are the first wave of a technological revolution that will overtake movie theaters. No longer will an underpaid projectionist struggle in the booth with ungainly cans of film. New movies will zip down from space and be projected into the screen with startling clarity. Digital video projection (jargon watch: "dijection") is being embraced by Hollywood, we read, because it will save the studios the cost of manufacturing and shipping prints all over the world.

But how good is digital projection? I saw it demonstrated last May at the Cannes Film Festival, and have read reports of those who've attended the custom *Phantom Menace* installations. A system offered by Hughes is not very persuasive, the witnesses say, but the Texas Instruments system is better; reviews range from "85 percent as good as a real movie" to "about as good." The special effects in *Phantom Menace* looked especially sharp, viewers said, and there's a reason: they were computer-generated in the first place, and so arrived at the screen without stepping down a generation to film. And because they depicted imaginary places, it was impossible to judge them on the basis of how we know the real world looks.

"Dijection" offers a wonderful new prospect, if it's for real. But it's not the only possible future. Far from the boardrooms of Texas Instruments, which has unlimited financial resources and wants to grab the world movie distribution market, there is an alternative film-based projection system that is much cheaper than digital, uses existing technology, and (hold onto your hats) is not "about as good" as existing film, but, its inventors claim, "500 percent better" That is not a misprint.

This system is called MaxiVision48. I have seen it demonstrated. It produces a picture so breathtakingly clear it is like 3-D in reverse: like looking through an open window into the real world. Motion is shown without the jumpiness and blurring of existing film projection, details are sharper, and our eyes are bathed in visual persuasion.

The inventor of MaxiVision is a Hollywood film editor named Dean Goodhill (he shared an Oscar nomination for *The Fugitive*). One of his partners is a manufacturer named Ty Safreno, whose company, Trust Automation, Inc., of San Luis Obispo, California, builds digital robotics systems for tasks which must be vibration-free, like the manufacture of Pentium chips.

Without getting into labyrinthine technical explanations, here is how MaxiVision48 works:

- It can project film at 48 frames per second (fps), twice the existing 24 fps rate, by fitting four frames into the film space that used to contain three. That provides a picture of startling clarity. At 48 frames, it uses 50 percent more film than at present. But MV48 also has an "economy mode" that uses that space differently, offering low-budget filmmakers savings of up to 50 percent on film.
- The MV48 projector design can switch on the fly between 24 and 48 fps formats in the same movie, allowing extra clarity for scenes that can use it. And it can handle any existing 35 mm film

format—unlike digital projection, which would make obsolete a century of old prints.

- MV48 uses a new system to pull the film past the projector bulb without any jitter or bounce. Goodhill says he can't go into detail while his patent is pending, but explains in general terms that MV48 completely eliminates the jiggle that all current films experience as they dance past the projector bulb. Watching it, I was startled to see how rock solid the picture was, and how that added to clarity.
- The result: "We figure it's 500 percent better than existing film or the Texas Instruments video projection system; take your choice," Goodhill told me.

It is also a lot cheaper, because it retrofits existing projectors, uses the original lamp housings, and doesn't involve installing high-tech computer equipment. MaxiVision's business plan calls for leasing the projectors at $280 a month, but if you wanted to buy one, it would cost you around $10,000. Estimates for the Texas Instruments digital projector, on the other hand, range from $110,000 to $150,000 per screen.

The contrast between the two systems is not limited to costs. Here are additional reasons why the death of film has been much exaggerated:

- The TI systems in the demo theaters bear no relationship to the real world. They're custom installations that do not address the problem of how a real film would get to a real theater. The source of their signal is an array of twenty prerecorded 18-gigabyte hard drives, trucked to each theater. This array costs an additional $75,000, apart from the cost of trucking and installation.
- Even so, a movie is so memory-intensive that these arrays must compress the digital signal by a ratio of 4 to 1. At a recent seminar at the Directors Guild in Los Angeles, however, digital projection spokesmen said that in the real world, satellite downlinked movies would require 40-to-1 data compression. This level of compression in movie delivery has never been demonstrated publicly, by TI or anyone else.
- The picture on the screen would not be as good as the HDTV television sets now on sale in consumer electronics outlets! TI's

MDD chip has specs of 1280 × 1024, while HDTV clocks at 1920 × 1080. For the first time in history, consumers could see a better picture at home than in a movie theater. A higher-quality digital picture would involve even more cost, compression, and transmission challenges.

- One advantage of a film print is that the director and cinematographer can "time" the print to be sure the colors and visual elements are right. In a digital theater, the projectionist would be free to adjust the color, tint, and contrast according to his whims. Since many projectionists do not even know how to properly frame a picture or set the correct lamp brightness, this is a frightening prospect.
- How much would the digital projection specialist be paid? The technicians operating the TI demo installations are paid more than the managers of most theaters. Hollywood is happy to save money, but are exhibitors happy to spend it?
- What about piracy? Movies will be downloaded just once, then stored in each theater. Thieves could try two approaches. They could grab the signal from the satellite and try to break the encryption (as DVD encryption has just been broken). But there is a more obvious security gap: at some point before it reaches the projector, the encrypted signal has to be decoded. Pirates could bribe a projectionist to let them intercept the decoded signal. Result: a perfect digital copy of the new movie. When the next *Star Wars* movie opens in 4,000 theaters, how many armed guards will Twentieth Century Fox have to assign to the projection booths?
- Film is harder to pirate than digital video, because a physical film print must be stolen and copied. An MV48 print would be even harder to pirate than current films; it would not fit the equipment in any pirate lab. Those fly-by-night operations, which use ancient equipment cannibalized over the decades, would have to find expensive new machines.

All of these are practical questions. They set aside the aesthetic advantage that MaxiVision48 has over digital. Once you've seen the system, you just can't get it out of your mind.

You have to actually go to San Luis Obispo, south of San Francisco, to see MaxiVision48 demonstrated. That's where the prototype projector resides, in Ty Safreno's facility. Not many Hollywood studio honchos have made that trek. On the day I visited, I was joined by Todd McCarthy, the chief film critic of *Variety,* and two leading cinematographers, Allen Daviau (*E. T., Bugsy*) and Dean Cundey (*Jurassic Park, Apollo 13*).

We saw a scene that had been shot for Goodhill by another camera-man who likes the system, Steven Poster, vice president of the American Society of Cinematographers. Poster deliberately assembled a scene filled with technical pitfalls for traditional film and video systems: We see actor Peter Billingsley walking toward the camera, wearing a patterned shirt. He is passed by another guy, wearing a T-shirt with something written on it. The camera tilts down as Billingsley picks up a hose to water a lawn. The camera continues to move past a white picket fence. In the background, a truck drives out of a parking lot.

Not great art, but great headaches for cinematographers, who know that picket fences will seem to "flutter" if panned too quickly, that water droplets will blur, and that the sign on the side of a moving truck cannot be read. All true in the old systems. With MV48, we could read the writ-ing on the shirt, see every picket in the fence, see the drops of water as if in real life, and read the side of the truck. Case closed.

McCarthy and the cinematographers praised what they saw. I was blown away. I've seen other high-quality film projection systems, such as 70 mm, IMAX, and Douglas Trumbull's Showscan process. All are very good, but they involve wide film gauges, unwieldy print sizes, and special projectors. MV48 uses projectors and prints which look a lot like the cur-rent specs, with costs in the same ballpark. Why, then, do we read so much about digital projection and so little about MaxiVision48? One obvious reason is that Texas Instruments has deep pockets to promote its system, plus the backing of propeller-head George Lucas, who dreams of making movies entirely on computers and essentially wants to show them on theater-sized monitors.

Another reason is that many Hollywood executives are, frankly, not much interested in technical matters. Their attention is occupied by proj-ects, stories, casting, advertising, and box office, as it should be. When they hear the magical term "digital" and are told their movies will whiz to theaters via satellite, they assume it's all part of the computer revolution and don't ask more questions.

Hollywood has not spent a dime, for example, to research the intriguing question, do film and digital create different brain states? Some theoreticians believe that film creates reverie, video creates hypnosis; wouldn't it be ironic if digital audiences found they were missing an ineffable part of the moviegoing experience?

Now that a decision is on the horizon, Goodhill's process deserves attention. One of the ironies of MaxiVision48 is that it's so logical and inexpensive—such a brilliant example of lateral thinking—that a couple of guys could build it in a lab in San Luis Obispo. If it were more expensive, it might attract more attention.

The big film companies like Kodak and Fuji should like the system, since it will help them sell more film. The directors who love celluloid, like Spielberg and Scorsese, should know about MV48. And there are other applications. Retail outlets use "video walls" to create atmosphere. Rain Forest cafes could put you in the jungle. NikeTown could put you on the court with Michael Jordan. No more million-dollar walls of video screens, but a $10,000 projector and a wall-sized picture.

But the industry has to listen. At the end of its first century, it shouldn't be so cheerful about throwing out everything that "film" means. And it should get over its infatuation with the "digital" buzzword.

When I told Dean Goodhill I was working on this article, he e-mailed me: "I'll make a special offer. We're leasing MV48 for $280 a month, but for $2,800 a month, which is closer to the per-screen cost of the digital system, we'll throw in a little chrome plate that says 'digital' on it."

THE MOST INFLUENTIAL FILMS
OF THE CENTURY

DECEMBER 30, 1999

The motion picture was invented before 1900, but "the movies" as we know them are entirely a twentieth-century phenomenon, shaping our times and sharing these hundred years with us. This was the first century recorded for the eyes and ears of the future; think what we would give to see even the most trivial film from the year 1000, and consider what a gift we leave.

This list of the ten most influential films of the century is not to be confused with a selection of the century's best, although a few titles would be on both lists. As film grew into an art form, these were the milestones along the way.

1. The Early Chaplin Shorts

In 1913, there were no Charlie Chaplin movies. In 1914, he made no fewer than thirty-five, in an astonishing outpouring of energy and creativity that made Chaplin the first great star. Stardom was to become so inseparable from the movies that it is startling to realize that many early films had unbilled performers. In the earliest days just the moving picture was enough; audiences were astonished by moving trains and gunshots. Then Chaplin and his contemporaries demonstrated how completely the movies could capture a unique personality.

2. Birth of a Nation

D. W. Griffith's 1915 film is a tarnished masterpiece, a breakthrough in art and craft, linked to a story so racist, it is almost unwatchable. This was the film that defined the film language, that taught audiences and filmmakers all over the world the emerging grammar of the shot, the montage, and the camera. At 159 minutes, it tilted Hollywood's balance away from shorts and toward the more evolved features that would become the backbone of the new art form. What a shame that it also glorified the Ku Klux Klan.

3. Battleship Potemkin

Sergei Eisenstein's 1925 film about a revolutionary uprising of Russian sailors was considered so dangerous that it was still banned decades later in some countries, including its native Soviet Union. It demonstrated Eisenstein's influential theory of montage—of the way images took on new meanings because of the way they were juxtaposed. *Potemkin* also demonstrated the power of film as politics, polemic, and propaganda—power that many regimes, not least the Nazis, would use to alter world history.

4. The Jazz Singer

"You ain't heard nothin' yet!" Al Jolson promised in 1927, and movies were never the same. The first talkie was released that year (actually, it was a silent with sound passages tacked on), and although silent film survived through 1928 ("the greatest single year in the history of the movies," argues director Peter Bogdanovich), the talkies were the future. Purists argued that sound destroyed the pure art of silent film; others said the movies were a hybrid from the beginning, borrowing whatever they could from every possible art and science.

5. Snow White and the Seven Dwarfs

Eisenstein himself called Disney's 1937 animated feature the greatest film in history. Excessive praise, but world audiences were enthralled by the first full-length cartoon. Animation was as old as the movies (the underlying principle was much older), but Disney was the first to take it seriously as a worthy style for complex characters and themes. Disney's features continue to win enormous audiences and have grown in artistry and sophistication; audiences, alas, seem resistant to animation by anyone else, despite some recent success by the geniuses of Japanese anime.

6. Citizen Kane

If *Birth of a Nation* assembled all the breakthroughs before 1915, Orson Welles's 1941 masterpiece was the harvest of the emerging art form. It was not the first to use deep-focus photography, or overlapping dialogue, or interlocking flashbacks, or rotating points of view, or trick photography, or a teasing combination of fact and fiction, or a sampling of genres (newsreel, comedy, drama, musical, biopic), or a charismatic director who was what the French later defined as an auteur. But in the way it assembled the pieces, it dazzled audiences and other filmmakers and so fully exploited its resources that *Kane* is often voted the greatest of all films.

7. *Shadows*

John Cassavetes' 1961 film was a salvo that shook Hollywood to its foundations. Renting a 16 mm camera and working with friends on a poverty budget, he made a film totally outside the studio system. That had of course been done before, but *Shadows* was the symbolic standard-bearer of the emerging New American Cinema movement, which gave birth to underground films and to today's booming indie scene. Cassavetes demonstrated that it was not necessary to have studio backing and tons of expensive equipment to make a theatrical film.

8. *Star Wars*

There had been blockbusters before, from *Birth of a Nation* to *Gone with the Wind* to *Lawrence of Arabia*. But George Lucas's 1977 space opera changed all the rules. It defined the summer as the prime releasing season, placed a new emphasis on young audiences, used special effects, animation, computers, and exhilarating action to speed up the pacing, and grossed so much money that many of the best young directors gave up their quest for the Great American Film and aimed for the box office crown instead. Now most of the top-grossers every year follow in *Star Wars'* footsteps, from *Armageddon* to *The Matrix* to *Titanic*.

9. *Toy Story*

This delightful 1995 computer-animated feature may have been the first film of the twenty-first century. It was the first feature made entirely on computers, which allowed more realistic movement of the elements and the point of view, and characters that were more three-dimensional in appearance. Someday, computer-animated movies may be able to re-create "real" human actors and settings. Whether or not that is desirable, *Toy Story* demonstrated that the possibility was on the horizon. If films shift from celluloid and flesh and blood to the digital domain, this one will be seen as the turning point.

10. *The Blair Witch Project*

Important not for its entertainment value, which was considerable, but for what it represented in technical terms. Released in the summer of 1999, it was the first indie blockbuster, a film made for about $24,000 and shot entirely on inexpensive handheld cameras (one film, one video), which grossed more than $150 million. The message was inescapable: in the next century, technology will place the capacity for feature filmmaking into the hands of anyone who is sufficiently motivated, and audiences will not demand traditional "production values" before parting with their money.

There is not one conclusion, but two. Films are getting bigger and smaller, cheaper and more expensive, both at once. While mass-marketed blockbusters dominate the market, independent directors have the ability to make their own films almost by hand. Digital techniques are crucial to both trends. Will the future belong to *Star Wars* clones made with *Toy Story* techniques? Or to films made in the tradition of the early Chaplin quickies (some shot in a day), the Cassavetes-inspired independents, and the *Blair Witch* technology? It belongs to both, I think. Which will be interesting.

IN MEMORIAM
Pauline Kael

SEPTEMBER 4, 2001

B etter than anyone else, Pauline Kael communicated the immediate, sensual, voluptuous experience of seeing a great movie. She was known for her harsh judgments, but it was in her praise that she stood alone, as the most influential American film critic—maybe the most influential critic of any art form—of her time.

When she died Monday, her spirit and passion were still being echoed in the words of a generation of film critics she influenced. She changed the way we talk about the movies. Eyes flashing, hair tossing, talking back to the screen, she wrote not from theory or ideology but from her own personal feelings. *I Lost It at the Movies,* she said in the title of her first book, and the more you thought about those words, the more you understood the transformational power the movies can have for some people.

After earlier years spent in San Francisco, writing program notes, contributing to film magazines, broadcasting on the local public radio stations, Kael emerged nationally in the 1960s, just a few years in advance of what became known as the Film Generation. She praised the best of the new movies from Europe, but wasn't a sucker for "art films," some of which she found phony and pretentious. She had an eye out for native art, for the new winds in American cinema.

After false starts at *McCall's* and the *New Republic,* she settled in as the film critic of the *New Yorker* under William Shawn, and championed a new generation of American directors. She hailed *Bonnie and Clyde* when it was generally dismissed, and wrote decisive early articles on Martin Scorsese, Robert Altman, and Francis Ford Coppola—she spotted them all right out of the gate. Her long article on Scorsese's *Mean Streets* essentially launched his career. Week after week she bashed Hollywood frauds and stuck up for the directors with distinctive styles.

"Sometimes people don't really seem to draw a line between the

381

movies that really enlarge their experience, and the movies that simply work them over," she said in 1975 in a lecture at the Arts Club of Chicago. "When a great movie like Altman's *McCabe and Mrs. Miller* comes along, one of the functions I felt as a critic was to discuss the ways in which the movie was new, and the wonderful things Altman was doing in it. But then when people are moved, and deeply moved, by trash like *The Trial of Billy Jack,* then perhaps the critic can help by explaining the ways in which trash can manipulate your responses, can work over your emotions in unworthy and dishonest ways."

She liked feelings in the movies better than ideas. She suspected message pictures, because she felt the best way to communicate messages was through the senses—through feeling, not preaching. She liked the way "Altman's movies are made up of moments that affect us in ways we can't fully understand—unconscious moments."

"Responsible artists," she said, "try to affect you sensually in a way that enlarges your experience. Altman, for example, has raised the sound track to a whole new level. He hears more perceptively than other directors. He hears Americans talking, and we talk more than any other nation in the world. When you come out of an Altman movie, you hear your environment in a new way.

"And sometimes directors can achieve a sensual affect that simply can't be explained. In Coppola's *Godfather II,* for example, after the scene where Robert De Niro, as the young Don Vito, kills the landlord, the extortionist, he walks down the street in such a way that the scene becomes incredibly moving and powerful—everyone I've talked to who has seen the movie was affected by that scene, and yet there's no way to explain why. I think Coppola got the power for that scene out of his own unconscious. I don't know if he could explain it, either."

In print she was a power, and in person she was a dynamo. I met her right at the beginning of my career as a film critic, at the 1967 New York Film Festival. She was open, friendly, and generous to me, and to many other new critics of that time—there was not a drop of snobbery in her—and I found myself invited along for the ride, crammed into booths in the back room of the Ginger Man, across from Lincoln Center, debating the films we'd just seen. There were late nights of talk in her apartment, and noisy dinners, and excited phone calls. And at screenings, where critics were not supposed to vocalize their feelings, there'd be Pauline's "Oh! Oh! Oh!" at something she detested. She wasn't expressing an opinion, but defending herself against a personal affront.

She gathered around her a salon of the new directors and writers. Wherever she went, she was surrounded. People loved to hear her talk. One night in the lobby bar of the Algonquin, she introduced me to a new director and his star: Brian De Palma and Robert De Niro. I'd never heard of them. She had. Another night, there was an Italian dinner with Pauline, De Palma, the writer Paul Schrader, and myself. Looking around the table, I realized Pauline was out of work (she'd been fired by *McCall's*), De Palma was broke after his first two indie films, and Schrader was a struggling screenwriter. I had a paycheck from the *Sun-Times,* so I grabbed the bill. Leaving the restaurant, Pauline was shaking with laughter. "You dope," she said, "Schrader just sold a screenplay for $450,000!"

Kael's reviews changed movie history. Her praise of Altman's *Nashville* was reprinted, word for word, in a double-truck ad in the *New York Times.* Her review of Bertolucci's *Last Tango in Paris* helped open the way for a new sexual frankness in the movies.

She blasted the prudishness of Jack Valenti's new MPAA ratings system, saying, "The problem for younger moviegoers is that the rating system has meant that kids haven't been free to go to the best pictures, unless their parents take them. How can they develop an appreciation for movies if all they're allowed to see are those dreadful, boring movies that are aimed at them? The best pictures are mostly those with the R ratings, and there have been pictures that got the R because of one forbidden word—when all you have to do is listen to kids talking today and you realize no four-letter word is going to come as news to them. In terms of the intelligence and invention that goes into them, the Saturday night shows on TV are a lot better than most G or PG movies."

While the MPAA wanted to protect kids in an artificially prolonged childhood, Pauline championed movies that would help them grow up. She lost it at the movies, and they should, too.

She wrote some of the most merciless pans of her time, but she was best writing about what she loved. "The critic's power is mostly positive, not negative," she told me once. "We can't stop the expensive trash with the millions of dollars behind it, but what we can do is help a good little film get shown, and direct attention to the best new directors, the ones who are fresh and exciting. John Leonard said the other day that critics were lice on the body of art. But art would never reach the public without the critics. I don't feel like a louse."

Playing with the sensual relationship Kael had with the movies, the titles of her books continued the sexual connotation of *I Lost It at the Movies*. They included *Kiss Kiss Bang Bang, Going Steady, Deeper into Movies, Reeling, When the Lights Go Down, Movie Love, Taking It All In, Hooked,* and *5001 Nights at the Movies*. Only *State of the Art* wasn't suggestive—maybe. She retired from the *New Yorker* in 1991, and in 1994 edited a vast collection of the best writing from all of her books. It was titled, suitably, *For Keeps*.

PART 7

On Film Criticism

INTRODUCTION

These are musings about the job. It is a curious job.

Critics are asked every single day how many movies they see in a day/week/month/year. "No matter what your answer is," Gene Siskel said, "they believe you." We are asked if we see them more than once (usually not, but if time has passed since a festival screening, I always try to see them again). We are asked if we ever change our minds about a movie (see above). The strangest question is surprisingly frequent: "Do you actually see those movies you write about?"

Of these pieces, two are not by me. Richard Corliss, a lifelong friend, wrote the 1990 article for *Film Comment* in which he lamented the directions he saw film criticism taking. I defended our television program, while agreeing with many of his laments. The wise Andrew Sarris stepped in to adjudicate. This may be a good time to observe that the giants of film criticism when I began—

Sarris, Stanley Kauffmann, Manny Farber, Donald Richie, Pauline Kael, Arthur Knight—were unfailingly friendly and open. No snobbery toward new kids. Maybe going to the movies for a living makes you into a small-d democrat.

TWENTY-FIVE YEARS IN THE DARK

APRIL II, 1992

For many years I remembered the name of the first film I ever reviewed, but now I find it has left my mind. It was a French film, I remember that much. I watched it from a center seat in the old World Playhouse, bursting with the awareness that I was *reviewing* it, and then I went back to the office and wrote that it was one more last gasp of the French New Wave, rolling ashore.

I was more jaded then than I am now. At the time I thought that five years would be enough time to spend on the movie beat. My master plan was to become an op-ed columnist and then eventually, of course, a great and respected novelist. My reveries ended with a deep old wingback chair pulled up close to the fire in a cottage in the middle of the woods, where the big dog snored while I sank into a volume of Dickens.

I now find that I have been a film critic for twenty-five years. I am not on the op-ed page, have not written the novel, do not own the dog, but do have the cottage and a complete set of Dickens. And I am still going to the movies for a living. My mother never knew how to handle that, when her friends asked her, "And what about Roger? Is he still just . . . going to the movies?" It didn't seem like a real job.

There is something not natural about just . . . going to the movies. Man has rehearsed for hundreds of thousands of years to learn a certain sense of time. He gets up in the morning and the hours wheel in their ancient order across the sky until it grows dark again and he goes to sleep. A movie critic gets up in the morning and in two hours it is dark again, and the passage of time is fractured by editing and dissolves and flashbacks and jump cuts. Sometimes I see two or three movies a day, mostly in the screening room upstairs over the White Hen Pantry. I slip downstairs at noon for a sandwich, blinded by the sunlight, my mind still filled with chases and gun duels, yuks and big boobs, cute dogs and brainy kids, songs and dances,

387

amazing coincidences and chance meetings and deep insights into the nature of man. Whatever was in the movies.

"Get a life," they say. Sometimes I feel as if I have gotten everybody else's. I have a colleague who describes his job as "covering the national dream beat," because if you pay attention to the movies they will tell you what people desire and fear in their deepest secrets. At least, the good ones will. That's why we go, hoping to be touched in those secret places. Movies are hardly ever about what they seem to be about. Look at a movie that a lot of people love, and you will find something profound, no matter how silly the film may seem. The real subjects of *Wayne's World* are innocence and friendship. That's what you get for your seven dollars.

In the past twenty-five years I have probably seen 10,000 movies and reviewed 6,000 of them. I have forgotten most of those films, I hope, but I remember those worth remembering, and they are all on the same shelf in my mind. There is no such thing as an old film. *La Dolce Vita* is as new for me as *Basic Instinct*. There is a sense in which old movies are cut free from Time. Paul Henreid and Curt Bois have died recently, and that means all of the major characters onscreen in *Casablanca* are dead, and the movie floats free of individual lifetimes. It no longer has any reference to real people we might meet at a gas station or the Academy Awards. It is finally all fiction. *Basic Instinct,* on the other hand, involves careers that are still developing, people who are standing behind the screen, so to speak, peeking at the audience from the wings.

I look at silent movies sometimes, and do not feel I am looking an old films. I feel I am looking at a Now that has been captured. Time in a bottle. When I first looked at silent films, the performers seemed quaint and dated. Now they seem more contemporary than the people in 1980s films. The main thing wrong with a movie that is ten years old is that it isn't thirty years old. After the hair styles and the costumes stop being dated and start being history, we can tell if the movie itself is timeless.

What kinds of movies do I like the best? If I had to make a generalization, I would say that many of my favorite movies are about good people. It doesn't matter if the ending is happy or sad. It doesn't matter if the characters win or lose. The only true ending is death. Any other movie ending is arbitrary. If a movie ends with a kiss, we're supposed to be happy. But then if a piano falls on the kissing couple, or a taxi mows them down, we're supposed to be sad. What difference does it make? The best movies aren't about what happens to the characters. They're about the example that they set.

Casablanca is about people who do the right thing. *The Third Man* is about two people who do the right thing and can never speak to one another as a result. The secret of *Silence of the Lambs* is buried so deeply that you may have to give this a lot of thought, but its secret is that Hannibal Lecter is a good person. He is the helpless victim of his unspeakable depravities, yes, but to the limited degree that he can act independently of them, he tries to do the right thing.

Not all good movies are about good people. I also like movies about bad people who have a sense of humor. Orson Welles, who does not play either of the good people in *The Third Man,* has such a winning way, such witty dialogue, that for a scene or two we almost forgive him his crimes. Henry Hill, the hero of *GoodFellas,* is not a good fella, but he has the ability to be honest with us about why he enjoyed being bad. He is not a hypocrite. The heroine of *The Marriage of Maria Braun* does some terrible things, but because we know some of the forces that shaped her, we understand them, and can at least admire her resourcefulness.

Of the other movies I love, some are simply about the joy of physical movement. When Gene Kelly splashes through *Singin' in the Rain,* when Judy Garland follows the yellow brick road, when Fred Astaire dances on the ceiling, when John Wayne puts the reins in his teeth and gallops across the mountain meadow, there is a purity and joy that cannot be resisted. In *Equinox Flower,* a Japanese film by the old master Yasujiro Ozu, there is this sequence of shots: A room with a red teapot in the foreground. Another view of the room. The mother folding clothes. A shot down a corridor with a mother crossing it at an angle, and then a daughter crossing at the back. A reverse shot in a hallway as the arriving father is greeted by the mother and daughter. A shot as the father leaves the frame, then the mother, then the daughter. A shot as the mother and father enter the room, as in the background the daughter picks up the red pot and leaves the frame. This sequence of timed movement and cutting is as perfect as any music ever written, any dance, any poem.

I also enjoy being frightened in the movies, but I am bored by the most common way the movies frighten us, which is by having someone jump unexpectedly into the frame. The trick is so old a director has to be

shameless to use it. Alfred Hitchcock said that if a bunch of guys were playing cards and there was a bomb under the table and it exploded, that was
terror, but he'd rather do a scene where there was a bomb under the table
and we kept waiting for it to explode but it didn't. *That* was suspense. It's
the kind of suspense I enjoy.

Love? Romance? I'm not so sure. I don't much care for movies that
get all serious about their love affairs, because I think the actors tend to take
it too seriously, and end up silly. I like it better when love simply makes the
characters very, very happy, as when Doris Day first falls for Frank Sinatra
in *Young at Heart,* or when Lili Taylor thinks River Phoenix really likes her
in *Dogfight.*

Most of the greatest directors in the history of the movies were already well known when I started as a critic in 1967. There was once a time
when young people made it their business to catch up on the best works by
the best directors, but the death of film societies and repertory theaters has
put an end to that, and for today's younger filmgoers, these are not well-
known names: Buñuel, Fellini, Bergman, Ford, Kurosawa, Ray, Renoir,
Lean, Bresson, Wilder, Welles. Most people still know who Hitchcock was,
I guess.

Of the directors who started making films since I came on the job,
the best is Martin Scorsese. His camera is active, not passive. It doesn't regard events, it participates in them. There is a sequence in *GoodFellas* that
follows Henry Hill's last day of freedom, before the cops swoop down.
Scorsese uses an accelerating pacing and a paranoid camera that keeps looking around, and makes us feel what Hill feels. It is easy enough to make an
audience feel basic emotions ("Play them like a piano," Hitchcock advised),
but hard to make them share a state of mind. Scorsese can do it.

Which of today's actors will become immortals? Not very many.
Nicholson and De Niro, and not many women, because Hollywood no
longer has a lifetime of roles for them. Compared to the great movie stars
of the past, modern actors are handicapped by the fact that their films are
shot in color. In the long run, that will rob most of them of the immortality that was obtained even by second-tier stars of the black-and-white era.
Peter Lorre and Sydney Greenstreet are, and will remain, more memorable
than most of today's superstars with their multimillion-dollar paychecks.
Color is too realistic. It is too distracting. It projects superfluous emotional

cues. It reduces actors to inhabitants of the mere world. Black and white (or, more accurately, silver and white) creates a mysterious dream state, a simpler world of form and gesture.

Most people do not agree with me. They like color and think a black-and-white film is missing something. Try this. If you have wedding photographs of your parents and grandparents, chances are your parents are in color and your grandparents are in black and white. Put the two photographs side by side and consider them honestly. Your grandparents look timeless. Your parents look goofy.

The next time you buy film for your camera, buy a roll of black and white. Go outside at dusk, when the daylight is diffused. Stand on the side of the house away from the sunset. Shoot some natural-light close-ups of a friend. Have the pictures printed big, at least 5 × 7. Ask yourself if this friend, who has always looked ordinary in every color photograph you've ever taken, does not suddenly, in black and white, somehow take on an aura of mystery. The same thing happens in the movies.

On the other hand, I am not one of those purists who believes the silent films were perfect, and sound ruined everything. To believe that, I would have to be willing to do without Marilyn Monroe singing "Diamonds Are a Girl's Best Friend," Groucho Marx saying, "This bill is outrageous! I wouldn't pay it if I were you!" Robert De Niro asking, "Are you looking at me?" Sound is essential, but dialogue is not always so. The big difference between today's dialogue and the dialogue of years ago is that the characters have grown stupid. They say what is needed to advance the plot, and get their laughs by their delivery of four-letter words. Hollywood dialogue was once witty, intelligent, ironic, poetic, musical. Today it is flat. So flat that when a movie allows its characters to think fast and talk the same way, the result is invigorating, as in *My Dinner with Andre,* or the first thirty minutes of *White Men Can't Jump.*

Home video is both the best and the worst thing that has happened on the movie beat since I've been a critic. It is good because it allows us to see the movies we want to see, when we want to see them. It provides an economic incentive for the prints of old movies to be preserved and restored. It brings good movies, new and old, to towns without good movie theaters. I get letters from people who live miles from any good-sized town, but rent the new foreign films through the mail.

Home video is bad because it has destroyed the campus film societies, which were like little shrines to the cinema. If the film society was showing Kurosawa's *Ikiru* for a dollar and there was nothing else playing except the new releases at first-run prices, you went to *Ikiru* and then it was forever inside of you, a great film. Today, students rent videos, usually not very good ones, and even if they watch a great movie, they do it alone or with a few friends. There is no sense of audience, and yet the single most important factor in learning to be literate about movies is to be part of an audience that is sophisticated about them.

I also hold it against home video that it has destroyed most of the repertory theaters. When I started as a film critic at the *Sun-Times,* there was a theater named the Clark, on the corner that is now an extension of the First National Bank. It showed a different double feature every day of the year, twenty-two hours a day. That's where I saw *Sunset Boulevard* for the first time, and *All About Eve*. On the other hand, when I started in 1967, there weren't many film festivals, and not many art museums that took film seriously. Today every medium-sized city has a film festival, where if you are lucky you will see a wonderful film you have never heard of before. And a lot of museums have excellent film centers.

What I miss, though, is the wonder. Anyone my age can remember walking into a movie palace where the ceiling was far overhead, and balconies and mezzanines reached away into the shadows. We remember the sound of two thousand people laughing all at once. And the screens the size of billboards, so high off the floor that every seat in the house was a good seat. Today you walk into a shoebox and peer around the head of the person in front of you, and in the quiet moments you can hear the sound effects from the movie next door, right through the wall. "I lost it at the movies," Pauline Kael said, and we all knew just what she meant. Now we can't even give it away.

But all is not lost. Scorsese is not the only great director to come along since 1967. There are Altman and Coppola, Herzog and Fassbinder, Bertrand Tavernier and Oliver Stone, Spike Lee and Jim Jarmusch. I went to Cannes last year and there was a twenty-three-year-old kid there named John Singleton who had made a movie, and he came out of thin air, but his talent was real. Things are opening up a little. In recent years we've started getting important films from blacks, Hispanics, women, and other groups that essentially made no films at all when I started reviewing.

When you go to the movies every day, it sometimes seems as if the movies are more mediocre than ever, more craven and cowardly, more skillfully manufactured to pander to the lowest tastes, instead of educating them. Then you see something absolutely miraculous. Something like *Wings of Desire,* or *Do the Right Thing,* or *Drugstore Cowboy,* or *Gates of Heaven,* or *Beauty and the Beast,* or *Life Is Sweet,* and on your way home through the White Hen Pantry you look distracted, as if you had just experienced some kind of a vision.

SYMPOSIUM

ALL THUMBS, OR, IS THERE A
FUTURE FOR FILM CRITICISM?

BY RICHARD CORLISS

(From *Film Comment,* March/April 1990)

Will anyone read this story? (It has too many words and not enough pictures.)

Does anyone read this magazine? Every article in it wants to be a meal, not a McNugget.)

Is anyone reading film criticism? (It lacks the punch, the clips, the thumbs.)

Can anyone still read? (These days, it's more fun and less work just to watch.)

My mother saves movie ads in which my name appears and magnetizes them to the door of her refrigerator. She judges my success as a *Time* film critic by the size and frequency of the blurbs publicists choose to promote their wares. Mom always taught me that if you can't say something nice about a picture, don't say anything at all. So if a month or two passes and I'm not quoted, she gets to fretting. "That Jeffrey Lyons," she purrs, scanning the ads, "he must be a *very* nice man. He seems to like everything." I have an image of Jeffrey Lyons's mother's refrigerator, festooned with rave quotes. It must be the size of a freezer at Hormel's main plant.

Jeffrey Lyons isn't a film critic, but he plays one on TV. The resident movie sage on PBS's *Sneak Previews* and superstation WPIX, Lyons has no thoughts, no wit, no perspective worth sharing with his audience. To anyone knowledgeable about pictures, he is a figure of sour mirth. But the other week he stumbled upon a truth about film reviewing at the end of this enervating decade. Appraising the movie *Internal Affairs,* Lyons said, "Sometimes, as an old showbiz adage goes, less can be more." No matter that the phrase was Robert Browning's (popularized by Ludwig Mies van der Rohe) and not Sam Goldwyn's. In today's movie criticism, less *is* more.

Shorter is sweeter. Today's busy consumers want just the clips, ma'am. And an opinion that can be codified in numbers, letters, or thumbs.

The star system (★ to ★★★★) is as honored in popular reviewing as it is in Hollywood. It is a way of summing up the critic's response to a film. But in less-is-all TV, the reviewer hardly has time for the basics: synopsize the plot, introduce an excerpt, and then (if he hates the movie) make a joke or (if he likes it) invoke the five W's—warm, winning, wise, wacky, wonderful. Traditional considerations of directorial style, social import, and the film's place in film history are luxuries unobtainable in a no-frills review. Words are so much hot (or dead) air; only the number matters. So Gary Franklin, Lyons's West Coast counterpart, pegs movies on a 1-to-10 scale. But, inflation being rampant in the rhetoric market, Franklin must give his favorites a 10+. On *Siskel & Ebert & the Movies,* the critics play Roman emperors and award a thumbs-down condemnation or a thumbs-up reprieve.

The new magazine *Entertainment Weekly* assigns a letter grade to each movie, television program, book, or classical record. *EW*'s editor is Jeff Jarvis, a self-proclaimed "cultural spud." As the TV critic for *People* until last year, Jarvis panned *Masterpiece Theatre* adaptations of the great novels he was forced to skim in high school. He argued that the top-rated TV shows had more artistic value than the bestseller list. In a review of *Nixon in China* he wrote: "I hate people who talk slowly and people who repeat themselves—ergo, I hate opera." Now Jarvis is the culture czar at Time Inc. And *EW* is the *reductio ad infinitum* of a tendency—ignited by *People,* stoked by *Entertainment Tonight,* and inflamed by *USA Today*—to reduce history to gossip and criticism to a voxpop brain scan.

"Real" critics—my colleagues in print, for whom films and film reviewing are just a little more complex—may think that Lyons and Franklin have no more in common with serious writing than belly dancers do with the Ballet Russe. At their most generous, print critics will say, "We're writers, they're performers," who must create a stern or goofy TV personality and look natural while cribbing from a teleprompter. The print guys will quote with approval the observation of ABC-TV's film and theater enthusiast Joel Siegel, who told *Theater Week* magazine, "Frank Rich got hired because he can write. I got hired because I can read." They will surely scoff at Lyons's prickly pretensions when he accuses his print brethren of "jealousy. They resent our money and exposure. They look down their noses at us. And that's the reason I make a point of being called a critic as opposed to a reviewer. It's my way of saying I'm doing exactly what they're doing."

Lyons is almost right. He's doing exactly what we may soon have to do. To editors at major newspapers and magazines, the brisk opinion-mongering of TV critics—the minute-manager approach to an art form about which there is so much to say—provides the maximum daily requirements to be consumed by a readership glutted with information. Isn't everyone in a hurry? TV certainly is, and TV sets the pace we live and think by. The nightly newscasts are offering more but briefer stories: not news in depth—news in shallow. Tabloid topics, sexy footage, lotsa graphics, hold the analysis: television news plays like the *International Enquirer* staged by MTV. In this cramped universe, the traditional film critic might as well be writing in Latin. The long view of cinema aesthetics is irrelevant to a moviegoer for whom history began with *Star Wars*. A well-turned phrase is so much throat-clearing to a reader who wants the critic to cut to the chase: what movie is worth my two hours and six bucks this weekend? Movie criticism of the elevated sort, as practiced over the past half century by James Agee and Manny Farber, Andrew Sarris and Pauline Kael, J. Hoberman and Dave Kehr—in the mainstream press and in magazines like *Film Comment*—is an endangered species. Once it flourished; soon it may perish, to be replaced by a consumer service that is no brains and all thumbs.

> [John] Huston's pictures are not acts of seduction
> or benign enslavement but of liberation, and they
> require, of anyone who enjoys them, the responsi-
> bilities of liberty. They continually open the eye
> and require it to work vigorously; and through
> the eye they awaken curiosity and intelligence.
> That, by any virile standard, is the essential to
> good entertainment. It is unquestionably
> essential to good art.
> —James Agee on John Huston, 1950

When Pauline Kael moved from San Francisco to New York in the mid-sixties, she called her archrival Andrew Sarris and suggested they meet. After the visit, Sarris told his friend Eugene Archer, "She wasn't exactly Katharine Hepburn." And Archer added, "Well, you're not exactly Spencer Tracy."

But they were, in a way. They raised the musty trade of film criticism to a volcanic, love-hate art. Their wrangles over the auteur theory had the excitement of politics and sport. The intensity of their debate lured people to see new films, and to see old (especially old Hollywood) movies in a new way. They opened eyes, awakened curiosity, aroused intelligence. They made film criticism sexy. Pictures were things that mattered; ideas were worth fighting over. Forget Tracy-Hepburn, Sarris and Kael were more like Ali-Frazier. Film criticism was the main event, and these two were the champs.

The important thing was not that they converted readers to their positions—after all, they ended up converting each other. Sarris came around to cherishing certain directors, like Huston and Akira Kurosawa, whom Kael had once chided him for attacking. And Kael became a more rigorous and predictable champion of a few younger filmmakers (Peckinpah, Kershner, Kaufman, De Palma) than Sarris had ever been of Hitchcock and Hawks.

Their true and lasting value was in the voices they devised for film criticism. Sarris's prose was dense, balanced, aphoristic, alliterative; he had taken more from the French than just the *politique des auteurs*. Kael's was loping, derisive, intimate, gag-packed, as American as Lenny Bruce. I can recall reading one of Kael's early pieces in *Film Quarterly* (1961, maybe) and being shocked—shocked!—to see she'd used a contraction. In those prim days, when most serious film criticism read like term papers in sociology and most popular reviews read like wire copy, Kael's writing was the battle cry of a vital and dangerous new era, the equivalent of Little Richard's primal "A wop bop a loo bop, a wop bam boom!" that announced the birth of rock 'n' roll.

I t's not as if no American had ever written about film in the vernacular, or with passion or intelligence. There had always been a freedom in reviewing a medium so pervasive and so déclassé. The critic needn't bring reverence to the job. He could speak in his own voice, at his own desired decibel level. In the late thirties and forties, Otis Ferguson and Manny Farber, writing for the *New Republic,* and Agee in the *Nation,* created a body of reviews that still make edifying reading. Another critic, Cecelia Ager, who appeared in the New York tabloid *P.M.,* established the bright, brittle tone that Kael would later make her own. Ager on *Citizen Kane:* "It's as though you'd never seen a movie before." Ager on the Bette Davis weepie *Deception:* "It's like grand opera, only the people are thinner." (Contractions! Wow!) Agee, Ferguson, and Farber finally had their film pieces collected in book form. Nobody's publishing film books anymore, but it would be lovely to see the work of this neglected critic between hard covers.

The difference between the best forties criticism and Sarris's and Kael's work two decades later was the difference between journalism— great journalism—and criticism. I once opined that Agee and Farber in their *Time* days were writing "haiku in the margins of film history," and Farber readily agreed. It's not that the short review is the assassin of wit and insight; a clever writer can shadowbox artfully in forty or sixty lines, sketch a line of argument, give hints of a directorial style, vacuum-pack ideas into assertions. But these wonderful writers couldn't take 9,000 words to demolish Siegfried Kracauer's theory of film, as Kael did in *Film Quarterly.* They couldn't erect the auteurist pantheon in sixty-eight pages of *Film Culture,* as Sarris did. Both generations of critics were film artists, but Agee and Farber were Tex Avery miniaturists; Sarris and Kael were muralists— Abel Gance, chronicling another revolution.

At first their publications had subscriber lists of just a few thousand, but soon the critics found larger audiences, Kael at the *New Yorker* and Sarris with his blossoming constituency at the *Village Voice.* Their occasional brawls were now broadcast in the *New York Times.* Considerations of Kael's collected pieces appeared on the front pages of the *Times'* book review. They also created, in their warring images, a generation of acolytes. They raised young readers into writers who, to this day, carry the cultural passions of Sarris or Kael, or both, like DNA. We were called Sarrisites (Wilfrid Sheed's wonderfully malign epithet: rhymes with parasites) or Paulettes (my phrase, for my sins). And like some juicy family feud, the old debates were reheated for new readers when our children's crusade marched into the available jobs. We were shouting at each other—because belligerence was the only sound we had heard as kids at the film-critical dinner table— but in the same language, the one Sarris and Kael had taught us.

For a while, it seems everyone spoke this language: Hollywood hacks who made "A Film by . . . ," moviegoers for whom "auteurs" now had marquee value, college professors ready to teach Lang, Murnau, and Curtiz—and maybe Larry, Moe, and Curly. Nearly every critic with a regular job published a book, often a scrapbook of his reviews. Someone must be reading this stuff. It must be the "Film Generation," the kids who would attend our wisdom, patronize our anointed directors, and, soon enough, make films tailored to our aesthetic prejudices.

That was delusion, of course—a typically American delusion of power and primacy. The French had started it all, defining and romanticizing the burly energy of Hollywood films. Then, from the early sixties, a batch of British renegades—among them Robin Wood, Raymond Durgnat, David Thomson, Peter Wollen—had been using another brilliant set of dialects. And in Wollen's influential case, dialectics. Sarris and Kael had validated the Hollywood film as a field of study, but their brand of interpretive scholarship never took at American universities; it wasn't sufficiently serious or rigorous or engagé. By the mid-seventies academe had been liberated or subjugated by semiology. Approaches to film were more fragmented. Semiologists claimed the high ground—the right to set the aesthetic, political, and moral agenda—while the Paulettes and Sarrisites found themselves loitering in familiarly dank territory, in the monarchy of midcult. We wouldn't be the next Truffauts, just the latest Bosley Crowthers. We weren't the only, and weren't the first. And we wouldn't last.

An excerpt from the basement video show *Wayne's World,* starring young Wayne Campbell and his friend Garth, and featured on *Saturday Night Live:*

> WAYNE: OK! Let's take a look at the movies, all right?
> GARTH: All right!
> WAYNE: Our first movie is *Back to the Future 2,* starring Michael J. Fox. I liked it! Garth?
> GARTH: Yeah, I liked it too.
> WAYNE: OK, let's move on! *Steel Magnolias,* starring Daryl Hannah and Dolly Parton. I thought it sucked! It's a *chick* movie! Garth?

GARTH: Yeah, it sucked.

WAYNE: OK, OK! *Valmont,* with that babe Meg Tilly—*growwwwwl!* Didn't see it. Garth?

GARTH: Didn't see it.

It remained only for somebody to claim the rich, fertile low ground. How inevitable, how irresistible, the rise of TV criticism now seems! We could write reams of descriptive, delirious, indignant prose. But we couldn't show you a clip from a movie. Sarris once said that much of Agee's famous *Life* essay on silent film comedy—his evocation of Chaplin's work or a Keaton gag—was gorgeously irrelevant, if you'd seen the films. The evidence was on the screen. I couldn't agree, because every Agee description offered implicit analysis; it was the art of gesture mirrored in the craft of writing. But Sarris was accurate, and prophetic, in spite of himself. Traditional film criticism was images reconsidered in words. First we told you what the picture was, then we told you what it meant; and on both accounts you had to take our word(s) for it.

The next step would be to analyze films on TV. Then you could literally *see* what we were talking about. And we could finally make good on auteurism's unfulfilled promise of mise-en-scène analysis. All we needed was the technology. And in the sixties, at the same time Sarris and Kael were clawing their way to prominence, TV sports directors were creating the crucial means of reproduction: the instant replay. Now there were "analysts" like Al DeRogatis (and, later, John Madden) who not only told you but showed you what happened and what it meant.

At the time, I was thrilled by the potential this powerful tool offered film scholarship. No more reliance on faulty, fractured memory—you could study a film as you would a painter's oeuvre, frame by frame. And at the Columbia University film school, one professor, Stefan Scharf, was teaching visual acuity by just this means. He would show, say, Chabrol's *Leda,* stopping each scene to note visual and dramatic composition. In the eighties, at film festivals, Roger Ebert would do the same with a print of *Citizen Kane.* Entertaining and illuminating, as only a *bon vivant* scholarshowman can be.

Yes, *that* Roger Ebert. Gene Siskel's costar on the long-running syndicated series *Siskel & Ebert & the Movies.* This is, shall we say, no film university of the air. The program does not dwell on shot analysis, or any other kind of analysis. It is a sitcom (with its own noodling, toodling theme song) starring two guys who live in a movie theater and argue all the time. Oscar Ebert and Felix Siskel. "The fat guy and the bald guy." *S&E&TM* is every kind of TV and no kind of film criticism. It's as tightly structured as a movie star's promotional visit to a talkshow: the requisite clip, the desultory chat. It shows you a couple of minutes from several new films so you can decide if you want to see them or, even better, talk about them at parties without bothering to see them. For moviegoers in a hurry, this is *Masterplots Theatre*.

The format, to be sure, was not designed to offer extended, enlightened commentary on pictures. It means mainly to answer two consumer questions about every movie: What's it like? Will I like it? A minute or two of discussion (which amounts to fewer words on the subject than one of Agee's, or my, *Time* blurbs), and break for commercial. *S&E&TM* is what it is. And it is successful enough for each of its stars to earn, it is said, an annual million or so dollars from the gig. Which nobody can deny a jolly good fellow like Roger. Whatever the gripes against their show, Siskel and Ebert do a tough job professionally. They give you movie clips and sound bites. They look at ease and in charge on the home screen—no small feat, as I can attest (and I've got the videotapes to prove it). They have triumphantly marketed TV-size versions of themselves. They are the very best possible "Siskel" and "Ebert." More money to them.

And less power. It's not that I'm embarrassed to see them shooting hoops in a poor-white-kids version of Michael vs. Magic on *Late Night with David Letterman*. That's just showbiz. I simply don't want people to think that what they have to do on TV is what I am supposed to do in print. I don't want junk food to be the only cuisine at the banquet. I don't want to think that all the critics who have made me proud to be among their number are now talking to only themselves, or to a coterie no larger than the one Kael and Sarris first addressed thirty years ago. They were Ali-Frazier; I don't want us to be Foreman-Cooney.

I hope there is a place in popular criticism for the seductiveness of a David Thomson sentence, with its snap, grace, and insolence. I hope Richard T. Jameson, the new custodian of this beleaguered magazine, will keep writing eloquently about what's on the screen and, as editor, encourage other critics to define their terms when they say a film is well or poorly made. Most of all, I hope there are still readers with the vigor, curiosity, and intelligence that Agee demanded of filmmakers and critics. We're in this fight together. To understand pictures, we still need words.

Did you get to the end of this story? Good. Maybe there's hope for both of us.

ALL STARS, OR, IS THERE A CURE FOR CRITICISM OF FILM CRITICISM?

BY ROGER EBERT

(From *Film Comment,* May/June 1990)

Richard Corliss is generally correct in his discussion of new developments in popular film criticism (*Film Comment,* March/April 1990). The age of the packaged instant review is here, and lots of moviegoers don't have time to read the good, serious critics—the Kaels and Kauffmanns. Thumbs, star ratings, grades, and the marvelous Franklin scale have made it unpopular, if not impossible, for critics to deliver an ambiguous or uncertain opinion of a movie (quick: *Last Year at Marienbad*—thumbs up, or down?). Newspaper editors around the country want colorful capsule verdicts on the new movies for their weekend pullout sections, and the TV stations in most major markets now have local personalities who narrate clips from the new releases.

What Corliss does not realize is that this is an improvement, not a deterioration, of the situation as we both found it in the mid-1960s when we started in the business of writing about films. That was a time when there was no regular film criticism on national or local TV. Film magazines did not exist on the newsstands, and although *Film Quarterly* and *Film Comment* were being published, few outside academia and the film industry knew about them. *Variety* was the showbiz bible, with the emphasis on biz. As a matter of policy, most daily newspapers did not publish film reviews. In general-circulation magazines, the great influential voice in the late 1950s and early 1960s belonged to Dwight Macdonald, in *Esquire,* the man who taught me that movies were to be taken seriously.

The single most influential event in the history of modern newspaper film reviewing took place as recently as 1963, when Twentieth Century Fox banned Judith Crist from its screenings after she attacked *Cleopatra* in the *New York Herald-Tribune.* This event so tickled the public fancy that it became necessary for the trendier newspapers to import or create their own hard-to-please reviewers. Before 1963, with the exception of a handful of papers in New York, Los Angeles, Washington, and a few other cities, newspaper film criticism existed on a fan magazine level, if at all. The proof of this was that most movie reviews were ghosted by various staff writers under a house byline (Mae Tinee in the *Chicago Tribune*—get it?). But by the middle years of the decade, any self-respecting newspaper had its own local critic, and every one of them had studied Kael's *I Lost It at the Movies* and Andrew Sarris's *The American Cinema*.

That was a good time for the movies, as who needs to be reminded. Something called the "Film Generation" made a newsweekly cover, and films like *The Graduate, Blow-Up, Weekend, Bonnie and Clyde, Persona,* and *2001* were opening. Revival theaters flourished in the larger cities. Film societies did standing-room business on every campus. Harvard students knew Bogart's dialogue by heart, and in Chicago the Second City nightclub cleared its stage on Monday nights for screenings of underground films.

Now all of that is long, long ago. It is probably true that today's average, intelligent, well-informed American university undergraduate has never heard of Luis Buñuel, Jean Renoir, or Satyajit Ray, and if you find one who can identify Hitchcock, Truffaut, Kurosawa, or Bergman, hang on to him—he's got the fever.

The death of the repertory and revival houses in most cities has been appropriately mourned, but who is there to grieve the death of campus film societies, which have shut down on one campus after another? Douglas Lemza of Films Incorporated, the largest 16 mm film rental company, tells me that classic and foreign film exhibition on the campus is dying or dead, replaced by videocassettes on big-screen TV. The campus auditoriums where once we saw *Ikiru* are silent now on Sunday nights, but down in the lounge of the campus dorm, the kids are sitting in front of the 50-inch Mitsubishi, watching *Weekend at Bernie's*.

The most depressing statistic I know about patterns in American film exhibition comes from Dan Talbot, the veteran head of New Yorker Films. He says that an average subtitled film will take 85 percent of its box office gross out of theaters in only eight North American cities, and will never play at all in most of the others. The vast chains like Cineplex Odeon have gobbled up the smaller local and regional exhibitors, and Chicago's

Biograph, which used to be an art house, was playing a Steven Seagal thriller the last time I drove past. The Cinema Studio, home of subtitled films, is the latest Manhattan art theater to close. In the late 1950s, more than forty college towns had theaters booked by the Art Theater Guild. Such a chain is unthinkable today. The growth of the Landmark chain of revival theaters in the 1970s was brought to an end by videocassettes. The bottom line is that mass-produced Hollywood entertainments dominate American movie exhibition, and most moviegoers seem to like it that way.

In the days of my youth and Corliss's, the film societies and art houses provided the environment where a serious film community flourished. People stood in line together, sat in the theater together, and hung out afterward to talk about the best new movies. Places where that kind of gathering can take place no longer exist in most cities. A few revival houses survive, and the largest cities have film programs at the art museums, or in subsidized cultural centers. There are more film festivals than ever before. Every city worth its salt has one, and specialist festivals like Telluride, Park City, and Mill Valley specialize in showcasing independent films. Even so, a young person seriously interested in film has little sense, these days, that he is part of a community. The collapse of campus film societies is the single most obvious reason for this. Serious discussion of good movies is no longer part of most students' undergraduate experience.

Now, what about film criticism in these dark ages? It is thriving. There is more of it than ever before. Richard Corliss can be forgiven, I think, for the elegiac tone of his farewell article; he is saying goodbye to *Film Comment* after many productive and valuable years, and his leave-taking must be painful because a large part of his life was invested in the magazine. But at least part of his discontent is a textbook case of mid-career crisis. He started with grand ambitions, he has achieved most of what he hoped for, and now he asks with Peggy Lee, is that all there is? Like many others his age (which is more or less my age), he finds the cause of his malaise in the general disintegration of everything in general and other people's standards in particular.

What strikes me as slightly disingenuous is his lament for serious film criticism; here is the brilliant critic of *New Times* in the 1970s, now a captive of the space and style restraints of *Time,* where the best way for a writer to get more space is to sell the editors on a cover story about a star, and then try to sneak criticism into the crevices of a personality profile. He praises my program *Siskel & Ebert* with faint damns (we are the best of a bad lot; I am personally a jolly chap, etc.) and then says, "I simply don't want people to think that what they have to do on TV is what I'm supposed to do in print." But that is not the real challenge facing Corliss, who might better have asked himself why what he has to do in *Time* is what he's supposed to do in print. This is particularly sad because, with this farewell article, Richard Corliss's distinctive critical voice may actually disappear from print: that isn't his own voice in *Time,* but a chirpy patois that he would not, I am sure, want to have collected under his signature. To put it another way, his manifesto would read more convincingly if he were leaving *Time* to join *Film Comment*.

Corliss's apocalyptic vision notwithstanding, good film criticism is commonplace these days. *Film Comment* itself is healthier and more widely distributed than ever before. *Film Quarterly* is, too; it even recently abandoned eons of tradition to increase its page size. And then look at *Cineaste* and *American Film* and the specialist fan magazines (you may not read *Fangoria,* but if you did, you would be amazed at the erudition its writers bring to the horror and special-effects genre). At the top of the circulation pyramid is the glossy *Premiere,* rich with ads and filled with knowledgeable articles that are not all simply puff pieces about the stars, although some of them are. It is Corliss's opinion that good film books are no longer published, but has he read David Bordwell on Ozu, Patrick McGilligan on Altman, or Linda Williams on pornography?

Kael, our paradigm, continues at the *New Yorker.* Kauffmann gets more sense into less space than any other critic alive, at the *New Republic.* David Denby is at *New York,* Jonathan Rosenbaum at the *Reader,* Hoberman at the *Village Voice;* Mark Crispin Miller has a cover story in the *Atlantic,* and on and on. The weekly *Reader* in Chicago, born in 1969, has spawned a new kind of national newspaper, the giveaway lifestyle weekly, and each of these papers—the *Phoenix,* the *L.A. Weekly,* etc.—has its own resident auteurist or deconstructionalist. Daily newspaper film criticism at the national level is better and deeper than it was in Corliss's golden age, no matter what his impression is. He mentions the invaluable Dave Kehr of the *Chicago Tribune.* Has he read Michael Sragow in San Francisco, Sheila

Benson and Peter Rainer in Los Angeles, Jay Scott in Toronto, Howie Movshovitz in Denver, Jay Carr in Boston, Philip Wuntch in Dallas? And what about the college newspapers, where the explosion in film education over the past twenty years has generated dozens of undergraduate film critics who already know more than some of their elders will ever learn? Yes, they are writing "journalism" for the most part, and, yes, their reviews will yellow with age as those of Corliss's fondly remembered Cecelia Ager also did. But then they are journalists. It is not dishonorable to write for a daily deadline.

No art form is covered more completely and at greater length in today's newspapers than the movies. A lot of papers review virtually every film released; many review no books at all. All of this film criticism has not resulted in a more selective North American moviegoing public, nor has it created larger audiences for foreign or independent films or documentaries. It exists in a time when alternative films, theaters, and audiences are in disrepair.

But what of movie criticism on TV? Is it the culprit? What about *Siskel & Ebert*? I am the first to agree with Corliss that the *Siskel & Ebert* program is not in-depth film criticism, as indeed how could it be, given our time constraints.* But Corliss has not bothered to really engage the program, to look at it closely and say what he thinks is wrong. He disapproves of the idea of *Siskel & Ebert,* but leaves it at that. (I wonder if Corliss watches *Siskel & Ebert* very much—he gets the title of the show wrong in his article and cites not a single moment from any show. He would be incapable of writing a movie review as unfocused as his dyspepsia about *S&E*.)

The weekly program takes two basic forms—the review shows, and the "theme" shows. The review shows are indeed as formatted as Corliss reports; a typical show involves reviews of five movies, with an ad lib discussion after the written portion of each review, and then a summary fea-

---

*Corliss might be surprised to discover, however, that he is not always right when he assumes that his magazine reviews are longer than the *S&E* treatment of a film. On *Blaze,* the *Time* count is 324, *S&E* 755. On *Blue Steel,* it was *Time* 267 words, *S&E* 864. On *The 'Burbs,* *Time* nudges us 603 to 471, and on *House Party,* 567 to 536, although, as Corliss points out, in addition to the words we also show clips from the films.

turing the famous thumbs. Although Corliss thinks he has heard us telling jokes, in fact we have a house rule against any deliberate or scripted jokes of any kind—especially puns on names. Nor are our reviews limited to Corliss's "five W's—warm, winning, wise, wacky, wonderful." In fact, his invention of this witty formula shows him using the very sort of jokey criticism he accuses us of practicing, although I will not deny the formula applies to many TV-based critics. Siskel and I have an advantage over many other critics on the tube in that we both still write for newspapers, where we have spent most of our time for more than twenty years. Most TV-based critics have never written a movie review longer than eight sentences.

I wish we had more time on the program. It would be fun to do an open-ended show with a bunch of people sitting around talking about movies, but we would have to do it for our own amusement because nobody would play it on television. The program's purpose is to provide exactly what Corliss says it provides: information on what's new at the movies, who's in it, and whether the critics think it's any good or not.

The program reaches audiences in nearly 200 cities, and from some of the smaller markets come letters like one saying, "None of these movies ever play within 50 miles of here, so thanks to your show at least we know what we are missing." In the golden age of the late 1960s, no film commentary of any sort reached most of the households in most of these markets, although faculty members on the local campus knew who Kael was, and huddled over the glow from their 16 mm projectors like monks in the dark ages treasuring manuscripts from far lands. When we review a film that is not being released simultaneously on 1,600 screens, our review is the only local exposure that film receives in many cities. When we have an opinion about a movie, that opinion may light a bulb above the head of an ambitious youth who then understands that people can make up their own minds about the movies. And when we try to explain why *Do the Right Thing* is a better film than *Driving Miss Daisy,* although admittedly less enjoyable, it is a message not previously heard in many quarters.

This is not deep criticism—it is informed and sincere opinion. We do it better now than we used to, and we are still trying to get it right. There is another thing we do on the *Siskel & Ebert* show that I am more proud of, and which Corliss does not mention. Over the past several years, we have devoted many "theme shows" to a single subject or issue. As a national program, we have been influential on some of these issues.

When we devoted thirty minutes to an attack on colorization in October 1986, we were the first national TV program to mention the subject, and for a year we were the only one. We have renewed the attack several times. We were the first program to illustrate the virtues of letterboxing (March 1987 and subsequently), contrasting it to the butchery of cropping and pan-and-scan. The TV medium was ideal for illustrating specific examples, such as the disappearance of Mrs. Robinson in her key scene with Benjamin. We devoted a show to Spike Lee in August 1989, while *Do the Right Thing* was still in theaters. We did an entire program in celebration of black-and-white cinematography in May 1989, and we filmed the show itself in black and white. It was the first new syndicated program shot in black and white in twenty-five years. We were the first program to feature Laserdiscs (May 1987) and demonstrate their features, such as simultaneous commentary on a parallel soundtrack. We attacked product placement on another program, with shots of the stars seen clutching their Cokes and sitting behind their Dunkin' Donuts boxes. In March 1987 we did a show explaining how the MPAA rating system was de facto censorship. We asked them to add a new "A" rating for films intended for adults, since the X rating is not controlled by the MPAA and means the automatic exclusion of a film from mainstream distribution and exhibition channels.*

Siskel & Ebert was the first and often the only television show of any kind to deal with many of these subjects. It would be fair to say that most mainstream Americans who have formed an opinion on colorization and letterboxing were inspired to do so because of our program. (Video retailers say the *Siskel & Ebert* program on letterboxing caused a noticeable swing in the opinions of their customers on the subject.)

Corliss regrets TV's lost opportunities for doing a "shot by shot" analysis of films, and I do, too. I continue to use the shot-by-shot approach for the close visual analysis of films at least five or six times a year, on cam-

---

*The MPAA's refusal in March to grant an R to *The Cook, the Thief, His Wife, and Her Lover* is the latest example of the way a film can suffer in distribution. Many chains have contracts with their landlords prohibiting them from playing X-rated or unrated films.

PART 7: ON FILM CRITICISM, A SYMPOSIUM ❧ 410

puses or at film festivals. This is partly to keep in training, which is also the reason I teach a film class; a mind that considers movies only at review length will atrophy. Laserdiscs make shot-by-shot analysis infinitely easier than the old stop-action 16 mm projectors did; Donald Richie and I made our way a shot at a time through the Criterion disk of Ozu's *Floating Weeds* last December at the Hawaii International Film Festival, and every frame seemed to reveal a new treasure. I would like to go through an entire film a shot at a time on television—or, more to the point, I would like to see a Scorsese or a Jarmusch go through one of his own films a shot at a time. Corliss and I both know this is not likely to happen. There is now the happy alternative of Laserdiscs with running commentary on the sound track.*

And yet television is a useful medium for showing things about film that cannot easily be explained in words. Gene Siskel and I have exploited the possibilities of the medium on many shows, as when we contrasted the colorized and black-and-white versions of the same movies, or when we showed the cropped and letterboxed versions of a film at the same time on the same split screen. Our show does more of this kind of hands-on analysis than an infrequent viewer might realize.

Of course our program could be better. Progress comes slowly. We no longer work with Spot the Wonder Dog, for example, and I for one was able to contain my grief when the little beast died of kidney failure. We no longer waste a segment on the week's worst movie—there are too many interesting movies to review. But I would like it if we took a scene by an interesting director and went through it with a voice-over analysis. And I would like it if we reviewed more independent and foreign films. If there is a malaise eating away at the heart of film journalism these days, I submit it should not be blamed on the reviewers who work on television. We are addressing a different audience from the passionate elite who followed the Kael/Sarris Wars of the 1960s. Some of the critics on TV address them better than others, and all of us operate under Sturgeon's Law ("90 percent of everything is crap"). There is room for improvement. Give me the opportunity and an audience that will watch, and I know where and how some

---

*The most detailed film criticism I've seen on American TV was the Richard Schickel PBS series where he led great directors through discussions of their themes and styles, and then showed what they were talking about.

of those improvements could be made. So do a lot of other people, but the daily reality of national television is unforgiving and not very flexible, and PBS provides even less leeway than our commercial syndication. Yet we are not the evil empire of film criticism.

I submit to Richard Corliss that he missed the real source of distemper in today's American film market, and that is the ascendancy of the marketing campaign, and the use of stars as bait to orchestrate such campaigns. Reviewers, after all, can only offer their opinions on a new movie. Some like it, some don't, and together they do not have the impact of a well-coordinated national campaign that lands a popular star simultaneously on the covers of a *People*-type magazine, a newsweekly, several glossy monthlies, and the talk shows. Hollywood has never been more star-driven than it is at this moment, and publishers and producers have never been more eager to get their piece of the star of the week.

Isn't it obvious that the auteur period is over with now—that we have passed through the age of the director, and returned to the age of the powerful studio and the star system? The most creative directors in America today mostly came from the 1970s; nobody since Scorsese has been better. For every 1980s director with a style and something to say—for those like Gus Van Sant, Jr., Spike Lee, and Jim Jarmusch—there are countless film school technicians who know how to manufacture glossy generic entertainments and would have been right at home on the B-picture assembly lines of the 1940s. (The difference is, in the 1940s, visual style was still prized; now most new directors depend on art directors for their visual impact, and give only perfunctory thought to camera style.) After a period in the 1980s when talented executives seemed to avoid studio jobs, the most successful Hollywood studios are now headed by men (and a rare woman) who demonstrably know what moviegoers want—up to a point, of course.

In the 1970s we went to see the new Altman, Coppola, Fassbinder, or Mazursky film. The 1980s mass audience goes to see a star, special effects, or a high concept. Martin Scorsese says the monster hit—the $200 million-plus movie—is a new genre, and he's right: the studios lob the blockbusters into the choice summer weekends, and lesser movies scatter out of the way. Today's average moviegoers follow the works of Tom Hanks and Michelle Pfeiffer in the way moviegoers used to wait for the new Hitchcock or Huston. Audiences cannot identify many directors, and hardly care. Just as in the days of Douglas Fairbanks, Charlie Chaplin, and Mary Pickford, stars are seen as the auteurs of their films—and why not, since what difference does it make who directed the next Schwarzenegger film when Arnold has the final authority?

Most big movies these days are packaged by agencies, who like to see their directors, writers, and actors working together. The director who has, God forbid, a personal vision to express will have to recruit support from an important star in the same stable to get his vision out of the agency doors and into production. Actors who regularly work at scale or discount for directors they believe in—actors like Matt Dillon, Jane Fonda, Morgan Freeman, Gérard Depardieu, Geneviève Bujold, William Hurt, Peter Coyote—are in effect subsidizing what's left of the auteur film.

In the meantime, popular film journalism has become starstruck with a vengeance. Not since the glory days of the glossy movie fan magazines have stars been viewed so uncritically, so fawningly. Where did it start, this rhetorical hyperbole that attempts to transform the star of the moment into something more than human? I was among the many admirers of Emily Lloyd's work in *Wish You Were Here,* but after reading some of the profiles I wondered how I had failed to properly appreciate her translucent skin, her sparkling eyes, her grace, her effervescence, her brilliance. We should fall on our knees in gratitude, that she should walk among us. Then Emily Lloyd went on to create more difficult performances (flawlessly using American accents unfamiliar to her) in two box office flops, *Cookie* and *In Country,* and where were her idolaters? Lighting candles before Laura San Giacomo and Julia Roberts.

In Hollywood's golden years, worship of the stars was usually confined to the cult-like fan magazines. Now it has infected the mainstream, as the media lines up and volunteers to be part of the hype. In the closing weeks of 1989, the hottest new movie was *Born on the Fourth of July* and its star, Tom Cruise, was the most desirable magazine cover subject in America. According to reports published a few months later, Cruise had promised his friend, *Rolling Stone* publisher Jann Wenner, an exclusive national magazine cover. But when *Born on the Fourth of July* turned out to be a powerful and controversial picture, his promise seemed unwise. *Time* magazine, for example, wanted Cruise for its cover. And so, according to the reports, Cruise asked Wenner for a favor—could he be released from his promise, so he could be on the cover of *Time*? And Wenner, aware that such a cover could help his friend's chances of an Academy Award nomination, agreed. Cruise's publicists then agreed to give him to *Time*—and not, for example, to *Newsweek*.

Do you see what's wrong with this picture? Any hardboiled old-time newspaperman could tell you. A publicist should not be able to give a newsweekly "permission" to run Tom Cruise on its cover. *Time* magazine should run who it damn well pleases on its cover, as it used to do. And if *Newsweek* wanted to run Cruise the same week, it should have. The key, of course, is that the favored magazine is being offered two carrots: exclusivity, and access to the star for an interview and photo session. It is never spelled out that the magazine's critics will subsequently give the movie in question a favorable review, but any reasonable publicist would assume that a magazine would not want to feature someone who was in a bad movie.

Here is the definition of an "exclusive interview" with a star: he will say the same things he always says, but for a two-week window he will say them only to you (and to one, but only one, of the morning TV talk shows). Usually this means the writer has his work cut out, since the editorial space available for a cover profile far exceeds what can intelligently be written on the subject, unless the star can be pumped up into a trend or a demigod. (The really interesting talkers—Teri Garr, Harry Dean Stanton, Albert Brooks— are not usually cover material.) In a process possibly designed to silence his own doubts about the newsworthiness of his subject, the writer then inflates the star-of-the-week with prose that approaches hagiography.* The superlatives used in *Time* to describe Tom Cruise would have seemed embarrassingly inflated if applied to a philosopher, poet, religious leader, or

---

*Corliss on Cruise: "The souped-up Chevy Lumina circles the track at North Carolina's Charlotte Motor Speedway. At the wheel is Tom Cruise, daredevil superstar. The hazel eyes that laser out of his handsome face focus on the thrill of speed and risk. Nor is this challenge confined to a roadway's hard curve; it applies as well to his career in the movies, even if it means taking dangerous curves toward roles that might confound his fans. This day, after a dozen laps, Cruise sees a dime, stops on it and emerges from the Lumina to say hello to a visitor. He extends a hand and flashes the million-dollar smile—or, to judge from the worldwide take of his past four movies, the $1.035 billion smile. He points to the car and asks, 'Want to go around?' America wants to go around with Tom Terrific—that's how he looks, that's how he makes moviegoers feel."

statesman. Whatever happened to the *Time* that used to be known for its sneaky puns and wise-guy cynicism? When did it join the packaging team?

Stars are marketed to local TV and newspapers in the same way. Lest anyone think I am singling out the newsweeklies, I hasten to confess that my own editors sometimes treat their entertainment writers as a journalistic version of the old Frank Buck radio program, *Bring 'em Back Alive.* No Sunday newspaper is complete without an endless "celebrity profile," and papers like the *New York Times,* where the critics do "think pieces" on Sundays and never interview anybody, are rare indeed. First the star sells the medium, and then the medium sells the star and his movie. Around and around.

There is little room in this circle for a movie without a star. That is why Hollywood stars are worth the salaries they are getting, and why some stars now make as much as a movie used to cost. The new releases used to open in New York and roll out across the country. Now they open everywhere on the same day, and in the seven days before they open you can see their stars on magazine covers in every checkout line and hear them talking on every interview show—backed up, of course, by TV spot commercials.

Then, on the Monday after the movies open, the box score appears in *USA Today.* We learn the "box office winners" of the previous weekend, and the "per-screen average" of the leading contenders. *USA Today* was the first to turn trade information into a national scoreboard, but now the totals are carried by the wire services and faithfully announced by disk jockeys. Corliss is disturbed that potential moviegoers only ask "What's it about?" and "Who's in it?" He should examine his feelings the first time he is asked about a film's per-screen average.

Do people still read and care about serious film criticism? That is the real question in the Corliss piece, and I think the answer is, yes, they do—the same people who always did, and probably a few more. To which we can add the greatly increased numbers of people who read and care about serious film journalism, as provided in *Premiere* and many other magazines and local newspapers. Are the movie critics on TV preempting the audience for such writing? No. They serve a different function, for a different audience, and in an age when celebrity puff pieces are a sponge soaking up the available media time and space, at least they offer critical opinions, not fan letters. Often, shows like *Siskel & Ebert* are the first contact a young moviegoer might have with the notion that films are to be thought and argued about, and not merely experienced. And they are the only way issues such as colorization will get wide national exposure.

Then why are the movies not as exciting as they used to be, and why are there fewer unconventional ones, and why is there no audience for repertory, revival, and campus film societies? Because (1) home video is killing 16 mm exhibition and all the film communities and programming that revolved around it, and (2) modern marketing techniques have consolidated exhibition patterns, so that movies can be block-booked onto thousands of screens at once, and sold in a media blitz.

Let's face it. The sad fact is that film criticism, serious or popular, good or bad, printed or on TV, has precious little power in the face of a powerful national campaign for a clever mass-market entertainment. The marketing of stars has become synonymous with the marketing of movies. Stars have become the brand names of the industry. Bring 'em back alive.

THEN AGAIN

(From *Film Comment,* May/June 1990)

I am grateful to Roger Ebert for responding to my article in the spirit in which I wrote it, as the opening of a civilized debate. We agree more than we differ, but that won't keep me from picking a few spats.

I do watch *Siskel & Ebert & The Movies,* and I watch it for the reasons most people do: to see the clips and enjoy the wrassling. I think the program has other merits, and said so in a sentence of my original article that didn't make it into type: "Sometimes the show does good: in spotlighting foreign and independent films, and in raising issues like censorship and letterboxing." The stars' recent excoriation of the MPAA's X rating was salutary to the max.

I don't see Fox's banning of Judith Crist as "the single most influential event in the history of modern newspaper film reviewing." (If so, what are we to make of Fox's brief banning of *Siskel & Ebert* this spring?) After all, 1963 was the year of Andrew Sarris's "American Cinema" rankings in *Film Culture,* of Pauline Kael's gnarly brilliance in *Film Quarterly,* and, on the mass-media front, of *Time*'s "Film Generation" story, with a photo of Roman Polanski's *Knife in the Water* on the cover. Those events surely influenced readers and editors at least as much as Fox's Crist-killing.

Whatever the causes, one result is clear. We now have more, and more knowledgeable, movie critics in the big slots (though some local reviewers have lost their jobs to make way for famous syndicated scribes like Roger Ebert). But we have less exciting movies to write about. And, as Ebert suggests, less excited moviegoers. "Serious discussion of good movies is no longer a part of most students' undergraduate experience," Ebert says. Go further: it's hardly part of anyone's experience. Popular taste, even sophisticated popular taste, is cramped and conservative—especially as it relates to film. TV critics can help persuade 40 million Americans to savor the supreme weirdness of David Lynch's *Twin Peaks*. Movie critics can't get a tenth of that number into the theater for any quirky independent or foreign film.

Not long ago, after I panned the popular film *Pretty Woman* in *Time*, readers barraged me with the overripe fruit of their scorn. "Please find someone," a correspondent wrote, "whose tastes are at least similar to a majority of the people who pay to see movies." Perhaps another swatch that didn't make it into my original *Film Comment* article will answer this reader. "The presumption is spectacular: that a critic's prejudices are supposed to reflect and anticipate the prejudices of every potential moviegoer. In this view we're not analysts, we're handicappers—not John Madden but Jimmy the Greek." The only solution, if a critic is both to speak his own mind and act as a bellwether of audience whim, is to write about a film, "It stinks. You'll love it."

That's still presumptuous. How do I know who'll love a movie? And who is "you" anyway? I'm not speaking to one reader, whose tastes I know intimately. My job isn't to predict what movies are going to be popular; that's what studio executives are paid for. And it isn't, primarily, meant as a consumer service. It's to enlighten the reader through my knowledge of movies and entertain him with my play of language. Which is what I try to do at *Time* and *Film Comment*.

Ebert writes about the straitjacket of space at *Time;* he even took the trouble to compare the word count of my shorter reviews with the verbiage expended on *Siskel & Ebert*. But space isn't the only dominatrix. Yes, *S&E* devoted more words on their show to *Blue Steel* than I did in *Time*. And still, I'd argue, they had less to say. Their discussion was pretty much limited to whether the film was a good or bad representative of the cop genre. Matters of style, of Kathryn Bigelow's fine directorial hand, of Ron Silver's hyperkinetic, antirealistic acting—the matters that mattered in *Blue Steel*—were ignored. In my 267 *Time* words, you would find those issues addressed. You'd just have to bring your magnifying glass.

When I came to *Time*, in 1980, I knew that the job offered different restrictions (of space) and rewards (of exposure) from my stints at *New Times* and *SoHo News*. One thing that made the tradeoff attractive was knowing that at *Film Comment* (where I've hung on in some editorial capacity or other for two decades now) I could continue to write at length on film issues and, just as important, assign others to write. Pretty good twin perks, which, I am assured by the magazine's current editor, will continue. So my critics piece is not a "farewell article"; I'll be at least as much a presence for Jameson's *Film Comment* as I was for Jacobson's.

Does this splitting of my work—into writing reviews for *Time* and criticism, if you will, for *Film Comment*—trigger a "mid-career crisis"? Well, I've had my share, though more at the Film Society of Lincoln Center than at *Time*. In a more general sense, I do accept Ebert's argument. I might even ask, "Have critics lost touch with movies? . . . I suspect that we, no matter what our ages, have reached a midlife crisis, a menopausal anomie. . . . We are beyond being shocked or impressed. The thrill of discovery is gone." In fact, I did raise these questions, in just those words, in a 1986 *Film Comment* article that eventually got around to considering *Out of Africa*. One of the pleasures of writing for this magazine is that you can take forever getting to the point, and then discover that the "forever" is the point.

O n Tom Cruise, the facts are simple: the relevant *Time* editors and I saw *Born on the Fourth of July*, thought the movie and especially Cruise's performance were worthy of cover consideration, sold the idea to *Time*'s managing editor, and received the star's cooperation for the interview that is usually part of such a profile. (We got no window of exclusivity, nor did we ask for one.) Cruise didn't tell us to do the story, and we might well have done it even if he had declined to participate. (We nearly came to that last year, when a proposed cover subject said he was too busy for us. "Let's do the cover anyway," said our managing editor, who is famously unwilling to be dicked around by publicists. To me he added, "I'd rather read what you have to say about him than what he has to say about himself.")

Time, in other words, was not in Cruise's control. It ran whom it damn well pleased on the cover—as it used to do, as it still does. And I wrote what I damn well pleased: a mixed review of the film encased in an assessment of Cruise's career. I'd summarize the piece on Cruise and *Fourth of July* as "liked him, wasn't crazy about it." Maybe the vivid prose in my lead reads like flackery to Ebert, but the flacks don't always take it that way.

They know that a *Time* cover does not guarantee a favorable review. In cover stories I've knocked *Field of Dreams, Fatal Attraction,* and the movies of Nastassja Kinski and Bette Midler. Our *Mississippi Burning* cover included a sidebar (not by me) lambasting the film as Hollywood whitewash.

Pretty brave, eh? Naaah. As Ebert indicates, the publicists of these films cared less about what *Time*'s critics said than that their clients got on the cover. They were interested in the quantity, not the quality, of the coverage. That's why they send pix to *Time* and clips to *Siskel & Ebert;* it's all free publicity. That may even be why some magazines employ some film critics. One respected periodical recently hired a reviewer known mainly for his effusive blurb-mongering. Howcum? The consensus belief: the writer's quotes get the magazine's name in movie ads. Devising copy for the publicity machine need not be a despicable craft (I still treasure *USA Today* critic Mike Clark's appraisal of some forgettable actioner: "Makes *Rambo* look like *Rambeau*"), but it's not what I'd put first on my job application.

For Roger Ebert, that function is even more confining. Ads usually yoke him to Siskel, Siamese-twin style, and quote him not with an adjective but with a thumb. I'll bet that, sometimes, he'd like it to be a finger.

As for *Last Year at Marienbad,* by the way, I give it a 10+.

AUTEURISM IS ALIVE AND WELL AND LIVING IN ARGENTINA

BY ANDREW SARRIS

(From *Film Comment,* July/August 1990)

A mixture of vanity and ideology has induced me to contribute to the recent soul-searching in *Film Comment* on the current state of film and film criticism in America. Still, my motives in questioning the conclusions of such esteemed colleagues as Richard Corliss, Roger Ebert, and (peripherally) David Thomson are not so much polemical as confessional. Since I am personally acquainted with all three participants in the imbroglio, and profoundly respect their opinions and achievements, I choose not to be excessively offended by their casual assumption that Andrew Sarris and auteurism are lost somewhere in the dear, dead past.

Quite the contrary. Andrew Sarris, like Miss Jean Brodie, is undeniably in his prime, and auteurism has become so pervasive that, like Gestalt before it, it is in danger of dying of success. When Corliss uses a review of *Miami Blues* in *Time* magazine to make a nuanced differentiation of the directorial styles of George Armitage and Jonathan Demme, and Ebert charges that David Lynch's Cannes Golden Palm—winning *Wild at Heart* is a shameless ripoff of Russ Meyer, auteurism is not only alive but actually more hyped-up than ever.

I doubt that this sort of esoteric analysis existed in 1936 when Sam Goldwyn fired Howard Hawks in the middle of *Come and Get It,* then hired William Wyler to finish it. No one worried back then about the identity of the major auteur. Many reviewers weren't even quite sure what a director did, if anything. This is not to say that any period of film history, including our own, qualifies as an era in which intelligent and insightful writing on film is unknown. I have already apologized in the *New York Observer* of November 27, 1989, for having made in the past "too many careless generalizations about American critics, without making the necessary

420

exceptions for Manny Farber, Otis Ferguson, Gilbert Seldes, James Agee, Robert Warshow, Meyer Levin, Frank Nugent, Seymour Peck, Robert Sherwood, et al." I would add also Cecelia Ager, Graham Greene, C. A. Lejeune, and Elliot Paul as English-language "influences" on my evolution as a movie reviewer. No man is an island, least of all a film critic.

From what I can deduce, Corliss and Ebert have been engaged in a generally genteel "debate" that has occasionally erupted into a barroom brawl whenever one has questioned the career moves of the other. Meanwhile, Thomson has been busily revising the American cinema—and America with it—through a series of highly speculative reinterpretations almost on a par with the micromanaged critiques of Raymond Durgnat and Garry Wills.

As much as I would like to assume a pose of Olympian detachment from the fray, I shall not be coy about the fact that I am much closer in spirit to Corliss than to Ebert or Thomson. Nonetheless, I would like to begin my own revisionist critique of my revisionist colleagues by correcting Corliss on a minor error he has made in an anecdote attributed to me.

As Corliss tells it (*Film Comment,* March-April 1990): "When Pauline Kael moved from San Francisco to New York in the mid-sixties, she called her archrival Andrew Sarris and suggested they meet. After the visit, Sarris told his friend Eugene Archer, 'She wasn't exactly Katharine Hepburn.' And Archer added, 'Well, you're not exactly Spencer Tracy.'"

Corliss goes on to say, "But they were, in a way. They raised the musty trade of film criticism to a volcanic, love-hate art. Their wrangles over the auteur theory had the excitement of politics and sport. The intensity of their debate lured people to see new films, and to see old (especially old Hollywood) movies in a new way. They opened eyes, awakened curiosity, aroused intelligence. They made film criticism sexy. Pictures were things that mattered; ideas were worth fighting over. Forget Tracy-Hepburn. Sarris and Kael were more like Ali-Frazier. Film criticism was the main event, and these two were the champs."

Grateful as I am for this enthusiastic tribute, I must note that it wasn't Eugene Archer I told of my encounter with Pauline Kael, but Marion Magid, a friend and confidante, and then as now an editor at *Commentary.* Marion was also a woman, and that is the point of my correction. She rightly reproved me for what she took to be my shameful lack of gallantry. Years later, Gary Giddins, one of Pauline's passionate admirers, scolded me in a similar fashion for my perceived sexism. Up to now I've never been able to get out from under this anecdote, but I'll try once more. Of course, I was thinking all along of that magical moment in *Woman of the Year* when Tracy walks in on Hepburn as she is adjusting her stocking in the newspaper editor's office where the two feuding journalists have been summoned to patch things up. Well, Pauline and I were two feuding journalists, and so why couldn't life be like the movies just this once? As it turned out, we weren't each other's "Rosebud" and we have sustained a healthy hostility to each other to this day, more than a quarter of a century later.

But that still isn't the point of the anecdote. I was genuinely surprised by the appearance of the motherly woman who wrote under the byline of Pauline Kael. Then as now, Kael wrote young and sexy in a provocatively conversational style that threw me and almost everyone else off balance. The time was the early sixties, just before the Kennedy assassination, when people were still trying to come to terms with pop, camp, the Nouvelle Vague, radical chic, homosexuality, and rock and roll. Pauline exploded on the scene with a Berkeleyish bravado acquired after a stint at Pacifica with a foulmouthed call-in program. She was on the cutting edge, the vanguard, though not necessarily the avant-garde.

I was no match for her in a straight-on polemic because she championed the popular cause of anti-theory in the movies. All I could do was lick my wounds, and return to the drawing board with the encouragement of Jonas Mekas to turn out the famous 1963 issue of *Film Culture* with the hilariously chained Goldwyn Girls from *Roman Scandals* as the metaphor for the Hollywood studio system. I must confess that I had nothing to do with the cover, and that at first I couldn't see the glorious humor of it. That's how green and uptight I was.

And why shouldn't I have been? Here I was, thirty-five years old, living in Queens with my mother, never having made more than a few thousand dollars in any one year, and beset by all forms of belittlers in print from *Variety* to *Cahiers du cinéma,* from Judith Crist to Claude Chabrol. I had become notorious without becoming rich and famous.

For her part, Pauline was a later starter than I was. And though everything went her way at first, and though she nurtured an impressive array of acolytes in movie-reviewing berths around the country, she soon found herself alienated from a large part of the cultural establishment that had initially embraced her as the scourge of the New Seriousness in Film Criticism.

Hence, the years Corliss describes in such glowing terms were no picnic for the people like Pauline and me grappling for a livelihood in the critical trenches. Who won? Who lost? Who knows? Who cares? The name of the game has become survival. Eugene Archer, with whom I began my endless adventure in film scholarship in 1954, died in a Los Angeles bathroom in the midst of preparing his first university course after a disastrous attempt to break into movie production in Paris. George Morris, one of my most dedicated auteurist allies, died in Texas from AIDS. Tom Allen, my dear friend and collaborator, and the man—more than any other—who dragged me screaming into the new horror genres and thus broadened my *politique,* died of a heart attack two years ago. But the dead are always with us, and auteurism continues evolving as a collective statement of many individual tastes in many countries.

I am not singling out Corliss, Ebert, and Thomson for their supposed slights to the contemporary applicability of auteurist doctrine. As an allegedly outmoded auteurist, I am the frequent target of the arcane semioticians flaunting such secret passwords as "aggregate" (the sublime Astaire-Rogers song-and-dance numbers) and "diegesis" (the sappy Astaire-Rogers spoken love scenes). I hardly wish to dismiss the entire structuralist and semiotic movements of recent decades, but I often suspect semioticians in cinema of being unjustifiably delighted with "insights" comparable to that of Molière's *bourgeois gentilhomme* when he discovers that he has been speaking prose all his life.

My abiding argument with semioticians is that they simply recycle the movies discovered by the auteurists. How can Laura Mulvey, for example, gaze on the obsessive meditations of Sternberg and Hitchcock as the work of "typical" Hollywood directors? Still, I cannot quarrel with the semiotic emphasis on social contexts. Even when I disagree with a witty semiotician (not entirely an oxymoron) such as Umberto Eco, I respect his ability to surround his subject and still penetrate it. To the commonsensical outsider, all the specialized jargons seem pointless and pretentious. We auteurists have been persecuted too long for imputing the glories of mise-en-scène to once-unfashionable filmmakers such as Samuel Fuller and Anthony Mann (not to mention Jerry Lewis, the big joke of francophobes) for us not to look past the buzzwords of semioticians for genuinely original formulations on the cinema.

The fact that I have always been too much of a journalist for the academics, and too much of an academic for the journalists, makes me especially sensitive to the deplorable noncommunication among various critical camps now on the scene. In this context, Kael and I at our most contentious at least spoke the same language. Nowadays many film departments dominated by semioticians have virtually excommunicated all mainstream film critics from the sacraments of "discourses" and "texts." This may explain some of the malaise of Corliss, Ebert, and Thomson, all of whom still write in mainstream English.

One must recall that the big brouhaha in film criticism took place more than three decades ago when auteurism was not yet even a word. This was a time when a new generation of cinephiles scattered in Paris, London, New York, and other cosmopolitan centers on the five continents cast off the socially conscious shackles of the thirties and forties in looking at movies. The late, great André Bazin was the spiritual father of this vaguely *vague*ish, unaligned assemblage of movie buffs; even he eventually issued paternal warnings against auteurist "excesses," though this revolutionary revisionism was never as monolithic as its detractors claimed it to be.

When I finally appeared on the scene as an underpaid guru of this "movement" in America, it was with the purpose of discussing a Bazin essay on "La Politique des Auteurs," which had appeared in the April 1957 issue of *Cahiers*. My own essay was entitled very tentatively—"Notes on the Auteur Theory in 1962"—and appeared in *Film Culture,* a specialized periodical that never had more than 10,000 readers. I prefaced my argument with a Søren Kierkegaard (1813–1855) quotation from *Either/Or:* "I call these sketches Shadowgraphs, partly by the designation to remind you at once that they derive from the darker side of life, partly because like other shadowgraphs they are not directly visible. When I take a shadowgraph in my hand, it makes no impression on me, and gives me no clear conception of it. Only when I hold it up outside the wall, and now look not directly at it, but at that which appears on the wall, am I able to see it. So also with the picture which does not become perceptible until I see through the external. This external is perhaps quite unobtrusive but not until I look through it, do I discover that inner picture too delicately drawn to be outwardly visible, woven as it is of the tenderest moods of the soul."

Kierkegaard, of course, died long before the movies were born, but, like Plato's Cave, his shadowgraphs seemed to anticipate the cinema. I was fascinated also by the idea of interiority on a graphic surface. By this time I had stayed in Paris long enough during the one impoverished bohemian interlude in my life to develop a passion for paradoxes and dialectics—for the bizarre notions that Raoul Walsh was to Poussin as Joseph Losey was to Delacroix, that Hitchcock plus cinema equalled Kafka and Dostoyevsky, and that Keaton plus cinema equalled Beckett. But nothing had prepared me for the polemical fury of Pauline Kael, who denounced me and my ilk as a bunch of closet queens with a passion for Howard Hawks action movies with barechested heroes—much as if we were all auditioning for the Sal Mineo role in *Rebel without a Cause.*

Since that time, the word "auteur" has seldom appeared in print without being accompanied by an undertone of derisive irony. When I was introduced to a slightly inebriated Budd Schulberg at a dinner party in the Hamptons a few years ago, he sputtered and stuttered furiously at me as the supposed glorifier of "auteurs." He seemed to blame *me* for all the trouble *he* had had on the set of *Wind across the Everglades* with that presumptuously self-styled director-auteur Nicholas Ray. Schulberg had both produced and written the movie, but he was merely the humdrum "author" whereas Ray strutted around as the godly auteur. Hence I was presumably responsible for the financial failure of the film. What a burden for a mere theorist to bear.

When I reread the article almost thirty years later, I feel very much like Mario Puzo when he remarked that if he had known so many people were going to read *The Godfather,* he would have written it better. If I had known my modest piece would be reprinted so frequently, as if it were a seminal statement comparable to Sigmund Freud's *Interpretation of Dreams,* I would have spent more time working on it—perhaps as much as thirty years, but even then I would not be ready for the last word on the subject.

As I wrote at the time, auteurism was the first step rather than the last stop in solving mysteries of the medium. Like all my other disclaimers, these words of caution were completely ignored by Kael. Perhaps it is just as well. If she had presented me as a reasonable person, I would have been filed away and forgotten. As a monstrous purveyor of Theories and Dogmas, I was magnified as a Menace to all that was enjoyable and worthwhile in movies. The estimable Dwight Macdonald went so far in that epoch to describe me as a Godzilla clambering from the depths. (I am gratified to say we later made up in print—something I cannot say about Pauline and me.)

I can see now and I can say now that my supposedly seminal article in 1962 was a nervy blend of bluff and instinct. I had a long way to go to understand fully the implications of what I was writing. At the time I grossly underrated Ingmar Bergman, and grossly overrated George Cukor. I had not yet integrated my special brand of auteurism with Sigmund Freud on Leonardo da Vinci, Northrop Frye on genre, Maurice Valency on romanticism, Lionel Trilling on Henry James and Theodore Dreiser, Roger Leenhardt and Alexandre Astruc on anti-style, and Bazin himself with all his blazing brilliance and his infrequent blind spots (notably on Hitchcock).

Through the sixties, I was journalistically trapped as an auteurist by feeling I had to rationalize the declining works of such still-living and active Pantheon directors as Alfred Hitchcock, John Ford, Howard Hawks, and Orson Welles. I was too sentimental to follow Kael's strong-willed practice of abandoning old favorites when their work ceased to please and astonish her. I was stuck also with a quintessentially American pragmatism that compelled any "theory" to prove itself in practice, and the more prophetically the better. Who's that at the door, dear? Oh, it's the Accidental Auteurist come to straighten out our reception of Rainer Werner Fassbinder. He has to get his tools: his Aristotelian anvil, his Bazinian hammer, and his Freudian flashlight.

There was nothing particularly new or original about what I did, but I did help correct some lazy, if widely held, assumptions about movies. Before auteurists came along, if a movie called *O Brother, Where Art Thou?* opened on the same day as a movie called *Bang, Bang, You're Dead*, the first-string reviewer would automatically be assigned *Brother* and the second-stringer would cover *Bang*. Nowadays, the reverse is more likely. A humanistic document with noble sentiments may well be dismissed as "Masterpiece Theatre" while a bloody special-effects extravaganza may be hailed as an advance in cinematic art. Indeed, this revisionist turnabout has gone to such extremes that I find myself vis-à-vis Kael defending the literate humanistic against her espousal of the brutal kinetic.

Hence, Corliss and Ebert should not be discouraged if their burgeoning feud does not achieve the impact of the now-legendary Sarris-Kael collision. Corliss and Ebert are much smarter and more sophisticated than we were, but so is everyone else, including presumably older-and-wiser Sarris and Kael. It is hard to imagine the sensation I created back in 1960 when I wrote a rave review in a proto-auteurist style of Hitchcock's *Psycho*. Dave Kehr alerted me to John McNaughton's much more gruesome but nonetheless brilliant *Henry: Portrait of a Serial Killer,* but neither of our rave reviews can create a sensation in today's genre-wise environment.

Typically, David Thomson's prolonged "rediscovery" of Robert Siodmak's *Criss Cross* in the same issue of *Film Comment* takes me and auteurism to task for inadequately appreciating still another film noir, of which there are an almost infinite number patiently waiting to have their quirky virtues and expressionistic virtuosities savored and recorded. Agee missed a few, and Farber caught a few, but it was the relentless search for auteurs that elevated the noir genres above the soleil genres once and for all. The rest is refinement and elaboration, and Thomson is as good at it as anyone around.

The bad news I brought back in the sixties was that even fun movies had finally been absorbed by an elitist culture, and nothing would ever seem the same again. Despite the resistance of the academic establishment, movies had become irrevocably one of the humanities. It has long been my dream to implant the cinema in the Columbia College curriculum. Still, there was more to my opening Kierkegaard quote than its prophetic aptness. It was the emphasis on a creation outside the creator that makes auteurism viable. If there had not been a multitude of good but unexplained movies, there would not have been any Pantheon auteurs to discover.

The movie's the thing, the message, without which the "personality" of the author is unimportant. Long before I knew anything about directors and direction, I was moved by movies. Auteurism is history, not prophecy. It seeks to understand the past, not to shape the future; for the mystery of artistic creation can never be completely understood. I have never been an activist critic like Pauline. I have ceased regretting what might have been to concentrate on what was and what is.

Finally, I do not share Corliss's despondency over the state of film criticism, nor Ebert's over the state of the film industry. It is simply too early to tell. Despite the prevailing media wisdom, more great films were made in the fifties than in the sixties, yet as I recall both decades, the former was considered the Dark Ages and the latter some sort of Renaissance. The cinema has been going to the dogs virtually since its inception, only to provide in retrospect one Golden Age after another. The nineties promise to be no different as we slouch with our press passes and film classes toward the third millennium.

As for the disputed career choices of Corliss and Ebert, I would like to remind all concerned that we live in a capitalist society and, lately, perhaps in a capitalist world. In any event, I would be the last person in this now-greediest world to condemn any critic for wanting to make a little more money. Besides, if Agee and Farber could write brilliant *Time* movie reviews in the limited space available, there is no reason Corliss should not use his considerable writing skills in the same endeavor. (The petty bickering over word counts baffles me. What ever happened to "Brevity is the soul of wit"?)

Having taught film a little myself, I would venture the opinion that both Corliss and Ebert tend to overestimate the educational value of frame-by-frame visual analysis. When facing an unsophisticated tabula-rasa audience, it is easy enough to elicit oohs and aahs with the most elementary demonstration of cinematic technique. This facility has been designated as the Slavko Vorkapich effect.

If I may be allowed to conclude by furrowing my brow to express mild concern over future temptations facing my colleagues: I would caution Corliss to avoid the sin of despair. And I would advise Ebert that what is at risk in his very accomplished Laurel-and-Hardy routines with Gene Siskel is neither his aesthetic integrity nor his emotional sincerity, but, rather, what I have perceived in private conversations as an irreverent wit being steadily eroded by too calculating a deference to the banalities of a mass audience.

Still, these are temptations we all face as we try to climb higher and higher on the movie food chain. The main thing for me is that the pillars of my Pantheon have stood tall, and that I have never had to revise my opinion downward on any Pantheon director. But there are many directors whom I have underrated, and still more whom I have neglected. The past is still rich with promise.

A MEMO TO MYSELF AND CERTAIN
OTHER FILM CRITICS

NOVEMBER 17, 1991

A new thriller has opened, starring Nick Nolte, Robert De Niro, and
Jessica Lange. There are supporting performances by Robert Mitchum and Gregory Peck. And those are the terms in which 95 percent of
moviegoers think of *Cape Fear*. But if you read the critics, you would have
heard about a man named Martin Scorsese, who directed the film, and
maybe something about Bernard Herrmann, who has been dead for fifteen
years, but whose musical score was used in the picture.

There is a gulf between people who go to the movies (the public) and
people whose lives revolve around them (critics, movie buffs, academics,
people in the business). For most people with seven bucks in their pocket
and an evening free, there is only one question about *Cape Fear* that is relevant: Will I have a good time? The "good time" may depend on whether
the moviegoer has an appetite for violence, or is a fan of one of the stars, but
it will not depend on whether the film was directed by Martin Scorsese.

That's why I question myself when I write a review like the one about
Cape Fear. I tried to say whether the filmgoer would have a good time, and
I had something to say about the actors. But my central concern was with
Scorsese, who I think is the best director at work in the world today, and
whose career is therefore the most interesting single aspect of my job. I
wondered whether it was good news or bad that he had a multipicture deal
with Steven Spielberg and Universal, that he was working with a $34 mil-
lion budget for the first time, and that he could use stars like Nolte, Lange,
and De Niro without asking them to defer their usual salaries. Would he
gain Hollywood but lose his soul?

Those are questions that may not be fascinating to everybody who
reads the daily paper. Maybe some were interested in the fact that Mitchum
and Peck had starred in the 1962 version of the same film, but I imagine almost nobody was interested in the fact that Scorsese had recycled the orig-

inal score that Bernard Herrmann wrote for the 1962 movie. And if I had written that Herrmann was also the composer of the music for *Citizen Kane, Psycho,* and *Taxi Driver,* would that have made any difference?

Writing daily film criticism is a balancing act between the bottom line and the higher reaches, between the answers to the questions (1) Is this movie worth my money? and (2) Does this movie expand or devalue my information about human nature? Critics who write so everybody can understand everything are actually engaging in a kind of ventriloquism—working as their own dummies. They are pretending to know less than they do. But critics who write for other critics are hardly more honest, since they are sending a message to millions that only hundreds will understand. It's a waste of postage.

Writing the *Cape Fear* review, I had to deal with my own fear that the director who is most important to me seemed to be turning away from the material he was born to film, big-city life in the second half of this century. Scorsese, whose *GoodFellas* was the best movie of 1990, has for 1991 made a movie that, in the long run, will not be very important to his career. It is a good movie, and he has changed the original story (good vs. evil) to reflect his own vision (guilt vs. evil). But Scorsese's soul was not on the line here.

In taking this director-oriented approach, I went through a sort of self-justification. I've written at length about every one of Scorsese's movies. I assume some of my readers have followed along, and share my interest. I can't write as if everybody was born yesterday, and doesn't know anything that is not in today's paper. One of the reasons I like the British papers is because they assume you know who "Thatcher" is, even if they don't preface her name with the words "Former British Prime Minister Margaret."

But there are no doubt many readers who couldn't care less about Great American Filmmaker Martin (*Raging Bull*) Scorsese. To them, I owe the responsibility of writing a review that will be readable—not jargon—and will give an accurate notion of the movie they are thinking of going to see. And I need to tell them that *Cape Fear* stands aside from other current thrillers like *Deceived* and *Ricochet* because it is made by a man with an instinctive mastery of the medium.

What I do not owe any reader is simplistic populism. Some newspapers have started using panels of "teen critics" as an adjunct to their staff professionals. These panels seem to be an admission of defeat by the editors; they imply that the newspaper has readers who cannot be bothered by the general tone of the editorial product, and must be addressed in self-congratulatory prose by their peers. A relative lack of experience and background is an asset.

What is happening here seems to be endemic in a lot of American journalism: people read the papers not in the hopes of learning something new, but in the expectation of being told what they already know. This is a form of living death. Its apotheosis is the daily poll in *USA Today*, which informs "us" what percentage of a small number of unscientifically selected people called a toll number to vote on questions that cannot possibly be responded to with a "yes" or "no."

Back to the movies. What if a poll discovered that less than one in twenty of the people attending *Cape Fear* know or care who Martin Scorsese is? Would that be a good reason I shouldn't write about him? I ask these questions here because I sometimes ask them of myself. Everybody who works for a mass-circulation publication has to ask them, at one time or another. I guess the answer is halfway between what you want to know and what else I want to tell you. Eventually you'll know more than I do, and then you can have the job.

EPILOGUE
Thoughts on the Centennial
of Cinema

1995
(Introduction to *Roger Ebert's Video Companion, 1996 Edition*)

> As I now move, graciously, I hope, toward
> the door marked Exit, it occurs to me that
> the only thing I ever really liked to do was
> go to the movies. Naturally, Sex and Art
> always took precedence over the cinema.
> Unfortunately, neither ever proved to be as
> dependable as the filtering of present light
> through that moving strip of celluloid which
> projects past images and voices onto a screen.
> —Gore Vidal, *Screening History*

We know more, much more, about Marilyn Monroe and Jack Nicholson than we know about Julius Caesar and Thomas Jefferson. We know what they looked like when they stood up and walked to a window, how they sounded when they were sad, and how they smiled when something struck them as funny. We know because we have seen them in the movies.

Oh, we have a lot of facts about Jefferson—but we don't know what he was *like*. In the everyday world we base our judgments of people on countless little clues of bearing, voice, and expression; we size them up and render a verdict, based on instinct and experience. That's why people never get hired from resumes, only after interviews, and why people can't really fall in love on the Internet.

The movies allow us to size someone up without ever meeting them. We sit in the dark, privileged voyeurs, watching actors express moments so intimate we rarely experience them in our own lives. If we go to the movies a lot, we can honestly say we've seen Gérard Depardieu or Jessica

Lange through more of the critical moments of life than anyone in our own families.

It has been only 100 years since "the cinema" became possible—a century, since the Lumière brothers in Paris patented the first projector. The invention had been a long time coming, and "moving pictures" were available much earlier in various forms, from flip cards to the spinning Zoetrope to Edison's kinetoscope, but the Lumières invented the cinema as we know it by combining the three crucial elements: a projector behind, an audience in the middle, and a screen in the front. Their 1895 film of a train arriving at a Paris station caused audiences, so it is said, to dive out of the way.

If the Lumières invented cinema, another Frenchman, George Méliès, invented "the movies," by using the medium to tell stories. He was the producer of *Voyage to the Moon* (1902), with its famous image of a space ship plunging into the eye of the Man in the Moon.

Although there are all kinds of movies for all kinds of reasons, for most people "the movies" will always mean sitting in a darkened theater with a crowd of strangers, watching imaginary stories on the screen. François Truffaut said the most moving sight he ever saw in a theater was when he walked up to the front and turned around, and saw all those eyes lifted up to the screen.

The twentieth century was the first in which we could fly, could send voices and pictures through the air, could peer into the soul of the atom and glimpse the most distant reaches of the universe. But the invention that most profoundly affected us may have been the movies. They allowed us to escape from our box of space and time, and they allowed us to see the past as it was actually happening.

The movies are still too young for the full impact to have settled in. But imagine what it would be like if movies had existed 500 or 2,000 years ago. If we could see moving, talking pictures of Jesus, how would that affect us? Would it enhance his stature in our imagination, or diminish it? If we could see Shakespeare's plays as they were originally performed, would we be moved, or only confused by strange accents and acting customs? What if we could see our great-great-great grandmother as a little girl?

Movies are pieces of time, Peter Bogdanovich said. Bogart is dead, but he still walks across the floor of Rick's Place and stops in the middle of a sentence when he sees Ilsa sitting next to the piano player. And he still has the power to move us in that moment. *Casablanca* is an experience that for many of us was as real as anything else that has happened in our lives.

"The fact is I am quite happy in a movie, even a bad movie," Walker Percy wrote in his novel *The Moviegoer.* "Other people, so I have read, treasure memorable moments in their lives: the time one climbed the Parthenon at sunrise, the summer night one met a lonely girl in Central Park and achieved with her a sweet and natural relationship. . . . I too once met a girl in Central Park, but it is not much to remember. What I remember is the time John Wayne killed three men with a carbine as he was falling to the dusty street in 'Stagecoach,' and the time the kitten found Orson Welles in the doorway in 'The Third Man.'"

Books and plays can provide us with stories. But the movies uniquely create the impression that we have *had* an experience. The key word is "we." I have seen a lot of movies by myself, but the experience is not the same as seeing a film with a large group of strangers. The greatest moviegoing experiences of my life—the premieres of *Apocalypse Now* and *Do the Right Thing,* both at the Cannes Film Festival—were great not just because of the movies but because nowhere else do more people gather in the same theater to see them. Together, *we*—a cross-section of humanity—had an experience, and because it mirrored our shared humanity, it was somehow spiritual; we were giving witness.

That is what movies can do at their best. At their worst, they can cheapen us, and make us think less of ourselves. Here I'm not talking about subject matter, because subject matter is neutral: it is possible to make a great, uplifting film about the most depressing imaginable subject (Spielberg did it with the Holocaust in *Schindler's List*) or a demeaning film about the most innocent (this would be true of movies that congratulate the audience on its stupidity).

The best movies are usually made because one person or a small group have a story they believe must be told, because it strikes a chord in their hearts. It can be a comedy, a musical, a drama, a polemic—the important thing is that they feel it.

The worst movies are made out of calculation, to reach a large audience. There is nothing wrong with a large audience, nothing wrong with making money (some of the best films have been the most profitable), but there is something wrong with the calculation. If the magical elements in a movie—story, director, actors—are assembled for magical reasons—to delight, to move, to astound—then something good often results. But when they are assembled simply as a "package," as a formula to suck in the customers, they are good only if a miracle happens.

Today movies are promoted with skillful advertising and marketing campaigns. A herd mentality encourages us to go to the "hits." This is the wrong approach. We have, after all, only so many hours in a lifetime to see movies. When we see one, it enters into our imagination and occupies space there. When we see movies that enlarge and challenge us, our imaginations are enriched. When we see dumb movies, we have left a little of our better selves behind in the theater.

A century ago "the movies" were invented, and allowed us to empathize with other people in a way never before possible. But like all inventions the cinema is neutral, and we decide whether it makes our lives better or worse. As the second century begins, our choices are about the same as they were in the beginning: we can fly to the moon, or duck to get out of the way of that train.

CODA
On the Meaning of Life . . . and Movies

JULY 2004

(Introduction to *Roger Ebert's Movie Yearbook, 2005*)

The new material in this year's edition was mostly written between August 2003 and July 2004. During the year I also went through some adventures with illness. I had surgery for salivary cancer in September, and in December spent a month in Seattle for radiation treatments. The surgery was not a big deal, but the side effects of radiation were not pleasant, and I didn't really begin to feel restored until May or June.

During that time I didn't miss writing a single review, nor did I neglect the *Great Movies* series or the "Answer Man" column. The *Ebert & Roeper* show continued without interruption; thanks to ingenious planning by our staff, we were able to tape several shows in advance to cover December and early January, and then I returned to the tapings. I also attended, as usual, the Conference on World Affairs in Boulder in early April, where we went through Renoir's *The Rules of the Game* a shot at a time during ten hours over five days. And I hosted the sixth annual Overlooked Film Festival in late April, before leaving for Cannes in June.

The radiation made it difficult for me to handle solid food, and I existed on a product named Ensure, which kept everything humming along. Very early on the first morning in Cannes I woke early, as I always do, and wandered, as I always do, down to the all-night café by the port, and ordered, as I always do, a croissant and café au lait. I dunked the croissant into the coffee, as I always do, and ate it, and that was the beginning of real food again.

I supply this information not as a medical bulletin, but as an entry into considering the way movies work for me and perhaps a lot of other people. Even during treatment in Seattle, I was able to attend screenings, catch movies in theaters, and write twenty reviews. One night I went to the local Landmark theater and saw Jean Gabin in *Touchez Pas au Grisbi* and found it so extraordinary it went into the *Great Movies* series. Some of my friends and editors said they were impressed that I continued to see movies and file reviews even during the more difficult days of January and February. I tried to explain that it would have been harder not to.

I was not in any great pain, although radiation caused several varieties and degrees of discomfort. My problems were serious but probably not life-threatening. Illness had its greatest effect on my sense of personal immunity. After enjoying extraordinary good health all of my life, I was faced with the fact that my body was fallible and my lifespan finite. Radiation causes erratic sleep patterns, and in the middle of the night, in addition to reading every one of the novels of Willa Cather, which were a consolation beyond all measuring, I had time to reflect on my mortality. I may have many years left, but I'd always thought I had forever.

These thoughts did not bother me while I was watching movies. I found myself drawn into them even more deeply than usual, as if giving myself over to them, healing in their glow. In a Seattle theater I saw the new P. J. Hogan version of *Peter Pan,* starring Jason Isaacs, Jeremy Sumpter, and the newcomer Rachel Hurd-Wood, and was struck by how delightful it really was—how they had tried to make something alive and special, instead of recycling the same familiar material. I had seen Denys Arcand's *The Barbarian Invasions* at Cannes, but now saw it again and was struck personally by its portrait of a difficult but irrepressible man in his sixties, surrounded at his deathbed by current and former friends and lovers, and presiding over the celebration of his own passing. "Dying is not this cheerful," I wrote, "but we need to think it is."

And in Jacques Becker's *Touchez Pas au Grisbi,* there's a scene where Max, the Jean Gabin character, a middle-aged gangster tired of risk and danger, is alone in his apartment contemplating how his best friend Riton has stupidly allowed himself to be kidnaped. He's less concerned about the loot he will lose, I wrote, than about his pal:

> He has a wonderful soliloquy, an interior monologue which we
> hear voice-over, as Max paces his apartment. He talks about what a
> dope Riton is, and what a burden he has been for 20 years: "There's
> not a tooth in his head that hasn't cost me a bundle." We under-
> stand that Max, who is competent above all things, almost values
> Riton's inability to live without his help. At the end of his solilo-

quy, instead of growing angry as a conventional gangster might, Max opens a bottle of champagne, plays a forlorn harmonica solo on his juke box, sits in a comfortable chair, and lights a cigarette. He treasures his creature comforts, especially when he might be about to lose them.

I appreciated that moment in Becker's film beyond all reason. I responded to the way it understood that a great movie can involve not plot but life and the daily living of it, and that although movies can amuse and excite us, their greatest consolation comes when they understand us.

A few months later, in June, I saw Julie Bertuccelli's *Since Otar Left*, a film set in the Eastern European republic of Georgia. The film stars a ninety-year-old actress named Esther Gorintin, who was eighty-five when she began her acting career. She plays a stubborn old lady who lives with her daughter and granddaughter. Her thoughts are focused on her son, Otar, who has gone to Paris seeking work. We know, but she does not, that Otar has died in Paris. The daughter and granddaughter try to deceive her that he is still alive.

"What is clear," I wrote, "is that this old woman has a life and will of her own. There is a wonderful scene while she is still at home in Georgia. She leaves the house alone, looks up some information in the library, buys two cigarettes, and smokes them while riding on a Ferris wheel. With a lesser actor or character, this would be a day out for a lovable granny. With Esther Gorintin playing Eka, it is the day of a woman who thinks she has it coming to her."

Moments like that glow with a special grace. Writing about them has its consolations, too. I find that when I am actually writing, I enter a zone of concentration too small to admit my troubles. Although I might feel uneasy or unwell when I sit down at the keyboard and feel that way again when I stand up, while I am working I feel—what? There is a kind of focus or concentration, a gathering of thought, language, and instinct, that occupies all the available places and purrs along satisfied with itself. I am known around the office as a "fast writer," but while I'm engaged in the process I don't feel as if I'm writing at all; I'm taking dictation from that place within me that knows what it wants to say.

This has been true all of my life. When I was fifteen and starting out as a sports writer at the *Champaign-Urbana News-Gazette,* I would labor for hours over my lead paragraph. Bill Lyon, who was a year older than me and would later become a famous columnist for the *Philadelphia Inquirer,* advised me, "Get to the end of the piece before you go back to revise the beginning. Until you find out where you're going, how can you know how to get there?" I took his advice and have never looked back. It condenses into a rule most writers discover sooner or later: the Muse visits during the work, not before it.

What I am trying to say is that I love my work. I love movies, I love to see movies, I love to write about movies, I love to talk about movies, I love to go through them a frame at a time in the dark with a room full of people watching them with me and noticing the most extraordinary things. On the Monday at Boulder, we showed *The Rules of the Game* all the way through and several people confessed they found it disappointing. Then we went through it for the rest of the week, a shot or even a frame at a time. By the Friday, they embraced it with a true passion. On Monday, we looked at it. By Friday, we had seen it.

Too many moviegoers look at movies and do not see them, but then it has always been that way. Movies are a time-killer or a casual entertainment for most people, who rarely allow themselves to see movies that will jolt them out of that pattern. The jolting itself seems unpleasant to them. I'm not a snob about that; anyone who enjoys a movie is all right in my book. But the movies don't top out; as you evolve, there are always films and directors to lead you higher, until you get above the treetops with Ozu and F. W. Murnau, Bresson and Keaton, Renoir and Bergman and Hitchcock and Scorsese. You walk with giants.

One of our grandchildren told me the other day that he knew why I didn't like *White Chicks*. It was, he said, "because you're not a kid. If you were a kid, you'd know how funny it was." "Yes," I said, "no doubt you're right. But if you were me, you'd know how bad it was." "But I'm not you," he said. "No, but you will be someday," I said. "I started out as a kid, and look how far I've come."

APPENDIX
Ten Best Lists, 1967–2005

1967
1. *Bonnie and Clyde*
2. *Ulysses*
3. *Blow-Up*
4. *The Graduate*
5. *A Man for All Seasons*
6. *The War Game*
7. *Reflections in a Golden Eye*
8. *Cool Hand Luke*
9. *Elvira Madigan*
10. *In the Heat of the Night*

1968
1. *The Battle of Algiers*
2. *2001: A Space Odyssey*
3. *Falstaff*
4. *Faces*
5. *The Two of Us*
6. *The Producers*
7. *Oliver!*
8. *The Fifth Horseman Is Fear*
9. *Rachel, Rachel*
10. *Romeo and Juliet*

1969
1. *Z*
2. *Medium Cool*
3. *Weekend*
4. *If. . . .*
5. *Last Summer*
6. *The Wild Bunch*

7. *Easy Rider*
8. *True Grit*
9. *Downhill Racer*
10. *War and Peace*

1970
1. *Five Easy Pieces*
2. *M★A★S★H*
3. *The Revolutionary*
4. *Patton*
5. *Woodstock*
6. *My Night at Maud's*
7. *Ådalen '31*
8. *The Passion of Anna*
9. *The Wild Child*
10. *Fellini Satyricon*

1971
1. *The Last Picture Show*
2. *McCabe and Mrs. Miller*
3. *Claire's Knee*
4. *The French Connection*
5. *Sunday, Bloody Sunday*
6. *Taking Off*
7. *Carnal Knowledge*
8. *Tristana*
9. *Goin' Down the Road*
10. *Bed and Board*

1972
1. *The Godfather*
2. *Chloe in the Afternoon*
3. *Le Boucher*
4. *Murmur of the Heart*
5. *The Green Wall*
6. *The Sorrow and the Pity*
7. *The Garden of the Finzi-Continis*
8. *Minnie and Moskowitz*

      9. *Sounder*

     10. *The Great Northfield, Minnesota, Raid*

1973   1. *Cries and Whispers*

     2. *Last Tango in Paris*

     3. *The Emigrants/The New Land*

     4. *Blume in Love*

     5. *The Iceman Cometh*

     6. *The Exorcist*

     7. *The Day of the Jackal*

     8. *American Graffiti*

     9. *Fellini's Roma*

     10. *The Friends of Eddie Coyle*

1974   1. *Scenes from a Marriage*

     2. *Chinatown*

     3. *The Mother and the Whore*

     4. *Amarcord*

     5. *The Last Detail*

     6. *The Mirages*

     7. *Day for Night*

     8. *Mean Streets*

     9. *My Uncle Antoine*

     10. *The Conversation*

1975   1. *Nashville*

     2. *Night Moves*

     3. *Alice Doesn't Live Here Anymore*

     4. *Farewell, My Lovely*

     5. *The Phantom of Liberty*

     6. *A Brief Vacation*

     7. *And Now My Love*

     8. *A Woman under the Influence*

     9. *In Celebration*

     10. *Dog Day Afternoon*

1976
1. *Small Change*
2. *Taxi Driver*
3. *The Magic Flute*
4. *The Clockmaker*
5. *Network*
6. *Swept Away . . . by an Unusual Destiny in the Blue Sea of August*
7. *Rocky*
8. *All the President's Men*
9. *Silent Movie*
10. *The Shootist*

1977
1. *3 Women*
2. *Providence*
3. *The Late Show*
4. *A Woman's Decision*
5. *Jail Bait*
6. *Close Encounters of the Third Kind*
7. *Aguirre: The Wrath of God*
8. *Annie Hall*
9. *Sorcerer*
10. *Star Wars*

1978
1. *An Unmarried Woman*
2. *Days of Heaven*
3. *Heart of Glass*
4. *Stroszek*
5. *Autumn Sonata*
6. *Interiors*
7. *Halloween*
8. *National Lampoon's Animal House*
9. *Kings of the Road*
10. *Superman*

1979
1. *Apocalypse Now*
2. *Breaking Away*

3. *The Deer Hunter*
4. *The Marriage of Maria Braun*
5. *Hair*
6. *Saint Jack*
7. *Kramer vs. Kramer*
8. *The China Syndrome*
9. *Nosferatu, the Vampyre*
10. *10*

1980
1. *The Black Stallion*
2. *Raging Bull*
3. *Kagemusha*
4. *Being There*
5. *Ordinary People*
6. *The Great Santini*
7. *The Empire Strikes Back*
8. *Coal Miner's Daughter*
9. *American Gigolo*
10. *Best Boy*

1981
1. *My Dinner with Andre*
2. *Chariots of Fire*
3. *Gates of Heaven*
4. *Raiders of the Lost Ark*
5. *Heartland*
6. *Atlantic City*
7. *Thief*
8. *Body Heat*
9. *Tess*
10. *Reds*

1982
1. *Sophie's Choice*
2. *Diva*
3. *E.T.*
4. *Fitzcarraldo/The Burden of Dreams*
5. *Personal Best*

6. *Das Boot*
7. *Mephisto*
8. *Moonlighting*
9. *The Verdict*
10. *The Weavers: Wasn't That a Time*

1983
1. *The Right Stuff*
2. *Terms of Endearment*
3. *The Year of Living Dangerously*
4. *Fanny and Alexander*
5. *Gandhi*
6. *El Norte*
7. *Testament*
8. *Silkwood*
9. *Say Amen, Somebody*
10. *Risky Business*

1984
1. *Amadeus*
2. *Paris, Texas*
3. *Love Streams*
4. *This Is Spinal Tap*
5. *The Cotton Club*
6. *Secret Honor*
7. *The Killing Fields*
8. *Stranger Than Paradise*
9. *Choose Me*
10. *Purple Rain*

1985
1. *The Color Purple*
2. *After Hours*
3. *The Falcon and the Snowman*
4. *Prizzi's Honor*
5. *Ran*
6. *Witness*
7. *Mad Max Beyond Thunderdome*
8. *Lost in America*

9. *Streetwise*

10. *Blood Simple*

1986

1. *Platoon*

2. *'Round Midnight*

3. *Hannah and Her Sisters*

4. *Sid and Nancy*

5. *Lucas*

6. *Vagabond*

7. *Trouble in Mind*

8. *Down and Out in Beverly Hills*

9. *Peggy Sue Got Married*

10. *Hard Choices*

1987

1. *House of Games*

2. *The Big Easy*

3. *Barfly*

4. *The Last Emperor*

5. *Moonstruck*

6. *Prick Up Your Ears*

7. *Radio Days*

8. *Broadcast News*

9. *Lethal Weapon*

10. *Housekeeping*

1988

1. *Mississippi Burning*

2. *The Accidental Tourist*

3. *The Unbearable Lightness of Being*

4. *Shy People*

5. *Salaam Bombay!*

6. *A Fish Called Wanda*

7. *Wings of Desire*

8. *Who Framed Roger Rabbit*

9. *Dear America: Letters Home from Vietnam*

10. *Running on Empty*

1989
1. *Do the Right Thing*
2. *Drugstore Cowboy*
3. *My Left Foot*
4. *Born on the Fourth of July*
5. *Roger and Me*
6. *The Mighty Quinn*
7. *Field of Dreams*
8. *Crimes and Misdemeanors*
9. *Driving Miss Daisy*
10. *Say Anything*

BEST FILMS OF THE
1980s
1. *Raging Bull*
2. *The Right Stuff*
3. *E.T.*
4. *Do the Right Thing*
5. *My Dinner with Andre*
6. *Raiders of the Lost Ark*
7. *Ran*
8. *Mississippi Burning*
9. *Platoon*
10. *House of Games*

1990
1. *GoodFellas*
2. *Monsieur Hire*
3. *Dances with Wolves*
4. *The Grifters*
5. *Reversal of Fortune*
6. *Santa Sangre*
7. *Last Exit to Brooklyn*
8. *Awakenings*
9. *The Cook, the Thief, His Wife and Her Lover*
10. *Mountains of the Moon*

1991
1. *JFK*
2. *Boyz n the Hood*

3. *Beauty and the Beast*

4. *Grand Canyon*

5. *My Father's Glory/My Mother's Castle*

6. *A Woman's Tale*

7. *Life Is Sweet*

8. *The Man in the Moon*

9. *Thelma and Louise*

10. *The Rapture*

1992

1. *Malcolm X*

2. *One False Move*

3. *Howards End*

4. *Flirting*

5. *The Crying Game*

6. *Damage*

7. *The Hairdresser's Husband*

8. *The Player*

9. *Unforgiven*

10. *Bad Lieutenant*

1993

1. *Schindler's List*

2. *The Age of Innocence*

3. *The Piano*

4. *The Fugitive*

5. *The Joy Luck Club*

6. *Kalifornia*

7. *Like Water for Chocolate*

8. *Menace II Society*

9. *What's Love Got to Do with It*

10. *Ruby in Paradise*

1994

1. *Hoop Dreams*

2. *Three Colors: Blue, White, Red*

3. *Pulp Fiction*

4. *Forrest Gump*

5. *The Last Seduction*

6. Fresh
7. The Blue Kite
8. Natural Born Killers
9. The New Age
10. Quiz Show

1995
1. Leaving Las Vegas
2. Crumb
3. Dead Man Walking
4. Nixon
5. Casino
6. Apollo 13
7. Exotica
8. My Family
9. Carrington
10. A Walk in the Clouds

1996
1. Fargo
2. Breaking the Waves
3. Secrets and Lies
4. Lone Star
5. Welcome to the Dollhouse
6. Bound
7. Hamlet
8. Everyone Says I Love You
9. Heidi Fleiss: Hollywood Madam
10. Big Night

1997
1. Eve's Bayou
2. Sweet Hereafter
3. Boogie Nights
4. Maborosi
5. Jackie Brown
6. Fast, Cheap, and Out of Control
7. L.A. Confidential
8. In the Company of Men

9. *Titanic*

10. *Wag the Dog*

1998

1. *Dark City*
2. *Pleasantville*
3. *Saving Private Ryan*
4. *A Simple Plan*
5. *Happiness*
6. *Elizabeth*
7. *Babe: Pig in the City*
8. *Shakespeare in Love*
9. *Life Is Beautiful*
10. *Primary Colors*

1999

1. *Being John Malkovich*
2. *Magnolia*
3. *Three Kings*
4. *Boys Don't Cry*
5. *Bringing Out the Dead*
6. *Princess Mononoke*
7. *The War Zone*
8. *American Beauty*
9. *Topsy-Turvy*
10. *The Insider*

BEST FILMS OF THE 1990s

1. *Hoop Dreams*
2. *Pulp Fiction*
3. *GoodFellas*
4. *Fargo*
5. *Three Colors: Blue, White and Red*
6. *Schindler's List*
7. *Breaking the Waves*
8. *Leaving Las Vegas*
9. *Malcolm X*
10. *JFK*

2000	1. *Almost Famous*
	2. *Wonder Boys*
	3. *You Can Count on Me*
	4. *Traffic*
	5. *George Washington*
	6. *The Cell*
	7. *High Fidelity*
	8. *Pollock*
	9. *Crouching Tiger, Hidden Dragon*
	10. *Requiem for a Dream*

2001	1. *Monster's Ball*
	2. *Black Hawk Down*
	3. *In the Bedroom*
	4. *Ghost World*
	5. *Mulholland Dr.*
	6. *Waking Life*
	7. *Innocence*
	8. *Wit*
	9. *A Beautiful Mind*
	10. *Gosford Park*

2002	1. *Minority Report*
	2. *City of God*
	3. *Adaptation*
	4. *Far from Heaven*
	5. *Thirteen Conversations about One Thing*
	6. *Y tu mamá también*
	7. *Invincible*
	8. *Spirited Away*
	9. *All or Nothing*
	10. *The Quiet American*

2003	1. *Monster*
	2. *Lost in Translation*
	3. *American Splendor*

    4. *Finding Nemo*
    5. *Master and Commander*
    6. *Mystic River*
    7. *Owning Mahowny*
    8. *The Son*
    9. *Whale Rider*
    10. *In America*

2004
    1. *Million Dollar Baby*
    2. *Kill Bill: Volume 2*
    3. *Vera Drake*
    4. *Spider-Man 2*
    5. *Moolaadé*
    6. *The Aviator*
    7. *Baadasssss!*
    8. *Sideways*
    9. *Hotel Rwanda*
    10. *Undertow*

2005
    1. *Crash*
    2. *Syriana*
    3. *Munich*
    4. *Junebug*
    5. *Brokeback Mountain*
    6. *Me and You and Everyone We Know*
    7. *Nine Lives*
    8. *King Kong*
    9. *Yes*
    10. *Millions*

INDEX

455